COMMENTARY
ON THE
NEW
TESTAMENT

COMMENTARY
ON the
NEW
TESTAMENT

E.M. BLAIKLOCK

FLEMING H. REVELL COMPANY
OLD TAPPAN, NEW JERSEY

INTRODUCTION

THE NEW TESTAMENT took shape nineteen centuries ago, over a span of forty years, unless, indeed, those scholars are correct who place the writings of John much earlier than the nineties, the decade of the apostle's extreme old age. It was the work of nine men, eight Jews and a Greek physician. The Jews were a varied band, fishermen from the Galilean lake, a tax official and a rabbi from Tarsus, a man of supreme intelligence and the heir of three cultures.

The New Testament contains history, oratory, closely argued theology, ethics, philosophy, letters and apocalyptic poetry. There is rugged prose like that of Mark, written in haste and reflecting the racy language of another, the splendid narratives of Luke, no mean historian, the passionate polemic of Christ's two brothers, James and Jude, Paul's packed disputation and sudden bursts of poetic writing, Peter's ripe wisdom, and John's delicate storytelling, marked by the touch of the eyewitness.

The New Testament, apart from any Christian context, is a priceless set of documents illustrating Greek and Roman life in the Mediterranean in the latter half of the first century of our era. As such it is receiving increasing recognition among classical historians. Little literature, in fact, survives from that tract of history in either Latin or Greek. Had the New Testament emerged recently, some spectacular discovery like the Dead Sea Scrolls, it would have been a major excitement for historians. The thought of myth or legend would not have occurred to them as they looked into areas of life in Athens, Corinth, Ephesus, back country towns like Lystra, or a tense Jerusalem lurching on towards the disaster of the Jewish Rebellion—fascinating revelations available from no other surviving source. Paul's travels, contacts, controversies and his person, as a Roman citizen who was also a leading rabbi and a cultured Hellenist, would have been examined with avid interest. So would daily life in the most turbulent of Roman provinces, life on the little farms and villages, among the rabbis and in the governors' headquarters . . . Rome's improvisings in a sensitive border region, the clever policies of the Herod family, a corrupt trial and a cruel persecution, the machinery of an appeal to Caesar—all these would have found interested attention.

And very soon any close reader of the newly discovered book would have observed that all its varied parts were bound together by one dominant theme—the extraordinary life, death and triumph over death of one whose followers rapidly penetrated the whole Mediterranean world, transforming men and women of all classes by the sheer passion of their conviction that God, no less, had revealed himself in one named Jesus. And no one unaware of the unique presumptions of New Testament criticism, would have imagined that the four evangelists were doing anything else than seeking to describe an experience they shared with one whom they knew, revered, yet failed to understand, until a tremendous event opened their minds . . . And was it all true, would be the question. It may be confidently said that many would find the evidence convincing.

The New Testament, and the faith which flowed from it, did not perish with the ancient world, when the tribes of the north broke the Rhine and Danube frontiers. It lived to form a bridge between the old world and the new, across the darkened centuries. The Empire, in its crassest act of folly, turned on the church, first at mad Nero's behest, and never, through three vital centuries, repudiated her policies of repression. It surrendered too late to ally its still undamaged strength to a more youthful church, and subdue the world as the legions never could, but Christianity and its book remained, and still remain, still challenging, still potent. Too often betrayed where it should be loyally served, too often divided when it should witness as one, the faith and the book have held within themselves those concepts of law and liberty on which western civilisation is founded. The ultimate truths are in the New Testament. It is no dead text. Its words rise from the page confronting, challenging, especially in a day when noisome things emerge from forgotten corners and the standards of two thousand years are eroded at their base. As the cultured man who wrote the Epistle to the Hebrews said: 'The word of God is alive and strong, more cutting than a sword of double edge. It can pierce clean between emotions and mind, to the very depths of the personality. It lays bare our real thoughts, our true motives.'

CONTENTS

THE GOSPEL ACCORDING TO ST. MATTHEW

The Book of the Tax Man

(Matt. 1: 1–25)

MATTHEW, the apostle, the converted tax official (9: 9), collected, according to tradition, a volume of the sayings of Christ, written in his native Hebrew, or Aramaic. At some later date, probably subsequent to the writing of the second gospel, a narrative sequence was added, and the whole turned into Greek. The obvious dependence of an apostolic document upon a non-apostolic Mark, in no way disrupts this tradition. Peter, according to equally firm tradition, gave apostolic authority to Mark, and the possibility of records earlier than both gospels is real. The mass of teaching in the words of Jesus in Matthew's gospel points to the tradition of dual format, and the book's preoccupation with Christ the King, and the fulfilment of prophecy, indicates Jewish origin.

To the Jew, alert for the messiah's credentials, the genealogy (1–17) was of great importance (cf. Ezra 2: 61, 62). It reveals the human lineage of Christ and his identification, 'after the flesh', with errant man. Consider the names, some of them faulty characters indeed. Two of the three women mentioned were aliens,

the third the wife of an alien and an adulteress. Royalty is stressed (Acts 2: 29–36; Rom. 1: 3; 2 Tim. 2: 8; Rev. 22: 16). It was important in Matthew's eyes (12: 23; 15: 22; 20: 30, 31; 21: 9, 15).

The story of the birth of Christ (18–25) cannot be torn from the text of Scripture without serious disruption. Luke investigated the beginnings of Christianity with time to interview, and with a scholar's mind. He confirms Matthew's story, probably with Mary's authority. The alternatives are stark. Is the woman, who has been honoured above all women, to be set down as a liar, covering girlhood fault or disaster with an audacious tale, or is she to be accepted, as she was accepted by those who knew her Son, as a true witness? The life of the Son to whom she gave birth is not without significance when Mary's veracity is tested. The story is set, as Luke will show, in a context of events capable of historical investigation. The issue is one of authority, on which liberal and conservative will differ. And that difference penetrates to the very heart of the past and future of the faith. That Christ's life had miracle at the beginning and the end, is not beyond belief to those who accept the miracle of the life itself. Observe that, whatever the Hebrew oracle of Isaiah 7: 14 may be made to signify, Matthew gives historic interpretation, and fixes the meaning of the word 'virgin'. The doctrine stands firm, to be accepted or rejected, and much of importance is involved in the choice.

From Bethlehem to Nazareth
(Matthew 2: 1-23)

BETHLEHEM, an ancient town of Judah (Gen. 48: 7; 35: 19; Ruth 1: 1; 1 Sam. 16: 1; 17: 12; 20: 6; 2 Sam. 23: 14, 15), was set down in an old prophecy as the messiah's birthplace (Mic. 5: 2). The cave under the Church of the Nativity, cluttered though the simple reality is by the unseemly eagerness of men to claim, adorn and spoil a holy place, is likely to be the true location. Hadrian, busy after the Second Jewish Rebellion (A.D. 132, 133) to extirpate the worship of the land, both Jewish and Christian, unintentionally marked and established the site with a grove to Adonis.

The Magi were astrologers, probably from South-east Arabia. Their study of the Judaean hope could go back to the visit of the Queen of Sheba (1 Kings 10). The gifts were characteristic of 'Sheba', or Arabia Felix (Ps. 72: 10, 11, 15). Their knowledge of the stars was used to honour a genuine hope. The questing Western mind, eager for rational explanation, has suggested Halley's Comet or some juxtaposition of Saturn or Jupiter. The date may reasonably be set down as 5 B.C. The wonder is that,

working back from A.D. 525, the Christian era was so closely dated.

Herod, who murdered the babes of Bethlehem in one of his last acts of fear and paranoia (13–18), the evils which dominated his last years, died in 4 B.C. Matthew's use of Hosea. 11: 1 shows his Jewish mind, imbued with Scripture and habitually building ideas round remembered phrases. The same habit of thought appears again in v. 18, where he quotes Jeremiah (31: 15). The plodding columns of exiles passed Rachel's tomb, and the poet pictured that 'mother of sorrow' weeping. She wept again, and history, so tragically cyclical, reproduced the grief of ancient days.

Joseph's emigration to Egypt (19–23), need not have lasted more than a year. Roman policy changed on Herod's death. Skilfully, he had served Rome and kept the sensitive Palestine frontier in comparative peace. Augustus now experimented with a system of tetrarchies. Herod's son, Archelaus, destined to reign only until A.D. 6, when Augustus, heeding complaints from collaborating aristocrats of both Judaea and Samaria, dismissed him, was a petty tyrant of whom Joseph might well have been apprehensive (22). A procuratorial administration followed his final banishment. Matthew, picking up the name of Nazareth, whither Joseph withdrew, found another poetic echo which is puzzling. Perhaps 'the prophets' (23), were non-biblical. Or does Matthew see an echo in Isaiah 11: 1, where the Hebrew for 'branch' (nezer) may have suggested a word-play? Was the assurance Matthew's own idea or some tradition? It cannot be said, but it is interesting to see a true Jewish mind at work.

Revival by Jordan
(Matthew 3: 1–17)

ALL the gospel writers agree that a great revival of religion swept the land before Christ began his ministry. The real significance of the Dead Sea Scrolls, discovered thirty years ago, lies in the people whose library they were—the community of Qumran. The Pharisees and Sadducees dominate the New Testament narratives, the former narrow exponents of the Law, the latter a cynical hierarchy, collaborators and simonists. But it is clear that there was a 'third force', a core of faithful folk, rebels against city corruption and organised Judaism, who sought, sometimes by a strangely exotic means, to keep true religion alive in a day of disillusionment and materialism. They had always haunted the background, 'the remnant', the 'seven thousand who had not bowed the knee to Baal', 'God's poor', brusque intruders into city wickedness, like Elijah or Amos. They reappear in the New Testament, the poor and rejected, Mary and Joseph, the fisherfolk of Galilee, one-time disciples of John.

It should, therefore, occasion no surprise that, around the time of Christ, a protest movement should have sought the wilderness. Isaiah's writings are prominent among the Scrolls, and a verse from Isaiah could have been the marching order of the Qumran community. 'In the desert make straight a pathway for your God.' (Isa. 40: 3).

Nor can it be accident that these very words find repetition in the recorded sayings of John the Baptist. He was 'a voice', he said, 'crying in the wilderness: Make straight a pathway for your God.' The desert preacher, whose whirlwind ministry forms a prelude to the Christian story (1–12), was obviously under the influence of the desert religious communities, or perhaps a member of them. His activities were centred a dozen miles from Qumran. His disciples, who became Christ's 'fishers of men', were converts who went back to their daily ways of living and carried into industrial and urban life the breath of the wilderness devotion.

John was, said Christ, the greatest of the prophets (Luke 7: 28), and his 'forerunner' (17: 12, 13). His fearlessness, his scorn of show, his identification of his own rôle, live in these verses, (7–12; Mal. 4: 5). His message was repentance (3: 11), faith (Mark 1: 15), judgment (11, 12), and finally the proclamation of his successor (John 1: 36).

John, stern and ruthless in his condemnation of sin, softens at the sight of Christ (13–17). He had known, it is clear, the perfection of his life, but had not yet recognised him as the messiah (John 1: 33). God's testimony to his son is composed of two messianic verses (Ps. 2: 7; Isa. 42: 1). Long years had passed in humble duties at Nazareth. Mary's family had grown, and could care for her, now, presumably widowed. Men in Israel, as never before, were conscious of sin and the demanding voice of God. There was a confluence of significant events. It was time for Jesus (1: 21), the Saviour, to identify himself with those he had come to save (15).

Temptation and the Galilean Ministry
(Matthew 4: 1-25)

ARID uplands lie west of the ruins of ancient Jericho, part of the grim valley wall of the Judaean wilderness. The tradition which places the scene of the temptation there, a few miles from the scene of the Baptism, is a sound one. Fierce assaults of evil can follow any great stand of faith, and Jesus, at we know not what climax of decision, had taken a firm step of committal. Nothing could alter that, but strife could rage over the future. His sensitive mind was assailed by wave on wave of shaking visions. That they were repetitive, continually restructured, varied, is shown by the changed order in Luke (4: 1-13). Should he use the power he discovered surging in him, for a selfish end? A miracle too, would remove any lingering doubt (3). He replied by Scripture (Deut. 8: 3). Or should he, remembering Malachi 3: 1 and Psalm 91: 11, 12, deftly quoted by Satan, begin his ministry by a spectacular demonstration? Another verse from Deuteronomy (the authority of which was seemingly accepted by Christ) provided the answer (6: 16). And was he then shown in imagination the Esdraelon plain, a familiar sight from the hills of Nazareth, Esdraelon, the marching place of ancient and modern

empires, where the brilliant mind of a boy might have seen the pageant of world history, and in the same dazzling vision seen world conquest if evil could be accepted as the means? Had Psalm 2: 8 not prophesied as much (9, 10, 11)? Deuteronomy 6: 13 gave the answer.

The story of the Galilean ministry, at first linked to John's (17), follows. Matthew, as was his custom, quoted an old oracle (Isa. 9: 1, 2) to join the covenants. Galilee was a significant choice, a crowded land, neighbour to great Gentile communities, the Lord's home ground.

The fishermen had been spiritually prepared by John's ministry (John 1: 35-42). They were able men, probably prosperous, for they were engaged in the most vigorous industry of Galilee, fishing the teeming lake. The new call (18-22) was joined to old training. The fishermen needs strength, endurance, patience, knowledge of his calling, of the ways of fish and the mood of his environment. He requires the proper skills, the correct bait.

The Lord chose his home ground (23-25). He chose, for beginning, the established order and opening—the synagogue, that wonderful organ of Jewish teaching and worship, which was one of the products of exile and dispersion. Galilee proved a good choice. Jerusalem, exclusive, proud, far to the south, felt the impact. So did the Ten Towns, where large Greek populations lived, east of the lake (25). The church was to 'begin at Jerusalem' (Acts 1: 8). The ministry of Christ, with equal logic, began in Galilee.

This Happy Breed
(Matthew 5: 1–48; 6: 1–7)

THE Lord began his ministry, as the psalms began, by describing the truly happy man. The element of suffering and rejection runs through all the Beatitudes (3–12). The 'poor' (Luke 6: 20) were necessarily the 'poor in spirit'. Isaiah said much of God's poor (3: 14, 15; 10: 2; 11: 4; 14: 30; 25: 4; 26: 6; 29: 19; 32: 7; 41: 17; 61: 1), and it was not by accident that the Lord chose Isaiah 61: 1 when he preached in Nazareth (Luke 4: 18). There he had known poverty. In Jewish minds the sense of rejection by God, and the denial of justice by men went with poverty. In Christ the poor find Perfect Justice. Grief can blessedly cleanse (3; Heb. 12: 11). The 'gentle' (5) have not yet 'inherited the earth', but their opposites, the arrogant, the loud and violent, have certainly not done so. Picture hunger and thirst in the context of a land which knew grinding poverty and the ferocity of thirst (6). Thus should we desire God. Mercy (7) is God's grace shown in human conduct, and the banishing of all duplicity, deception, carnality (8), a condition for knowing God. Peace (9) is more than the absence of war. The peace of God is the peace of those who have fought down evil, and carry and communicate God's peace. The persecuted are a wider group than those who have withstood violence for Christ. They are those who have confronted evil and paid a price for good. They are 'the Few', who are ranged with the persecuted Christ, and have scorned the cruel pressure of the conforming crowd, the contempt of sin's 'Inner Ring', the academic sneer, the brute's hostility (11, 12). They are the salt which preserves society from its final corruption (13). In salt two violent elements cohere to make a compound which gives savour, creates thirst, and functions only when pure from alien mixture which corrupts (14). They are like Safed or Hippo, whose high-lifted lights could be seen by all Galilee. And for what other purpose is light than to show men the true shape of things (15), and point to a goal (16)?

Christ came to be such a light (John 12: 46). He showed the true nature of the Law (17–19), darkened by the Pharisees (20). He revealed the penetrating demands which legalism had shallowed into external formalities (21; 6: 4). The Law had lost its savour, its power to sting and penetrate (21–24), its attenuated morality scorned even by common justice (25, 26). Evil is not external (27, 28), but a cancer within, to be excised even at cost of loss and pain (29, 30). God's demands had been made ludicrous by foolish codifications (31–37), misinterpreted (38, 39) by men eager for their rights, and niggardly in generosity (40–42). Some, by their own precepts (43) had blasphemed God. The Lord is quoting a Qumran text from the Dead Sea Scrolls.

But set the true vision of God before a man (48), and littleness (44), selfrighteousness (45), introverted, narrow selfishness (46), racialism, class consciousness (47), posing and exhibitionism in charity (6: 1–4), and in prayer itself (5, 6), vanish. In God's presence conduct and devotion fall into the proper shape, purged, sanctified (6: 1–7).

Prayer and its Consequences
(Matthew 6: 8–34; 7: 1–11)

THE mention of false prayer turns the Lord to the theme of real prayer. It must be in private. Any peasant's house had a storeroom (6) where the humblest could find a place to be alone. In the headings which follow (9–13), all forms of prayer are covered, devotion (9), aspiration (10), petition (11), repentance (12), longing for holiness (13). No proper desire, no legitimate aspiration, no true intercession, is excluded, if the suppliant allows the mind to play round these simple themes. No one hears but God, and nothing is small to him (Neh. 9: 32). Such prayer admits no 'playacting' ('hypocrite' is from the Greek for 'actor'—2, 5), and needs no chanted repetition (1 Kings 18: 26; Acts 19: 34), but only utter sincerity (14–18).

To such suppliants comes true reward. What is the recompense for anyone who seeks God or good? Surely success in their quest. God is found, by those who sincerely seek (Heb. 11: 6). Those who, by carnality in the holy place, seek a lesser prize, gain it (2, 5; Ps. 106: 15). In life, men commonly gain what they seek, the fragile, perishable goods of their blind and selfish questing (19), or that which

shall prove eternal (20). The quest itself purifies and straightens the life (21). Blurred vision distorts the message which the eye conveys to the mind. He who does not see aright travels crookedly (22). Thus it is with the heart and mind. If corruption, dwells in the personality, if ambitions are bent, and desires distorted, the damage is like physical blindness. The truth is obscured, the path impossible to find (23). In fact, how can any man pursue contradictory aims? He must choose who or what shall govern his life (24).

That is why it is better to look to God than self. The Lord is speaking in the strong hyperbolical language of the East (cf. 5: 39–42). He is not counselling irresponsibility, but childlike trust (25), and a quiet confidence that man is God's most precious creature (26). Can we grow taller than genetics predestine (27)? God, who lavishes beauty on the humblest flower, is surely able to provide, if his children will but trust (28–31). Israel, of all peoples, had been taught such dependence (32). If life's dominant preoccupation be that God rules supreme, with awesome regularity the rest follows (33). Such is the armour against 'future shock' (34).

That is why our moral concern must first be with the condition of our own life (1, 2). Dust, or fragments wind-blown from threshing floors were common enough, but imagine, says Christ, again in the language of hyperbole, a man with wood in his eye, presuming to remove a speck from the eye of another (3–5)! These are precious truths, not to be boasted about, but to be demonstrated visibly (6). Prayer calls for persistence. 'Keep on asking, keep on seeking, keep on knocking,' run the Greek imperatives, for God delays to purify prayer, to discipline supplication, to promote self-examination. This is not vain repetition. God's answer may be surprising; it could be different from that which is anticipated. It will probably be greater (Eph. 3: 20). It will not be a mockery (9–11).

The One Foundation
(Matthew 7: 12–29)

IT has been alleged that these chapters are a haphazard collection of striking sayings. On the hillside above Tabgha the Lord, no doubt, had more to say than Matthew recorded, but the links between theme and theme are obvious. At 7: 12 the Lord began some concluding remarks. Their order and nature could have been determined by questions or remarks from the crowd. He sums up his whole appeal and his attitude to the Law (12). He offers no easy path. He who travels must travel hard, and not follow the crowd (13). The true followers of God are always a 'remnant' (14). There have been always those who teach otherwise, pretenders and deadly (15). The test is simple. What do the claimants produce in terms of good or godliness? Every peasant in the congregation had the answer on his little farm (16–20).

Let them, therefore, test the self-appointed teachers. The religious leaders, the experts in the Law, the proud Pharisees, the worldly Sadducees pass without mention, but no listener would doubt the meaning of the simple words. Profession must be backed by reality (21–23). Life is like building. Character needs foundations. The word for rock used here is *petra* (24), and implies a rocky pile, a crag. The picture is probably that of a man who builds on the high side of a dry river valley, a *wadi*, as the Arabs call the desert water-course. Such a house has foundations, and stands above the level of the storm-born freshet which can fill the whole wide channel of the valley.

He who builds on the sand has taken a risk (26). There might be years between the floods, and it is easy to build on the level *wadi* floor. Trade and human fellowship travel that way. It is not lonely, not conspicuous, frequently profitable, certainly cheaper, thus to site one's habitation. It is a vivid picture of the man who lacks foundations and takes no thought of them, until 'the day reveals it', in tumbled ruin.

Life is like that, with its gales of grief, its floods of trouble, its waters of death, its tempests of temptation (27). Only then are the foundations tried; only then, when the realities are stripped and exposed for what they are. We do well to be founded on Christ (1 Cor. 3: 11). Without the Saviour of that other Mount, the Sermon on the Mount is no more than a haunting vision of what man might be.

On Both Sides of Galilee
(Matthew 8: 1-34)

THE next two chapters seem chronologically arranged and geographically sited. Their theme is nine authenticating works of Christ arranged in groups of three. The first three (1–17) show his authority already demonstrated in word (7: 26), visible in action, and confronting deadly disease, leprosy (1–4), paralysis (5–13), and fever (14–17).

The leper came confidently, but humbly and reverently (2). His disease was one of horror and devastation. The Law, and all that scribal diligence had added to the Law, cast him from society. Jesus touched him—another identification with sinful man. Matthew passes immediately to a case of healing from a distance, as though to stress that no physical contact was necessary. Note how the Roman's soldierly bearing comes through (6–8). The officer was probably a picked man, seconded from the Tenth Legion for a difficult liaison task in Herod's territory. All the five centurions in the New Testament seem men of ability and strength, especially appointed to Rome's most difficult province. Here (11, 12) is the first glimpse in Matthew of the wider gospel, so prominent in Luke. Peter's wife's mother is the next patient. She rose and served them (15). Healing should have no other sequel. With the Sabbath done, the Lord's ministrations became general. Typically, Matthew quotes the Old Testament.

Escape across the lake was im-perative. The Lord had no wish to precipitate public excitement in a politically difficult area (18). The scribe's emotional response (19), promptly reduced to reality by Christ (20), revealed the peril which was abroad. The Galileans were a volatile group. Another man accosted him on his way to the shore. He too would serve, but only when his father was no longer alive (21). His father was not ill, and might have had many years to live.

The next story (23–27) showed the 'Son of Man', as he has now styled himself (Dan. 7: 13, 14), commanding the obedience of violent Nature. Such storms, born of the north wind sucked down the great Jordan Rift by the heat over the Dead Sea, are common (Ps. 89: 8, 9).

Matthew speaks, in the next story (28–34), of two maniacs, Mark of one. Peter, who provided Mark's material, was there. Matthew, not yet called (9: 9), was close to events. There is no contradiction. The larger number included the lesser. To see in such stories diagnosable mental illness, does not relegate supernatural evil to ancient superstition. The man was healed, and if it took the sacrifice of a herd of swine, rushing into one of the rabbinical 'gates of hell'—the sea—to convince him, the question emerges: 'How much is a man's soul worth?' The geographical difficulty is negligible. Gadara was six miles from the lake, Gerasa thirty miles, but any locality can show territory held outside its own administrative borders by all kinds of municipal authorities. A rented Gerasene enclave in Gadarene lakeside areas could account for the difficulty (28). Observe the preference of the local population. They chose swine (34).

The Response of Galilee
(Matthew 9: 1–38)

THE scene is Capernaum (Mark 2: 1), 'his own town'. Determined friends brought the stricken man to Christ. Friends can do no more. From then on it is a matter for the afflicted and the Saviour. The rabbis' reaction was not because Christ began with sin and forgiveness (2). They actually believed that all illness was a result of sin. The sick man, too, must have been convinced that he was paying the price of sin, and he could not have been cured until he was conscious of forgiveness. What stirred the question was that a man should presume to pronounce such forgiveness (3). It was 'blasphemy', an insult to God. The demonstration provided by the cure apparently did not impress them (4–7). The people at large saw something new and real (8).

'His house', (7) was probably Matthew's house, but Matthew was writing the gospel. What Matthew owned was Christ's. Hence the guests (10). The 'publican', was an officer of the hated tax system. Taxes were farmed out by auction to collecting agencies which, to recoup their outlay, proceeded to collect all that extortion could accomplish. The tax system, whether it was Herod's or Caesar's in this case, was also a symbol of bondage to the Jew. No Jew of standing or self-respect would lend himself to such a trade. It meant contempt for his people, readiness to do anything for gain. Behind cynicism and hardness, as the Lord knew, lies sometimes self-loathing and wistful longing to be free (9–13).

Christ has been accused of blasphemy (3), base association (11), and now of impiety. Was he not John's successor? Why not, then, fast? (14). The reply was twofold. First came the covert thought that the era of the Law was ended. Fasting, reduced by Pharisaism to a mechanical ritual, had now no meaning. It was a time of joy, not grief. Then with swift apprehension, the Lord foretold of stress to come (15). Let the disciples of grace rejoice in the brightest years of life. They were all to suffer much. The second point is that, though the Law would merge with the gospel, it could not, like unshrunken cloth, be patched on to the new material (16). So, too, with wineskins (17).

An interruption ... One rabbi was in dire need (18) which met prompt response (19), an errand disastrously (Luke 8: 49) delayed. Delays which God permits are meaningful (John 11: 4, 21, 32). The rabbi needed this ultimate demonstration, if he was one of the critics of the earlier incident. He had come in desperation, for his closest associates were sceptics (24). Nothing in what God does, or in how he does it, is without meaning. Observe the prime rôle of faith—breaking down pride and self-esteem in one dissolving moment of agony (18); reaching out from a pit of dark rejection (Lev. 15: 25–27) and fear (21); grasping dimly a mere title

(27). This group of stories all lead to a refrain (26, 31, 33). Unprecedented events, the healing of the afflicted, the blind, the dumb (22, 30, 33) and the raising of the dead, set a seal on the messiah's ministry. The response was vicious blasphemy from dedicated evil (34). The Lord looked on a suffering population, cursed with such false leaders (36), and cried for men to stand with him.

The Apostles Go Forth
(Matthew 10: 1–42)

THE Twelve were varied in social background, personality and skills. None of them, by common estimate, were distinguished in standing or ability (1–4). They were sent out with a commission commensurate with their abilities. Not yet trained or equipped to deal with Gentiles, they were to minister only to the Jews (5, 6). The Lord himself had no such inhibitions (see Luke 10: 30–37; John 4: 4–32). They were sent to carry on what they had seen begun (7, 8), in complete dependence (8–10) upon friends (11–13). They were to waste no time in barren argument (14, 15), to be wise in the face of persecution (16), but to expect no justice or mercy (17, 18). Their defence could only be, as Paul found, their message (19, 20. Acts 22: 1–21; 24: 2–23). They must have no illusions. The proclamation of the gospel would divide men (21), provoke opposition (22).

(The difficult v. 23 can refer only to 28: 18–20, when the resurrected 'Son of Man' widened his commis-

sion. Matthew must have meant this or, writing anything from thirty to forty years later, he would have made the Lord say what he knew to have been unfulfilled. This he would not have done.)

The commission resumes. Can the disciple expect more justice than his teacher (24), less falsehood or insult (25)? They need never fear that truth can be silenced. History shows that persecution, death, or the powers of Hell cannot prevail against it (26). How true! Before Matthew died the message had penetrated the Empire, and we know not what lands beyond it (27). The proclamation called for heroes (28), but heroes who knew their worth in God's eyes (29–31), and the reward which would follow faithfulness (33; 2 Tim. 4: 7, 8).

Christianity is stern soldiering (2 Tim. 2: 1–4). It brings strife, as well as peace (34. John 14: 27; 16: 33). A strong stand for Christ can divide families (35, 36) and produce a situation in which the dearest ties of life must loosen before the claims of God (37). The cross is a heavy burden, but Christ bore it (38). Death is not the ultimate of evils. Denial of Christ nothing can remedy (39). The beautiful closing verses rank the disciple with his teacher, the Christian with his Lord, and make the reward of service equal to all who serve as they are able (40–42).

Jesus on John
(Matthew 11: 1–30)

JOHN's fate was grim. In a dungeon at Machaerus, John, denied full information, still haunted by his views of a conquering messiah, fell into despair and doubt (2, 3). The Lord answered by a re-affirmation of his credentials (5) and a reference to Isaiah, the prophet whom John knew so well (6). Apparent abandonment, by a God who seems to act contrary to all expectation, is the sternest test of faith.

The messengers gone, the Lord turned to the theme of John. Why, he asks, did all the land stream down to Jordan? Whence this moving of the Spirit? Why this pilgrimage to the reed-lined river? (7). No prince or prelate 'riding triumphantly laurelled to lap the fat of the years' gathered multitudes to the steaming valley (8). They sought a man who spoke God's word (9), for a 'prophet' is no less. One favoured generation had seen the greatest preacher Israel had ever known, and lived through the land's most challenging revival (10). And yet John himself was not to know the consummation in Christ. He was Elijah of prophecy (14; Mal. 4: 5) if they could but comprehend (15). The revival continued. Hence the strong metaphor of v. 12. People, 'publicans and sinners' included, were surging like a storm-ing party against the ramparts from which a false hierarchy had repelled them. Men were desperate for truth, and with John's ministry they laid hold on it.

But there was also confusion. The reference to the children, at odds over some game, perhaps in some scene visible to those who listened, is not clear. Some found a contradiction between John, aus-tere, passionate, fiery, and Christ,

'gentle, and quiet in spirit' (29). Ultimately, truth emerges, for it is deeds which justify the wisdom be-hind them. Time will tell (19).

The land was polarised. Hosts had stormed heavenwards. Others, like some of the religious leaders (9: 34), like whole communities (20, 21), had displayed a hardness, a fierce rejection, worse than pagan in its depravity (22–24; 8: 34). The poor accepted him (25), the leaders, the learned, those who should have received him, turned away. They saw in him the liberator, the lifter of loads (23: 2–4). 'My yoke fits easily,' he said (30), perhaps with crafts-manship of a workshop in Nazar-eth in mind. 'I will not load you with more than you can carry.'

The Conflict Begins
(Matthew 12: 1–50)

THE narrative quickens as Mat-thew moves on to the clash with the hierarchy. To eat the casual handful of corn by the path through the fields was part of the mercy of the Jewish code. To pluck this on the Sabbath was 'harvesting', a practice forbidden by Pharisaic elaboration of the law (1, 2). The party must have been under close surveillance, itself significant. The Lord countered, a trifle ironically, with arguments native to scribal thought—the historic incident in which David, desperately hungry, ate the Bread of the Presence (Lev. 24: 5–9; 1 Sam. 21: 1–6), a per-quisite of the priests; then the fact that the necessary work of the temple went on (3, 4) . . . He then summed up the principle of all ritual and regulation with a telling text (7. Hos. 6: 6; already quoted in 9: 13), and put both sacred temple and revered Sabbath in place in two audacious phrases (6, 8). In v. 6 RSV chooses the neuter of the likeliest reading: '. . . something greater than the temple'—that is a needy human being, a 'temple of the Holy Spirit', infinitely more precious than building or institution. Thus interpreted, 'son of man' (8) can mean simply 'man', as the phrase does over a hundred times in Ezekiel—and possibly v. 32.

Arriving at the synagogue (9) the Lord illustrated the principle again (9–13). He gave a human being his health, and, if, as the apocryphal *Gospel of the Hebrews* says, the man was a mason, he gave him livelihood, dignity, usefulness, all gone with his paralysed limb. Hatred was rising now to explosion point. The Sabbath was the core of Pharisaic regulation. Both Antiochus and Pompey had taken Jerusalem because Jews would not fight on the Sabbath. Christ never confused courage with foolhardiness, nor sought perilous publicity (14–17). He withdrew, according to the character Isaiah had outlined (17–21. Isa. 42: 1–4).

Desperately, the Pharisees sought to counter his influence by ascribing his good works to the devil, a blasphemy easily answered. 'Can any Kingdom fight for two incompatible ends, any house pursue two policies and remain one?' (24–27). Referring to Isaiah 49: 24–26; (29) (and perhaps, after John's preaching, Isaiah was particularly well-known) the Lord bade them ob-

serve that he was defeating Satan, and that the Kingdom of God was 'on its way' (28). Let them therefore take sides in a duel in which there is no neutrality (30). And let them understand that, though man may malign man (taking 'Son of man' to mean 'man'), or alternatively to malign Christ himself as a man (taking 'Son of man' in its commoner sense), and if evil becomes so woven with the mind, so dominant and accepted that a man can ascribe the doings of the Almighty to the Prince of Evil, then dedication to sin has become so intractable that the sinner is past salvation (31–34). Let them watch their words for the lips betray what is accumulated in the personality (35–37).

A 'sign' then, they demand. It was a Jewish preoccupation (1 Cor. 1: 22). 'They shall have one,' he replies, 'the resurrection' (40). They have one also. Evil Nineveh, citadel of Assyria's bandit kings, heard the faulty Jonah, and lived (41). Sheba's queen saw the faulty Solomon and became a believer (42). That generation had the responsibility and opportunity of the sinless presence of the messiah. And if the religious leaders, sequestering the Law and making it a burden, had betrayed them, they had still known the vast cleansing of John's revival. If, thus blessed, they should reject Christ who fulfilled the Law and consummated John's revival, their condition would be like the man who tastes truth and deliberately puts it aside, an acute piece of psychology (43–45. Heb. 6: 4–6).

The final story perhaps represents a sequence of events (46–50. 47 is not a well-attested verse).

Mary, no doubt, believed in him. His brothers did not (John 7: 5). But all were by now anxious for his safety.

The Parables

(Matthew 13: 1–52)

To the surprise of his disciples (10), Jesus turned suddenly to open air preaching (1) and to parables. 'Look,' he began, 'the sower . . .'. It is a definite article. As he did so often, he plucked an illustration from the immediate environment (e.g. 6: 28). Observe that one point only is contained in each parable. The fate of the seed, and the variety of the harvest (4–8), is the lesson. There is no suggestion that some lives are fated for rejection, some gifted with fertility. Ears come with listening (9). The parable was designed to encourage the seeker for truth, to thwart the mentally lazy, and baffle the curious. Those bent on storming the stronghold of truth (11, 12) will be enlightened, because truth, like the stained glass window, can be seen only from within. A 'mystery' (11), in the New Testament, as in Greek religions, is truth made plain to those within the circle. But all can enter that circle (11: 28, 29). Those who climbed the Mount heard the Sermon. That is why, as Isaiah said in a moment of despair (12–17. Isa. 6: 9, 10), preaching seems to harden those who will not hear, and to confirm their condemnation. If this is sometimes the result of preaching, it is not its purpose.

The despoiler of the seed (19) in the interpretation (19–23), suggests another rôle of the enemy. Like its predecessor the parable of the tares (24–30) is straight out of the environment. The darnel, like the sham Christian, grows up unrecognised, until 'the day reveals' him (3). And speaking of seed, what of the tiny mustard seed, a figure for smallness among the Jews, but which produces a tree big enough for nesting birds. So, from a dozen men, came the church, a force working among men like the leaven in the meal (33). (Leaven usually is a figure for creeping corruption.) The disciples, passing the test of sincerity, real desire, and eagerness for truth (17), are given the meaning of the second parable also (34–43).

He continues. There are good things in life worth sacrificing all else to possess (44–46). Or, 'Look yonder to the lake,' he seems to say (2) and see the catch drawn in (John 21: 11). Some great movement of evangelism, some organisation like the church, encloses a varied host. Only the judgment day can separate good and bad, those with whom the experience is deep and transforming and those with whom it is a passing gust of emotion. Matthew only reports the saying in v. 52. 'New and old' refers to the familiar and age-old facts of life and nature, set in a novel context of spiritual instruction. It points, too, perhaps to the fact that a true student of Scripture does not throw away the past (e.g. the Law) when he grasps new truth. The scribal critics of Christ produced only the old, the stale, and even what their own hands had spoiled. Christianity can absorb and transform all truth.

Retreat from Herod
(Matthew 13: 53—14: 36)

THE scene in Nazareth is a common one. 'We know him, we know his family. How then, can he be different?' (53–56). The illogicality is obvious. They were eager for the spectacular, a sad failing of man. God glorifies the ordinary, meets us in everyday things, haunts the common scene. He asks us to look and listen, to be alert, swift to follow him, jubilant of feet. Two remarkable verses close the episode. One (57) sums up a sad, general truth. The other (58) states a spiritual principle. God thrusts himself on no man. To do anything he must have in man a bridgehead of faith.

Herod Antipas, one of the first Herod's four sons, now enters the story (14: 1), and Matthew takes occasion to tell of the murder of John. Antipas had stolen the wife of Philip, not Herod's fellow tetrarch, but another brother. an obscure expatriate living in Rome. Herodias, carnal and ambitious, saw a future for herself when Antipas visited Rome in A.D. 23. She fled to Palestine with the weakling, and sparked a frontier war which angered the emperor, when Herod's rightful queen fled to her Nabatean people in the rock city of Petra. That is why Herod was in the fortress of Machaerus. He could not leave Herodias in Tiberias, for John's brave voice was known and heard in all that valley. Hence the contrived situation. The woman knew her husband's vices, and trained her vicious daughter well (3–12). Herod's fear (2) was danger-ous. Hence the Lord's withdrawal (13, 14).

The scene is somewhere east of the lake near Bethsaida (Luke 9: 10), not too far for crowds to walk round north of the lake from Capernaum. The story of the meal is regarded as of prime importance. All four gospels mention it. It enshrines a principle. God's creative work in human life seems to need some surrendered fragment upon which to work. Given that, he can astoundingly multiply (15–21). Each disciple was equipped, as Jews were, with a food basket. Hence the twelve of v. 20. The women would be few in that male-dominated society, and would also be serving (21).

The 'other side' is not back to Capernaum, which was Herod's territory whence they had withdrawn. Mark says Bethsaida was their destination (6: 45). Luke says they were at Bethsaida (9: 10). Matthew says they were in the deep countryside (15). The accounts reconcile, if the picnic took place near Bethsaida, but across a bay. The Lord intended to walk over the hills. He sent his men with the boat across a curve in the shore (22). After the day's toil and tension he needed quietness (23). Meanwhile the boat was in trouble, and in trouble because it was on course. A contrary wind (24) not infrequently indicates that the bow is set according to orders. The uncanny incident (24–27) shows that they were not forgotten. Peter's adventure (28–31) is omitted by Mark. Peter was behind Mark's account, and sought no prominence. 'Beginning to sink' is a common experience (30). It is then time to cry for aid. They 'landed at Gennesaret' (RSV 34). This is Chinnereth, a small plain north-west of the lake.

The Conflict Sharpens
(Matthew 15: 1-39)

THE watchers never relaxed. The 'washing' (2) which the disciples neglected was not a simple act of cleanliness but a ritual with the amounts of water measured by the egg-shell, with the movements of hand in hand, and the flow of the water from wrist to elbow and the rest prescribed and formulated. Hence the Lord's reply (3-6). To declare any property 'Korban' (a gift) was to sequester it effectively from the most humane and sacred obligations of generosity (5). 'Tradition', in other words could counteract the Law, and the most solemn sanctions of the law (6). Quoting Isaiah (8, 9) again with devastating effect, he called the legalists 'play actors', turning religion into tragic comedy. Let common sense prevail (10, 11). The food laws of the Pharisees were too ridiculous, Christ says in effect, to be taken seriously. The Pharisees, none the less, did take them seriously (12), but the report led only to a sharp denunciation. The Pharisees were no creation of God (13), they would, in consequence, suffer the fate of any weed, and meanwhile could only stumble on like blind leading helpless blind (14). What matters, he said, continuing his stern word of v. 11, is what lies in the depths of the personality, and issues in word and deed (15-20).

The unexplained visit to Tyre (21-29) was the Lord's one excursion out of the territory of Israel. A track led over the hills out of Galilee to a point near Tyre, now closed by the Lebanese border. In Tyre there is a well-laid first century pavement on which the Lord may have trodden between the columned arcades of a shopping street. But why did he make this northern journey? All day, the men who walked with him may have murmured about the Gentiles—these 'dogs' unworthy of 'the children's bread'. They disliked the foray into Phoenicia. Then in the Tyrian street the foreign woman importuned him. Dark-faced, the disciples looked on. The quick-witted Phoenician saw their opposition, and caught the warmth of his kindliness. He had brought them north perhaps for precisely this lesson. Turning to them, he spoke the words of v. 26, with a note of sorrow and irony in his voice: 'I mustn't take the children's bread and give it to—dogs.' The woman caught his words up cleverly and said, with a side look at the disapproving men: 'To be sure, but the little dogs eat of the bits which fall from the—children's table.' Imagine a slight ironical emphasis on 'children's'.

The feeding of the 4,000 is not a garbled repetition of the earlier incident. The first incident took place in spring, the second in summer. The second incident was in a Gentile area (31). The name for 'basket' is different. A 'sphuris' used here was a hamper, a Gentile basket, not a *'kophinos'*, the Jewish container for 'kosher' food (14: 20).

Confession at Banyas
(Matthew 16: 1-28)

THE Sadducees, the sceptical and powerful priestly group, now join the Pharisees in demanding a sign in the sky (1). The delicate irony of Christ, noted in the last chapter, appears again. They were observant enough to note that, since the rain-belts came out of the Mediterranean, red in the sky (a 'sign from heaven') varied in significance according to the points of the compass (2, 3). The truth about their feet, of Christ, of his coming, of the sinister drift of history, eluded them. Were they duller than Nineveh, which heard Jonah and repented? (4).

Leaven, commonly, signifies a corruption which spreads and contaminates an environment. The curious little incident of verses 6–12 was based no doubt on the Lord's amusement about the disciples' care for bread and the petty rules which surrounded eating. Let them beware, he said, whither such trifling can lead—to the corrupting care for minutiae of ritual, or to a worldly-minded religion. The 'leaven' of the two religious sects could damage them in two ways.

Caesarea Philippi, the modern Banyas, one of the sources of the Jordan, is a beautiful area of northeast Israel. It lies under Hermon and the Lord sought rest and withdrawal in the quiet villages among the hills (13). The conversation is revealing. Some identified Christ

with the hero of the Great Revival, some with the fearless Elijah, some with the agonised Jeremiah (14). Peter alone had grasped the blessed truth, that the past and its figures had gone, and that they were faced with the consummation, the messiah of God. Where the spring of Jordan burst from a rock crag (*petra*) a temple to Pan was built into the rock (hence Banyas from Panias). This was the basis of the play on words (*petros* and *petra*). Peter's confession was the 'crag' (18). The 'gates of Hell' mean 'the authority of Hell'. Lot sat in the 'gate' of Sodom (Gen. 19: 1), and archaeology can show the place of assembly and justice, the exercise of rule and judgment, inside many ancient gates. The 'church' was the assembly of the faithful (*ekklesia*— 'those called out'). A 'key' was a symbol of free entry and exclusion (Rev. 1: 18, 3: 7—both deriving from Isa. 22: 22). Peter fulfilled this function of opening in Acts 2: 41, and Acts 10 and 15. He was to 'allow and to forbid' a function he visibly exercises in his first epistle. V. 10 was a commission of vast responsibility. Peter abundantly fulfilled it.

At the same time, Christ was under no illusions about their distorted and inadequate views of messiahship. He could not trust his men to proclaim them (20) and, when he set out to teach what to them was a grim contradiction (21), it was Peter himself, who showed how far his conception of the messiah fell short of the truth (22), and touched a sensitive relic of the Lord's own temptation (23). The way of Christ is the way of those that follow him, a death and a resurrection (25, 26). A judgment follows and another life (27). And some of them did see the risen Christ and the beginnings of his triumph (28).

Transfiguration

(Matthew 17: 1–27)

THE snows of Hermon were no more than a dozen miles from Caesarea Philippi, and the high slopes must have been the scene of the event which haunted all of Peter's life (1 Pet. 5: 1) and John's long memory (John 1: 14). The transfiguration had deep significance. The great law-giver, and the first great prophet unite (3) to link the present Christ to all the past of Israel. The chosen trio misunderstood. Peter thought of three rallying points. 'To your tents, O Israel', was the call to resist (1 Kings 12: 16), and Peter was stirred by some wild hope that the messiah's uprising was at hand (4). The 'cloud' was part of Israel's history (Exod. 13: 21, 22; 34: 5; 40: 34). It is difficult to visualise it. The 'cloud' which 'received him out of their sight' (Acts 1: 9), was not the piled and lofty cumulus of medieval art. It was more likely a dazzle, a shimmer, which made all else invisible. However imagination seeks to picture it, the cloud was a symbol of the divine presence (5). The prohibition to speak was again a precaution against a mass acclaim which could have sparked rebellion and reprisal (9). Peter's foolish suggestion (4) had shown how close nationalism was to eruption.

Was this vision, they ask, coming down to Caesarea Philippi, a fulfilment of the prophecy of Malachi (10, 11; Mal. 4: 5, 6)? The Lord replied that Elijah had come unrecognised (12, 13). See also 11: 14. At Caesarea Philippi a scene of failure was waiting, a scene more fully described by Mark, who had the story from Peter (14–18). The disciples had been empowered to deal with cases like this (10: 1), but some alien element in their endeavour, perhaps a desire to impress the local notables (20, 21), had enfeebled them, and the stricken father was without help (16). The Lord's words of v. 17 reflect his disappointment in his men. 'How long must I stay with you before you understand?' is the purport of his words. They lacked true faith. The 'mountain' is not to be taken literally (20). It was a common rabbinical metaphor to describe the removal of difficulty. The logical Western mind, used to abstract speech, frequently finds the coloured, concrete, hyperbolical language of the Eastern mind a stumbling block.

Vv. 22 and 23, suggest an interlude after the return journey from Hermon and Caesarea Philippi, in which Jesus, about to make the last visit to Jerusalem, seeks again to prepare the disciples' band for the looming ordeal. They come to Capernaum and are faced with the demand for the temple-tax. The didrachmon required was a coin equivalent to the Jewish half-shekel, a poll-tax obligatory on every Jew over twenty. It was a post-exilic due based on Exod. 30: 13–16, and collected in March. Observe that the authority of Peter is recognised by the authorities (24). Peter is prompt in accepting obligation and goes in to report. Mindful of the developing jealousy among them (18: 1), Jesus anticipated Peter's assumption of authority (25). It is a fact that the Galilee mullet, the 'Saint Peter fish', rectify a physical imbalance, suffered when they expel their young from the protection of their mouth, by picking up a pebble —or in this case a lost coin.

Moral Training
(Matthew 18: 1–35)

THE last few weeks had revealed some weaknesses in the party. These are dealt with over the events of the next two chapters. Ambition was the first fault to earn rebuke, ambition so naively expressed (1) that it must have gravely tried the Lord's patience. He called a child, perhaps Peter's child (Matt. 8: 14; 1 Cor. 9: 5). Unless, he told them, they reversed the direction of such thinking (3) and learned the humility (4), trust and dependence which mark the child, they could not begin to learn what the rule of God in the life of a man signifies. The child probably remained happily with them, and provoked further teaching. In the heavenly Kingdom the strong do not trample, but exalt the weak, and the direst sin is that of making the path of the humble more difficult to tread. Pride, self-assertion and insensitivity among those who profess Christ can harm others, block the path to Christ, and create infidels. It is better to die than to harm others (6). Many mill-

stones, the upper shaped like a cone and turned by an ass harnessed to a pole, the lower cupped to receive it, lie today among the ruins of Capernaum. Perhaps some such were in view. No weight could sink a drowned victim more deeply and irrecoverably than the great cone-shaped upper stone, pierced to take the beam thrust or pulled by the circling donkey.

Sin is abroad in the world, a grim reality (7), but the sinner's personal responsibility remains. Let no one blame the result of his own evil choice or surrender, on 'society', upbringing, genetics or aught else. To tear out a root or cause of sin, a recognisable source of temptation, might be like losing eye or limb, but it must be done (8, 9). To be ruthless with oneself is better than being a peril to others (10), for when we drive another away from a God who would save, we frustrate the very work of Christ, the Shepherd who cares and suffers for even one lost from the flock (13). God treasures all (14).

The chapter reads like the notes of a long discussion. The question of wrong done to another rises. First, resentment must not rankle. It must be above ground, reduced to size by frankness (15), subjected to others' judgment (16) and finally, if proved intransigent, brought to the collective judgment of the Christian community (17), who have power to lay down that which is allowed and disallowed (18). The agreement of two in matters of vital spiritual import (19), does not provide a magic formula to force the hand of God. It merely leaches prayer of selfishness and creates the purged and tested petition which the Lord can answer. Two or three can, with God, form a society.

Peter interrupts, and such intrusions make Matthew's recollection of the long discussion very real. Forgiveness has no numerical limits in a society to which the condition of entry is forgiveness immeasurable (22, 23). As we have freely received so must we freely give (23-35). Here lies the test of sincerity and truth.

On to Jerusalem
(Matthew 19: 1—20: 16)

THE last journey began besieged by need (1, 2), and the Pharisees opened their campaign. In the matter of divorce they had two characteristic objects—to trap him into contradicting Moses, and to make him take sides either with the conservative school of Shammai, who interpreted Deuteronomy 24:1 strictly, or with the 'permissive' disciples of Hillel, who, by their laxity, made havoc of marriage (3). Implicit in the creation of one man and one woman, he replied, was the thought that each was for each and none other (Gen. 2: 23, 24). Therefore there was fundamental ungodliness in divorce (5, 6). Moses was not promoting divorce, but seeking to mitigate its evils (7, 8). Like much of the Law (e.g. 'an eye for an eye') the regulation restricted an evil which declension from original holiness had injected into society. The new society should return to holiness (9), a standard which his own chosen followers found it difficult to accept (10). Only those

who accept the Christian ethic, Christ continues, can face the enormous demands of such self-discipline. There are those, he remarks, who by physical defect or the inhumanity of man are denied marriage, and there are a few who, in obedience to some rare and demanding call, deny themselves (11, 12). Perhaps Matthew thought fit to follow this austere passage with the story of the children to suggest that the Lord was a lover of children, no withdrawn ascetic, and beloved by parents. If the sequence was not Matthew's choice it was happy coincidence.

The rich young man caught a glimpse of this truth. The discovery stirred him. Here on the road was the One who could help him. He cast reserve aside, ran, and kneeled. 'Good Master,' he cried, 'what must I do to win eternal life?' In this story (13-22) note several points. The first is the unwillingness of Christ to take advantage of emotional excitement (Mark 10: 17). Abiding conviction must be based on reason. It must count the cost of decision, and follow calm choice. Christ saw that the youth kneeling in the road (Mark 10: 17) was overwrought. He proceeded to strip the self-deception away. '*Why* do you call me good?' he asked. The emphasis is on the interrogative, and no disclaimer of goodness. Christ paused, and prompted the silent young man. '... There is no one good but God.' (17) The right answer lay ready. 'Master, have I not heard what one of your men said: "Thou art the Son of the Living God."'? And you accepted the word. I call you good because

God is good, and you and He are one. This is no courtesy I might use to any rabbi.' On such a foundation the Lord might have built. All Christianity must begin with the recognition of the deity of Christ. The young man failed adequately to reply. The Lord, still determined not to by-pass the will of the enquirer, turned to a familiar pathway (17). He quoted the fifth to the ninth command nents (18), adding 'defraud not,' a precept from Deuteronomy (24: 14) referring to prompt payment of wages, relevant in the case of a man with a large establishment. Again he might have replied correctly. Had he conceived the Law aright, he would have replied: 'Master, I know the Law, and have sought as long as I can remember to meet its demands. All I find is despair and frustration. The Law does not save me from sin, it underlines my sin. I need not a code but a Saviour.'

He said none of this. The puzzled face looked up. 'Master, I have done all these things.' The Law had not done its work of conviction. Morality for him was passive, a mere abstaining. It was not active, a drive to do. The Lord 'looked at him and loved him' (Mark 10: 21). There is yearning in the phrase, and a longing to break through and make the self-satisfied youth see and understand how shallow was his outer rectitude. He exposed the truth by a last demand and revealed that, if it came to sacrifice, the poor young man was bound to earth (21, 22).

Hence the question of v. 25. Riches bind a man, make him blind too often to his need (Rev. 3: 17)

and make salvation difficult (24). The needle's eye has given rise to odd interpretations. It has been suggested that the word used was 'cable' not 'camel', and that a word for cable in the original language was, as in English, not phonetically far removed from the word for camel. The words were probably Eastern hyperbole. Peter's characteristic intrusion (27) earns a gentle rebuke. Surely they shall receive a reward (28), but so shall others (29), and none must presume (30).

The chapter division which cuts v. 30 from the parable is not a happy one. It is a vivid little cameo. There was a crisis in the grape harvest, a spell of heat and a rapid ripening, and labour had to be hired in quantity. The farmer was a generous fellow. He had done well with his grapes, and like a good Israelite was in a mood to pass some bounty on. Perhaps he was a kindly fellow like Boaz in the story of Ruth.

It was hot weather, perhaps with a sirocco blowing (20: 12), and the work was hard, but, said the Lord, God does not love the legalist, and Peter's niggling question provoked this slightly ironical reply. God does not measure out reward. He rather pours out his wealth.

Christ's Disappointments
(Matthew 20: 17-34)

THE road was crowded. It was the eastern route to Jerusalem, down the Jordan, then west through Jericho. Christ sought privacy and told his men again what was awaiting. It was the third warning

(17–19; 16: 21; 17: 22). He sought some fellowship with them to ease the heavy burden of this journey, but encountered only the proof of how little they had understood, or how vagrant had been the attention to a lesson he had for several days been seeking to teach them (18: 3 and onwards). Zebedee's children included John, no doubt in the hands of an ambitious mother, herself crude in her misunderstanding (20, 21). The Lord sought to disenchant them. 'Cup', in Hebrew can imply both good and ill (Ps. 96; 23: 5). The two aspirants for office were convinced that it was full of good, and, speaking as naively as Peter (19: 27), were sure they could drink it (22). Perhaps, indeed, they were so to suffer, he continued (23), but it was not his to bend the processes of history and predetermine the ultimate plans of God. The tension in the group, clear in all four gospels, was grave (24), and it must have been with a heavy heart that he turned from his deep preoccupations to reiterate the long unheeded lesson of humility. They were picturing the kingdom of Heaven, he says, like a segment of the Empire, with some procurator or puppet king uplifted and both subject to the prince in Rome (26). The rules of his realm ran in the opposite direction (27, 28).

They were over the Jordan now and into Jericho, the most ancient of all fortress towns, where in forgotten centuries some nomads walled in a spring, and the tragedy of frontiers began. The three synoptic evangelists tell the story of the healing of the blind (29–34). Matthew speaks of two, Mark and Luke of one. Matthew and Mark place the incident as they left Jericho, Luke at the entering (Mark 10: 46–52; Luke 18: 35–43).

Those anxious to discover 'contradictions' in Scripture have made much of this. If the three accounts are read precisely as they are set down, it will be clear enough that three or perhaps four men were healed, one of whom was named Bartimaeus. Incidents took place on both sides of the town. What is more likely than that the news of the first healing, and the words which claimed attention, should spread through the crowd and provoke other requests? Others see confusion between Old Jericho, the mound which covers the Canaanitish city-fort, where the excavations may be seen today, and New Jericho, Herod's foundation, the modern tree-filled town. There is no careless reporting. It is the brevity of Scripture which causes misunderstanding.

Into Jerusalem
(Matthew 21: 1–22)

THE long climb of 4,000 feet up from the Jordan to Jerusalem reaches its highest point on the Mount of Olives (1) over which the ancient road seems to have run to offer the pilgrim coming from the east and south the sudden magnificence of Jerusalem, fronted by its temple, spread before him. The Lord probably had some arrangement about the ass. He deliberately fulfilled a prophecy of Zechariah (9: 9) when He chose the ass for His triumphal entry into Jerusalem.

It was on an ass that the ancient monarch rode when he came on a mission of peace. A horse was the beast of war. On that momentous day, He was offering himself to Jerusalem, not as the messiah of war, which their carnal expectation desired, but as the Prince of Peace. He wanted no illusions (2–7).

The cheering multitude saw the coming of One who would perhaps lead them to victory over the occupying power, and who would form a rallying point for the proletariat against the priesthood and the collaborating aristocracy. Hence the change of mood a week later.

The cleansing of the temple (12, 13) is dealt with at greater length under the comments on John 2. Christ was left, it seems, in sole control of the temple court whence the pollution of the hierarchy had been banished, and at first the mood was such that the entrenched authorities were baffled.

Bethany enters the story (17. John 11: 18), the Lord's place of rest. The return across the Kidron into the city was marked by the blighting of the fig-tree (18–22). It was a parable in action. Eastern teachers taught by actions as well as words. There are many illustrations in the prophets, who married wives, hid girdles, made yokes, and gave many other object lessons. The Lord, too, 'set a child in the midst' (18: 3), and in parable, as well as indignation, drove out the money-changers (12). Only a few weeks before (Luke 13: 6), he had used the barren fig tree to illustrate Israel's fruitlessness. Now he significantly repeated the lesson, and made it wider in its meaning, for it

also illustrates the spiritual truths of the Sermon on the Vine (John 15: 6). Here was the tree, like many a man, green with the leaves of profession, but with no fruit of rich reality beneath. It was a living hypocrisy. By its withering, the Lord showed that visible death and ugliness, apparent for all to see, is the final end of backsliding. If we cease to produce the fruits of the Spirit (Gal. 5: 22), though the outward habits and formalities of our religion may maintain appearances for some brief time, inevitably the sham must ultimately be exposed. In the national application, the destruction of Jerusalem, when Roman Titus was 'the axe' (Isa. 10: 15), was the outworking of the prophetic lesson.

The Duel with the Usurpers
(Matthew 21: 23—22: 14)

THE Sadducees had organised by the time he reached the temple, and sought to discredit him (23–27). It is well, if controversy is thrust on a Christian, for him to note that the Lord parried question with question, and was not driven to the defensive. The abiding influence of John's revival among the rank and file is apparent. The following parable relates to this (28–32). The first son represents the outcast multitude who repented and found salvation under John's preaching. The unctuous elder brother, like the green fig tree, made much profession but gave no evidence of reality. V. 32 links the damaging parable to the question of John's authority.

In the second parable Israel is the

vineyard, a figure from the well-known prophet Isaiah (5: 1, 2), the scriptural basis of the revival. God is the owner, and the tenants the religious leaders. The son is the messiah and, in the context, obviously and boldly, Jesus. The sequence is natural. John the forerunner is prominent in the first parable, and now it is the Lord. Prophecy intrudes (35, 36), for the long chain of rejected prophets is to end with the rejection of the messiah. The application is clear, and immediately capped by a felicitous quotation (Ps. 118: 22, 23). Hence forfeiture of privilege, and a clear' note, not common in Matthew, of a global gospel (43). The imagery of the rejected stone is allowed to run on into another verse (44), and the Pharisees see the point. They fear, none the less. Jesus inherited the standing of John, and as yet the multitude had hopes of the messiah of their mistaken dreams.

The third parable of the trilogy has similar import (22: 1–10). The bidden guests were the religious leaders, the outcasts, John's converts who bypassed the tyrannous hierarchy. The king was giving a feast in recognition of his chosen son. The chosen guests were those most reasonably expected to accept him. The notion of rejection again arises. The small appendage (11–13) is quite logical. Augustine was surely right in his suggestion that those who had come in by the proper door, received the appropriate garment by the grace of the king. Anyone, then, improperly arrayed, would be an intruder. In every revival, and John's was no

exception, there are those who, for their own ends, follow a crowd. V. 14 is a conclusion to the trilogy of parables.

The Unholy Alliance
(Matthew 22: 15—23: 39)

THE land had been ruled by procurators, officers directly responsible to the emperor, since A.D. 6. Roman rule was therefore immediate and clear. The tribute was the sharpest and most irksome symbol. It was the silver denarius, bearing Caesar's head and titles, and issued for the purposes of taxation. The Jews accepted the fiction that the coins belonged to Caesar (Tiberius at this time) and that therefore Caesar merely received back his own. The Jews, therefore, were not directly paying tribute to the alien, nor accepting a graven image. It required a subtle legal mind to accommodate thus to reality, but the collaborating hierarchy were not lacking in legal-mindedness. It tried the conscience of some, for all that, and the question levelled at Christ offered a deadly dilemma. It would have been fatal to answer either way. The reply was brilliant. It established a principle of life, and reminded the malicious priests that man also bore an image (Gen. 1: 26)—that of God, defaced and soiled (17–22).

The Sadducees were a worldly sect, liberal in their theology, and the core of collaborating Jewry. They accepted only the five books of Moses and rejected the resurrection. The question was intended to throw ridicule on this belief. The dignified reply showed that their crude attack was itself ridiculous. The other life is no pagan paradise, an extension of this life without pain. Such is the fault of all philosophies which limit man's understanding to the data of five defective senses. See 1 Cor. 2: 9 (23–30). Characteristically, the Lord took the offensive and silenced them with a text which, by their own methods of exegesis, was decisive.

The Pharisees were listening, for an alliance was growing between the two groups who were commonly at odds. They were there in force (34. Ps. 2: 2). The test question elicited nothing unorthodox but a reiteration of Deuteronomy 6: 5 and Leviticus 19: 18 (34–40). Then, in the pattern of riposte observed before, the Lord asked for their view of a key messianic text, Psalm 110: 1. If the coming one was more than David's son, must he not be more than another David? The words struck deep at the root of the common belief in a conquering king (41–46).

In chapter 23 some suggest that Matthew has gathered together numerous sayings uttered in criticism of the Pharisees. If so this is a chapter from the collection of sayings which was traditionally the first form of Matthew's gospel. At the same time, the location of the speech is appropriate, and there is no evidence that it did not crown the day-long contest with the legalists. The discourse has sequence. The exponents and guardians of the Law had a proper function (2), but one too commonly perverted (3). They made religion difficult for common men (always a mark of

error), but provided themselves with a corpus of escape clauses calculated to lift the burden from themselves (4). Pride, the basis of all sin, prompted this tyranny (5–7), and destroyed the humility which is the prerequisite of faith (7–12).

Eight 'woes' follow, against those who obscure the simplicity of faith (13), the greedy hypocrites (14), the self-seeking sellers of their own corrupt religion (15), and the absurd casuists (16–22). Christ's superb common sense blows over the 'religious' nonsense of the day like a cleansing gale. Tithing, reduced to petty legality, can be as debasing (23). For 'faith' read 'faithfulness' (Mic. 6: 8), and, in v. 24, 'strain out'. External religion is like dirty utensils, or the tombs, whitened to save ritual pollution in any who accidentally touched their exterior (26–28). And as for tombs, what of the pious plastering of the prophets' sepulchres, good men done to death by such religion as theirs (29–32)? History has not paused. It never does (33, 34). It moves to crisis and climax (35, 36). The ending is exquisite. The last crisis had not come without a final and wondrous opportunity. Jerusalem, like Judas, could still repent. They had chosen desolation by long tradition (37), blind to the day of their last chance (38, 39).

The Coming Catastrophe
(Matthew 24: 1–51)

THE temple, a glorious pile of white marble on a superb site, excited the wonder of the disciples. Perhaps, distraught by the conflict with the Pharisees, and conscious that he left the great building for the last time, Jesus appeared preoccupied and unappreciative of the grandeur around him (1). He could see the future too vividly. Archaeology in the last few years, especially round the south-west corner of the great Herodian walls, has shown the shocking ruin of fire and destruction which came in A.D. 70 (2).

They pause to look back to the superb view on the slope of the Mount of Olives (3), and the puzzled disciples, still obsessed by the unveiling of the messiah in conquering glory, hazard some questions, prompted by the closing words to the Pharisee (23: 38, 39). The Lord began with a warning (4). Mistaken views had led dupes to death before, and would lead them again (Acts 5: 35–37). War, and the threat of war, poisoned the air for the next generation, and conflict erupted in A.D. 66 (5, 6), but the discourse roams wider than the tiny corner of the world where these words were spoken. There is a timelessness about the Lord's apocalypse, and the whole future of man is encompassed, the war-ridden world, famine, again an emerging reality, and a grim feature of the first century (7), the persecution of the remnant (9), apostasy (10), the perennial deception of false teachers (11) and the fate of their dupes (12), vast missionary endeavour (13) and the antichrist (15). At this point the theme narrows. The coming ordeal of the land was a microcosm of global affliction (16–20). These words saved many Christian lives when the Great Rebellion came from 66–70. The church fled to

Pella. The words were true of trampled, ruined Palestine, but contain a hint of darker, wider application (22, 23). In A.D. 132, in the second rebellion, Bar Kochba was such a desert messiah (26), and the tortured land suffered its second desolation (21–27). The true advent of Christ will be unmistakable. The eagles of the legions closing on Jerusalem were the sign of the city's death, not the coming of God's deliverer (28).

A difficult passage follows (29–31). Jerusalem's horror was but one of the historical disasters which were to torment the earth. The language of poetic apocalyptic literature was familiar to the Jews (29. Isa. 13: 10; 34: 4; Amos 8: 9; Ezek. 32: 7, 8; Joel 2: 28–32). Stress was world-wide. Rome and Italy were devastated by civil war in A.D. 69, in the midst of Israel's suffering. Vv. 29–31 cannot be made to set the second advent of Christ immediately after Israel's disaster. It did not happen. But it was only after the ruin of an old order (29), that the world became aware of the power of the gospel. Christ's 'angels', his messengers, if we thus interpret, were the heralds who brought the new faith, like a summoning trumpet blast, to the world, and it is historic fact that Christianity changed the course of history.

Twofold warning, in this intertwined prophecy, follows. That 'generation' did not 'pass away', until many had seen the downfall of the land. That 'race' (the second, meaning of the word) has not passed away (34), and will not pass away, until the final and secondary meaning of the oracle is revealed. His words stand (35), but no juggling with utterance or event can pinpoint a date (36). The warning abides for those who care. For the rest comes sudden disaster (36–41). The Christian, first century or twentieth, has one duty—to watch, understand, be ready (42–47), and not, grown faithless and apostate, presume (48–51).

Last Judgment

(Matthew 25: 1–46)

THE closing words of the apocalyptic prophecy suggest the parables of this chapter. The theme is continuous, and this chapter division might have been made at 24: 42. The parable of the girls with the lamps (1–13) shows how necessary it is to distinguish between parable and allegory. A parable has one point to press. Pictorial details merely make the story. To seek further meaning in this exhortation to vigilance and preparedness (24: 42–46) would be to sanction selfishness and niggardly disregard of another's need. (Observe the stages of Jewish marriage—first the engagement, a contract between parents, then the betrothal, a formal ceremony of great sanctity. A betrothed girl was regarded as a widow if the man died before marriage. The marriage took place some time later, and the formal procession of the bridegroom and his friends to claim his bride from the parents, is the ceremony envisaged in this story.)

The church, however, has more to do than passively wait. Hence the second parable (14–30). There are duties to pursue. All the servants were judged trustworthy, but of unequal ability. Hence the distribution. It was 'after a long time' (19) that the master returned and commendation was given to those who had used well the little or the much that had been entrusted to them. Condemnation, and dire condemnation, fell upon the negligent and inactive, especially when he blamed his master for his supineness (24, 25). Note that even one talent was a very considerable sum. God does not undervalue anyone's usefulness.

A poetic description of the last judgment follows (31–33). The goat was recognised in the Mediterranean for the sinister beast he was, a disaster to living vegetation. See Ezekiel 34: 17. The goat deforested Greece and Asia Minor, and modern Israel seeks in vain to discourage Arab goat-herding. Goats, like evil men the world over and through history, ravage, spoil, destroy and blight the environment.

The pronouncement of judgment closes the chapter (34–46). As with the negligence of the virgins of the first parable, the inactivity of the useless servant in the second, so here, it is the sins of callousness, neglect, and lovelessness which win condemnation. Uselessness earns merited destruction.

Looming Agony

(Matthew 26: 1–75)

THE plot was afoot and Jesus was aware of it (1–5). It was a tense and turbulent province, as the

Romans knew, and the Romans' collaborators had no friends among the rank and file. Jerusalem was crowded, and many a zealot had slipped into town. That was how the terrorist Barabbas was apprehended. The priests wished to do their work quietly and, if Matthew's account is set with John's (which see), the whole texture of the plot is clear. The Galileans, of all Israel, were perhaps the most difficult.

It was a singularly happy chapter division which placed Mary's (John 12: 1-11) symbolic act in the same chapter as the Passion story (6-13). It was a 'beautiful deed' (10), said Jesus. She alone had caught the pathos of the moment and in one lovely poetic act showed that she understood. The sacrifice was very expensive. Just such a jar of ointment had once been presented by Cambyses, emperor of Persia, to the king of Ethiopia. The disciples were gruff with women (15: 23; 19: 13). There was a growl of protest, headed, says John, by Judas (12: 4). 'It is not at all surprising', remarks Malcolm Muggeridge, 'that the villain among the disciples should appear as the most socially concerned. The wicked are much given to collective moralising . . .'

'Judas', writes Alexander Bruce, 'could not breathe easily amid the odours of the ointment and all it emblemed.' Perhaps, indeed, this scene was the last straw in some process of disillusionment with so disappointing a messiah. He went his way, and played into the plotters' hands (12-16).

It was not without the knowledge of his Master as the story of the Last Supper shows (17-30). Some arrangement appears to have been made (18), unknown to the disciples, so that Judas should have no knowledge of the place. His betrayal had to be open, as John 13: 30 indicates. The dish (23) was probably a customary mixture of dates, figs, vinegar and spice, the colour of mud, to remind them of Egypt's brickmaking. What is so awesome is the Lord's full knowledge of the coming ordeal, and his complete command of the situation.

The same calm mood continued as they left the city, crossed the Kidron, and came to Gethsemane (30-36). Some of them had caught a fragment of his meaning but Peter's protestations (35) only made his loneliness more intense. All through the time of overwhelming agony under the olives he was utterly alone (37-45). The story of the arrest needs no exposition. No words could be more poignant—the flare of torches under the trees, a traitor's kiss to form a symbol of treachery for all time, Peter's slash at one of the priest's attendants, and universal abandonment (47-56).

The Sanhedrin was in makeshift and illegal session (57), desperately shamming a regular trial (59, 60) without success (61, 62). At last the high priest put his prisoner on oath over the question of messiahship. An answer had to be given, for his whole life's claim was now involved. Continued silence would be denial (63, 64). Caiaphas had his evidence and called for sentence (65, 66). The fear and tension under which the Sanhedrists were committing their crime, and their consciousness of the illegality of the whole process, erupted in base and undignified violence (67, 68). The scene shifts to Peter's ordeal and denials. One act of betrayal, as is the way, led to another. He was known, his dialect was plainly Galilean, defective in gutturals, it is said. And the cock crew. Whether 'cockcrow' was the name for the trumpet call signalling the last watch from the Tower of Antonia cannot be said with certainty.

On to Calvary

(Matthew 27: 1–56)

PILATE had, it appears from John's intimate account, promised already a death sentence (1, 2). Matthew breaks the story to tell of Judas' fearful end (3–10). It was no doubt the sight of Jesus being led, chained and battered, to Pilate which broke Judas. The tragic attempt to give the money back, and the legalistic subterfuge of the priests, are a striking stamp of reality on the narrative. After his habitual fashion, Matthew finds two prophetic echoes in the Old Testament (Jer. 32: 7–9; Zech. 11: 12, 13). There is no clash between the account in Matthew and that in Acts. The 'field of blood' was doubly so after Judas' suicide there. His suicide was obviously followed by the ghastly ruin of his body, undiscovered as it hung in some cleft and destroyed by its fall as the rope broke or was cut. So traitors end, rejected and despised by those who accept their betrayal.

Obviously, the priests had made much capital of an alleged claim to royalty (11). It would weigh with Pilate, whose one commission was to keep peace in that sensitive military corridor and border area. It was obvious that Pilate was not open to protestations of innocence, or an explanation of a mystic kingship, but the prisoner's dignified silence impressed him, and he sought escape from what was becoming a dilemma (12–14). Perhaps they would accept Jesus as the prisoner customarily released to celebrate the Passover? The priests' hidden reasons for the trial were also apparent to him. Hence an appeal to the gathering crowd. 'This man or Barabbas,' the popular terrorist? The crowd were now with the priests. The so-called messiah had disappointed them. He had suffered indignity without resistance. Let him die. Let the rough strong man be freed. The priests were active among them, and calling the tune. So Pilate failed in his two-pronged attempt to spite the priests, and do justice cheaply (15–18). His wife was no help. Claudia Procula, if that was her name, must have known of a corrupt bargain with the Jews, slept with the shame of it on her mind, and dreamed disturbingly (19). Pilate, stirred by her message, and uneasy, continued his attempts, but he was in the grip of some base compromise, and could not afford a riotous Jerusalem at Passover. The year 66 showed what a city tumult could ignite (22, 23). The washing, and the crowd's awful reply, have become symbols of human sin and folly (24–26).

Scratched on the stones of the Pavement are the marks of a soldiers' game. It is to be seen beneath the Convent of the Sisters of Zion. The details are obscure, but the soldiers' play used Jesus, arrayed as king, as a piece or a pawn. He stood weak and bleeding on a square where B ('*basileus*'—, king) is still visible (27–31).

The Lord refused the anaesthetising drink (34) and was nailed to the crossbeam of what was probably a T-shaped cross. The 'hand' in spite of medieval art, would not have held the weight of the body on the nails. 'Hand' was used to include wrist and forearm. A skeleton discovered in an ossuary in 1968 showed scratched bones in the forearm, damaged as the victim writhed in agony. The nails had pierced the forearm above the wrist. The beam was lifted on to a permanent stake (the word 'to crucify' (22) means 'to stake'—and see 1 Pet. 2: 24). They divided his garments as Psalm 22: 18 had uncannily foretold, and an inscription savagely directed by Pilate against the Jews, was set in place (see John 19: 19). Two criminals, possibly members of Barabbas' gang, died with him (Isa. 53: 12). The events which followed are simply told with rapid, poignant realism—the callous priests, vile in their hour of triumph, the cowardly, silent majority, vocal now (40–43), the quotation of Psalm 22: 1 (46), the kindly soldier who stuck his spear in a sponge, (see on John 19: 29) and offered the sufferer a drink of the squad's ration wine ... Then the last cry, its meaning inaudible to Matthew (50), but clear to John standing by the cross ... Three strange events are recorded—a sinister darkness (45), the tearing of the temple veil by some seismic shock (51), seen by the writer to the Hebrews as a symbol (Heb. 6: 19; 10: 19). Only Matthew mentions the strange appearance of past saints in Jerusalem, a mark of the conquest over death. The centurions of the New Testament were chosen men assigned to a difficult province. The officer in charge of the execution party (54) was typical, and overawed by the hour's events (John 12: 32).

Empty Tomb
(Matthew 27: 55—28: 20)

THE women followed from the cross to the grave (55, 56). Joseph, a rich man (57) from Ramathaim-Zophim (1 Sam. 1: 1), actually a member of the Sanhedrin (Mark 15: 43; Luke 23: 50), courageously secured proper burial for his friend, 'in his own tomb' (58–60). Pilate gave gruff (65) permission to the priests to set a guard. It was ironical (66).

The Sabbath over, early on the first Christian Sunday (28: 1), the same two women who had witnessed the burial (27: 61) came to the tomb and were involved in a sudden storm of events they found hard to describe. How long the happening listed in vv. 2–7 took, cannot be said, probably less time than it takes to read them—women and guards overwhelmed by the shudder of the earth, the blaze of a presence about the tomb and the rock; a voice, a statement, a command. Emerging sharp and clear was the memory of an empty tomb. The actual rising of Christ is not

described, and it is manifestly
wrong to visualise this cluster of
events in the forms and tradition of
medieval art.

To clarify their dazzled minds the
risen Lord met the women and told
them of his rendezvous in Galilee
(9, 10). There is no obligation to
choose between a set of appearances
in Jerusalem and a set in Galilee.
John, also an eyewitness, mentions
both. The priests, who had accepted
Pilate's charge (27: 55, 56) were in
a dilemma. Their own guards were
involved, easily bribed, and as
ready as they were to propagate a
story (13) if necessary. They hoped
for the best (14) and succeeded.

The tale took root, and, if the
Nazareth Decree is evidence, was
abroad in Rome in A.D. 49.

Matthew's brevity is disconcerting, but a roll of papyrus had
its limits, and when his gospel was
set in final form, Luke's account
and Paul's were common knowledge. The doubt mentioned in v.
17 suggests that the occasion
included many more than the eleven.
Perhaps it was the occasion of 1
Corinthians 15: 6. Some were
baffled by the sheer wonder, some
under the curious spell which held
the two of the Emmaus road (Luke
24: 16). The book ends with a
mighty promise.

THE GOSPEL ACCORDING TO ST. MARK

Mark and his Swift Story
(Mark 1: 1–45)

MARK, Simon Peter's 'son in Christ', wrote this gospel. It is possible that it was in the sinister summer of A.D. 64, which saw the Great Fire of Rome, and the beginning of the Empire's lamentable policy of persecution, that Peter saw the gathering storm, and called Mark to write his brief, clipped account of vital events. There must have been a jealously-guarded oral tradition (1 Cor. 11: 23; 15: 3; Phil. 4: 9; 2 Thess. 3: 6), and possibly even a written tradition of which the puzzling fragment discovered at Qumran might be a part. (See also Luke 1: 1.) For writer, says old tradition, Peter chose John Mark, son of Mary, the widow of Jerusalem, in whose house the Lord and his men met on the betrayal night, and where the first Christians gathered (Acts 12: 12). Mark was associated with the first missionary ventures of the church, quarrelled with Paul over some feature of policy, and withdrew (Acts 12: 25; 13: 5, 13; 15: 38, 39). Restored to usefulness, and ultimately to the friendship of Paul, Mark found at last his real calling, and wrote a gospel (1 Pet. 5: 13; 2 Pet. 1: 15, 16; Philem. 24; 2 Tim.

4: 11). They were perilous days. Time was short. Hence the brevity of the book; perhaps also a lost ending. The Greek is rugged. There are echoes of Peter everywhere.

Mark plunges straight into his story (1–8), linking the ministry of Jesus with the great religious revival which, as Malachi had foretold, swept through a people starved in spirit by the worldly Sadducees and the legalistic Pharisees (Mal. 3: 1). There is growing evidence that John the Baptist was part of a strong religious stream which never ran dry in Israel, from Elijah and Amos to the shepherds of Bethlehem, and such wilderness cults as that of the Essenes and Qumran.

Mark crowds the story of the Lord's baptism (Matt. 3: 13–17; John 1: 30–34), like Luke, into two verses (9, 10), and compresses the story of the temptation into three (11–13). (cf. Matt. 4: 1–11; Luke 4: 1–12).

Similar brevity marks the tale of the Galilean mission. Jesus waited until John's ministry was obviously ended (14), began to preach 'the Kingdom of God', and chose his disciples—men from the prosperous fishing industry of the Lake, and probably converts of John (15–20; John 1: 35–42).

The events in the Capernaum synagogue seem to have been regarded as a notable beginning (21–32; Luke 4: 31–37). Mark was Luke's authority here as a comparison will show. Mark's authority was recognised and promptly used.

Mark widens the circle, passes to the incident Peter so well remembered (30, 31), and then to the cool of the evening and the gathered population of the town (32–34). The land, long oppressed by puppet rulers, the occupying forces and the collaborating priests, over-populated, its soil exhausted, was haunted with physical and mental sickness. It is a fact which obtrudes in the story. To heal, to help, to preach, drains the spirit. Jesus withdrew and the clamant need drew him back (35–37), but good and blessing are to share (38, 39).

The next incident is not without connection. Vv. 16–34 record, almost with breathless haste, a typical day in the Lord's early ministry. It must have been intensely exhausting, and he needed peace from the noise and jostling, and renewal of strength. He knew of no better therapy than solitude and prayer. Back with the people the next morning (40), he meets and heals a leper (41–43). Why was silence enjoined? (44). The man had committed an illegal act by coming to town at all. The sooner healing was authenticated the better. But Peter must have marked a crucial moment when the scene of ministry had to avoid the larger assemblages of men. But observe that the careful respect for the law shown by Jesus has relevance.

Stir in Capernaum
(Mark 2: 1–28)

CHRIST could not be hidden (7: 24). When he is in a house others know. He was a resident now of Capernaum (Matt. 9: 1; Luke 4: 31). The Galilean tour over (1: 38, 39), he was home again and besieged (1, 2). Aware now of his presence, the local hierarchy (or an investigating group from Jerusalem cf. John 1: 19; Luke 5: 17) were watching (6). A sick man was lowered by friends through the roof. Perhaps it was the practical Peter's suggestion, with ropes borrowed from his boat. Diagnosing the situation (5), Christ passed by the physical malady and struck at the spiritual cause. The critics, without pity for the dire human need before them, lapsed into theological quibble (7), quickly met and confounded (8–12). Their reasoning, of course, was sound. If Christ was not divine, he was a deceiver. He left no other alternative open to us. He was either what he claimed to be or a creature to be rejected with pity or with scorn. 'The Son of Man' (cf. v. 10) was a recognised messianic title, and a claim was in the phrase (Dan. 7: 13; Luke 19: 10).

Levi, also called Matthew (Matt. 9: 9), as a tax officer of the hated Herod's administration (Luke 23: 6, 7), was trebly outcast, a renegade from Jewry, a participant in the immoral tax-farming system, and an associate of sinners (16). Again, Christ looked past the outward appearance (1 Sam. 16: 7). As with Paul's conversion (Acts 9), the climax only is shown. The concealed agony, self-loathing and desperate reaching for God (cf. Luke 18: 13, 14), is not revealed. God never fails to see it. The first instinct of the truly converted is to share the blessing (15). Matthew did, and his Lord received biting criticism. They failed to see that one who has become Jesus' friend has ceased to be a sinner. For this reason Matthew had abandoned his loathed way of life. Hence the irony of v. 17. 'There is none righteous' (Rom. 3: 10–27). Their boasted righteousness had forgotten Isaiah 64.

Levi's banquet sparked criticism on a wider scale. John's disciples had conformed to scribal rules of fasting. Leaving him to follow Jesus (John 1: 35–37), they found a code less strict. Was this a scorn for the Law beginning to form a pattern? (1: 26; 2: 23). Was it a challenge? (18). The hour, Christ sanely replied, was a time of joy (20), but such hours are not the norm of history. Then cryptically he suggests that old forms, like old garments (21) and dried bottles (22) could not contain the intrusion of new things, be it a strong patch on worn cloth or the ferment of new life.

Surveillance soon found another charge (23). Thousands of petty rules hedged the Sabbath. Plucking corn was allowed (Deut. 23: 25) but not, by rabbinical law, on the Sabbath. They were 'reaping'. The charge was one of ignorance (24). What sort of teacher was this? (John 7: 15, 49).

The answer came on two levels. First the Lord casually cast down a precedent (25, 26). They could never answer such arguments. Then, on a

higher level he stated an immortal principle (27) and made a bold claim (28). They dehumanised God's beneficent provisions by their code, and denied God's son his standing. The gauntlet was obviously down.

The Unpardonable Sin
(Mark 3: 1–35)

SEE the comments on Matthew 12: 10–14 for the story of the man with the withered hand. The Pharisees' response was shocking. The man was a test case. His healing could have waited till the next day, but Christ decided on the confrontation which, in any case, was inevitable. Too calloused in heart to sense the urgency of human need, they stood publicly condemned. Deliberately to refrain from doing good is to do evil (5. Jas. 4: 17).

The Pharisees were also isolated and felt the public hostility enough to seek a partnership with the Herodians. Mark only mentions this group here (Matt. 22: 16). This society was composed of those who recognised Herod's house as a bulwark against Roman domination. Indeed, for a whole century, the able and ruthless family was precisely that—all five of them known to us. The Pharisees looked upon this wealthy, shrewd and largely Sadducean group as traitors and collaborators. Their desperation is revealed in this expedient accommodation (6).

Disciples were gathering from beyond the Jordan and from the Phoenician coastal towns of the modern Lebanese littoral (7, 8). The synagogue was obviously closing, but the open air was free. Along the coast south of Capernaum there is one crescent bay where a ship could lie offshore as if in the orchestra of a Greek theatre, and where thousands could listen on the curved sloping shore (9, 10). Healing, too, continued, and in the midst of this surge of popularity the Lord sought to quench unnatural enthusiasm (11, 12).

Mark's headlong narrative rushes in a few verses over the Sermon on the Mount (13), the choosing of the Twelve (14), their commissioning (15), and the list of their names—a varied group, as any church must be. It was at this time that Christ's family became concerned about him (20, 21; 31-35). Perhaps Matthew 10: 35-40, placed in this same context, was the Lord's reaction. And see Matthew 12: 46-50.

The Pharisees' reaction prompted a terrible rebuke (see comments on Matt. 12: 24-29). The unpardonable sin is no commonly listed sin (1 Cor. 6: 9-11). Consider the background. The Holy Spirit prompts men to consider Christ. The effect is an overwhelming consciousness of inadequacy (Luke 5: 8). Christ does not depart. He draws near when the heart is anguished thus. Penitence follows, and forgiveness. But reverse the process. Dogged refusal to listen to the promptings of the Holy Spirit (Gen. 6: 3), in pride of heart or nourished hatred, results in an inability to see the beauty and challenge of his perfection. That inability stifles all sense of sin. The sinner so paralysed cannot repent. He cannot therefore be forgiven. It is self-willed hard-

ness, not a form of words, which constitutes blasphemy against the Holy Spirit.

This was the situation with the Jerusalem Pharisees on their visit to Capernaum. They identified Christ's work with the Devil's work. They declared in measured and deliberate terms that the healing he had brought to tormented lives was the activity of evil powers. To lie thus, thus to misrepresent and corrupt goodness and truth, was to demonstrate evil so determined and ingrained, a spirit so lost to good and grace, a conscience so seared, and a heart so wilfully hardened that Christ (but only Christ) could declare that such men were lost, 'of their father the Devil and doing his desires' (John 8: 44). Like the friar in Dante's Inferno, their souls were in Hell while their bodies still walked the earth.

The Parables
(Mark 4: 1-41)

SEE comments on Matthew 13: 1-17 for the parable of the sower. The marks of the environment are often on the teaching of Christ. He sat on the ship facing his lakeside audience. Some farming operations would be visible on the hills around. So he won attention, but at the same time deliberately sifted out the indolent, the thoughtless and the merely curious. The country audience was thus bidden to think and seek the deeper meaning of things. Those who caught his meaning saw the figure on the boat merge with the sower, saw their hearts and minds as the receiving earth, and left under challenge to self-examination and soul-searching (1–20).

For was he not uplifting a light (21)? The new style of preaching was designed to make clear all that needed clarity (22), and to inform those who chose to listen (23). They understood, when they looked attentively, that the listener received only what he deeply desired to receive (24), and once he had, by earnest thought, laid hold on truth, so truth multiplied (25). Once planted, the seed grew. There is acute psychological insight here. Set in the mind's depth, and implanted at the core of the personality, the seed germinates. God needs only a bridgehead to invade the life (1 Cor. 3: 6; Phil. 1: 6; 2 Pet. 3: 18). So comes the true harvest (26–29).

So the seed, be it ever so small a hint of good, of true surrender, of longing for Christ, produces what it was appointed to produce (30, 31). Perhaps a small mustard tree stood nearby with birds perching in it (so v. 32—not 'nest').

For the story of the storm see comments on Matthew 8: 23–27. The notable fact about association with Christ is the growth of the disciples' awe. Friendship with him brought no disillusionment, none of the common adjustments of tolerance, no pardoning of faults. It was growing wonder.

The Man who was Legion

(Mark 5: 1–43)

IT was night when they reached shore (4: 35). It was not a pleasant time to hear a cry from a homi-

cidal lunatic. He was emerging from the scattered tombs (5) around the limestone rocks, with fragments of the bonds upon his hands by which the terrified townsfolk had sought to bind him (4).

He was possessed by 'an unclean spirit' (2). The statement is not to be lightly dismissed. There are phenomena of evil not adequately explained by psychologists. Voodooism, for example, with the sudden seizure of bystanders by some alien influence, a visitation which destroys individuality, changes the voice, imposes patterns of behaviour remote from normal—such manifestations of something unseen are not fully to be explained by known processes of the mind's working. They may be paralleled by similar corruptions of the personality in pagan cults, ancient and modern. To dismiss them as 'an extensive complex of compulsive phenomena' is only to say in more words what the Bible says in few.

The afflicted man knew that immense and manifold evil gripped and filled his soul (6, 7). A legion, Rome's unit of six thousand men, had become for him an awful symbol of himself (9). Perhaps he had run madly from his village, a little shrieking boy, when a Roman patrol closed round it to wreak reprisals for the murder of some member of the local garrison.

Perhaps the memory of his parents, dead in the dusty street, drove him to consuming hatred, and breakdown of reason. Occupying forces of foul presences held his mind and heart in cruel subjection. And there, among the Roman tombs, he saw the word 'Legion', carved, as archaeologists have found it, on stone after stone until he raved and tore things apart. What had they to do with Christ, such a regiment of horror (7)? Some undamaged corner of the man's will cried out for salvation. But how could Christ convince so shattered a soul that it was cleansed and free? It costs much sometimes to effect salvation. The price is not always mentioned. It is set down in this story, and it cost two thousand swine (11–16).

How long this took is impossible to know, but the local citizens, preferring swine to Christ, drove their dangerous visitor away (14–17). The healed man was sent back to the community which had feared him. He was the first missionary to the Gentiles, for the Decapolis was full of Greeks (18–20. See Matt. 8: 28–34).

On the story of Jairus' daughter see the comments on Matthew 9: 18–26. Mark adds a few details and one seems sometimes to hear Peter's voice—as in v. 16 ('They heard about the pigs too'). Observe the touch of scorn in v. 26, which physician Luke omits (8: 43), and note the words of v. 30. We cannot be touched and healed by Christ privately (33, 34). He will not allow it. He is never too late, however late it looks (35). He will not work amid scorn and unbelief but desires a community of faith (37. 6: 45). Peter's memory again records the actual Aramaic words (41).

Herod's Last Chance
(Mark 6: 1–56)

SEE the comments on Matthew 13: 54–58 for the visit to Nazareth, back in the hill country of Galilee some miles west of the lake (1–6), and on Matthew 10 for the sending out of the Twelve (7–13). See comments on Matthew 14: 1–14 for the grim story of Herod's crime, but observe in Mark's account one or two points of interest (14–29).

The mission of the Twelve through the villages of Galilee stirred the guilty conscience of Herod Antipas, the tetrarch of the land, the contemptible son of Herod the Elder, the scoundrel of the Nativity story. 'It is John the Baptist,' whispered the ruler, when he heard of Christ, 'John the Baptist whom I beheaded, risen from the dead.' (14–16) And Mark adds a curious detail: 'For Herod feared John, knowing that he was a just man and an holy, and he observed him; and when he heard him he did many things and heard him gladly.' Or to paraphrase in simple English: 'Herod respected John. He knew that he was a just, good man, and paid attention to him. He listened willingly to John's preaching, and John's words deeply influenced his conduct' (20).

It is a strangely moving picture of what might have been. The New Testament has little good to say of the five Herods who move through its pages, and to Herod Antipas the Lord had no word to say. 'That fox' (Luke 13: 32), he called him in one phrase of scorn. And yet here is the memory of a brighter hour, with desire for good, and admiration for a good man, still active in a life which became utterly corrupt. Here too is a conscience moving, and the sting of remembered sin. Here is the puppet prince of Galilee with the disguises torn away and the defences stripped, a frightened man tormented by a memory, alone with God.

Herod could still have been redeemed, even after the flesh had betrayed him (22), and sensuality had brought him to the bottom rung of moral disaster. The way back goes far down the slope. The grace of God reaches infinitely low. Herod had only to treat with scorn the laughter of vicious men (26). He had only one step of right to take, and it might have saved his feet from catastrophe. He failed to take it, and when he at last met Christ, Christ himself had no point of contact, no single word which the ruined man might have understood (Luke 23: 9). Here was Hell indeed, self-created.

For the story of the lakeside picnic (32–44) and the adventure on the lake (45–52), turn back to the comments on Matthew 14: 13–32, but observe one or two marks in the story of the vivid memory of an eyewitness—the utter weariness of the disciples (35, 36), the memory of green grass (39, John 6: 10, written thirty years later), and especially v. 40. The Greek reflects Peter's Aramaic construction. He remembered how, on the green grass, the people looked like 'flower beds' and that is what Mark wrote ('groups', 'companies', 'rows', 'parties', 'squares', say the translators timidly).

For Gennasaret see comments on Matthew 14: 34–36.

Confrontation and Retreat
(Mark 7: 1–37)

MATTHEW 15 contains the major portion of the teaching and narrative of this chapter and the comments given there apply here. Christ was back in the area patrolled by the Pharisees' envoys, and meets the old problem of their unrelenting surveillance. They attacked the Lord first through his disciples (2, 5) not infrequently a more vulnerable avenue of assault, and then turned on him directly (7). It was a deadly retort to show how tradition could actually contradict basic Scripture (6–13), and it may have silenced the legalists temporarily (14).

It is saddening to see how difficult Christ's own men found it to understand him (18). It was his intention to leave to these men, prone to misunderstand (8: 16), hard of heart (16: 14), the promotion of his gospel. The mind is the danger point for man (19), and what mind, from then till now, has not needed the Interpreter (John 14: 26)?

A hostile frontier makes Tyre remote from Galilee today. In those days communication was open (3: 8). Converts had come and gone. The story of the deaf-mute can be better understood against its background (31–37). Cutting back over the hills to eastern Galilee and then across the lake, the traveller entered another area, that of the Ten Towns, where the population, like that of

Tyre, was predominantly Gentile. The lesson the disciples had learned in Tyre now had relevance. This was the country of the maniac named 'Legion'. The man appears to have done his work well (33. Matt. 15:30). The needy were waiting. Matthew dismisses the story of the visit briefly (15: 29-31), but it made a greater impression on Peter. Christ used, in order to awaken faith, a superstition that the spittle of a good man had healing power (33. cf. John 9: 6). The Aramaic word (34) suggests that the man was a Jew.

Round the Lake
(Mark 8: 1-38)

THE feeding of the 4,000 (1-9) is not a duplicate, as was pointed out in the comments on Matthew 15: 32-39. Two gospels directly in touch with eyewitnesses place the events close together. The audience could, in fact, have been largely Gentile, the fruit of the missionary efforts of the Gadarene. The word for basket is not that describing the Jews' food container, and authenticated even by a Roman satirist's account of a Jewish slum (Juvenal 3: 14). It is the word used for the big basket used in Paul's escape (Acts 9: 25). Probably the Twelve did not this time replenish their own food supplies (14), but the local population filled the seven hampers which were available (9).

The visit to Dalmanutha, an unknown locality, was spoiled by the Pharisees calling for signs (11-14). The same cause can still spoil and frustrate. V. 12 should be taken to heart by those who preach the gospel (10-13). Musing on the incident, and grossly misunderstood (16-21), the Lord warned how corrupting and pervasive the Pharisees' ritualism, legalism and deadening conformities could be—even in little Dalmanutha. Leaven is commonly a figure for seeping evil (1 Cor. 5: 7). In Luke 12: 1 it is explained as hypocrisy. See comments on Matthew 16: 1-12. Herod (15) was devoted to earthly power. He had gained it by evil, subservience, utter selfishness. Let the disciples beware lest they so misconceive the Kingdom of God.

Bethsaida was abandoned (Matt. 11: 21-24) but mercy was still available to those who sought it. Observe the eyewitness' mark in v. 23 and refer back to 7: 33. The restoration in this case was slow. It often is when Christ heals, but he will continue patiently if the healed one trusts ... Bethsaida still lay under its penalty (26).

See the comments on Matthew 16: 13-27 for the significance of Peter's confession and the Lord's discussion with his men at Caesarea Philippi. This is the first of three occasions when he sought to make the coming ordeal known (9: 31; 10: 32).

On the Mountain and Below
(Mark 9: 1-29)

SEE Matthew 17: 1-8 for the story of the transfiguration (1-13). The Valley of the Shadow lay ahead. Peter, James and John were to be the leaders in that ravine, and the Lord sought in a special way to fortify their souls for the ordeal (2).

In Peter's second epistle, written a generation later, there is reference to the awesome experience (2 Pet. 1: 17, 18. Add perhaps 1 Pet. 5: 1). Mark, too, has homely features in his account which catch the sound of Peter's voice as he detailed the tremendous story. The expression, 'exceeding white, so as no laundryman on earth could whiten them' (3), is in Mark alone, and Mark bluntly reports that Peter's suggestion about the three tents were made by a man 'not knowing what he said' (6). It was always Peter's way to hide tension by saying anything which sprang to his mind. It was a frequent source of folly.

Testing and temptation were to take two forms in the coming weeks of trial and misery. First they were to be tempted to think that they had been wrong about Christ. For minds steeped in the O.T. there was overwhelming significance in the appearance of Moses and Elijah (4). Those trained to see the analogies and parallelisms of past history would remember that both Moses and Elijah died strange deaths, both east of Jordan, that two mountains, Horeb and Nebo were in the story of one, while two mountains, Horeb and Carmel, were in the life of the other. The cloud that misted Hermon would recall the clouds of Sinai into which Moses went, and the cloud which came up out of the sea after Elijah's victory. Moses was the leader of the exodus, and in the Greek text of Luke's account we read that Moses and Elijah spoke with Christ of the 'exodus he should accomplish at Jerusalem' (Luke 9: 31). Elijah, like Christ, knew an ascension. Moses was the great Law-giver, Elijah the first of the prophets. The Old Testament was embodied in them. Words, too, would echo in the minds of the three, oracles chanted in the synagogue, and heard on the rabbis' lips a thousand times. Verses from Deuteronomy (18: 15–19), words uttered to Moses, would spring into the memory: 'I will raise up a prophet from among their brethren like unto thee, and will put my words in his mouth . . .' And from the last of the Old Testament writers, Malachi (3: 1; 4: 5, 6): 'Behold I will send you Elijah, the prophet, before the great and dreadful day of the Lord . . .' (11–13).

The second shape of their coming testing was the temptation to despair, to imagine that God had lost control, and that evil was triumphant. In that temptation lies the darkest hour of the soul. That is why Christ, so soon to hang broken and bleeding on the cross, was revealed as 'the Beloved Son' (7). And we are 'accepted in the Beloved' (Eph. 1: 6).

For the story of the impotent disciples (14–29) see the comments on Matthew 17: 14–21. Mark adds some touches of vivid narrative from Peter's memory. The spotlight turns upon the desperate father. There is a note of hopelessness in his voice (21, 22). 'If you can . . .' The tone is flat and disillusioned. The Lord looked at him and said: 'If you can believe! All things are possible to one who believes.' At the words, the man's heart caught fire. 'Lord,' he cried, 'I believe. Help my unbelief' (24). So KJV and Moffatt. 'I have faith. Help me where it fails,' Rieu renders. 'I do believe. Help me to believe more,' says J. B. Phillips. Or translate: 'I believe, I believe, pity my faith's feebleness.' So cried the man, and put a magnificent prayer into history, a prayer which, of all prayers, can claim an answer.

From Caesarea to Jericho
(Mark 9: 30—10: 52)

THE route should be followed on a map. The Lord sought to use every minute but found cause for sorrow in the disciples' attitude. (See the comments on the parallel passage in Matt. 17: 22, 23; 18: 1–10.) Mark's account leaves out the story of the tribute, perhaps part of Peter's deliberate attempt not to make himself too prominent in the story. One or two sharp details grace Mark's story. He 'took the child in his arms' (36). The future in v. 35 probably renders the Aramaic tense which formed an imperative: 'Let him be...' Vv. 38–41 is obviously a crude interruption. John was quick tempered ('son of thunder'). Perhaps he had burst in with the news, and anxious to report, had interrupted a tender speech. The result was the expression of a principle (40), to be held in wise tension with that of Matthew 12: 30. The rest of the chapter contains much repetition of words spoken on the mount of the famous sermon (Matt. 5–7), no doubt in sight at the time of the discussion. A good teacher believes in repetition (Matt. 5: 13, 29, 30). The same reminiscence continues some days later (10: 1) as they drew near Judaea by the road east of Jordan (Matt. 5: 31, 32. See also comments on Matt. 19: 1–9). The Pharisees of the Judaean heartland were closing in (10: 1–12). The Lord did not reject Moses, but went behind him (as did the writer to the Hebrews). Moses was permissive. There was a sterner ethic for Christians.

The disciples sometimes screened their Master from the crowd (13. John 12: 21, 22). Perhaps the action was well-intended, but it is not a Christlike quality to be inaccessible to common people. The disciples again misunderstood him (14). Children, in his eyes, were models of trust, innocence and dependence. The story of the rich young man adds nothing to Matthew's narrative (see comments on Matt. 19: 15–30). To want is not enough. We must want enough. 'If with all your hearts you truly seek me...' (Jer. 29: 13). He was 'sad' (23), but one who found the costly pearl (Matt. 13: 46) 'joyfully' sold all he had. Painstakingly the Lord, for the fourth time, raised the theme of coming trials (32–34) only to be saddened again by James and John (see comments on Matt. 20: 20–28). Mark does not mention a fact found in Matthew (20: 20), that the masterful wife of Zebedee was ambitiously behind her sons. How ironical is the fact that when the Lord 'entered into his kingdom', 'on the right of him and on the left' (37) were two bandits (15: 27).

For the story of Jericho's blind men see comments on Matthew 20: 29–34. Mark adds a few of Peter's details, the man's name (46), the haste with which he threw his cloak aside and ran (50. cf. John 4: 28).

Into Jerusalem
(Mark 11: 1–33)

THE long climb from the Jordan cleft is over. The triumphal entry, the cleansing of the temple and the parable of the withered fig tree (1–21), appear in almost identical language in Matthew. See the comments there (Matt. 21: 1–21). The Lord regarded the temple as a place of instruction (2: 49) and of prayer (17. Luke 18: 10). It was the concept caught up by the first disciples (Act 3: 1, 11). Perhaps the barren fig tree was not unrelated to what he actually found in the shrine. In Mark's account (20–26) he uses the tree as an illustration of effective prayer. Only Mark mentions Peter as the speaker (21). Amazement followed at the rapid effect of the curse on the tree (Matt. 21: 20). Cursing, in such a context, was a divine prerogative of judgment. It is not for us (Jas. 3: 10). But the incident did provoke some words on the power of prayer and a stress on grace received as a condition of grace besought (Matt. 18: 32, 33).

Opposition was organising. Crowds frequented the temple (Matt. 21: 23). His authority, in the eyes of the Pharisees, was a vital question (28). Adroitly he identified it with that of the leader of the great revival and left them in a deep dilemma, a dilemma created solely from a complete unwillingness to face patent truth which conflicted with their prejudice. It is important, and saving grace in a man to be ready and willing to confess he has been wrong. A man who will not accept the truth must end by becoming a living lie.

The Duel
(Mark 12: 1–44)

SEE comments on Matthew 21: 33–46 for a discussion of this parable of rejection based on Isaiah 5: 1–7; (1–12). They readily admitted that their forbears had misused the prophets (Matt. 23: 30), but the Lord's words extended the guilt to their generation. There is awesome force in vv. 6–8. They killed the son precisely because they recognised him for the son, and in the crime attacked the father (John 12: 44). An additional point in Matthew's version (21: 41) seems to make the Lord turn to the crowd, which, swept along by the vivid story, declare their assent. It is all in the manner of eastern preaching, notable for crowd participation. Turning to his opponents the Lord cast a text at their feet, a word from a Passover psalm much in evidence that week (Ps. 118: 22, 23). The suggestion involved provoked rage (Matt. 21: 43). Paul and Barnabas stirred similar reaction by similar words (Acts 13: 46–50).

The question about the tribute money was intended to place Christ on the horns of just such a dilemma as that in which he had placed them (11: 27–33). Full comments will be found in Matthew 22: 15–22. Contrast the smooth hypocrisy of v. 14 with the sincerity of Nicodemus (John 3: 2). The principle of the brilliant reply is a basis of Christian citizenship. The Pharisees and the Herod society had tried the political question (18–26). Incongruously the politically minded Sadducees are left with the theological question. (See the comments on Matt.

22: 22–33.) Observe the gentle irony of the reply to men who were talking of a resurrection in which they did not believe, and the quiet mention of angels whose existence they denied, and the subtle thrust of the remark about Exodus 3: 6 and 15.

For the scribe, his question and the answer, see the comments on Matthew 22: 33–40. Summarising Israel's basic religion, the Lord added the Shema of Deuteronomy 6: 4, 5 and Leviticus 19: 18. In passing, observe that 'liberal' rejection of the authority of Deuteronomy as genuine scripture heavily involves the authority of the Lord. The scribe was compelled to express his admiration (32, 33), but must have been taken aback by the Lord's reply. It must not be imagined that all of the hierarchy failed to find Christ. Some were convinced ... (34. John 12: 42; 19: 38, 39; Acts 6: 7). The question on Psalm 110: 1 (see comments on Matt. 22: 41–46) found no orthodox answer and left Christ conqueror on the field, to the joy of the common folk who held no brief for their religious leaders (37). Perhaps the pompous scholars withdrew, and, looking after their retreating figures, he addressed a few remarks to the crowd (38–40). And, exquisitely, the revelation of true religion came —a widow with two tiny coins (42). The investment still bears interest.

The Prophecy on Olivet
(Mark 13: 1–37)

READ the discussion of the parallel passage, Matthew's chapters 24 and 25. They were on the slope of the Mount of Olives from which a glorious panorama of Jerusalem is to be seen, looking back perhaps from the summit as they walked over to Bethany. The temple stood in white and golden splendour on the massive rock platform which Herod's engineers had built over the summit of Mount Moriah. It was difficult to imagine such disaster as the Lord foresaw. The Lord's first object was to persuade his men that the temple signified nothing in itself, a point Stephen remembered from the report of this conversation which he must have heard (Acts 7: 48–50). The new faith was not to be a sect of Judaism (1–4).

False claimants to his authority would rise (5, 6), in the same evil world of strife and conflict (7, 8), a world hostile to their challenge as it was to his (8, 9), and in which doggedly, against the agony of persecution, betrayal and hatred, they were to preach the gospel (10–13). These are steadying thoughts, applicable today as ever. The fulfilment of such prophecies moves in concentric circles. Bar Kochba was a 'messiah' who set the final seal on the ruin of the land a century later (21–23). V. 9 can be illustrated from the events of Acts to those in troubled lands today.

The 'abomination of desolation' (14) is an apocalyptic phrase (Dan. 9: 27; 11: 31; 12: 11) for a symbol of blasphemy. Two close fulfilments are recorded. At the climax of the first rebellion the Roman armies with their 'idolatrous' symbols, the eagle and the emperor's medallion, invested Jerusalem (A.D. 70). After the suppression of the second rebellion in A.D. 134, Hadrian, changing the name of Jerusalem to Aelia Capitolina after himself (Aelius Hadrianus) and Jupiter, whose shrine stood on Rome's Capitol Hill, set a memorial statue of Jupiter in what still stood of the temple (14). Flight undoubtedly saved many (15–20). What wider circles of fulfilment remained, or still remain, can be seen in history, and could still be seen.

False teachers (22, 23) were to arise (see on John's First Epistle). Deceivers still, as C. S. Lewis subtly put it, cover Puzzle the Ass with a lion's skin and call it Aslan. The vision widens (24–27), for human time is irrelevant here, with the turmoil of falling rulers and the din of history, as applicable to the advancing doom of Rome as it is to the clash of tribe and tribe, race and race, nation against nation today (24–25). No date is given, only the hint that, like any good husbandman, God's people should be alert for signs (28–32). The Coming is sure and that fact calls for watchfulness (33–37).

Last Evening

(Mark 14: 1–72)

THE plot was taking shape and Judas gave it the last touch of treachery (1, 2, 10, 11). (See comments on Matt. 26: 1–16 on the interweaving of Mary's symbolic act with Judas' perfidy.) Simon the leper's home would appear to be also that of the Bethany family, Eliezer, Martha and Miriam (Lazarus, Martha and Mary.) Perhaps the patriarch of the house lived somewhere in isolation as Uzziah did in his own palace (2 Chron. 26: 21). Matthew (26: 8) and John (12: 5) are more detailed about the gust of disapproval. God, who values the mite (12: 43) treats extravagant expense with tolerance . . . We can do with more mites and more spikenard, for it is what both mean· that matters.

See comments on Matthew 26: 17–29 for the events of the Supper (12–25). There were obviously unknown disciples on whom the Lord could rely (13. 11: 2), people who had little to offer, but who offered it all. Such small services may, at the right place and time be an essential part in a plan. Perhaps Mark still found it wise to conceal the man's name. It was, in all likelihood, Mark's own home (Acts 12: 12). It is only John, in a better position to observe (13: 26), who gave the final details of the drama at the table (20). For the agony in the Garden and the arrest, followed by the illegal arraignment at night before the Sanhedrin, see the comments in the parallel narrative in Matthew 26. It is moving to find that in this 'Petrine gospel', the story of Peter's failure should have been recorded in ruthless detail. Simon, the Lord calls him in v. 37. Peter (the Rock) was hardly the word for this occasion. Peter's name is prudently not mentioned in the story of the attack on the attendant (47). Peter gives the fuller account of the charge (57–59). He was by the brazier in the yard. Peter's fall was the doom which can fall on rash confidence. Perhaps the steps can be traced (29, 31, 37, 50,

54). As a recognised leader he may have been self-betrayed by a rough attempt to lift the sense of doom which lay on the party.

Vv. 51, 52 are peculiar to Mark. It is not unknown for ancient writers to 'sign' their books by a touch of personal narrative, and that is what Mark is probably doing here. Perhaps the background may be imaginatively reconstructed ... In the long room on the roof of the house of Mary, the rich widow lady of Jerusalem, the Lord and his band meet for what was to be the Last Supper. In his room below, awake and alert, for he sensed the danger which lurked about the house, lay Mary's son, John Mark. He heard the hurried steps of Judas on the stairway without, and listened with sharper care. And then the noise of feet, and the rest depart.

On a sudden impulse the boy seizes a linen sheet from his bed, wraps it round his body and follows. He watches under the olive trees, sure that some crisis is at hand. A flare of torches, and the betrayer is there. With a boy's reckless loyalty he shouts some protest, and angry hands lay hold of him. Slipping out of his sheet, Mark escapes. Perhaps he bore a cruel and mutilating sword-slash across his fingers, for an old tradition says that in the early church Mark was called 'the Stumpfingered'. Shall imagination be followed a little further? Did the savage blow and the cry of his young friend stir Peter to draw his long fisherman's blade and slash back at the offender? (And see a comment on Acts 13: 13.)

Via Dolorosa
(Mark 15: 1-41)

THE trial before the governor (equally the trial of the governor) is more briefly told in Mark than in Matthew. Mark, conscious of the brevity of time, is hastening to the end. He even abbreviates the inscription above the cross (26). Like Matthew he omits the attempt to unload responsibility on to Herod (Luke 23: 6-12). Mark omits the vitally interesting message from Pilate's wife. The hostile mob was doubtless assembled by the priests. Crowds can be fickle (Acts 14: 13, 19) but they can also be manipulated (Acts 17: 5; 19: 29). The host which welcomed Christ (11: 9, 10) were not in the streets. The priests sought to bypass this awkward eventuality. There were antagonistic elements from whom the priests could pick their demonstrators (John 10: 19-21). It was the demonstrators who finally daunted Pilate. He was bitterly angry at the dilemma forced on him (9, 10) and unsuccessful in his attempt to appeal to the crowd (Matt. 27: 24). The street was too carefully packed.

V. 21 is another detail unique to Mark. Cyrene was an important Libyan city with expatriates in Jerusalem (Acts 6: 9). 'From the country' means probably 'from abroad', making Simon a pilgrim on a visit to Jerusalem. If he was a local resident of Cyrenian origin the phrase could bear the meaning 'from his farm'. The curious reference to his sons suggests that at the time of writing, the men were known to the Christian community.

Was Rufus the man mentioned in Romans 16: 13?

The scene at the cross is part of the meaning of the Atonement. God, in permitting the crucifixion, revealed two truths—first that God is involved in human sin (2 Cor. 5: 19). If God suffered in Christ, it makes it difficult to sing such fierce hymns as:

'Jehovah drew his awful sword
He sheathed it Lord in thee.'

The sombre scene also goes far to explain the elusive mystery of pain. Pain can be infinitely fruitful. The second truth revealed is the depth of human evil (29–37). The scene catches mankind at a moment of dark self-revelation—priests of God (31) mocking a man in agony, the conformists taking their tone from the leaders (29, 30), the great silent majority, and God's remnant standing by the cross (John 19: 25). Man's fall cannot be doubted. Neither can God's involvement in it be set aside. There is more here than rampant evil and pure tragedy.

The Tomb

(Mark 15: 42—16: 20)

IT was growing late on the day we call Friday. The sabbath began at sundown. Hence some haste to bury the body before the holy day properly began. Part of Friday, however small, would be one 'day and a night' by the curious Jewish reckoning. Joseph was known to the synoptic evangelists, Nicodemus only to John (19: 39). Both were Sanhedrists (John 12: 42), rich men

(Matt. 27: 57; John 19: 39), and obviously of sufficient standing for Pilate to consider it wise to grant so small a favour.

The rapidity and brevity of Mark's ending, even in a book noted for the clipped haste of its narrative, is a little disconcerting. It is curious that in a story derived from Peter, Peter's own run to the tomb, told by John with all the authentic marks of the eyewitness, should have been eliminated (John 20: 1–10). And why the larger omission of Peter's rehabilitation? (John 21). Peter had clearly not forgotten this (1 Pet. 2: 25). He chose to say no more.

The great problem remaining is whether Mark ended at v. 8. The whole book seems to finish in a hurry with a portion, a little clumsily added, by another. Mark was writing in Rome, perhaps round A.D. 67 (2 Tim. 4: 11). It was a dangerous time. It is easy to imagine sudden interruption, a raid on a hidden lodging, the hasty thrusting of an almost finished manuscript into a place of concealment, and the end . . . Was this the story?

There is much to support the contention that vv. 9 to 20 were a later addition. Characteristic expressions of Mark are absent from it, and words not occurring elsewhere in the Gospel are found in it. No less an authority than Jerome states that the verses were not in most of the Greek Testaments of his day, and Eusebius supports him. The verses are wanting in two of the most ancient manuscripts one of which is the authoritative Codex Sinaiticus. An Armenian codex of the tenth century, which may retain an ancient tradition, includes verses 9 to 20 after a break and heads them, 'By the Presbyter Aristion'. It is to be admitted that the close of v. 8 is an abrupt ending to the Gospel, but it is equally true that if Mark left his book unfinished that would itself constitute a temptation to some over-zealous copyist to supply an ending, and vv. 9 to 20 would be just the sort of ending that such a person might make up from the other gospels and from Acts. Consider v. 18 in relation to Paul's adventures on Malta, and few would care to put the rest of this verse to the test. It is for this reason that on both external and internal evidence most informed and orthodox scholarship regard the whole of the closing section indicated as apocryphal.

THE GOSPEL ACCORDING TO ST. LUKE

The Book of the Physician
(Luke 1: 1–80)

LUKE, the Greek physician from Philippi, who first joined Paul at Troas (Acts 16), was, as a careful assessment of his second book demonstrates, an exact and careful historian. Luke probably collected his material in Palestine during Paul's enforced period of inactivity in Caesarea (Acts 24–26). After the manner of a Greek classical historian, Luke begins with a polished and elaborate paragraph (1–5), before slipping into the vernacular of more common communication (6). His style is nevertheless lucid and good.

Herod's cruel and sanguinary life was hastening to its end in madness and murder, but there were good men in the land—the perennial 'remnant' (1 Kings 19: 18). Of such was Zecharias' family, faithful in the midst of corruption. All members of Aaron's tribe took turns to make the daily sacrifice and bless the multitude (6–10. Exod. 30: 7, 8). It was a high moment, and Zecharias came with heart awed and prepared for the wonder which met him (11–14).

John fulfilled a prophecy (17. Mal. 4: 5, 6). The Lord himself identified the fiery John with the fiery Elijah (Matt. 11: 14; John 5: 35). Voiceless and overwhelmed, the good Zecharias continued and concluded his duties. He gave the people their blessing, and somehow conveyed his news to them. Observe that, in beginning a new era, God used the machinery of the old —a priest, the temple and a prophecy link the Testaments (18–23).

On the birth of Mary's son see the comments on Matthew 1:18–25. Luke's account agrees entirely with Matthew and with John (35. John 1: 14). Luke probably received the facts from the aged Mary (26–38). Mary, too, was of 'the remnant', and it is only a misguided worship of the Virgin which has denied a wondrous woman the reverence she merits. She faced a breakdown of life and happiness (Matt. 1: 18), the slander of men (John 8: 41), pain untold (24–37). Mary was stirred to song, a psalm full of the poetry of the O.T. Compare Hannah's hymn, which the Virgin remembered (1 Sam. 2: 1–10). Mary spoke as one of the common folk of Palestine (51, 52). In that land of deep poverty and deprivation it was among the poor that the strongest currents of faith ran. (See notes on Matt. 5: 1–3). From Elijah to Amos, God had spoken through simple people. The

Bible has its men of substance, from
Barzillai to Joseph of Arimathea,
but wealth won little blessing from
Christ, and scorn from James—not
because of what wealth brings, but
because of the temptation it carries
(53). Note in this chapter the careful
construction of speech and fact,
poetry and prose. They illustrate
Luke's ordered mind (1: 3).

John means 'God's gift' or 'God
is gracious' (58–65), and in gratitude for the gift the old priest
breaks into his hymn of praise. It is
language laced with his pondering
over the great scriptures of his race,
solemn with the cadences of
psalmist and prophet. Rich dependence on the Bible always marks
the great hymn (66–79). And John,
the chapter concludes, was in the
wilderness (80), the refuge, often,
of those who sought God (Isa. 40:
3; Heb. 11: 1). The Qumran
community has thrown much light
on this 'third force' in Israel.

The Nativity

(Luke 2: 1–52)

PAPYRUS fragments of public
notices confirm that the Roman
census required householders to
report back to their hometown
authorities (3). The census of
Quirinius presents no dating difficulties, if the tardiness of communication and the facilities for tempo-
rising in such situations are
sufficiently considered.

Luke, telling a story gathered
from Mary, introduces the shepherds of Bethlehem. The shepherds
were part of the old unspoiled stock
of Israel, and it was appropriate

that the announcement should by-
pass the hierarchy and come to
them (4–15). The stable was the
innkeeper's second best. He was
merely the manager of a shepherds'
khan (Jer. 41: 17) and no doubt
Bethlehem's distinguished son, Hillel the Pharisee, occupied the guest
room (16–20).

Joseph was a simple man who
always did that which he ought to
do, honestly and uncomplainingly.
Hence the offerings which the Law,
in its mercy, accepted from the poor
(Exod. 13: 12; Num. 8: 17; Lev.
12: 8). Jerusalem was on the way
home and so the Babe came to the
temple (21–24) and the Holy Family
met another of the 'remnant', an
aged man whose faith had penetrated their secret (25–28). His
poem of praise is an echo of Isaiah
(29–35).

And after Simeon came Anna.
She was eighty-four. She gave herself to prayer, the last aid the very
aged can give. It is a fair inference
that she had been always a woman
of prayer. God's plan for the
evening should be the concern of
the afternoon (36–40). Man commonly shows then what he has
been.

The remaining section of the
chapter shows the Nazareth family
journeying to Jerusalem, probably
in special preparation for Jesus'
reaching responsible age. This was
at thirteen years. A boy became 'a
son of the Law' and assumed a
dress more proper to maturity.
Mary must have told Luke the
story, and it remained in her mind
(51) because in some deep fashion
it underlined her growing conviction that her son was utterly differ-

ent. In civil law and everyday usage Joseph was counted his father. Luke saw no contradiction between vv. 48 and 49. V. 49 contains the first quoted words of Christ. In the latter verse the RV rendering 'in my Father's house' is correct.

John's Revival
(Luke 3: 1–38)

READ the comments on Matthew 3: 1–17 and John 1: 19–34. Observe how Luke, the careful historian, sets the events in the framework of Roman and Middle Eastern history (1, 2). John's wilderness revival was a prelude to the ministry of Christ. That the city was aware of the witness of the wilderness is shown by the fact that Jerusalem went out to the preacher (7). John did not seek the crowds; they sought him, listeners of all types—proud Pharisees, soldiers, the hated tax gatherers. The land was hungry for truth. John's preaching was no comfortable experience. Picking his metaphors from the rough Jordan countryside, the scrub fire with the quick vipers escaping (7), the felling of trees in the jungle (9), the winnowing of the corn, and lacing all with quotation, John lashed his audience. Perhaps the times called for such fierce preaching. John was such a man, and God used the tool which lay ready to his hand. The whole land was moved by John's preaching. There had been arid and barren years, but revival was afoot, and men in their multitudes were seeking God. And God was found along the ancient paths.

John's call to repentance was no abstract doctrine. He demanded demonstration in conduct and each day's living (10–14), fitting the conduct to the person's peculiar temptations and walk of life (14). Conscious of the nature of his ministry, John was clear in his repudiation of any other rôle than that of forerunner (15–18).

On Herod see comments on Matthew 14: 1–12 and on the genealogy comments on Matthew 1: 1–17. Luke's genealogy (22–38) differs from Matthew's. It is obvious that Matthew and Luke, with access to the same information, and writing in the same generation, would not knowingly contradict each other. It is clear that they must have followed different plans. Matthew gives Joseph's line, while making it clear that Jesus was not Joseph's son, because Joseph was Jesus' legal father, a point important for more than one reason in Jewish law. It was also necessary to establish the fact that Mary married within the tribe. Legislation mentioned in the closing chapters of Numbers shows the necessity for this to be clear. Luke almost certainly gives the genealogy of Mary. Joseph, not Mary, is given as the immediate descendant of Eli because Joseph authenticated Mary's inheritance by the Numbers legislation (27: 1–11, 36: 1–13). It is probable that more exact information would establish some ritual of adoption in such cases. Note that Matthew takes the line back to David; Jesus was King. Luke takes it to Adam; Jesus was the Son of Man, the world's Saviour, not the Jews' alone. Luke, the friend of

Paul, has the world in view. He has just spoken of the baptism, necessary only as the sign of the identification of the Sinless One with sinful man.

From the Temptation to the Galilean Ministry

(Luke 4: 1-44)

SEE comments on Matthew 4: 1-11. The subtlety of the temptations lay in the way they corrupted what was harmless or good. There was nothing evil in a desire for food. The sin lay in satisfying hunger in Satan's way. There was no sin in a wish to govern men for, good, and to hold such power over warring nations that the gift of peace should be theirs. Augustus had been acclaimed by poet and orator for no other gift. There was no sin in a desire to be accepted for what he was, the Holy One of God, and to initiate his ministry with convincing miracle. The sin lay in coming before men after the fashion of Satan's suggestion. All Satan asked was that legitimate aspirations should be channelled through him.

Temptation is repetitive, varied, resourceful. It has its origin in a malignant mind, organising attack, confrontation, ambush, probing for the undefended point, switching the thrust. Nor was this the only episode (Heb. 4: 15; Matt. 16: 23). V. 13 says literally: 'When he had ended every possible kind of temptation he departed until a suitable time'.

Luke begins the story of the Lord's ministry in Nazareth, but much had already happened, probably all the events up to Matthew 8, Mark 6, and perhaps John 4. Isaiah (17) was in the minds of men after John's revival, and the Lord read Isaiah 61: 2 with a phrase from 58: 6, which may have been in the same passage in the roll from which he read. He thus took up the theme of John, with the significant variation that, whereas John preached judgment, the Lord stressed the fact that the day of grace continued. Dramatically he broke off in the middle of a verse (19).

Christ in no way sought to correct his forerunner. The messages were complementary. Grace is for those who repent. The vision of sin, and the condemnation which lies upon it, must always prepare the way for the forgiveness of God. The people of Nazareth recognised the power of the Lord's words (22), and the winsomeness of the message. But was he not their townsman? Was he not Joseph's son? Was he not ordinary, small like themselves, without authority? Such littleness of mind denied Nazareth its blessing, for it created pride, and pride is a poison which inhibits faith (23). The Lord pointed out to his jealous townsfolk that theirs was the attitude which had more than once denied God's people the good which might have come to them (25-27). A Phoenician woman and a Syrian soldier won blessing which Israel had forfeited for lack of faith. At such reproach jealousy turned to violence, and Nazareth sought to anticipate history and murder the messiah (29, 30).

The Lord departed as he did from Gadara. Capernaum gained by

Nazareth's loss (31, 32). There was a gust of popularity (33–37). He put hands 'on each of them' who gathered round as the hot day waned and Sabbath ended with sunset (40), meeting each, as he does, at the place of need.

Mission to Galilee
(Luke 5: 1–39)

THE low shore of the lake runs from Capernaum to Tiberias in a wavering line and one bay in particular forms a perfect auditorium for a speaker moored offshore. Peter, weary from a fruitless night's work, saw little meaning in the command but obeyed (1–5). His first reaction to the great catch was like that of Isaiah—a sense of unworthiness and inadequacy (Isa. 6: 5). Ever ready in moments of stress to rush into speech (Mark 9: 5, 6; John 21: 3), he uttered the prayer of v. 8. He who touched the stricken leper (13) was not likely to shun the contrite fisherman. Peter's spoken prayer was unanswered, but his heart's desire was met (Ps. 37: 4). It sometimes happens thus. Our words are not a true rendering of the soul's real wish. God answers, not the hasty words, but the aspiration of the soul, incoherent and fumbling, but known by him.

Having healed the leper the Lord bade him conform to the regulations of Leviticus 14, and enjoined secrecy (14). He was anxious to avoid a mass movement or an epidemic of emotional enthusiasm both of which could invite official repression. The crowds were nevertheless on the move (15) and the religious leaders were taking notice (17). On the remaining incidents of the chapter see the comments on Matthew 9 and Mark 2.

Christ must have known the self-contempt and longing for a clean heart which no one else could see in the tax collector of Capernaum (27–29). He calls no man who has no desire to follow him. Matthew 'left all' and responded. Unlike the rest of the chosen, he abandoned for ever his livelihood and his possessions. Fishing was an honourable craft, and could be resumed without fault (John 21: 3). When Matthew left his office he knew that he could never go back to it. Decision for Christ sometimes calls for the utter rejection of a manner of life. Matthew's first act was to testify in his own society (29). If testimony cannot be given there it is useless to seek other spheres of witness. There was small privacy in the ancient world and the Lord was observed among the guests in Matthew's house (30). Hence the irony, for there are none righteous (Isa. 64: 6; Rom. 3: 23). Observe the subtle attempt to divide John and Jesus (33), and the Lord's own first reference to his death (35).

The Mission Continued
(Luke 6: 1–40)

FOR the clash with the Pharisees over Sabbath-breaking (1–5), and the story of the man with the withered hand (6–11), see comments on Matthew 12: 1–14. With v. 11 the sinister shadow of the plot touches the edge of the story. Weary and revolted by the conflict, the Lord withdrew for a time of communion with God, from which he always drew strength. Abraham 'went to the place where he stood before the Lord', Habakkuk sought his 'watchtower' (Gen. 19: 27; Hab. 2: 1). He had the task of choosing (John 15: 16) a special group, all busy men as far as can be judged, not without property and successful in their way of life. These were the men who were to change the world (12–16). In this intimate circle the Lord blended Matthew, the one-time outcast, Simon the resistance fighter, the dynamic Peter, the sceptical Thomas and Philip.

The crowds gathered as he came 'to the plain' (17, 18) and repeated the sermon of Matthew 5, 6, 7—timeless words for Christ's followers, challenging, flatly contradicting common values. Luke records in a balanced pattern—three general benedictions (20–22) and one related to the active spite of men (23), then three general 'woes', (24–26) and one related to spiteful speech of men. Luke concentrates on the most penetrating and paradoxical parts of the sermon. The language of paradox is not, however, the language of impossibility. To transform evil, demands the sturdiest faith, but that requirement is not intended to daunt and discourage, but to lead to a nobler plane of Christian living. Nor is the command to love our enemies beyond the reach of man. The remark (27) is a direct contradiction of teaching detailed in a Dead Sea Scroll. Such love is the attitude of mind which consistently, unwaveringly, seeks another's good. Note too an important fact. The natural affections are

spontaneous. We sometimes love in spite of ourselves. To love an enemy demands a movement of the will, an act of faith, a deliberate Christlikeness (28, 29, 35).

On the passage generally consult the notes on Matthew 5, 6, 7. Of the closing parable (47–49) Matthew gives a clearer picture (7. 24–27). The figure is that of a man who notes the level sweep of sand in a summer river-bed, emptied by the season's drought. It is easy to build there but only the fugitive from toil and the man without foresight do so. The man of sense seeks the solid rock, for he knows that the winter freshets and the sudden flood from some cloud-burst in the hills, will sweep over the level sand of the dry water-course, and carry away whatever thoughtless optimism has built.

More from Galilee
(Luke 7: 1–50)

SEE on the story of the centurion's servant comments on Matthew 8: 5–13. Among the stacked stones on the synagogue site in Capernaum is a piece which could easily be from the first building on the site. It bears the emblem of the Tenth Legion, two stylised eagles, an 'idolatrous' symbol tolerated perhaps by the Jews in gratitude for a synagogue (5). In an atmosphere of hate and bitter nationalism, this man had set out to win the friendship of a subject race. He had admired, and probably adopted, their religion. And note his gentlemanly concern for another's convenience (6), and his willingness to remain in the background (7). Observe his love and care for a man in a lower station, his sturdy, simple faith. Nain lies ten miles as the crow flies, from Nazareth, across the eastern extension of the Esdraelon plain (11). Shunem lies a few miles to the south-west, where Elisha brought a boy to life (2 Kings 4). Endor is in the contrary direction, scene of Saul's grim encounter with death. The widow would walk ahead. Women led funeral processions because, said the rabbis, 'they had brought death into the world'. The rock-cut tombs outside the village may still be seen (12). The narrative sparkles with marks of truth (13–15). Luke had, he claims, carefully researched his facts (1:3). Artless marks of truth make 'mythology' impossible. This incident happened and in v. 13, Jesus is called Lord for the first time (16, 17).

On John's agony (18–29) see the comments on Matthew 11: 2–15. It was a noble tribute. John's ministry outweighed the ministries of the great men of the O.T.—Elijah, Isaiah, Ezekiel, Jeremiah. And yet the desert preacher, who led the great religious revival was no frequenter of courts of kings, like Isaiah and Jeremiah. He was a son of the people, influenced rather by the communities of the wilderness, than by the Pharisees and the urban experts in the Law. His ministry had sharpened the deep contradictions of society, and bared the insincerities of the leaders of religion. The ascetic evangelist was dismissed by them as mad, and, blinded by prejudice, they rejected him. The Baptist held them in scorn (Matt. 3: 7–12). The outcasts of society (29) saw in John's message the

truths which the theologians were unable to perceive. Who was truly wise, the repentant rebel, or the proud religious leader, was obvious from the event (35).

The incident of vv. 36–40 is not that recorded in Matthew 26: 7–13; Mark 14: 3–9 or John 12: 1–8. Simon the cleansed leper is not Simon the Pharisee. There are twelve Simons in the N.T., twenty in Josephus. The incident takes place in Bethany but the woman is not Mary, as in the other stories. The background may be envisaged. The courtyard of a big house where summer meals were eaten, was open to the passing stranger. The Jewish leaders were accustomed to such publicity, and indeed were flattered if the ordinary people sought the sound of their wisdom. Hence the presence of the poor woman seeking the Lord in an agony of need. The reason why Christ was there is more difficult to assess, until one remembers the ways of man. The Pharisee was publicly entertaining the Lord, but had neglected the simple courtesies of the Jewish host (44). Clearly, he was hesitant before the public, was prepared to patronise, but shunned too obvious a committal. He deserved his rebuke (41–45) but failed to see that forgiveness could come by diviner ways than the Pharisees' contact with God (48–50).

From Galilee to Gadara
(Luke 8: 1–50)

VERY much of the material which Luke records in this varied chapter has been the subject of comment earlier. The narrative covers much from Matthew and Mark, or from the common source of all three evangelists. (See comments on Matt. 5: 15, 16; 8: 23–27; 28–34; 9: 18–26; 12: 46–50; 13: 1–23; Mark 4: 1–20; 22–23; 36–41; 5: 1–12; 22–43).

Galilee, overpopulated, and more crowded then than now, was not an easy mission field for preachers on foot (1). Response was not only among the rank and file. It reached high, as it also did later in the Gentile world, where, before the death of the last apostle, Christianity had penetrated the imperial family. Women are prominent in Luke's narrative. His references flowed from his own investigations in Palestine (2, 3. 24: 10).

The Lord's brothers and sisters are several times mentioned (Matt. 12: 46; 13: 55, 56; Mark 3: 32; 6: 3; John 2: 12; 7: 5). The story that these relatives were cousins, or children of Joseph by an earlier marriage was an invention of Jerome and others in the years when non-Christian views of marriage were invading the church. Note that this story (19–21) contains no harshness. There are fifty-six words in the Greek text and no evidence of dismissal or rejection. The events merely frame the saying.

Jairus (41) must have known that the hierarchy was turning against the Lord. His associates among the rabbis would disapprove but he was desperate, especially when the crowds blocked the way, and when the Lord lingered to treat an ailment and to make a woman confess her healing (43–49). Jairus' priestly friends were in the house (53), but

into the room where Jairus' daughter lay he allowed only the reverent. The scornful are not permitted to see the mysteries of God. Scorn and contempt build barriers and inhibit insight and perception. Christ's touch could have given life to the little girl in any place. The scoffers were excluded because they were, unworthy of the revelation. God reveals himself to faith and to humility and Jairus had fulfilled those conditions. As a leader of orthodox Jewry, he must have been aware that publicly to seek Christ's aid was to challenge the prejudice of those in high places. It was a confession of need, and an act of trust. On such levels God will meet a suppliant. In fact, he will meet him nowhere else.

Galilee and Caesarea Philippi
(Luke 9: 1–62)

THE events of this chapter's narrative have been reviewed in notes on Matthew's and Mark's gospel. (See, in sequence, Matt. 10: 1–12; 14: 13–21; 16: 13–20, 21, 22–28; 17: 1–8, 14–21, 22, 23; 18: 1–5, 18–22; Mark 6: 7–13, 30–34; 8: 27–30, 31, 32; 9: 1, 2–8, 14–20, 30–32, 33–37, 38–40; Matt. 8: 18–22.)

A few additional comments may be made. Rudolf Bultmann has suggested that the story of the mission of the Twelve (1–9) was placed in the N.T. to justify the evangelism of the church. The suggestion is typical of much in N.T. studies which would be dismissed as quite ridiculous in any other sphere of literary criticism. Note that 'shaking off the dust' was the habit of a rabbi in leaving Gentile territory (5). The story of Herod may have come from Joanna (7).

A comparison with Matthew and Mark will show that Luke omits, after v. 17, a block of events, recorded in Matthew 14: 22 and 16: 12, Mark 6: 45 and 8: 27. The edges of the gap are joined at v. 18. In his second book Luke's habit of drastic abridgement, when he was seeking space to expand elsewhere, is very obvious. There were limits to one roll of papyrus. The journey to Tyre must have been tempting to one of Paul's global outlook, but perhaps he was conscious of no fresh details, and the need to include new material which he had collected was pressing upon him. Such priceless passages as the story of the Prodigal Son were part of that unpublished narrative.

That is why Luke does not make it clear (23-26) that the confession of Peter was part of the story of several weeks of preparation for the cross, while the party lingered in the beautiful north-east of the land, where the Banyas spring of the Jordan bursts from the rock.

Some further details: Luke has six references to Jesus' prayer habits unmentioned in the other narratives. (18. 3: 21; 5: 16; 6: 12; 9: 18, 29; 11: 1). Of v. 27 there are three suggested interpretations— the resurrection, the transfiguration, or the destruction of Jerusalem. The third may be eliminated. The eight days of v. 28 is not a mistake. Matthew and Mark say six days, but Luke uses the inclusive Roman reckoning. 'Decease' (31) is 'exodos', also used in 2 Peter 1: 15, a

touch of authenticity for that disputed letter. V. 35 quotes Psalm 2: 8 and Deuteronomy 18: 15. In v. 41 Luke uses a word for 'perverse', which he repeats at Acts 20: 30 (the related verb is in Acts 13: 10). It means 'crooked' or 'bent', in the sense in which G. M. Hopkins and C. S. Lewis use the adjective. Curiously it is found in the medical writer Hippocrates. The quarrel of v. 46 was the shocking reaction to v. 44.

At v. 51 Luke begins a tract of narrative not, except for minor details (e.g. 57-61), matched in the other evangelists. From 9: 51 to 19: 44 there is an account of the Lord's words and doings as he moved back to Galilee, down the Jordan and up to Jerusalem. His mood was stern (51, 53), and even may have provoked John's rash suggestion (54). Perhaps they saw the messiah of their mistaken dreams emerging.

From vv. 57-62 three types are mentioned. The man of unconsidered impulse (57, 58), a scribe according to Matthew, a man with conflicting duties unresolved— Philip, according to tradition (59, 60), and a man with divided mind. He dallied prepared to expose his desire to contrary arguments.

Moving out of Galilee
(Luke 10: 1-42)

GALILEE was to see no more of Christ but was not, for all the hardness of many (13-16), left behind without a final mission (1-12, 17). The mission of the seventy, however, covers more than Galilee (to which area the mission of the twelve [Matt. 10] was confined). It may have extended to Judea. The seventy, like the seventy members of the Sanhedrin, had a mission of preparation. Jerusalem's Jewry had neglected the Transjordan area, and if these preachers moved ahead down this southward road (1), they touched new territory, the lower regions of the Decapolis, already invaded across the lake. It was a brief pioneering foray so detailed preparation was not necessary (3, 4). There was no time for the elaborate ceremony of the east (2 Kings 4: 29), no room for scrupulous observance of dietary taboos (5–7). The Lord's progress was slow, for the seventy went and came as he moved through Galilee. He checked too optimistic a jubilation with a reference to Satan's fall through pride (17, 18, 20). The apocalyptic reference of v. 19 would not be taken literally by minds accustomed to that type of poetry. Let them, he hints, think rather of privilege than power (20). V. 22 is in the vein of John 3: 35 and vv. 23, 24 is echoed in John 8: 56.

The lawyer's question was to trap Christ and justify himself (25). V. 26 implies a reproach. Embarrassed, the questioner returns to the attack (29) and provokes the story of the Samaritan. Luke's 'parables' are stories from life. The Jericho road, running from Jerusalem 2,600 feet above the sea to Jericho, in the rift valley almost 4,000 feet down, was a notorious haunt of bandits. The priest feared ceremonial defilement if the still figure by the path should prove to be dead (Num. 5: 2). The Levite was perhaps afraid of a trap. Modern men might similarly shun

involvement in some urban situation of assault or violence. There is no indication that the victim was a good man. The Samaritan did all that which the others failed to do. As a visitor from the hated north, he lacked the Jew's knowledge of the Scriptures. Samaria had only the books of Moses, and it is ironical that Leviticus 19: 18, which counsels love for one's neighbour, was part of the Samaritan Bible, and was probably worn in a tiny leather case on the scribe's waist when he posed his question. The legalists, after the age-old fashion of their kind, had a way out of such obligations. They defined 'neighbour' to suit their prejudice and convenience. The splendid and challenging common sense of the Lord's reply cut through their nonsense. The lawyer cannot bring himself to utter the word 'Samaritan' (37).

Chronologically these central chapters of Luke present some problems, but no careful chronology is intended. This tract of narrative preserves material collected by Luke alone, and appears to be associated with the time between the Galilean ministries and the last visit to Jerusalem. It is suggested that the incident of Mary and Martha took place on a visit to Jerusalem other than that of the passion story. Perhaps an unexpected visit took Martha by surprise, and she reacted as an anxious housewife might. Martha is not blamed, but gently shown that the service which frays the temper is not to be preferred to quiet attention to important counsel. She 'stood over them', says v. 40 literally. Unruffled attention to what the Master has to say leads to truest service. The rush of business, however laudable, can destroy the spirit's calm, and so mar spirituality that service loses effectiveness. Mary had realised that 'man lives not by bread alone', and there is no truth that she needed more. Without this 'good part' (Gen. 43: 34) the feast of life loses its spiritual vitamin. The service begins at the feet of Jesus.

Teaching Continues
(Luke 11: 1–54)

ON the Lord's prayer see the comments on Matthew 6: 9–13. The disciples had asked to be taught how to pray (1). The prayer gives all the headings of prayer, includes all our needs, and covers all types of prayer. The opening vocative alone opens the door to all the supplications of God's children (2–4). A homely little story, another Lucan 'parable', follows (5–10). In the interpretation of parables we must disengage the main theme, and set the pictorial details in their proper place. The story does not suggest that God is like the hesitant man in bed, importuned to rising against his will by his insistent neighbour. Nor does it mean that the obstinate pressing of a request forces God to act. It does mean that we should continue doggedly to pray for that which we truly need, and which only God can give. The verbs 'ask', 'seek', 'knock' are in the continuous or linear present. We must 'go on asking, go on seeking' (10). Herein lies the discipline of prayer. God appears to

tarry and to withhold his answer. But, unlike the man in the closed house, he has his answer ready. The suppliant who passionately desires the object of his petition, in continuing doggedly to pray, is drawn into the purging of his motives and the examination of his life. When the answer comes it comes to a better man and carries more than he asked (Eph. 3: 20). God's fatherhood is no mockery. If man can give in love, God can give in love that is perfect and, above all, love allied with perfect wisdom (11–13).

On the shocking charge of v. 15 see the comments on Matthew 12: 22–37. It is a part of the viciousness of human nature to shut the eyes to good. Some perversity of mind bends the whole outlook of the obstinately evil man and produces a diabolical ingenuity in the rejection of good. Unable to deny the visible demonstration of fact, a base explanation is sought for it (14–23). The curious little parable of relapse in the next three verses (24–26) is spiritually and psychologically true. Sin is not to be simply repressed, it must be replaced. Hence the doctrine of rebirth. The forgiven sinner must be a new person, with new ideals, a new purpose to live for, a new heart. That which has occupied and crowded the centre of the being, polluting thought, corrupting speech and poisoning all the personality, must not only be expelled but replaced by the indwelling Christ.

The Jews forever 'sought a sign' (29. 1 Cor. 1: 22). They had a sign more potent than Jonah's preaching (30), more winsome than all Solomon's wisdom (31), sought so eagerly by Sheba's queen. Nineveh was their rebuke (32). From Galilee down to Jerusalem the light he had mentioned on the hill above the lake (Matt. 5: 15, 16) was shining with no attempt at concealment, but they were blind as Bartimaeus, waiting down at Jericho (33–36). If illumination is to flood the mind, the eye must receive and transmit the conditions without. God's grace is the waiting light of the sun. The eye is the faith which receives. The eye can be closed, and so determinedly kept closed, that it can lose the capacity to see. Let them beware lest the faculty for perceiving truth die not.

Washing the hands was not a simple act of hygiene (38). It was a ritual act. In their passion for prescribing the correct procedure for every process of life, the legalists had laid down rules for washing. The water was to be special water, free from all possible chance of ritual uncleanness. The amount was laid down in exact measure. The manner in which it was poured, and the very movements of each hand were precisely specified. The story does not suggest that the Lord went with unclean hands to his host's table. It does demonstrate his contempt for the idle and vexatious formalities into which the Pharisees had distorted true religion. V. 46 is the core of the charge. The 'lawyers' had made a beneficent code a complicated web of regulation too difficult for ordinary people to follow. And it remains true that any system of interpretation or teaching which removes religion from the reach of the mind or practice of common man, may be forthwith dismissed as

wrong. For the denunciation of the Pharisees (39–54) see comments on Matthew 23: 13–35.

Teaching and Parables
(Luke 12: 1–59)

IT is impossible to say whether Luke collected a number of related sayings and illustrations here or whether he gives a summary of one day's teaching or one long address. Any teacher is repetitive. Echoing his conversation in the house of the Pharisee (11: 37), Christ warns the great crowd to avoid the vice of the Pharisees—the concealment of an unsanctified life behind an exterior of complicated and exhibitionist holiness (1). All hypocrisy ultimately betrays its sham (2). Therefore let truth be boldly spoken, and evil speech cherish no illusions (3). Fear is an inhibiting force (4) but should take second place to reverence towards God (5). Gehenna, the valley of Hinnom, where Jerusalem's trash was burned (Josh. 15: 8; 2 Kings 23: 10; Jer. 7: 31) is used metaphorically for the life which ends as rejected rubbish. God cares for the frailest life committed to him. Two a penny, said Matthew, five for twopence, says Luke—an extra carcass for a larger sale, so small in worth were the tiny birds (6, 7). Even such trivial death does not escape God. Much less his own (8). Denial is also noticed (9) and perilous because it can harden into an irreversible habit of heart which is impervious to God's Spirit (10). Amid such solemn words came a tactless and insensitive interruption

(12–15). Deaf to immortal words which might have shown him loftier values, the man could think only of his financial problem. In Christ's rare and passing presence, all he could think of was money.

The thought provoked another story (16–20). The rich man lived entirely for himself. It was 'my barns', 'my fruits', 'my goods'—and 'my soul'. He was an able farmer, and no doubt had produced his bumper crops by good agriculture and sound management of his property. He had probably earned and deserved the prosperity he won. He could point to hard work and skilful planning in a difficult land. For all the story tells us, no one had any reason to accuse him of dishonesty towards others or unfairness in his relations with his labourers. And yet the Lord called him a fool. Why? Because it was crass folly to plan life as if he could control the future. It was folly to confuse his body with his soul. Could he not enjoy his food, his prosperity, his days? He had failed to note the tokens of mortality. That night some vital organ of the body failed and he learned the truth.

The thought flows on with teaching from the Sermon on the Mount (21–35), full of the Lord's contempt for money, with the insistent warning emerging that we should be ready for God's call.

The expectation of the Lord's coming does not paralyse energy (35) but strips for ready action (John 21 7; Eph. 6:14; 1 Pet. 1:13). V. 40 disposes for ever of perverse schemes of date-fixing. On the other hand the coming of Christ is sure and can catch evil by surprise (42–48. 2 Pet. 3:4; Mal. 3:1–6; Prov. 29:1).

Vv. 49–53 must be taken in context. Christ brings inner peace (John 14:27; Phil. 4:7), peace between man and God but a new-born loyalty can clash with old allegiance. 'He who is near me is near the fire', is a saying of Christ quoted by Origen and fire must be approached with due calculation. Aslan in Lewis' Narnia books 'is not a tame lion'.

There is a division before v. 54. These words are addressed to the crowds. They were alert enough for the signs of the weather. The wind out of the west rolled in such water-laden clouds from the Mediterranean as Elijah's servant saw (1 Kings 18:44, 45). Out of the Arabian desert the south and west wind brought the scorching heat. Worldly wise in such matters of simple observation and common prudence, they shut their eyes to 'the signs of the times'. Hence the designation used: 'hypocrites'. There was pretence, the blindness of obstinacy and pride. Like a man doggedly determined to push a bad or a hopeless case to the last arbitrament of the law-courts (57, 58), instead of seeking a just and reasonable accommodation out of court, the people were blundering on towards the disaster which lay ahead. The signs of the coming Great Rebellion of A.D. 66 to 70 multiply in the N.T. This warning is one of them. Wilfully blind, the Jewish people refused to heed the voice of prudence, and beat their nation to pieces against the iron wall of Rome. Among the few who survived in liberty were Christians who heeded such words as these.

Teachings on the Way
(Luke 13: 1-35)

THE innocent Galileans who died were probably protesters against Pilate's using a temple fund to provide a very necessary aqueduct into Jerusalem. It was typical of the procurator's brutal handling of his office. But, said Christ, they, like the victims of a city disaster, were under no special judgment. If being a godly person ensured divine protection, then it would be actually profitable to be good, an impossible situation for faith, viewed from the point of view of either the sincere or the insincere (1-5).

And, regarding repentance (5), the whole nation, whose ancient image was a fig tree (Isa. 5: 1-7), should remember that its time was short (6-9). It had, in fact, barely forty years to live, but made its choice not long after these words were spoken (John 19: 15).

The woman (10, 11), as Dr. Rendle Short pointed out, had an arthritic spinal deformity. Luke spoke the language of his day (11), and the Lord used no formula of exorcism (12, 13). Satan lies in the near or distant background of human ills (16) and Christ's words are merely the language of ultimate truth, and no concession to superstition. Hypocrisy always stirred the Lord's anger (Matt. 23), and the leader of the synagogue was one who accepted Talmudic rules about the Sabbath watering of livestock, and had no pity on an afflicted woman who came bent and agonised to the place of prayer (14-16). For the mustard tree and the leaven see comments on Matthew 13: 32,

33. Leaven is commonly an image for insidious corruption (12: 1; 1 Cor. 5: 6-8; Gal. 5: 9), but the context here seems to suggest a variant use for beneficent penetration.

The burden of the following discussion is dire urgency. The Lord is moving south down the Jordan valley with the cross in full view (22). An irrelevant question (23) sparks a reply like v. 6 (24). 'Strive' is the word rendered 'fight' in 1 Timothy 6: 12. V. 25 seems to envisage a night wedding feast with a doorman checking guests. Vv. 28 and 29 introduce an unexpected allusion to Gentiles in God's plan, an allusion for which Luke was alert (cf. Isa. 49: 12; 45: 6).

Herod's territories embraced Galilee and Peraea, and they were still within these boundaries when the message came from the Pharisees (31). Whether they were well-wishers, or merely sought to drive him into the hands of the Jerusalem Sanhedrin cannot be said. The allusion to Jerusalem caused Luke to anticipate in time the lament from the Mount of Olives (see 19: 41-44).

Table-Talk
(Luke 14: 1-35)

THE question of healing on the Sabbath had been so effectively answered (13: 15-17), that, when it arose again, there was merely sullen silence (1-6). The gathering was a crowded one (1), and, watching whimsically the guests' strife for the smallest social advantage, the Lord told an ironical story (7-11). 'Do not always invite your friends' (12), his advice runs, and look rather to the Banquet of the Righteous (14, 15). A sanctimonious comment (15) provoked another story of a feast (cf. Matt. 22: 1–10). Israel received the first invitation through the prophets (16, 17). Jesus and John brought the second invitation which came as a reminder, in Eastern practice, to those who had been forewarned. The first man (18) was insincere. Who would buy a farm which he had not inspected? He wanted to enjoy the farm, a natural desire, but a faulty priority. So, too, with the second man. He was too absorbed with his way of life to heed the call (19). The third man hid behind a Mosaic regulation (Deut. 24: 5), as did many of those who heard Christ's words. The house had to be filled, and vv. 21 to 24, again to Luke's special interest, prefigure the Gentiles thronging into Israel's heritage, and accepting the invitation Israel scorned.

If the Lord was moving through Peraea, he was in territory where he had not ministered before, and crowds (25) came from genuine curiosity. He sought to purge out the insincere by some stern words on the cost of discipleship. Vv. 26 and 27 are Eastern hyperbole. The earlier story (16–24) had shown the folly and sin of reversed priorities (18, 19). Priorities can be painfully difficult. Suppose, for example, the call of God conflicts with the demand of a parent? Who comes first? (12: 51, 52). He who bade us love our enemies would not command literal hating of our nearest. Christianity is toilsome. It is like a building project, with need for scrutiny of cost (28–30), like a battle

with strategic considerations (31, 32). Paul picked up both metaphors (1 Cor. 3: 10–14; Eph. 6: 11–17). Christ must hold pre-emi ence in all true committal (33). For the figure of the preserving, antiseptic salt see Matthew 5: 13.

Lost
(Luke 15: 1–32)

THE pitiless attitude of the self-righteous Pharisees (1, 2) provoked three stories based on the pathos of the word 'lost'. The story of the lost sheep (4–7), perhaps suggested by Ezekiel 34: 1–6, speaks of a creature lost in witless folly and thoughtless preoccupation with petty needs, like the guests of 12: 18, 19. The compassion of the shepherd, is the dominant thought (19: 10; Matt. 9: 36). To the Eastern shepherd sheep are individuals, not anonymous flocks, as they were to 'the false shepherds of Israel' (Ezek. 34: 1, 2; John 7: 49; 10: 12). The woman in search of the lost coin (8–10), lost from no fault of its own, among the rushes on the floor, makes a similar point. The ten coins were probably her dowry, worn about her neck, and she had no joy in the remaining nine while one was lost. And so with God— each soul is of infinite importance.

The story of the prodigal son could be from life. A papyrus letter survives from the end of the century, in which a rebellious boy, reduced to shame and rags, begs his mother to pity him, using the very phrase of v. 18—'I have sinned'. The 'far country' (13) need not have been geographically remote. Across the lake and the Jordan lay the ten towns of the Decapolis, with a largely alien and Gentile population. The ruins of Jerash, the ancient Gerasa, one of the Ten Towns, reveal the pomp and splendour of these cities of the easterly trade routes. As Samson found the pagan Philistines fascinating, so perhaps a young Jew from Galilee found the brilliant Greeks. The world welcomes, drains dry, and cynically rejects (14). Cruelly the worldling sent the Jewish boy to feed pigs (15. Lev. 11: 7) and need drove him to self-realisation (16, 17). It was a low motive on which to return home (18-20), but God accepts any movement of the mind which turns the feet in the right direction, and the lost boy was welcomed (21-24) and even given honour.

The elder son was as remote from his father's heart as his brother. He was the image of the Pharisee, full of hate to see the scorned and rejected finding a saviour in Christ (25-28). Laboriously, grudgingly, painfully, like the leaders of Jewish religion, he had served. But he had no sense of sin, no knowledge of his merciless heart. 'This son of yours,' he snarls (30). 'Your brother,' the father replies (32), and 'kept entreating him' (28). Service had been rendered without love, and whether the sin was remedied we do not know.

Two More Parables

(Luke 16: 1-31)

FROM the papyri which have been recovered from the rainless sands of Egypt, many scamps like

the bad farm-manager of vv. 1-8 have emerged. It is obvious that the world of the first century had its bribery, embezzlement and fraudulent manipulations of money. This story again could well be from life. The final verse (8) has been misunderstood. The lord who thus praised the dishonest fellow is not the Lord Jesus. He has no capital L. He was the steward's own lord, his master, his employer. Rich enough to laugh at the loss of a few barrels of oil and wine, the owner dropped some words of rueful praise for the smart dealing of which he was the victim. And this is the parable's point: the rogue of the world will leave no stone unturned to gain his end. The world will watch and grimly praise him, as he turns the world's resources to his purpose. What of this enterprise in a nobler sphere? Cannot Christians scheme as indefatigably for the kingdom's sake? 'Make friends', the Lord concluded, 'by means of the Mammon of Unrighteousness.' If rascals can use money to build themselves comfort, cannot others use it for God? 'Mammon' (9) is an Aramaic word for money, plain cash, not 'true riches' (11). For 'hate' (13) see 14: 26.

The Pharisees were stung by the story (14). Compact groups in religious circles from then till now can provide a common market and a mutual aid society, which can be financially very rewarding. The Pharisees were an illustration, and they were generally prosperous. They paid their tithes, to be sure, but this can mean nothing in terms of true godliness (18: 9-14). In the same debate, here strongly compacted, some controversial reference to divorce must have intruded. For v. 18 see comments on Matthew 19: 3–11.

The rabbis looked upon riches as a special mark of God's favour. Hence the story of vv. 19–31. Parables must be read in the light of their main point and intention. This story is designed to teach that opportunity is here and now, and that the measure of earthly prosperity and social standing in no way indicates a man's acceptance with God. The parable does not teach that Paradise and Hades are visible each from the. other. The phrases 'Abraham's bosom' (22), 'this flame' (24), the 'great gulf' (26) and the rest, are apocalyptic images. The story continues the theme of Pharisaic pitilessness which has run on from 15: 2. The rich man's callous carelessness (21) was like the elder brother's cold anger (15: 30). Nor is misery a path to heaven. It is not implied that Lazarus found the way by any other path than that of grace accepted in faith. Note the clear indication of the continuance of personality beyond death (24, 25, 28), and the assumption that the O.T. points to Christ (29).

Various Teachings
(Luke 17: 1–37)

THESE are chapters in which Luke seems to gather and record sayings from the last discourses of Christ which might otherwise have been lost. It is not always easy to recover context and background. Indeed, from a literary age, we may have here, as we have in many

chapters of Aristotle, the notes of listening disciples (1: 1, 2). At the same time Luke's intention may be discerned, and loose links observed between areas of thought and comment. This may be better seen if chapter and section headings, and even the enumeration of verses can be forgotten. The story of the rich man, prepared to allow a helpless beggar to lie in unrelieved and unpitied need, could have prompted vv. 1–4. It would have been better to drown deep before piling a weight of guilt heavier than any stone about his neck. But pity and mercy go together, and Christ's men should carry forgiveness beyond the rabbis' 'three times'.

Faith, remarks someone, is needed for such sensitivity (5), and faith, the Lord replies is a rare but potent force. The language is Eastern. No one who uprooted the mightily rooted sycamine (the black mulberry) would wish to plant it in the sea. The figure of speech merely suggested vast power and the drive to face and to accomplish the seemingly impossible (6).

A difficult little parable follows (7–10). It is again a scene from life, and it is what commonly happened (7, 8). The servant was expected to 'labour on, spend and be spent'. The master was not a picture of God. Again the parable makes its point. It is not an allegory, in which all details have significance, and the point is here that man can surely give to God that which man, without complaint, on any farm, gives to man. For the untold last chapter see Revelation 3: 20, 21.

Perhaps vv. 11–19 are misplaced. From 9: 51, 52 and 13: 22 it appears that this series of events took place on the Jordan valley route from Galilee to Jerusalem. V. 11 is correct in RSV. The Samaritans refused passage (9: 51-53) so he passed from Galilee through Bethshan, crossing the river where it winds through the level valley plain south of the lake, and then down the eastern bank to a point opposite Jericho. Somewhere on the borders of Galilee, a band of lepers provided this lesson in ingratitude. 'Gratitude', said Samuel Johnson, 'is a fruit of great cultivation. You do not find it among gross people.' Cicero described it as the parent of other virtues. The thankless heart, in fact, cannot know humility, and therefore can scarcely repent and surrender. There are mean souls which find it difficult to utter thanks, but are eloquent in expressing reproach. The problem of unmerited suffering evokes thousands of words. How seldom does the problem of unmerited blessing arise (Ps. 50: 14; 100: 4; Phil. 4: 6; Col. 2: 7).

A highly compact eschatological passage follows to be placed beside Matthew's fuller treatment. No one can predict the coming of the Lord, as one can predict, by careful observation, the coming of sunrise and sunset (20). If they had eyes to see, the kingdom in reality was there, in Christ's person (21). It will appear to recede (22), and false messiahs will appear to baffle and mislead, men like Theudas (Acts 5: 36) and Bar-Kochba, leader of the last mad revolt in A.D. 132 (23). There will be no doubt when God's Day dawns (24) but the passion of Christ must come first, and the vast rejection

(25). Then with a telescoping of the ages between two verses, the end of the age of God's grace, and time's consummation breaks in (26-30). Tangling with events at the end of history, is the closer prospect of judgment on Jerusalem, Matthew's double thread of eschatological language. Let those who would live watch the gathering eagles. The eagle stood on the standards of the legions.

Various Parables and Teaching
(Luke 18: 1-43)

THE story of the unjust judge (1-8) is to be set beside that of the importunate neighbour (11: 6-10). The magistrate 'regarded neither God nor man' but gave the widow justice when she plagued him. She 'kept coming' (3). She 'gives me a black eye', he said (5). Neither of these little stories in any way suggests that God is like the judge or the annoyed neighbour. Nor do they suggest that God can be driven or cajoled into granting that which he would otherwise withhold. What the Lord does mean is that in human relationships people are not put off by delay or even by a first refusal, if their desire is keen enough, and if their confidence in the ability of the one they approach to grant their petition is deep enough. 'If you, being evil . . .' the Lord remarks. Unjust judges and dour friends can be approached with persistence and hope. How much more should they, who feel that God can help and who are aware of no evil in their petition, wait before his feet in confidence, so that, in his own wise way and in his own good time, he will answer? 'The Kingdom of Heaven', wrote Dante, using another text, 'suffers violence from warm love and live hope.'

The vivid little story of the Pharisee and the tax official (9–14), a hated officer of the fiscal contractors and loathed by nationalistic Jews as a symbol of subjection, is told in Luke's best style, brief, pungent. It no doubt reflects the teaching manner of the great teacher. There is a poignant detail lost in KJV under a mis-translated article. It is a not uncommon fault in KJV (as also at John 3: 7) to confuse definite and indefinite article, (RSV perpetuates the error both here and in John 3: 7). The Pharisee according to common custom prayed aloud. The tax official, as he was intended to do, heard him. In humility he prayed: 'God be merciful to me the sinner'—the sinner described. 'Justified' (14) is Paul's great word. The penitent who looks for mercy finds it (14: 11).

Luke seems at v. 15 to rejoin the thread of Mark's story. On vv. 15–30 see comments on Matthew 19: 13–30 and Mark 10: 13; 31. Vv. 31–34 are the seventh reference to the coming ordeal in Luke (5: 35; 9: 22, 43–45; 12: 5; 13: 32, 33; 17: 25). On vv. 31–43 see comments on Matthew 20: 17–19; 29–34. Also Mark 10: 32–34; 46–52.

West and Up to Jerusalem
(Luke 19: 1–48)

THEY crossed the Jordan a few miles from Jericho, and traversed the lush plain to the rich little town by the oasis, the place where man first fortified a spring, created the first frontier in the Middle East, and called a natural resource his and his alone. So began Jericho, the oldest city on earth. In the first century it lay on an artery of trade. Hence the presence of tax officials, levying customs and transit dues. Jericho was a rich place, perhaps cooler and less oppressive in humidity and heat, 2,000 years ago.

Zacchaeus was eager to see the Lord (3–5) an indication, perhaps, that, like Matthew, he longed for something better than his despised calling, with its temptations, corruption and ostracism. Luke tells the story with his usual vigour. Forgetful of dignity, the small man outstrips the crowd and climbs a tree to see the Lord pass. It would be interesting to know whether Zacchaeus himself first wrote the narrative down. The numerous 'ands' suggest an Aramaic original. Zacchaeus wanted a glimpse of a cleaner world, and Christ opened the vision wide (6, 7). That world lies always near to common life. Christ comes into no house without cleansing it (8, 9). It all illustrates 18: 24, 27. Zacchaeus repays on the scale of Exodus 22: 1 rather than on 22: 4, 7, 9; Leviticus 6: 5; Numbers 5: 7.

The parable of the absent nobleman (11–27) is based on history. When Herod the First died his will divided the kingdom between his sons. Judea was part of the portion of Archelaus, and this was why Joseph and Mary, returning from Egypt, did not go back to Bethlehem, but went north to Nazareth in the realm of Herod Antipas (Matt. 2: 22, 23). Archelaus, who had a full share of his father's vices, without the first Herod's diplomatic astuteness, began his rule over Judea with the sanguinary suppression of disorders in Jerusalem. A widespread Jewish uprising necessitated the intervention of Varus, the governor of Syria. It was at this time of tension that Joseph and Mary returned from Egypt, and the disturbed state of the country was reason for their change of residence. But it was vital for Archelaus to have his authority confirmed by Augustus in Rome, and necessary, in consequence, for him to hurry to the capital before reports from Palestine, and especially the despatches of Varus, presented the condition of affairs in troubled Judea in too unfavourable a light. A Jewish embassy, and Herod Antipas in person, opposed Archelaus' appointment. Augustus, surprisingly, did confirm his title to Judea, but refused the appellation of 'king'. Archelaus, then, was the 'nobleman' who went abroad to 'receive a kingdom', and it was natural enough for the Lord to use the incident as a parable in Jericho, because this was his starting-point. Archelaus had a large palace in Jericho, and the sight of its white marble and terraces suggested the story. It is a further illustration of the necessity of dissociating the machinery of a parable from the moral or doctrinal significance. There could be no greater contrast between the Lord, leaving behind him his followers with responsibilities, and the villain of the Herod family, whose tyrannical rule until

A.D. 6 altogether failed to justify the confidence which Augustus had placed in him.

Archelaus, bitter at Augustus' refusal of the royal title, may have acted as v. 27 describes. A conversation as they left Jericho, and began the long climb to Jerusalem, prompted the use of the incident. The reason for telling the parable is in v. 11. The Twelve were in a state of high excitement, in spite of the warnings they had received. (Mark 10: 32–45). The parable hints at long delay, but also inevitable judgment on what has been done or left undone with life's opportunities of service. V. 23 echoes a traditional saying of Christ: 'show yourselves approved bankers'. (See Eph. 5: 16; Col. 4: 5; 2 Tim. 4: 1, 2.)

On vv. 28–40 see comments on Matthew 21: 1–9 and Mark 11: 1–10. With sombre insight the Lord saw Jerusalem from the crest of the Mount of Olives as it was to be in less than forty years, the walls scarred and crumbling under the bombardment of the Roman ballistas, the slopes of the mount blackened and bare. And worse was to follow—fire, demolition, ruin, ashes and death. The south-west corner of the great Herodian walls is visible from the Mount of Olives, and recent Israeli clearance has shown the calcined ruin of first-century streets and shops. He descended the hill and entered the city (45–48).

From Mark 11: 11 and 15 it appears that Jesus crossed the Kedron, entered the city, and went straight to the temple. It was only a few hundred yards to the left of his place of entry. The old abuses had crept back to the holy place since the earlier occasion, described by John (2: 13–17), when he had driven out the traders and money-changers. He then retired to Bethany, came back to the city the next morning, and cleansed the temple afresh. The Sadducean priesthood, who authorised this lucrative bazaar in the Court of the Gentiles, were hesitant to act because of the support for the Lord among the multitude. They waited cunningly for the onset of disillusionment in those who had expected a spectacular demonstration of messiahship.

Teaching in the Temple
(Luke 20: 1–47)

MUCH of the story of this chapter covers familiar ground. On vv. 1–18 see comments on Matthew 21: 23–27, 33–46; Mark 11: 27–33; 12: 1–12. There is a vivid detail in v. 1. The group from the Sanhedrin 'came upon him', and the verb used is that of 10: 40 describing Martha's exasperated approach to Christ. It is used again in 21: 35. The dexterous parrying of question with question is sound debate. The opponent of Christ has many unanswered questions.

The vineyard parable is closer to true allegory than most parables are, for the vineyard metaphor is woven deeply into O.T. scripture and was a commonly accepted figure for Israel (Deut. 32: 32, 33; Ps. 80: 8–16; Isa. 5: 1–7; Jer. 2: 21; Ezek. 15: 1–6, 19: 10–14; Hos. 10: 1; Joel 1: 7). History was woven bitingly into the story. Those who were entrusted with the guardian-

ship of the vineyard looked upon it as their private preserve. The parable passed from history to prophecy in vv. 14 and 15. V. 17 is from Psalm 118: 22, a song said to have been sung at the completion of the walls of Jerusalem in 444 B.C. The Lord showed the true content of the words. The early church remembered this (see Acts 4: 11; 1 Pet. 2: 7, 8; Rom. 9: 33).

For the incident of the silver denarius (19–26), see comments on Matthew 22: 15–22; Mark 12: 13–17. The Pharisees, pre-occupied with authority, retired defeated. Now came the Sadducees with an absurd theological and eschatological dilemma (27–38). See comments on Matthew 22: 23–33; Mark 12: 18–27. Pass on, for vv. 39–47 to comments on Matthew 22: 41–46; Mark 12: 35–37. The prophecies of the O.T., with their clear indications of Davidic descent, were much more significant as arguments in a Jewish context (2 Sam. 7: 8–29; Isa. 9: 5–7; Mic. 5: 2; Ps. 110: 1, etc.). It is well to remember that a messianic meaning in these places is not precluded by some other or local significance. It is often the case that a passage has both primary and secondary meaning. The Lord was also speaking within the context of the Jewish interpretation of the O.T., and confounding his critics with their own doctrine and methods of exegesis.

Last Things
(Luke 21: 1–38)

ON vv. 1–4 see comments on Mark 12: 41–44. He 'looked up and saw' (1), as though he had been sitting exhausted with the hateful fray, with downcast eyes. The tiny gift (there were 128 lepta to a denarius) refreshed him. See comments on Matthew 24 and 25 and Mark 13 for the Olivet discourse. The 'goodly stones' were the marble walls, not the Cyclopean blocks with which the great rock platform was sheathed and best visible today in the length of the 'Wailing Wall'. There was a table of gold from Ptolemy of Egypt and a golden vine from Herod, among other costly objects in this 'shrine of immense wealth', as Roman Tacitus described it. There had been warning enough (Lev. 26: 31–33; Deut. 18: 19; 32: 35; 1 Kings 9: 6–9; Mic. 3: 12). The warning of v. 8 was the point of these remarks. The next forty years saw abundant calamity, natural and man-made, through the world of the Mediterranean. Vv. 12 and 13 are for men called to stand and be true before there was a book of rounded doctrine. Simple men and untrained (Acts 4: 13) were called upon to face the subtle arguments of authority and learning. The practical directions of v. 21 saved many Christians from imagining that the fortress walls of the superbly placed city were a strong refuge. V. 25 makes it clear that the Lord is using apocalyptic language, that species of poetry used to express transcendental truth. The sea has been an image for the restless surge of nations in more than one language. The heavenly bodies are an image for those in authority (e.g., Gen. 37: 9). The rise and fall of kings and tyrants has been a commonplace of history, but seldom more striking than in the first

century and the twentieth. The remainder of the chapter has adequate comment in the parallel passages of Matthew and Mark.

Betrayal Night
(Luke 22: 1–71)

COMMENTS on Matthew 26, Mark 14 and John 18 cover the main events in this long chapter. It remains to touch on a few features of the narrative peculiar to Luke. Jewry, gathered in multitudes round Jerusalem, was a formidable force (Mark 14: 2). The vast numbers in Jerusalem for the Passover are grossly overestimated by Josephus, but on the most conservative estimate the population must have swollen to seven or eight times the basic city population of perhaps 25,000 or 30,000. Many thousands would be from Galilee. It was a horde to be reckoned with (6).

The house honoured by the Lord (7–13) was probably that of Acts 12: 12, the home of Mark's mother, and if Mark's father was the man of v. 10, it must have been one of the last deeds of his life, thus to arrange for the Lord's privacy. Aware of Judas' plotting, he sought to conceal the meeting place for as long as was necessary.

The order of events at the supper (14–20) varies a little from that given in the other synoptists and in 1 Corinthians 15. A Syrian manuscript of Luke preserves the same order as in Matthew, Mark and Paul, and may represent an ancient Lucan order. There is no significance in the variation. Of all people, Luke would know what Paul knew.

Snatches only of the conversation are given, and there was tension at the table as the footwashing of John 13 shows. Somewhere between the events of vv. 21–30 some scramble for precedence (14: 7–11) provoked the Lord's act. There was a range of age as v. 26 suggests. Peter was a married man with his own home when he joined Christ (4: 38). He calls himself an 'elder' in the sixties of the century (1 Pet. 5: 1). John, who lived till the death of Domitian in A.D. 96, was probably the youngest.

V. 30 is apocalyptic language, as all would know, and v. 31 a reference to the dramatic opening of Job. Note the use of 'Simon', the name of frailty. He was also speaking in apocalyptic symbolism when he spoke of the sword in vv. 36–38. Since the Lord later that night repudiated the use of force (49–51) he cannot have been speaking literally. He turned away with weary words at the sight of their puny weapons, and before their dull misunderstanding (38). 'Enough,' he sighed.

Only John, writing between thirty and forty years later, reveals that Peter was the assailant of v. 50. It was safe then. John, too, with access to the high priest's house, knew the servant's name. It was a characteristic of Peter to turn to action in bewilderment.

Who reported the prayer? (41–45). The three intimates (see Matthew and Mark) possibly heard much of it. Mark, if he was the young man in the linen sheet, may have heard it all (Matt. 26: 37, 38; Mark 14: 51, 52).

Luke, not a Jew, and not a member of the apostles' band omits some of the more reprehensible details of Peter's betrayal, in understandable reserve.

Luke tells of five trials of Jesus (63–71); comparison of this first one with Mark 14: 53–64 suggests that the Sanhedrin met with Annas to draw up their charges against Jesus, and then (as they were not supposed to meet by night) the morning's business was a mere formality. Even so, the proceedings were irregular. Witnesses for the defence should have been summoned first and solemnly adjured to speak from knowledge; the meeting should not have been held on a feast day; sentences of condemnation should have been held over for twenty-four hours. V. 69 would recall Psalm 110: 1.

In v. 69 the Lord again uses apocalyptic language. It refers to the resurrection. The phrase 'Son of Man' was a recognised messianic title (Dan. 7: 13) and was so taken by those who heard. Hence the direct question of v. 70. Mark renders the same reply: 'I am'. This is indication enough that the formula of v. 70 is one of assent. See also Acts 2: 33–35; Romans 8: 34; Hebrews 1: 3, 4; 1 Peter 3: 22; Revelation 3: 21, 12: 5. It is important to understand how, and in what sense, the Sanhedrin took Christ's words. Western minds are prone to literalism and to logical statement. The East spoke in imagery with greater ease. The important point is that the Jewish leaders clearly understood that Jesus claimed to be the messiah.

From Pilate to the Tomb
(Luke 23: 1-56)

LUKE adds a few touches of light to the story as it appears in Matthew 27, and Mark 14 and 15. See also John 18 and 19. Herod was too practised a diplomat to be the victim of Pilate's attempt to shed responsibility. He was in Jerusalem for the festival, diligent, as ever, to keep up appearances with the Jews. How the refusal to oblige dissipated the unexplained feud between Herod and Pilate is not known (12). Four times Pilate insisted that Christ was blameless (4, 14, 15, 22; John 18: 38; 19: 4, 6). The obvious course was acquittal with, at most, some show of official displeasure that tranquility was in any way broken (16). Barabbas, the significant choice, was some resistance fighter (19, 25), and it was ludicrous to set such an enemy free. Pilate was coerced by the Jews who had cleverly used his mistakes in office to corner him. He could not afford further appeals to Caesar. His mandate was, at all costs, to keep a turbulent frontier and a restless province quiet. Tiberius wanted results, not explanations.

The reference to the women is characteristically peculiar to Luke (28), and the inscription is given differently by him. If Matthew's version is turned into Latin, Luke's into Greek, and John's into Aramaic, the lines are of almost equal length, a matter of importance to the signwriter. John says that the inscription was trilingual, as are notices so often in the Middle East today (John 19: 19). Luke's eye, and he could have seen the notice or a copy, would turn naturally to the Greek. John would more naturally read the Aramaic. No case can be made for Matthew's more readily reading Latin, save that, if his post was in the Roman tax-system, he might have been accustomed to scanning Latin communications. Mark, of course, abbreviates.

In vv. 39-45 there is no clash with Mark. Both criminals fell into abuse (Mark 15: 32). One, awed by their fellow-sufferer, repented (42). His acceptance is prime illustration of Ephesians 2: 8. On the symbolic significance of v. 45 see Hebrews 9: 3-8, 11, 12; 10: 9-22.

Empty Tomb
(Luke 24: 1-53)

LUKE reports the appearances of Christ associated with Jerusalem and its environs. Alleged discrepancies are of small consequence. Luke mentions two presences, Mark (16: 5) only one. He was writing in feverish haste, and mentions only the spokesman. Two, at all events, contains one (1-11). On v. 12 see comments on John 20: 3-10. Note that there were two apostles (John 20: 2). Luke mentions only one. Luke's informants are apparent. Joanna (8: 3) probably supplied details here, as at 23: 8-12. The women were a stable group, and probably available around 59 and 60 when Luke was combing Palestine for facts. Luke's reading peeps out at v. 11—'idle tale' is a medical term for the babblings of delirium.

The exquisitely told tale of the

Emmaus road is one of Luke's discoveries. Nothing could be more eloquent of the broken despair of the disciples—so remote from the 'discernment situation' imagined by some theologians, in which myths emerge from heated enthusiasm, to turn with a promptitude unknown in history into facts sharp and clear enough to transform life and inspire martyrdom.

A stretch of Roman road beside the church seems to confirm the traditional site. Parallel with the modern road, but 100 yards to the north of it, is undoubtedly an ancient road, along with the ruins of some ancient houses and an oil-pressing factory. There is a long length of heavy stone paving intact, cambered and channelled with a narrow raised footpath like the streets of Pompeii and other Roman ruins.

Realisation burst upon them as he broke the bread. Perhaps it was only then that they saw the torn and ravaged hands. Perhaps a familiar gesture revealed him. Weariness forgotten, they hurried the seven miles back to Jerusalem to find the Eleven. The experience on the Emmaus road was no illusion. It was no group of deluded enthusiasts who were thus transformed. If the tomb was not indeed vacated by a risen Christ there is no Christian faith, and theologians who deny the fact might more appropriately seek less compromising employment. Note the clear and specific report of events in vv. 22 to 24. These were not gullible men. They admit only what their eyes have seen.

Observe that it is a matter of concern with Luke to establish that Christ was real (39, 42). On the other hand, his body was strangely different. He appeared and disappeared. It is seventy years since James Orr hazarded the guess that 'physicists are not so sure of the impenetrability of matter as they once were'. Physics since then has demonstrated that matter is only apprehended by sight and touch in the form appropriate to those senses. Its overwhelming proportion of empty space, if that term itself makes sense, the fantastic motion of seemingly motionless material, all emphasise the fact that we see only that which we see, and that there is an order of existence beyond comprehension on such levels of evidence. This does not explain the resurrection appearances of the Lord, but does suggest the thought that there are other orders than those of common experience.

Luke's brief ending points to his intention to write another book. He began with the Lord's ascension.

THE GOSPEL ACCORDING TO ST. JOHN

The Word Made Flesh
(John 1: 1–51)

THE fourth gospel was written by John, the apostle, in the nineties of his age and in the nineties of the century, the most remarkable work of an aged man in all literature. The authority of the book has been assailed with varied ingenuity, but it can no longer be relegated to a late date nor to another than the traditional author. If papyrus fragments of the book were discarded, worn out, in Egypt, in the principate of Hadrian, there can be few valid objections to the first tradition that it was written in Ephesus in the century's last decade, by the last of the apostles, to answer the deviant doctrines of the first Gnostics, who were tampering with basic teaching on the deity of Christ. Competent scholarship maintains that the book contains some of the oldest historical material in the Christian tradition. It bears the marks of an eyewitness. Recent archaeology has vindicated authenticity, establishing place and personal names. The leading ideas are rooted in the synoptic narratives.

The prologue (1–18) contains all Christianity. 'The Word' was a Greek concept, as old as Heraclitus, himself of Ephesus (500 B.C.). It signified the reason which permeates the universe. The Stoics adopted the idea, and so did Philo, the Alexandrian Jew (20 B.C.–A.D. 50), who sought to show that the Jews had anticipated much Greek philosophy (Prov. 8). Philo came near to identifying the Word with God. John did so: 'In the beginning was a Mind which expressed itself . . .'— a mighty argument for God's existence, in which a mind may rest (1). That primal Intelligence was personal, and expressed itself in the order of Creation (2, 3). It became incarnate in Christ (4, 14), who alone can interpret God to man, in whom alone God can be made intelligible to man (18).

So came light to see by, and it had not been quenched by Jew or pagan. The night 'had never overtaken it'. So v. 5, using the same verb as 12: 35. Turning abruptly to history, John claims his namesake, the Baptiser, as a witness to Christ's messiahship. He who was baptised in Jordan was the pre-existent Word. John Baptist's purpose was thus to testify (6–8). He was to point to Christ, 'the one who should come'. 'He came to his own things,' runs v. 11, 'and his own people rejected him.' (One's 'own things' is a Greek phrase for 'home'. It recurs at 19: 27). John's witness is underlined (15, 29–36). John, the writer, adds his own here (14, 16, 17), and in the covering letter which accompanied the gospel (1 John 1: 1–3). His fellow apostles are called (38–51), the two who heard John, one of whom was Andrew (36–41), then Peter (42), Philip (43–45), the sceptical Nathaniel (46–51), convinced by a mysterious reference to devotions 'under the fig tree'. Was Nathaniel in meditation on Jacob's story (48) and an open way between man and God? (Gen. 28: 12, 13). 'No guile' (47), and the angelic traffic (51), both refer to Jacob. The Lord's words turned a doubter into a devotee in one moment of conviction (50). He saw such 'glory' as John saw, 'as befitted the Father's Son' (16. NEB) and 'grace in his life which gave grace to others'. They all entered into Paul's experience—the inadequate law, the all sufficient Christ (17).

There is the ring of truth in the story of the Pharisees' deputation. They were rude, and were curtly answered (21). When, fearing for their mission, and dropping their discourteous neuter ('what' of v. 21), the Sanhedrists ask more politely, John replied with words from Isaiah (23), and with prophetic emphasis (26, 27). The Baptist himself, expecting a very different messiah, and saddened by his own obtuseness (31, 33), becomes a decisive witness to the person of the Lord—no human Jesus, son of Mary and Joseph, into whom the Christ came at Jordan only to desert him on the cross, but God in flesh appearing. Thus was the 'liberal', Cerinthus, answered.

The Commanding Christ
(John 2: 1–25)

PERHAPS the 13 members of Christ's party had not been included in the original budgeting. When once they arrived, Eastern hospitality would compel an invitation (2). Hence Mary's urgency (3). The Lord's reply (4) has been misunderstood. 'Woman' is not a harsh vocative. Contexts from Homer onwards show it to be gentle and affectionate. 'What to me and to you?' is the literal meaning of the question, and this can mean a repudiation of fellowship. The whispered reply was possibly: 'What is that to me and you?' It was misunderstood when turned from Aramaic into Greek, and alone among English translations, George Lamsa's renders it correctly. 'Mother, what is that to us?' is a fair translation. 'This is not my feast'. 'Hour' can have no eschatological meaning, for he promptly acts (5–8). The relieved witticism of the bridegroom's friend shows a touch of reality. In such simplicity Christ's course began (9–11).

At this time Mary and her now numerous family moved to Capernaum (12). Joseph was dead. The visit to Jerusalem, in the first Passover of his ministry (13), saw the scene in the temple—not the later 'cleansing' of the Passion Week narrated by the three synoptists. Evil reasserts itself. Cynically, the Sadducean priests turned the temple to profit, with a market for sacrificial beasts, and an exchange bureau to provide 'clean' Jewish money (14). Observe that no criminal charge followed Christ's drastic action (18). It follows that he did nothing indictable. He collected discarded lengths of rope and stood twisting them into a scourge—symbol of authority over beasts (15). His stern and silent presence spread uneasiness. Perhaps an old oracle was whispered (Mal. 3:1, 2). Uneasiness is easily communicated to animals. Nervously handled, some ox breaks loose. The herd stampedes. The pens break up. The tables scatter. The doves in their cages were not involved (16). Of course, 'he drove them out'. He was the prime cause. He, at that moment, stood for the holy place. Hence his remark (19), misunderstood by those who failed to understand holiness (20–22).

Rebirth

(John 3: 1–36)

V. 25 of the last chapter made a statement which the story of Nicodemus illustrates. That story also shows how 'regeneration', known well enough to Paul and Peter, entered the teaching of the church. Nicodemus sought privacy (2), for he was no coward (19: 38, 39). He, the great rabbi, the meticulous Pharisee, came in sincerity, with polite exordium (2). He was about to ask the burning question: 'When will Israel be liberated?' when Christ interrupted him with words about the only Kingdom which mattered, whose citizens must be men remade (3). Nettled, Nicodemus pretended not to understand (4). He did, for a scholar of his standing knew the prophets by heart. He realised that Christ spoke

in mystic language (6, 7) and referred to Ezekiel 36: 25–27; 37: 1–14. Christ deftly showed that he was aware of Nicodemus' understanding by referring to the wind (8. Ezek. 37: 9). Surrendering now to the argument, Nicodemus asks when God will thus act. Christ gently chides him. 'Are you the teacher of Israel? . . .' The article is definite. (To change definite for indefinite article is a common fault of KJV.) The answer lies in another story—Numbers 21: 5–9. He who looked lived. So Nicodemus had his answer. Israel will regain the kingdom, when Israel is reborn, rebuilt of new-made men. That is what God in grace can do? When? When men in desperation lay hold of grace by faith (15).

This, John comments, is universal truth (16). God has offered grace. He who believes 'shall not perish but have the very life of God'. Or 'shall not destroy himself', for the verb can be what Greek calls 'middle'. And those who refuse God's offer do 'destroy themselves'. John condenses the rest of the conversation, down to v. 21. The invitation is universal. 'Whosoever' comprehends, and cannot exclude (17). Judgment is already passed (18), but stands confirmed only when men, seeing the light, actually prefer darkness (19), shrinking from self-revelation and painful exposure (20). If a man follows the faintest gleam, stumbles after truth, and desires good, for all his failure, he finds it (21).

V. 22 begins a section. Jesus and John overlapped (22–24). Hence the ironical comment of some Jew (25. The word is singular): 'Which of you is right?' John's greatest words follow, spoken to some disciples who could hardly bear to utter Jesus' name (26). He was quite clear about his task (27, 28). The work of the '*shoshben*' was to bring the bride to the bridegroom (29), no more, much less keep the bride. 'He must go on increasing, I must go on decreasing.' Thus the words, stressing the Greek linear tenses. It is a rule for Christian living.

John's comment fills the last six verses. Christ is God's last word. God's wrath is a fact of Scripture and must not be anthropomorphised. To choose evil is to repudiate God, and step into the realm in which his repudiation lies.

Samaria

(John 4: 1–54)

THE shortest of the three possible roads to Galilee ran along the upland spine of the land, through the province of Samaria. Depopulated by the Assyrians, a century before Judah's fall, the area had been resettled by mixed stock, which had gradually conformed to a primitive Judaism, and which a more active evangelisation from Jerusalem might have done much to modify and reform (2 Kings 17: 24–41). Instead, Judah withdrew from her contaminated neighbours, and when, after Judah's own exile and restoration, Samaria offered aid in rebuilding the temple (Ezra 4: 1–3), the Jews made the rift complete by rejecting co-operation. The events recorded in Nehemiah deepened hostility.

'He knew what was in man' (2:

25). First it was the cultured Pharisee, now the alien woman. The Lord was leaving Judea to avoid comparison with John, and found work to do in Sychar (1–6). Nicodemus came by night. The Samaritan faced Christ in the blaze of midday (6–8). He asked her for a drink and broke a barrier down (7). The woman could not resist some sarcasm: 'You, a Jew, asking drink of me, a woman and a Samaritan? Jews do not use the same utensils as Samaritans' (9). Without annoyance the Lord touched her curiosity —a foible old as Eve, but this time salutary: 'If you knew . . .' (10). 'How?' she asks and it is a fact that the well is a hundred feet deep. (She did not know Isa. 55 and Ezek. 47. The prophets were not in the Samaritan tradition.) He merely looks at her, and unable to bear the quiet scrutiny, she runs on, with a small thrust about Jacob, their common sire (11). When she can think of no more who drank at the well, he adds another word (13, 14) which provokes a desperate witticism. 'Such water would be fine. I should not need to keep coming here' (15). It is time to break her. By some means, doubtless perfection of faith and fellowship with God, the Lord could tap some source of knowledge. 'Call your man,' he says ('husband' and 'man' are the same word). She finds she cannot lie (16–18), and tries defensively to provoke a theological argument about Gerizim (19, 20), and Jerusalem's more complete tradition (21–24). She tries then to end the conversation (25), and hears Christ's ultimate claim (26). The disciples arrive (27) and he prolongs the conversation until the blur of white along the road showed what he had waited for—the curious crowd (35) stirred by the woman's word (28–39). The fishers of men became reapers of souls (40–45).

Work waited too in Galilee where Herod's officer (46), a movingly human suppliant (49), received answer to his prayer (50).

Bethesda

(John 5: 1–47)

ANOTHER story of Christ and the individual follows. The incident leads to another clash with the hierarchy, and, on a human level, what Christ did and said this day cost him his life. In 2: 13–20 he antagonised the Sadducees. Now it is the Pharisees. V. 4 is a gloss. Important ancient manuscripts do not contain the verse, and it is an obvious explanatory note ('gloss') on v. 7, which became tangled with the text. The Lord takes no notice of the tradition of the moving water, which could have been a thermal phenomenon, the bubbling of a natural spring, or water periodically pumped from the temple. Nor are such competitive miracles found in the Bible.

V. 7 contains a principle. God has nothing for the half-hearted (Jer. 29: 13; Luke 17: 32). Perhaps the man had adjusted damagingly to his position. He was limiting God's help to his own narrow prescription. Besides it was the Sabbath. How intensely did he desire healing? It appears from vv. 10–18 that the man was under surveillance by the authorities, and reported

details to clear himself from the charge of Sabbath violation. This led to the confrontation between Christ and the hierarchy which occupies the rest of the chapter.

Vv. 19–26 amounted to a claim to be the son of God. The words 'the son' are used eight times in these eight verses and only five times in the rest of the gospel. V. 19 restates 1: 18. It is also a principle of living. All scientific research, after all, consists in finding what the Mind behind phenomena has already determined (1: 1), and all technology applies its principles. To break the moral law, interwoven with all life, is similarly, in the final issue, to 'kick against the goad' (17, 19–21). That is why Christ alone can be the ultimate judge. He has shown 'in small letters' what is 'written large' in the universe. He has shown God's life in man, the life available to faith. He is the standard, and can therefore be the judge (27. Heb. 4: 15). And judgment, like the incarnation, is a point in time (28. Acts 17: 31), and judgment will be just (30).

It follows that God vindicates the one through whom he reveals himself. John had, indeed, told the truth about him, and they had seen the splendour of God in John (35), but the whole weight and drive of ultimate truth convinced all open to truth that God was speaking in Christ. Their very Scriptures, for those who would see and search, thrust towards the same end (39, 46). All that stood in the way was the pride of rebel man which stiffened the will against surrender (40). Pride, their daily habit, in fact inhibited the surrender which gives life (45). The practice of pride and self-assertion was a destructive principle, and ironically it was linked with their very study of the law (46, 47).

Bread of Life
(John 6: 1-71)

THE story of the meal by the lake is told by all four evangelists, by John because it led to the sustained metaphor of the living bread. The scene is on the Golan Heights (3), east of Galilee, and John, his memory always vivid, recalled the grassy upland (10). Characters stand out—Philip always facing hard facts (5-7. 1: 46; 14: 8), Andrew's witticism, rapidly withdrawn (9). Men predominated, as they do in a Jewish crowd at the Wailing Wall today (10). The few women would be helping. Observe v. 12: '... that nothing be wasted' contains the verb, in the same mood and tense as 3: 16 ('perish'). It might as legitimately be used there ... 'should not be wasted but have real life'.

The response was prompt. This was the sort of king they wanted. And in trying to force him to be such a king, they lost both the king and the kingdom (15, 26, 27). He withdrew further up the heights, 'himself alone', says John (15), using significantly a phrase he uses nine times. He dismissed the crowds, according to Matthew (14: 22) and Mark (6: 45). One can imagine his saying: 'Oh go away, go away, you do not see what this means?'

Obediently the disciples put to sea. With a contrary wind (Mark 6:

48), it took all night to fight their way north-west up the lake. The wind was against them because they were keeping course as bidden. After the rejection of the crowd's homage and the night's toil they needed him—and he came. It was then that the great Rift Valley gale dropped and they were home.

And now he tries to tell them that what they needed was not mere food but another bread, a different kingdom, truer water. And that came by simple faith—the only 'work' we can do (27-30). Prove it then, they say, by another miracle (31-33). He, in truth, was their bread. Like the woman at the Sychar well (4: 15), they reply ironically (34). Man, he goes on to say, needs a lasting satisfaction and all may have it (35-37). God's will for man was another sort of life, fuller living, reality (38-40). They did not want this at all (41). They were small-souled, petty-minded. They knew his parents. How could he be aught to wonder at (42, 43)? Blindly they refused to see the inner meaning of his words and so God could not draw them into the circle of his grace (44-59). His was a 'hard' word (the adjective of Matt. 25: 24; Acts 26: 14; Jas. 3: 4), hard, not because he baffled their minds but because he challenged their lives. He had dedicated followers, sympathisers and some who were loosely attached. His demanding words showed clearly enough that he was to promote no political action, and the realisation sifted out the true. 'Does this stumble you?' he asks. 'What when they kill me?' (62). This was the signal for many to 'go to the things behind' (66—

literally. See Phil. 3: 13). Such things may have been harmless—fishing, farming, trading—but they involved withdrawal. The sad question (67) produced one of Peter's magnificent words. He told them of 'a life different from every other kind of life'.

The Festival of Tents
(John 7: 1–53)

REJECTION was the theme of the great Isaian oracle (53:3) and the Lord suffered it on all fronts (1: 11; Matt. 12: 24; Mark 5: 17; Luke 4: 28, 29). Rejection by his own family was the direst test. It was part of his temptation (1 Pet. 2: 6–8; Heb. 4: 15). In this and the following chapter the enemies of Christ are mentioned ten times. His life was in danger. Hence the decision not to go to the Camping Festival with a caravan of excited Galileans, which, for their own ends, his family desired. Nor did he court publicity (3, 4). The 'proper time' (8) had not yet come. There was no deception involved—only a refusal to share his plans with unsympathetic people (15: 15). He did not leave Galilee till halfway through the festival, arriving apparently on the last day (10, 37). He had been teaching in the temple for some time before people recognised him (25). It was, in fact, becoming perilous to associate with him. Hence the whispering (12).

His teaching astonished them, for he was attached to no rabbi (15). The comment was that faith began with a moral choice (17). The hostile mind receives no compelling revelation, but a reaching for good and God is fertile in understanding. Scepticism blinds the mind to truth. It inhibits search. In spite of clear prophecy (Mic. 5: 2; Matt. 2: 3–6), the rabbis taught that the messiah would come unawares. After the experience of Matthew 2: 13–16 Mary spoke little of Bethlehem, and Nazareth became associated with Christ. The truth was available. There was long debate, perhaps a full day, in vv. 14–36, the common duels over the law (19–24), the controversy among the people (25–29), followed by the fumbling attempts to arrest him, when the Pharisees caught the echo of the crowd's wonderment (32). Events were moving as Christ expected (33, 34). The Pharisees cared little for the Jews of the Dispersion and breeds outside the law (35). Their arrogance was apparent.

Part of the current ritual was the thanksgiving for water. Water was drawn from Siloam in a golden ewer, and Isaiah 12: 3 formed the hymn. Hence the sermon (37) and wide persuasion (40–42). The very officers of the Sanhedrin postpone (44), and then abandon the ordered arrest (45). Apart from some exasperation, the hierarchy accepts the open disobedience (47–49). Nicodemus makes a formal defence (50, 51), but is silenced by an illogical academic argument. 'No one who is of any standing, no one of us, have believed in him.' Any academic can recognise the tone (52). Nahum came from Galilee, where Capernaum may·bear his name. He was dismissed as the mere author of a triumph song. Jonah came from Galilee—but he preached to Gentiles (52). As for the crowd, who did not know the 613 commandments, God's curse on them (49. Deut. 27: 26). V. 53 is subtle irony.

Stones in the Courtyard
(John 8: 1–59)

Vv. 2–11 are not included in some important ancient manuscripts. This does not diminish the authenticity of the story, or its right to a place in the text. Even if the doubtful claim to stylistic differences could be sustained, the conclusion would be that John included a passage by another hand. The narrative has the ring of truth, and must be set beside the story of the tribute money as an attempt to discredit Christ. Observe his mental and moral preeminence. KJV's weakness over the definite article is again apparent in v. 7: 'Let the one without sin among you . . .' There was a shaft of irony in the words. In a group so zealous, surely one was perfect. The mysterious writing in the dust seems to have sent them out in order of precedence (9). What did he write, and did he, still ironical, deal with them in the precedence they loved? Where was the man who must also have been discovered? (4). The law said both must suffer (Lev. 20: 10; Deut. 22: 22). Was there provision for escape in the plot? V. 11 reads: 'Nor am I passing sentence on you', a forgiveness beyond the grasp of the ascetic copyists who omitted the passage from the text.

V. 12 follows. His presence had been a revealing light that day. The riposte of the defeated Pharisees was feeble (13. 5: 31). He rebuked their literalism as he did Nicodemus (10–19. 3: 12). So too in vv. 21 and 22. As though remembering Nicodemus, he again turns to Num. 21 (24–30). He is speaking later to his converts (31, 32), when listening foes rudely interrupt (33). Disregarding the fact that the Jews had been subject to Egyptians, Babylonians, Persians, Greeks and at that time were under Rome, they claim unbroken freedom. Patiently the Lord defines freedom again, shows how unworthy they were of their ancestor, stingingly shows their true paternity (44), and moves to the astonishing challenge of v. 46. It went unanswered and the fact casts a light on the power of his presence. An unrepentant piety could not be sustained by a mere man. Abuse was all they could offer (47) and the confrontation led to an open claim to deity (58. Exod. 3: 14). They saw the point, and violence, evil's last resort, was the response (59). The same daunting presence (9) held their hand. 'My word' (52) means 'all my teaching' (34, 43, 51, 52). 'Keep' means hold as a treasure, not merely nod assent. John uses the verb eighteen times here, and seven times in the first letter.

Blind
(John 9: 1–41)

A blind man provoked a theological argument. The rabbis taught that 'there is no death without sin, and no suffering without iniquity'. On the basis of Genesis 25: 22, they accepted the possibility of prenatal sin. On Exodus 20: 5, they based the thought of parental guilt (1, 2). With sharp impatience the Lord dismissed theology. The man was a spectacle of need. KJV grossly mispunctuates: 'Neither this man sinned, nor his parents. But if he is to demonstrate what God can do, we must do God's work while day lasts. It is later than you think' (3, 4). The use of the clay was no superstition (5, 6). The blind beggar had little knowledge of God. The tags of popular theology in his duel with the Pharisees are witness to that. Something was needed to awaken a spark of faith, and spittle, especially 'Sabbath fasting spittle', was considered by the rabbis a healing thing, and the dust of the earth was a symbol of creativity (Gen. 2: 7). The man is then told to do something (7). The psychology is perfect.

Debate broke out. The man answered simply (8–12). But it was a religious question. Mixing and anointing fell under scribal Sabbath prohibitions (5, 13, 14). Sensing the hostile context, the man suppresses detail (15). The Pharisees divide. One group begins with the Sabbath-breaking, the other from the visible miracle (16). They turn helplessly to the man, and receive a clipped reply (17). After John's common fashion the man is well characterised. John had entry to the high priest's house (18: 16). The first position was that the healer did not come from God, therefore the miracle did not happen. They ignore the evidence. There must be a flaw. So v. 18. They call the parents (19), timid, respectful of authority, anxious not to be 'involved', even

for their son (20, 21). 'He is of age' (anything over thirteen years and a day) (22). The verdict is given (24). The man, however, has their measure. He picks up the pompous 'we know' and no doubt with such mimicry as he dared repeats it twice (25). Baffled, they revert weakly to questioning (26) and elicit a bold but slightly impertinent testimony. 'Surely you do not want to become his disciples too?' (27). They use their authoritarian 'we know' twice more (29, 30) and are worsted by the reply: 'Yes, a marvellous thing is this that you do not know . . . we know that God does not hear sinners . . .' The parody is perfect and the response prompt (34). To be 'cast out' is sometimes to find Christ (35–38. Heb. 13: 13). Christ's presence lights up reality (5). Who was really blind? (39–42). It is a perfect example of John's method. His choice of incidents illustrates great words.

The Good Shepherd
(John 10: 1–42)

THE brush with the hierarchy provoked the discussion on shepherds, an image as old as psalms and prophets. It is found in Sumerian literature. God (Pss. 23, 80; Isa. 40: 10, 11), the king (Ps. 78: 70–72) are shepherds. They were bad shepherds (Isa. 56: 9–12; Jer. 23: 1–4; 25: 32–38; Ezek. 34: 1–10) 'such as', in Milton's words, 'for their bellies' sake, creep, and intrude, and climb into the fold' (1). It was a long discussion, here contracted. The Lord appears as the shepherd (2), and the door (3). The eastern context must be borne in mind. The sheep follow, they are not driven. They know their pastor's voice, so that a call can separate commingled flocks (3–6, 14, 26, 27). There are those who ravage the flock left unprotected (10–12). Perhaps 'the wolf' was Rome whose ancestral Romulus was suckled by a wolf. Vv. 1–18, parabolic teaching which bypassed the thoughtless, as it was intended it should do (6. Matt. 13: 10–16), are the complete answer to those who allege that John omits this facet of Christ's teaching. He gradually sifts from the parable the picture of himself, ready to die (11, 15), the caller of a wider flock (16), commissioned (17), and in control even of the coming mystery of death (17, 18). Hence the division (19–21).

The argument was resumed in the Colonnade (23. Acts 3: 11; 5: 12) where, sheltered from the winter cold, Christ taught during the Feast of Dedication (22), the festival commemorating the last great deliverance of the Jews and the re-dedication of the temple after the defeat of Antiochus Epiphanes in 165 B.C. The thoughtful, the seekers, the willing, had already been separated from the cavillers, the shallow and the self-seeking (24). They had only to look and believe (25). 'Miracles', in a word, cannot be avoided. To 'demythologise' Christ is to demolish him. Hence the exasperation of the unwilling (23–32), and the defensive argument of vv. 33–39. Such dexterous word play confounded the Pharisees (Matt. 21: 41–46; Mark 11: 27–33; Luke 20: 39–44). Psalm 82: 6 likened the judges to gods, exer-

cising the power of life and death. Then why cavil if the psalm can in any sense apply such a word to men, especially when he whom God sent claims it? (33–39).

Wearied with such confrontation, he sought the place of old victory (40–42).

Lazarus
(John 11: 1–57)

JOHN was free, no doubt after Lazarus' death, to tell this story. Even had Lazarus moved to Ephesus, world Jewry was coherent and vocal through the whole century (Acts 20: 3; 21: 27) and could have menaced him (12: 10, 11). Peter, Mark's informant, besides, may have been in Galilee. He is not mentioned between 6: 68 and 13: 6 (cf. Matt. 19: 27 and 26: 33; Mark 10: 28 and 11: 21; Luke 18: 28 and 22: 8). The dual origin of Matthew's gospel—first sayings, later interpolated with narrative, could be another explanation of omission.

There was no direct plea for aid. Note in v. 5 that Martha is mentioned by name, and Mary unnamed. Perhaps John wearied of misinterpretations of Luke 10: 38–42. Notice 'therefore' in v. 6. Characterisation is sharp in this chapter. Thomas remembered the peril (10: 31). He was a man aware of such circumstances, no facile optimist. It is true courage to see danger and still face it (16). V. 9 has hinted that Christ was not stumbling in darkness. He knew what he was doing.

Lazarus, when the party came to Bethany, was four days dead. The

Jews had a belief that the soul stayed three days near the grave, and on the fourth day came a climax of mourning. This was what Christ encountered as they came up the Jericho road to Bethany (19). That is why he stayed outside the village. Observe the consistent characterisation of the sisters (20), and the strength and faith of Martha. Let Martha be remembered for v. 27. At the spectacle of death, Jesus grieved (33, 35). There is no need for remote explanation for Jesus' grief. He was Jesus, perfect man, as well as Christ, victor over death. In true manhood there is place for understanding, sympathy, horror at death's grim intrusion, the agonised sharing of sorrow. For the rest, the story tells itself... Perhaps Mary's emotional needs were greater (31, 33, 35), but it is Martha who is in charge.

John had access, in some way, to the councils of the Sanhedrin (47–55). Hence the intimate report, even to the well-known rudeness of the Sadducees (49). The 'place' (48) of Caiaphas' cynical speech was either Jerusalem, the temple, or the eight-ton stone, marked 'The Place of the Trumpet', found recently. It has a place for a trumpeter (Caiaphas or his deputy) to stand at sunset, and announce, berobed and jewelled, the coming of the Sabbath. The Romans levered it from the wall top. What Caiaphas sought to avert by murder, came to pass. So, ironically, did v. 50.

V. 25 is the saying which lay behind John's choice of the Lazarus story. Another life, it means, cannot be a tenet of real faith apart from Christ. Life, as life should be understood, has no meaning apart from him (2 Tim. 1: 10).

The End of Christ's Ministry
(John 12: 1–50)

THIS may be the story of Matthew 26: 6–13 (Mark 14: 3–9), set at Bethany in 'the house of Simon the leper'. Was he the father, in seclusion because of his affliction? (Uzziah lived in seclusion while Jotham reigned). Luke 7: 36–50 was in Galilee. Simon was a common enough name. John tells the story to prepare the way for Judas' betrayal. His motive perhaps appears—disillusionment, as the ambition for an earthly kingdom faded (1–8).

The choice of an ass, the animal of peace (Zech. 9: 9), confirmed Judas' decision (14). The crowd seized on Psalm 118: 25, 26, one of the cycle of Passover psalms. Palms signify victory (Rev. 7: 9), and adorn Jewish coins from 140 B.C. to A.D. 70. The crowd again were acclaiming kingship, to the consternation of the hierarchy (17–19).

Keeping the resurrection in full view, John introduces the story of the Greeks. The purest of the Greek 'mystery' cults was that of Eleusis near Athens, where the myth of Demeter was celebrated. The goddess, 'entertained unawares', gave the young prince a corn of wheat with directions to place it in the ground to die. Thus it would rise again, and feed mankind. Eleusis built a ritual and a creed of spiritual regeneration on the story. It is as though Christ pointed to a fragment of truth the Greeks may have already apprehended (20–25). A gush of temptation followed. If the Jews rejected, would the Greeks receive? Read a question at 'hour' in v. 27. V. 31 meant that Calvary finally convicted man. Sin did its worst, and was defeated. 'Lifted up' (32) is used four times in this gospel, always of the cross, and the spectacle of sacrifice is Christ's universal appeal (32). There is no other gospel, no other offer. It can be received or rejected. The words offend 'the crowd' (here mentioned for the last time). They chose darkness, so failed to see (35, 36. 3: 19; Isa. 50: 10). Their obtuseness amazed John (37–43) and he turned to Isaiah for explanation (Isa. 6: 10; 53: 1; Acts 28: 28; Rom. 1: 24–28). Vv. 44–50 are the last words recorded by John of the Lord's public ministry. He himself, the Word, is God's last utterance to man. Only a wilful choice of darkness blinds those who might see but will not.

At Table

(John 13: 1–38)

THE journey up from Jericho had been marred by bitter quarrels over precedence (Matt. 20: 20–28; Mark 10: 32–35) and in the symbolic fashion of the East the Lord sought to break the pride of his men, so slow, to the end, to comprehend. John adds the moving details to the already recorded story of the last supper. His act broke the tension which marred fellowship. Peter was led to whole-hearted surrender, and one of those spontaneous words which so often delight (9). But Judas was hardened in his contempt for such a leader. It was Christ's last appeal so to wash his feet. For the rest, their hearts were right. All they needed was cleansing from the stains of the way (10).

He told them the meaning of what he had done. He spoke again of betrayal, another appeal to Judas, and traced it to prophecy (Ps. 41: 9). It filled him with agony of mind (21. 11: 33; 12: 27). It was the vision of death which, in all three cases, occasioned the struggle. He was about to dismiss Judas on his errand of evil, but gave him yet another chance. The 'sop' a choice morsel, was a mark of friendship (26). He saw Judas' eyes harden. He left, and John, watching in horror, remembered, sixty or more years later, the oblong of dark as the door opened and closed. It was like the theme of darkness and light which runs through all his writings. The door closed—for ever (30). Can this be other than the word of an eyewitness?

The Lord's final words to his men begin with v. 31, and with one interruption (14: 31) continue to 16: 33. V. 31 uses the word 'glorify' in the sense in which John uses it several times (7: 39; 12: 16, 23; 17: 1). He had long forseen this moment (2: 20, 21; 3: 14; 6: 51; 10: 11), but his words had not been grasped. Hence the present shock and apprehension, more felt than understood. They lacked unity, a prime necessity in the coming ordeal. One force could bind them—love. It was a commandment old but new (34. 1 John 2: 3; Lev. 19: 18).

Christ the Way
(John 14: 1–31)

THE choices lie between indicatives and imperatives for 'believe'. KJV is probably best (1), but for v. 2 read: 'Had it not been so, would I not have told you?' 'Mansions' is literal Latin for the Greek word (*monê*) in Jerome's Vulgate, and means 'resting places', 'pauses on the way', or even 'rooms'. Thomas, a deeply honest man, could not reconcile v. 4 with 13: 33 and 36. He elicited the beautiful logion of v. 6. Christ bridged the gap between man and God (Eph. 2: 13, 14; Heb. 10: 19, 20). The first Christians took the words in the sense of 'a way of life' (Acts 9: 2; 19: 9, 23; Ps. 27: 11). Truth, the quest of all healthy thought is seen best from the centre Christ provides. His light illumines life. He is life, for severance from him means death. Philip sought some theophany (8–11. Exod. 24: 10; Isa. 6: 1) and Christ replied with an expansion of 1: 18. Such words would be deadly indictment if he who uttered them were less than he claimed to be. 'In his name' (13) means with regard to his person. To 'believe in his name' means to believe he is what he says he is. To pray in his name means to trust him to overrule beneficently all prayer.

Four times John calls the Holy Spirit 'the Paraklêtos' sometimes Englished as 'Paraclete' (16, 26; 15: 26; 16: 7). As in 1 John 2: 1 it should be rendered 'advocate', a word which suits all contexts. It means a helper, summoned to the side of one in need. V. 23 is a verse to ponder. God and the Son are present in the Spirit. The Trinity, a concept to enable us to grasp a transcendental truth, must not be mechanically divided. Great heresies and lamentable misunderstandings arise from that attempt. See also 2 Corinthians 5: 19. 'I will not leave you orphans', says v. 18—desolate, forlorn, bereaved. Then, as though time was too short, the Lord rose suddenly, and left the upper room (31). He seemed to be briefly thwarting Judas, due to return with the temple guards at any moment.

Abiding
(John 15: 1–27)

HE probably led them to the temple court, the last place where Judas might expect to find them. The clue is the metaphor of the vine, for a sculptured vine, figure of Israel, gilded and glorious under the paschal moon, overhung the gate of Herod's building. Pruned, cleansed, fed by a noble stock, the branches can bear abundant fruit. It is listed at Galatians 5: 22, 23 (1–3).

Abiding, is that unbroken attitude of mind in which we lay aside all that which we seek to derive from our own strength, to draw all from Christ by faith (4–7). It is the application of 14: 20. It issues in identity of aim, purpose, desire, and that is obedience (10). Such committal is based on love (11–14). The word rendered 'ordained' by KJV (16) is literally 'put' or 'place' (Ps. 8: 3 shows a similar literal translation of Jerome's Latin. The KJV translators had an eye on the Vulgate). The meaning here is that

God 'so places' the surrendered soul that it can act and be fruitful. No conditions are listed. He who 'abides' is free. The Husbandman sets him in the soil and place where he can best produce the fruit he is fitted to produce, and which the Husbandman would have of him. The approval of a pagan society is not to be expected (18). A world which crucified Christ is not likely to be gentle with his followers (20). 'Stop trying to make yourselves like the society you live in,' said Paul with these words in mind (Rom. 12: 2). Note how, in v. 19, 'the world', the great non-Christian organism of evil, is mentioned five times, as though to fix it in the listeners' minds. The world did not know God (21), had deliberately refused to know God and the burden of that ignorance was fearsome (22). They had seen and rejected (24) the last and deadliest sin (Mark 3: 22–30).

The Holy Spirit
(John 16: 1–33)

THE chapter break is arbitrary, for the daunting theme of persecution goes on to v. 6. The coming ordeal would leave them exposed to hatred as well as to apparently irreparable bereavement (1–6). But only thus could a vast plan be consummated. Only thus could the first witnesses explain the faith which they were to preach, learn by personal experience the truths that God keeps, guides, indwells (7), and only thus could they acquire that authority of speech and power of conviction which would challenge the world (8–11). The spirit's

presence in the conscience was to take the place of Christ's illuminating presence among them. He was so to shape and fashion understanding, deepen insight and reveal truth, that the gospel would take form. The result was to be the New Testament and Christian theology (12–15).

The Lord then spoke in veiled and mystic terms of the coming shock, his death and the desolation to follow. 'A little while' puzzled them, but the resurrection made it clear. It would be like a mother's travail, pain swallowed in joy at the emergence of new life (16–22). V. 23 repeats an earlier promise. We ask in another's name only that which we know will command that person's approval. Christ was perfectly holy, unselfish, loving, wise. No base, selfish, hate-ridden, foolish prayer can be made, therefore, in his name. This does not, as his model prayer shows, inhibit simplicity, the simplicity with which any child can come to a loving parent. God will answer the innocent plea, but in perfect love and perfect wisdom. He sees what we cannot see, the ultimate effects of an answer, and commonly answers in a way not prescribed, but infinitely more imaginatively, fruitfully, wisely than the ignorance of the petitioner imagines (Eph. 3: 20). His words, at last, brought comfort (24–33).

The Lord's Other Prayer
(John 17: 1–26)

THIS prayer is not for imitation. No disciple can claim to have glorified God. Unrepentant piety is not for man. Such calm and confidence in such a context is hardly of this world. For a saint of earth thus to pray would be to negate all holiness, and manifest an arrogance which would repel. Christ was what he has claimed in these three chapters to be, or else unworthy of regard. But these were not the words of a deluded man, much less a deceiver. Nor, curiously, has hostility made a point of this. Human prayer may be set before God with confidence (Heb. 10: 22) but such prayer can hardly omit the note of repentance and gratitude for sin forgiven. Neither are in this prayer of Christ.

The raised eyes (1) were a human posture (11: 41; Mark 7: 34; Luke 18:13). 'Father' ('*Abba*' of Mark 14: 36) is a title man is privileged to share. In v. 3 'eternal life' is defined, the knowledge of God in Christ (perhaps John interpolates these words into the prayer). It is part of the great mystery, that Christ found 'glory' in the cross ('When I survey the wondrous cross . . .') but so it came to pass.

The main part of the prayer concerns the disciples (16–19), the conclusion contains the church—us (20–26). He has delivered his message (8), trusted them with his 'glory' (10). For his sake the 'world' rejects them (14). It is their lot to remain and face the gales of hate (14–16), reinforced by the truth they hold (17). To sanctify is to set apart for holy use. In such fashion Christ 'set apart' himself for the looming task. His act was purposeful—to enable his own thus to be set apart from a doomed and vicious system. The solemnity of

the divine fusion of Son and Father and church is awesome (24).

Arrest and Trial
(John 18: 1–40)

HE had said now all he had wished to say to his men and rose to face the end. He knew that Judas, finding the upper room empty, would proceed to the Garden of Gethsemane (Matt. 26: 36; Mark 14: 32; Luke 22: 39). Thither came the traitor with a band of temple guards and a small reinforcing detachment of Roman soldiers. John brings out the majesty of Christ (4–8). Such was the dignity which surrounded him in the gloom and the glare of the torchlight, that at the words 'I am' there was confusion, as the front men stumbled back (Exod. 3: 14). Peter is now named as the defender with the sword (Mark 14: 47). It was not safe to do so when Mark wrote (9–11). 'The cup' is mentioned in the other gospels. It was part of the prayer of agony (Matt. 26: 39; Mark 14: 36; Luke 22: 42). The metaphor is often used in contexts of suffering and wrath (Ps. 75: 8; Isa. 51: 17, 22; Jer. 25: 15; Ezek. 23: 31–33).

John gives a more detailed analysis of the examination and trial scenes than the other evangelists. With his apparent access to the priestly palace, he was in a position to do so (14–18). Was v. 21 an invitation to Peter, visible by the fire, to step out and testify? He was able to remedy his denial (17) but repeated it (27). Next came the trial before Pilate on 'the Pavement' (19:

13), where he could be heard and seen from thé road which borders it. The opening of the trial was in the form which the accusers should have expected, the normal request for a formal charge (29). The request seems to have astonished them (30). The only explanation of an omission so extraordinary with clever lawyers, is that Pilate must have undertaken to omit all formalities, and issue a condemnation. Why, if that is the case did he change his mind? The only ready explanation is that his wife, who knew of the corrupt arrangement and detested it, dreamed a disturbing dream. Hence her intrusion into the trial (Matt. 27: 19). A Roman would take notice of such a portent. Off balance, and fighting for time, Pilate retreated to proper formality. He was no doubt under threat, and could not bring himself to do what should have been done —dismiss the charge. The priests had the upper hand, and the procurator could not afford a third appeal to Caesar. He was directly responsible to the dour Tiberius who demanded peace on the frontiers. His bafflement is apparent (31, 33–38). He made a last attempt at escape but the Jews were ready for that. With tragic irony they chose Barabbas. It was a choice of death (39, 40).

The Cross

(John 19: 1–42)

A scourging (1) was a fearsome experience which often ended in death. It probably caused the damage which produced the fluid in the thoracic cavity (34) revealed by the spear thrust. The crown (2) was part of the cruel game of the soldiers, of which the scratchings on the floor of the Pavement under the Convent of the Sisters of Zion are an archaeological relic. One square is marked B for '*basileus*'— 'king' (3). Pilate thought to stir pity by the shocking sight, salving his conscience at the same time (4, 5). The priests were now ready and had their answer prepared in the roar of their minions in the street (6), and in the malicious thrust against Roman prohibitions (7). Pilate fought hard, caught in the dilemma, his wife's fears, his Roman instincts, and his apprehension over previous appeals to Caesar, had built (8–11). The clever priests held him, trammelled by his own arrogant past, and he was forced to be content sardonically with hearing them cry allegiance to Caesar (12–16), and with an insulting title on the cross (17–22). John read the Hebrew (or Aramaic) which ran as he quoted it (19).

John's intense pre-occupation with exact reporting appears in his account of events at the cross (23–30). Comparison with the other narratives, shows that John, who actually stood by the cross, omitted a sequence of events. They were those which took place while he took Mary home (25–27). He did as his Master commanded, and must have come back, penetrated the crowd, and heroically resumed his place of vigil. He was there to see the end, and the proofs of actual death. The legs were broken (31, 32) to prevent the convulsive actions of a crucified man, rising on his nailed feet to expel the air from his lungs. The nailed arms lifted the chest high, and prevented normal action of the intercostal muscles, while the weight of the body was on the arms. The legs once broken, the build-up of carbon dioxide speedily brought suffocation. Vv. 33 to 35 are John's attestation. The resurrection was not resuscitation. Nor was it to be a miracle such as the Pharisees might have explained by reference to 2 Kings 13: 21. The tomb was new (41) and was near (42).

One flash of humanity lightens the dark hour. A soldier stuck his spear into a sponge, dipped it in his jar of ration wine, and offered it to the dying victim. Hyssop is a twisted shrub, but a rare word for spear is '*hyssos*'. There is little manuscript evidence, but the translation makes sense (29). Those at the back of the crowd saw only the haft of the spear (Mark 15: 39).

Empty Tomb
(John 20: 1-31)

IT was about the same time as John was writing in Ephesus his moving account of Christ's death, that a Roman aristocrat, Pliny, destined a few years later to govern Bithynia and meet the Christians there, was busy writing for his friend, the historian Tacitus, a factual account of his uncle's death in the eruption of Vesuvius in A.D. 79. The two narratives may be set side by side. They are similar, attempts to set clearly down known facts about a loved one's death. Both are history.

Remembering that there were no lines ruled or chapters numbered by John, read right on to the story of the empty tomb in the garden. The nature of the writing does not change. Prose does not become poetry, nor history myth. The story, therefore, cannot be examined unless it is accepted for what it claims to be—an attempt to describe an event. At this point only it becomes possible to ask whether the writer told the truth, deceived or was mistaken.

Look at the detail, where evidence for truth or error lies—the startled response of Mary, and the two men she approached. Observe the reality of the run to the tomb, and the order of arrival, and the reaction, true to both characters, at the awesome sight. Note v. 7 with the detail of the head bandage, only apparent when one penetrated the twilight of the cave. Consider Mary left alone (15). She could not move a body. No one has satisfactorily explained v. 17. The words were not invented, or they would have been intelligible (1-18).

The stamp of the eyewitness is on the whole chapter. Thomas is true to character, a man prone to gloom (11: 16), difficult to convince (14: 5). His cry (28) rings poignantly true. Fiction would have set here a speech of contrition. John hoped to end with v. 29, as a message for his 'children' (1 John 2: 1; 1 Pet. 1: 8). He was old and weary with a task so exacting. He had one purpose, and it was fulfilled (31).

On the Beach
(John 21: 1-25)

AND then, because of a rumour that the last of the apostles was destined not to die (23), John was compelled to tell of one more encounter with the risen Lord (20: 30). With characteristic impatience and desire for action Peter turned to his old life (3). As they came shorewards in the murk of the morning, Christ stood, as they had often seen him, on the shore. Note the truth to character of the disciples' response, John's quicker apprehension and Peter's translation of realisation more quickly into action, a moment he was to remember (7. 1 Pet. 1: 13). John, always preoccupied with figures, counts the fish. (On an unchecked statement of Jerome that Oppian, an obscure poet, Cilician or Syrian, of the second or fourth centuries, claimed that there were 153 kinds of fish in the sea, some critics have imagined here an allegory—the unbroken net the hopefully undivided church, and the fish all the nations of earth. Such speculation could have been avoided had someone questioned Jerome's assertion and counted the fish mentioned in Oppian's dull 600 lines. Counting molluscs, shellfish and sponges the total is 152).

John told the story (1–14) because it led to the conversation with Peter. There is no mystery over the three questions, the three affirmations, and the three commissions (15–17). Peter is given what heart and mind required, a chance to wipe away the memory of three denials (Matt. 26: 69–75; Mark 14: 66–72; Luke 22: 54–62; John 18: 15–27). He remembered the commands (1 Pet. 5: 2–4). John signs off (24) and is not too old to end the writing of the New Testament with a gentle quip (25).

THE ACTS OF THE APOSTLES

The Ascension and the Sequel
(Acts 1: 1–26)

THE Acts of the Apostles is one of the most important books of all time. It is an important document of first-century history. It links the ministry of Christ with the letters, which interpret his life, death and resurrection to the world. It provides us with one glimpse, through the ministry of Stephen, Philip, Peter, and supremely Paul, of the first surge of that life which was to transform the human story, fuse the contributions of Palestine, Greece and Rome, and lay the foundations of the civilisation of the west.

It was written by Luke, writer of the first gospel, and participant in many of the events he relates. Luke, as this century's archaeology has strikingly demonstrated, was a first-class historian in his own right. He wrote, probably, over a period of years from Paul's imprisonment at Caesarea in the late fifties, to his sojourn in Rome in the early sixties. The exact date eludes, and Luke disappears without trace.

The book was addressed to Theophilus (1) and continues the gospel addressed to him in what seems more formal language (Luke 1: 3). It follows the risen Christ through the undoubted fact (3) of the resurrection, on to the ascension, and his presence in the church. He 'began' his work and teaching on earth (1). It still continues. The disciples, still bewildered by the sweep of events (6), were given preliminary orders (4, 5, 7) and a pattern of evangelism which is still valid (8). The 'promise of the Father' (4), an assurance of enablement, refers to Joel 2: 28–32; Luke 24: 49; John 14: 16, 26; 15: 26.

The ascension must not be visualised in the forms of medieval art. He took them out to Bethany (Luke 24: 49–52), which is just over the summit ridge of the Mount of Olives, spoke the words of v. 8 while Jerusalem was still in view— and disappeared, in what they could only describe as a cloud, a blurring of outline, an upward movement, and a bewildered searching up and around (9–11). Some such act was necessary to initiate their new life.

They returned to the upper room (note the definite article, 13), all save Judas (16–18), and Peter, ever the man of action (cf. John 20: 3; 21: 3), suggested filling the empty place. Note Peter's manner. He is shown in sermons and letters ever ready with an authoritative quotation from the O.T. (Ps. 69: 25).

There is no contradiction between vv. 18–20 and Matthew 27: 3–10. The priests, typically, bought the field in Judas' name. The suicide, the broken rope, the sequel, are part of the same story. Matthew heard Peter (13). We hear no more of the good Matthias (23–26). Legend places his death in Ethiopia. Peter was still living in the O.T. (Lev. 16: 8). It was before Pentecost (John 16: 13) and clearer enlightenment.

Pentecost

(Acts 2: 1–47)

FIFTY days after the presentation of the 'wave-sheaf' at Passover, came the harvest festival of Pentecost (Lev. 23: 15–21). Those who thought habitually in the symbols and language of the O.T. would undoubtedly see a connection between the death of Christ 'our Passover' (1 Cor. 5: 7) and the 'first-fruits' of the church (Jas. 1: 18). Wind and fire (2, 3) were symbols of the powerful and cleansing drive of God's spirit. This was a unique moment of history, not to be repeated.

On 'tongues' (4) observe several points. Those listed in vv. 9–11 were Jews, resident aliens of the Dispersion, living in urban communities among the peoples named. They understood two languages, Greek and Aramaic, with perhaps Latin for the Italian Jews (John 19: 19). They would be as unlikely to know the dialect of the countryside as a bilingual South African (Afrikaans and English) would be likely to know Zulu. No multiple

gift of language was therefore necessary. If, as many assume, this was the case, it was a gift rapidly withdrawn. Neither Hebrew, Aramaic, Greek nor Latin served Paul in his great linguistic emergency, and no miraculous understanding of Lycaonian came to his aid (14: 11–14). This was a passing phase of ecstatic utterance (Acts 10: 46), and unlike the Corinthian phenomenon (chs. 12 and 14). It seems that one must reject the view that recognisable but unknown languages were spoken. Further, the phenomenon made for clarity. It did not destroy it. Penetrating clarity and compelling precision are sometimes achieved by simple men in moments of high emotion. There was certainly some miraculous emancipation of tongue and mind, and men perhaps heard words, which caught and expressed their own unutterable longings, in such a fashion that everyone heard them speak 'his own language'. This explanation would fit the narrative.

The audience was composed of 'devout' men (Luke 2: 25; Acts 8: 2). It is a Greek word meaning 'cautious' or 'discreet'. Luke elevates it to mean 'godly', but not without a suggestion of reliability as witnesses.

Peter dismisses the crude explanation of the disciples' ecstasy (13–15). On the authority of Exodus 16: 8, scrupulous Jews drank wine only when eating flesh. They ate bread in the morning, flesh only in the evening. Peter's theme was obviously for a Jewish audience, and in terms of messianic expectation (18–21). Boldly, he faced the crowd of the Passion Week, those who had

cried: 'Hosanna'... 'Barabbas'...
'Crucify', and drove home the facts
(22–24). He quoted familiar Scripture (25–28. 1 Pet. 1: 10–12) and
applied it (29–31). Observe his
assumption that they accepted the
empty tomb (32). It remained only
to stress its significance (33–36).
Scripture interweaves his speech
(Ps. 16: 8–11; 110: 1). V. 36 returns
to the fearless thrust of v. 23. The
appeal was simple (37–39), the
result spectacular. V. 39 is the first
apostolic vision of a wider gospel
and the first mark of Luke's
attempt to link Peter's teaching to
that of Paul in a doctrinal sequence.
V. 40 suggests that records of such
sermons were preserved. The age
was thoroughly literate. An attractive picture of the first church
follows, united, clear-cut in belief,
ardent and held somewhat in awe
by a watching world (42–47). The
experiment in communal living was
soon abandoned. Nor was it universal. The tenses in v. 45 are imperfect: '... they used to sell ... used
to divide...' The final words
should be rendered: '... those who
were being saved.' (47).

Peter's Second Sermon
(Acts 3: 1–26)

PICKING up a word from 2: 43,
Luke illustrates by an event at
the temple gate. He is also supply-
ing the background for Peter's
second sermon, and the Sadducean
persecution which followed (1–11).
It is a vivid narrative, which reminds a sensitive reader of the style
of Mark's gospel. As Peter was

behind Mark's narrative, so he is
behind this. Ch. 12 is similarly
reminiscent. It is absurd to dismiss
the story as a fabrication because
faith is not stressed. V. 6 is the test
of faith. The words 'Jesus of
Nazareth' had recently been read
over a malefactor's cross. To res-
pond as the man did, called for
trust.

Peter's address is a vigorous
utterance, summed up in Luke's
best manner. First came a bold
proclamation of the Lord's messiahship (13). 'Servant' should be
read in vv. 13 and 26, not 'son'. It is
a reference to the moving 'servant
songs', which close Isaiah. To
minds familiar with those messianic
chapters, Peter stresses the shocking
contrasts—God glorified his servant; the Jews betrayed him (13).
Pilate 'had determined' (RV) to
acquit him; the Jews denied him
(13). He was the holy one and just;
the Jews chose a bandit (14). The
Jews killed him; God raised him
from the dead (15).

Then, exactly in the manner of
the first sermon, Peter turned from
strong accusation to appeal (16,
17). It was, nevertheless, foretold, so
hope remained (18). Therefore,
repent (19). Then in a manner a
trifle remote from Western thinking, but exactly in the manner of a
Jewish preacher, Peter turns to the
prophets (20–26). A lofty Chris-
tology, first expressed in v. 13, is
taken up again. All that Paul and
John were to preach and express in
their writings, all the major doctrines, are latent in this speech.
Under John the Baptist and under
Christ, Peter had absorbed the O.T.
It was coming to life in his new

situation. This was no 'unlettered' Galilean (4: 13).

Luke's object in this chapter, as the companion of Paul and the historian of his ministry, is to do justice to the 'acts of Peter', and at the same time to show that Paul was anticipated by the senior apostle in his evangel, his methods and his reception. This is one theme in the first half of the book.

The First Persecution
(Acts 4: 1–31)

THE Sadducees, who rejected belief in immortality, were sensitive about the resurrection (1, 2). As the murderers of Christ, they had political reasons, as well as doctrinal, for persecution (3). A familiar situation was taking shape. It was after the resurrection of Lazarus that the Sadducees took precedence over the Pharisees as the persecutors of Christ (John 11: 47–50; 12: 10, 11). They run true to character (Matt. 26: 59–63), sly priests seeking to tangle simple men in their words (5–7).

With considerable art, Luke succeeds in ninety words in conveying the point, power and purport of Peter's fearless speech (8: 12). He is courteous, but firm. The rejected stone was an ancient symbol (Ps. 118: 22; Isa. 28: 16), appropriated by Christ (Matt. 21: 42; Mark 12: 10; Luke 20: 17) and taken up by Peter (1 Pet. 2: 7), perhaps because of his own name (*petros*—a stone). Peter's style is not obscured by the brevity of the report. He touches on the hearers' experience, the basic facts (the man who was healed was 'standing' among them (14)—note Luke's word), the appeal to Scripture, and the application—as he did in earlier addresses.

Vv. 13–18 illustrate Luke's muscular brevity. He touches on their unwarranted assumption that those without the orthodox education were therefore ignorant (13). Hence a dilemma before the facts—the apostles' skilful use of Scripture, and the living evidence of the man (14). They catch a glimpse of truth —they 'realised that these men had been disciples of Jesus'. Luke then reveals their bafflement (15, 16). An honest course was obvious, but like Pilate, they were prisoners of their own preoccupations and past choices. Hence the rather futile decision. 'Straitly threaten' reflects a Hebrew or Aramaic construction. Was Paul there? Did he tell Luke? Was this a living echo of what the Sanhedrists said? (17). The threat was met with vigour (18–22). Evidence is here for the strength of the church and the 'loss of nerve' among the authorities before it. The fact of the empty tomb must have been beyond dispute. But defiance was not arrogant and called for prayer (23–31).

The Church in Unity and Division
(Acts 4: 32—5: 16)

THE suggestion that vv. 32–37 are a naïve repetition of 2: 44, 45 illustrates the obtuseness of some N.T. criticism. Luke was no simpleton in historiography. Before telling of the doings of Ananias and Sapphira, he provides the background.

The experiment in community of goods had led to selling of property for the relief of want. Barnabas appears to show that selected property could be thus disposed of for the common good. Observe too, a literary device of Luke. Three times he makes prior announcement of a person about to move on to the stage (6: 5; 7: 58).

(Before leaving this matter of property, note that the experiment was evidently abandoned as impracticable. A similar immaturity in the interpretation of the teaching of a second advent led to social problems at Thessalonica, which called for Paul's strong intervention. James deals with the problem in the context of sanctified common sense to which it was soon reduced. It is also a fact that the reckless dissipation of property by the Jerusalem church led to a poverty-stricken Christian community, for whose needs Paul collected all over the world. To be sure, much of the property, thus turned to present use, disappeared in the disaster which fell on the city and the land, forty years later.)

Peter was stern, but his severity must be seen in the context of the terrible situation (5: 1–11). He had diagnosed a plague in the healthy body of the church. He remembered the Lord's words to hypocrites (Matt. 23). Observe the conspicuous honesty with which Luke turns from four chapters of triumphant witness to a story of sordid deceit. All love, trust and sincerity were at risk in the deliberate plot (9) of two mean souls to buy a reputation for sanctity and sacrifice with lies. To conspire thus

in such an atmosphere demanded some hardihood of wickedness. It was like a second fall of man. The serpent was in the new Eden. Told in the manner of the O.T., the story omits details which the antiquarian would be glad to know – such matters as burial regulations, notification of death, and so on. Thus it came about that the first church burials were those of hypocrites.

At v. 12 Luke turns with relief to a continuing story. It is like a scene from the first ministry of Christ. The Christians gathered like the Greek philosophic schools in public buildings (e.g. the Stoics in the Stoa Poikile – the 'painted cloister' or 'porch'). No one was lightly associated with them (12, 13) but their reputation sent a wave of conviction, as well as overtones of superstition, through the community (15, 16). Such phenomena are often on the fringe of a genuine religious movement.

The Second and Third Persecutions

(Acts 5: 17—6: 15)

THE Sadducees, their worst fears realised (4: 17), move again (17). The Romans, political opportunists, wanted only peace in a turbulent province on a sensitive frontier. They chose to work through the Herod family, and a collaborating hierarchy. The collaborators were sensitive to any threat of tumult in a volatile and dangerous proletariat.

Hence the apostles' arrest and imprisonment (18). The miraculous escape challenges the inbred scepticism of the modern mind, but why must any disturbance of the natural be necessarily impossible (19–28)? A believer is not called to credulity, but is, by his very convictions, called to faith. The events are those surrounding a great intrusion of God into human history, the resurrection of Christ and the founding of the church on that fact. Observe, too, three points. First, after the tragedy of Ananias, the church needed encouragement, and received it, for the vigour of the apostles' testimony and the firmness of their affirmation is notable (29–33). Secondly, Gamaliel should be heard. The Pharisees were on the scene again, and this learned and wise man was clearly daunted by events (34–39). Thirdly, Luke has earned the right to be regarded as a careful and notable historian, and he had his facts from Peter and Paul. Peter won the day (40–42).

Some touches of authenticity are embedded in the text. Peter's own vocabulary is interesting. In 4: 28 Peter's word 'determined' is found (2: 23; 10: 42; 13: 29; 1 Pet. 1: 2, 20; 2: 4–6). Similarly observe his word for 'tree' in 5: 30 (*xulon*). It means timber, or cut wood (1 Cor. 3: 12; Rev. 18: 12) and by extension a club (Matt. 26: 47, 55). It could, in later Greek, mean a living tree (Luke 23: 31; Rev. 2: 7). Now the Greek for the instrument of crucifixion was 'stake', referring to the fixture at the place of punishment of an upright post, arranged to take the cross-beam which the victim carried (John 19: 17). The 'cross' was like a capital T rather than its traditional representation. Peter's

'tree' implies that cut-off tree trunks commonly served for the 'stake' (1 Pet. 3: 24).

Opposition, bipartisan (34), was being organised. An historic moment had passed. Christians were beginning nineteen centuries of physical suffering for faithfulness (40, 41). The experience tangled with all Peter's teaching (1 Pet. 2: 20, 21; 3: 14, 17; 4: 1, 12–19). The 'disciples' (6: 1) likewise saw the challenge to organise. The apostles' perceptive eyes saw a potential rift between proud metropolitan Jewry, represented in the church, and the Jews of the Dispersion, whose chief language was Greek rather than Aramaic. The solution (2, 3) was wise and practical. Those entrusted with social service, the seven (3), all bore Greek names. They are not called deacons but functioned as such, without preclusion from other ministry (8). Luke, after his manner, took occasion to introduce Stephen, a link with Paul, who was soon to emerge. Stephen's interpretation of the O.T. led to controversy (8, 9), familiar slander (11. Matt. 26: 60, 61), arrest (12) and false accusation (13, 14).

Stephen's Historic Address
(Acts 7: 1—8: 4)

A Hellenistic Jew was liable to return to the narrower environment of metropolitan Jewry with a mind broadened by contact with Greek culture. Stephen, like Paul, whom he decisively influenced, saw the Jews within the pattern of wider history, shaped to serve mankind,

not called to self-esteem. With
clearer understanding, Stephen saw
the wider sweep of a divine plan in
history, and how inconsistent with
its significance were the pretensions
of those who turned a noble religion
into a nationalist cult, itself a
travesty of the code they professed
to honour.

With knowledge, logic and irony,
an irony typically Greek, Stephen
returns, like the writer of the Epistle
to the Hebrews (cf. 3: 1–6; 9: 18–20;
12: 24), to Abraham (2–8), whose
call preceded that of Moses, and like
the call of Moses was in a foreign
land (2–4; 39–44). Joseph (9–16),
like Moses (40–43), suffered the
spite, callousness and pride of the
people he sought to serve. Moses,
'in whom they trusted' (John 5: 45–
47), had 'come to his own' (35.
John 1: 11), Moses who prophesied
of Christ (37), and had suffered
rejection. Note the stinging and
skilful use of Scripture. '*This*
Moses . . .', Stephen says (35, 37,
38, 40. Exod. 32: 1). '*This* Jesus . . .'
they had said in scorn, following
their rebel fathers (6: 14). A similar
doom was on them. Scorning their
deliverer, they fell under the judgment of blindness (39–43). Perhaps
the subtlety of the next few verses
(44–50) is that, whereas Moses, by
divine command, built the beautiful
tent in the desert, symbolic of God's
unseen presence, his law, his mercy
and the blood of sacrifice, the
temple, the home of their cult and
their idol, was a royal whim,
tolerated by God. It was significant
only as an emblem, but they, wor-
shipping form rather than reality
(51), unable to bear truth (52),
violated their own law (53).

Catch the touches of authenticity
which close attention to language
often shows. V. 14 says seventy-five
as against the seventy of Exodus 1:
5. The Greek Jew is quoting the
Greek Septuagint which preserves,
as the Qumran Exodus text shows,
the Hebrew reading of the first
century. 'Exceeding fair' (20) and 'I
have seen, I have seen' (34), like
'straitly threaten' of 4: 17, preserve
the Hebrew emphatic use of the
Hebrew infinitive absolute. Luke
had this report from Paul, who was
present (58), in Aramaic or Hebrew.
'Church' (38) is incorrect. '*Ekklesia*'
means 'assembly' in Greek. Stephen
views Israel as a Greek state.

The effect was devastating. Paul
never forgot the speech (13: 14–41;
17: 29). He sought uselessly to
shake off the memory in persecution (8: 1, 3). The church was
scattered, its witness multiplied,
and the dominance of Jerusalem
salutarily broken. Stephen died,
remembering Christ (Luke 23: 34).
Paul was shattered, though none
knew it yet. Pilate, still in Palestine,
but, with his corrupt patron,
Seianus, dead and disgraced in
Rome, increasingly timid in his
precarious situation, chose not to
interfere in contrived riot (57, 58)
and murder (59). The stage was set
for the next movement of Luke's
theme.

Philip's Ministry

(Acts 8: 5–40)

THIS section is an interlude
touching on the ministry of
Philip, another Hellenistic Jew.
Luke, before returning to Paul, is

showing that the global ministry of the apostle to the Gentiles was no innovation of Paul's own, but had begun before he was converted, and continued, independently of him, after that notable event. Luke is also seeking a transmission from the ministry of Peter to that of Paul. Philip resembles both Stephen and Paul, and is notably like Paul in his evangelism. Like Stephen he was emancipated from the Jewish vice of nationalism (5. John 4). In Samaria he met the sinister Simon (9), a charlatan professing a special unction from God (10), and acquiring, as such creatures do, a following among the credulous (11). Whether his professed conversion was part of the sham (12), it is impossible to say, but at this point the two apostles arrived to assess Philip's ministry (14). Still a little bewildered at the turn the gospel was taking, Peter and John seek some form of confirmation (15–17). The clash with Simon was immediate. His faith was based on miracles and their reproduction (13, 19, 20). He coveted such wonder-working (18) and put a name into the language, 'simony', for traffic in sacred things, another Balaam (2 Pet. 2: 15). Such exhibitionists and self-seekers have not disappeared with Simon. He merited Peter's denunciation (20–23). Since the deaths of Ananias and Sapphira, evil in the church was a raw spot in Peter. Whether Simon did repent is not clear (24). That the Samaritan church was accepted in Jerusalem is an indication of how far the apostles were moving.

And let us, Luke appears to say, follow Philip in a wider arc of adventure. The story was probably told to Luke by his host twenty years later (21: 8). It is reproduced in Luke's best manner. Philip was urged to take the desert road to Gaza (26), the old strategic route in and out of Egypt as all history shows. It bypassed the new Roman port. It was customary for a lonely traveller to attach himself to a larger company and the Ethiopian courtier would have had a considerable retinue (27). The man, evidently a proselyte, was reading the 'servant songs' of Isaiah. As was customary, he was reading aloud (28). That is how Philip knew what he was reading (30). The officer was probably heir to a millennium of tradition. Trade routes, connected Southern Arabia with Jerusalem. Hence the visit of Sheba's queen. And Southern Arabia had close contact with Ethiopia across the strait. Many legends connect Shabwa, Sheba, Ethiopia and Solomon. The Magis' gifts suggest that they came from Arabia Felix and also that some messianic tradition lingered there. Hence the Ethiopian's visit to Jerusalem and a notable piece of personal evangelism. His question was a natural one (31–34). Philip's reply was not only immediately effective, but set its seal on a line of interpretation (35). V. 37 is not fully backed by ancient authority but no doubt contains the truth. Such would be the formula for baptism, and it needed no great lapse of time to take shape. It was fundamental to the apostles' gospel. Vv. 39 and 40 need not imply a supernatural removal, no more than a prompt withdrawal in obedience to a compelling urge. Azotus, the old Philistine Ashdod, was not far away.

The Damascus Road
(Acts 9: 1–30)

PAUL was a 'young man' (7: 58), a description available until the age of forty. Saul may have been between thirty-five and forty. He was born in the ancient city of Tarsus—'no mean city', he calls it, quoting Euripides. Tarsus was in Cilicia, an ancient seat of administration back to Persian times, a centre of learning, the home of a philosophical school, and the hub of a linen industry. It was a confluence of East and West. That is why Paul could think like a Greek. Educated also in Jerusalem, under a famous scholar, he was at home with Jewish thought. As a member of a privileged group in Tarsus, he held the coveted Roman citizenship. In his own right, Paul, as he was called in Gentile contexts, was an intellectual of the first order, probably the finest mind of his century, and ranked with Plato by the classicist T. R. Glover of Cambridge. It was 'no mean man' who fell on the Damascus road.

Paul was an ardent Pharisee, and it was his sectarian zeal that drove him to persecution of the Christians, an ardour accentuated by the conviction, born of Stephen's death, if Luke read aright, that the Christians held the truth. Fierce action can be assuagement for a tormented mind. The fastest route to Damascus ran north through Nablus, swung west and crossed the Jordan south of the Galilee lake, traversed the Golan Heights, and then turned north-east to Damascus. Somewhere on this road, and at some time during the week the journey would take, the bitter Pharisee was halted by God's challenge (3). The words were snatched out of Paul's own mind (5). He knew that he was acting like a recalcitrant ox (22: 20). This was no hallucination, no trick of a disordered mind. The intellectual achievements visible in Paul's career and writings, show a consistently active, superbly sound and magnificently creative mind, undiminished by hardship, and powerful till death.

Three days of broken bewilderment followed, probably referred to in 2 Corinthians 12: 1–4; (9). Paul was nursed back to calm and health by the brave Ananias (10–18). His blurred vision cleared (18) and he stayed in Damascus briefly (10: 48; 15: 36; 16: 12; 24: 24; 25: 13). His superb expertise in the Scriptures, destined to colour all his activities through an arduous life, was now in the service of Christ (20–21), with results which he must have known would follow from his late associates (1, 2, 23, 24). In Jerusalem the gentle Barnabas undertook the ministrations of Ananias (26–29), and Paul, accepted in Jerusalem, returned, as was right, to Tarsus (30).

Peter's Gentile Ministry
(Acts 9: 31—10: 48)

CHAPTERS 9 and 10 cohere to form an introduction to what follows. Peter passes from view, and Paul moves to the centre of the stage. It is important to show that Peter, the great leader of Jewish Christianity, himself opened the door (Matt. 16: 19) to the Gentiles. Peter's sweep through the old Philistine country of the coastal plain must not be seen in the light of a Gentile invasion. In Maccabean times the Jews had made it a point of national honour to occupy the area in force, and Peter, in visiting the church at Lydda (mod. Lod, Tel Aviv's airport), was merely fulfilling the function of episcopal supervision which had taken him to Samaria (8: 14). The stories of Aeneas (32–35) and Tabitha (36–42) are told to authenticate his ministry (Matt. 9: 23–26; Mark 5: 38–43; John 5: 6–9). Peter was the guest of a tanner (43), an unclean trade, and therefore striking evidence of progress in Peter's spiritual pilgrimage. Luke is subtly preparing his readers for Peter's coming adventure—quite in the manner of 7: 58.

Joppa is by the sea, today a southern extension of Tel Aviv, and the tanner had made his weary guest comfortable under a leather awning on the breezy roof. Peter prayed and dozed, his last conscious view the awning of skins bulging down from its corner fastenings, his last thoughts a half whimsical, half wondering pondering on where he, once so orthodox, was resting. Hence his dream, fashioned of the stuff of homely circumstance (9–16), Peter's very protest (14) being true to character (Matt. 16: 22; John 13: 8). And Luke, following the manner by which Ananias and Saul were simultaneously prepared (9: 10–16), tells of Cornelius (1–8) and

Peter (17–22) brought together. Caesarea, the Roman port and garrison town some score of miles up the coast, was a present of Herod to his Roman protectors, a magnificently fortified beachhead equipped with docks and all the facilities of a praetorian headquarters. Luke tells his story with leisure. He can be ruthless in his brevity at times. With events he considers important, he can resort to repetition (30, 31). Peter stresses the truths of earlier emphasis (36–42). The audience was overwhelmed and spoke in the ecstatic language of the early converts. Their 'tongues', observe, were intelligible (46). Peter ordered baptism. To avoid creating factions the apostles abstained from personally conducting the ceremony (1 Cor. 1: 13–16). It may be noted that an Austrian inscription, dated A.D. 69, mentions an 'Italian cohort' (1). They were a detachment assigned to special duties. Cornelius was a respected officer.

Report to Jerusalem
(Acts 11: 1–30)

LUKE considered Peter's report to Jerusalem revealing for several reasons. For example, it revealed the hesitation with which the Jewish Christians in the mother city of both faiths moved toward a global religion in which the old Israel would be merged in a wider community. At first they had no idea that the old 'apartheid' was finished (2, 3). They envisaged a cleansed and reformed Judaism, into which Gentiles would be welcomed as they were always welcomed into the synagogues, especially those of the Dispersion. They thought, no doubt, that the numbers would be small and the movement soon terminated by the Lord's return. It is difficult for us to imagine the enormous reappraisal that Paul's evangel demanded. He himself occasionally wavered. Peter had a fierce struggle (Gal. 1: 11–2: 14). Peter's careful report (4–17), together with his apt quotation (15–17), brought a somewhat grudging acceptance.

The dispersion of the church following Stephen's death, brought Antioch into history as the second capital of the church (19), with Jerusalem taking her supervisory function naturally for granted (20–22). The gracious Barnabas, who had first sponsored Paul, now becomes the agent by whose quiet planning the great apostle, after unrecorded years, moves into his mighty ministry. It was subtle diplomacy to entrust Paul with the funds contributed by the Gentile church for famine relief in Judaea (27–30). The dispersal of Christian capital in the communal experiment twice mentioned already, had left that area peculiarly vulnerable to the hard times which fell upon the world. The Sahara determined the climate of the Mediterranean, and abnormal conditions there had before shifted the rainbelts.

It was at Antioch that some official in the Roman records office became aware of a sub-group among the Jews, and from his enquiries set them down as Christians (26). The name recurs twice (26: 28; 1 Pet. 4: 16).

Herod Agrippa's Persecution
(Acts 12: 1–25)

HEROD Agrippa I, grandson of the first Herod, friend of the third emperor, the mad young Caligula, had retained the confidence of the middle-aged Claudius, Caligula's successor, and so had the areas of Judaea and Samaria added to the old domains of Herod Antipas already granted him by Caligula. The clever Herod family had contrived to satisfy the Romans and satisfactorily control the Jews for half a century, and the new attack on the church was a policy move to please the two major sects, the Pharisees and Sadducees (1–3). Hence the assault on Peter, immediately after the events of the last two chapters. Seeing no sign of political overtones, nor withdrawal from the Jewish establishment, the two sects and the hierarchy were beginning to manifest a tolerant attitude towards the dissident Christian minority. They kept them obviously under close surveillance, for Peter's visit to the coastal plain and his report seemed to alarm the hierarchy, and provoke persecution. Hence death (2) and imprisonment (4).

The vivid narrative of Peter's imprisonment and escape bears all the marks of an eyewitness account. Observe vv. 8, 12–17. Thus, with a touch of drama, Luke dismisses a great Christian from the story of evangelism, slipping down the dark street, muffled in his cloak, to some hiding-place not known to us. He is to reappear only once more, as a mediator (15: 7–11). Herod stayed in view a little longer. The Greeks, with their doctrine of 'hubris', that self-exaltation and arrogance which brings divine destruction on presumptuous man, would have accepted without question that Herod died for blasphemy. The stricken man's violent intestinal seizure (23) is diagnosable. The visible and agonising peristalsis is described by a Greek adjective used by the botanist, Theophrastus, of 'worm-eaten' plants. It was evidently also a contemporary medical term.

The Beginning of World Evangelism

(Acts 13: 1–52)

IT was necessary that Antioch should take the lead. Jerusalem was doomed. Antioch had been the capital of one of the four successor states of Alexander's empire, broken up over three centuries before. Its wavering borders had at times touched the edge of Egypt, the Persian Gulf and the Aegean. Antioch had headed a world power. It had clashed with Rome, and proved Rome's doughtiest eastern foe. It was natural that the church there should think in terms commensurate with a wider world (1, 2).

Cyprus, Barnabas' old home (11: 19, 20), was the first objective. It was an ancient meeting place of Mediterranean culture, a proconsular province, as Luke, ever exact with official names, notes. (7; 'deputy' is 'proconsul'). Sergius Paulus, like many aristocratic Romans of his day, was given to eastern wizardry and wonder-mongering (6–12). The name seems to be archaeologically authenti-cated, a proconsul named Paulus appearing in a North Cypriot inscription.

The party traversed the island from Salamis in the east to Paphos in the south-west. Paulus seems to have been a convert. There is abundant historical evidence for the penetration of the upper ranks of Roman society by the faith during the first century. Luke at this point is in one of his moods of brevity. Paulus, like Felix (24: 24), may easily have had further conversation.

The next verse covers the move to Pamphylia on the south coast of Asia Minor, an area evangelised only on the return journey (14: 25). Some obscure tension led to the withdrawal of John Mark, nephew of Barnabas. In Galatians 4: 13 Paul speaks of a debilitating illness which marred his visit to the south Galatian churches of Pisidian Antioch, Iconium and Derbe, and the idea of passing by Perga, and proceeding inland to the elevated and healthy back-country, may have been motivated by Paul's physical condition. Pamphylia had an unhealthy, probably malarial coastal climate, and it has been argued with some cogency that Paul's 'thorn in the flesh' (2 Cor. 12: 7) was the malaria endemic in the place. Antioch of Pisidia stood at 3,600 feet. The route was arduous and bandit ridden (2 Cor. 11: 26), but the place was the central Roman bastion of defence in Asia Minor, a hint of Paul's emerging strategy. Luke puts all this into v. 13.

It was probably in the late summer of A.D. 46 that Paul and Barnabas took their seats in the Antioch synagogue, and, after the lesson, which may have been Deuteronomy 1 and Isaiah 1, received the customary invitation to speak. Clearly regarding the speech as historic, Luke becomes detailed. Similarities to Stephen and Peter are clear, but also the emerging characteristics of Paul. The history of Israel, Paul states, becomes meaningful in Christ. Misreading all their history (17–23), disdaining the forerunner (24, 25), the Jews of Jerusalem rejected Christ (27–29), but thereby fulfilled a plan (30–41).

The theme of the message does not seem to have roused opposition. The Jews of the area were liberal in their outlook, appear even to have intermarried with Gentiles (16: 1), and to have included many proselytes (42, 43). It was this which led to a Gentile contact and the awakening of a latent Jewish nationalism (44, 45). History was repeating itself. As in Palestine, so in Asia Minor, vested interest was ranged against Christ. Vv. 46–49 record a great turning-point. The evangelists 'turned to the Gentiles'.

Observe that v. 48 is no charter for Calvinism. The Jews had already, of their own choice (46), rejected Christ. Among the Gentiles they found 'those who set themselves in place for eternal life'. This correctly renders a middle verb. (In this tense middle and passive coincide.) 'Ordained', of course, of KJV's rendering, is not theologically loaded. It meant 'to set in place' in the English of the time (Ps. 8: 3; John 15: 16).

The Jews had influence with the authorities in very many urban centres of the day, and the status of women in all the Asia Minor provinces, as in Macedonia, was high (50). Numbers of them were in the synagogues. Tradition has it that Pilate's wife, Claudia Procula, and Poppaea, empress of Nero, were Jewish adherents. Juvenal, at the end of the century, satirises the trend.

Back to Antioch
(Acts 14: 1–22)

ICONIUM, modern Konya, rich in history, strongly Romanised, bore in its population Jews, Greeks, Romans—the three groups among which Paul, heir to three cultures, moved most easily. There would, of course, be an Anatolian substratum as Paul found disturbingly in the more rustic Lystra.

Luke is brief again, for events took the same course as at Antioch (3). Some time, however, seems to have been spent in Iconium, for the place became a centre for the diffusion of the gospel. The legendary story of Paul and Thekla, a second-century fiction, was set in Iconium. Legend usually contains a core of history, and the legend of Paul and Thekla implies a stay in Iconium of some duration. Contrived riot and official intervention (2, 4) ended a successful mission.

Lystra was an obvious refuge, a colony founded by Augustus with a core of Roman citizens. Lystra is another illustration of the Empire's working. Popular superstition, based on a local legend of a theophany of Zeus and Hermes (8–18), led to an attack on two visitors by a disappointed rout of native Lycaonians. The two gods in the story visited Lystra incognito and were churlishly received. The rustic proletariat were not disposed to repeat the mistake. They did not take kindly to Paul's denial of deity and were fuel for the Jews' rabble-rousing (19). There was no riot-squad to rescue the victims (22: 23, 24), no city clerk voiced concern in a popular assembly (19: 34–41). No proconsul noted the outbreak of lawlessness with nicely calculated inaction (18: 12–17). It was a remote edge of the Empire, a border town with highland territory beyond, where pacification was marked rather by the absence of armed turbulence than by Roman-ised or Hellenised living. Cicero, in Cilicia a century before, Quirinius on the central plateau, half a century earlier, had dealt with back-country banditry by force of arms. 'Perils of robbers' (2 Cor. 11: 26), formed a traveller's hazard in the Asia Minor peninsula, and it seems clear that Rome did not expect completely to police its remoter borderlands. It might in passing be noted that the Lycaonians spoke a primitive Gallic dialect (11), if Jerome is to be believed. They could have been a surviving ethnic remnant of the wandering Gauls who, centuries earlier, had invaded the region and given it the name Galatia. It is clear that the mys-terious 'gift of tongues' was not a miraculous proficiency in foreign languages.

Derbe is passed with little notice. It was a rustic community on the edge of civilisation and probably with little contact to offer Paul with the chosen objects of his evangel-ism. His message would doubtless be what he offered the Lystrans (14–17), an appeal based on natural theology, and which, in much more sophisticated terms, he brought to the Athenians (17: 22–32).

The Watershed of Acts
(Acts 14: 23—15: 31)

THE party returned by way of Perga and ministered there (25). The report to Antioch on Gentile evangelism (26, 27) disturbed the Jerusalem Christians who sent envoys (15: 1) who 'set about teaching' the necessity for Judaistic observances (the imperfect tense implies a consistent campaign). There was a serious division. 'Dissension' is 'stasis', that sinister word in Greek history of which more than one city-state died. Authoritative guidelines became necessary (2), and a conference was mooted. The patient acceptance of the primacy of the Jerusalem con-gregations, obstinate in the face of a clear movement of history, under-lines the grace and statesmanship of Paul. (See comments on Gal. 2: 1–14.)

The Pharisaic minority led the opposition (5, 6) countered boldly and nobly by Peter, who took full responsibility for Gentile evangel-ism. Luke regards this chapter as the keystone in the arch of his book, and Peter's words an historic watershed. And yet he sees the terrain continuous over the water-shed between the Acts of Peter and the Acts of Paul.

James summed up (13–18), and a delegation carried the proposed compromise (19–21) to Antioch (22–29). Its moral demands, and its deprecation of practices loathsome to the Jews, made the letter reasonable, though it is clear from the rise of the Galatian heresy that the rigid minority (11: 2) did not long observe it. The Jerusalem church grew more introverted. Paul felt himself under its disapproval (21: 20–26), and it was only the grim march of history which broke the power of the Jerusalem church by destroying the city itself. Jerusalem's Judaic form of Christianity precariously survived as the Ebionite heresy until the fourth century.

The Second Journey
(Acts 15: 32—16: 40)

FAITHFULLY, as ever, Luke records a serious difference of opinion between Paul and Barnabas over John Mark. A strong word is used in v. 39—'paroxusmos'—and KJV is correct when it adds the adjective 'sharp'. Mark had probably disagreed with Paul in the matter of Gentile evangelism when Paul chose Pisidia over Pamphylia, and Paul was sensitive over laggard service (Phil. 2: 20, 21). The story, fortunately, had a happy ending (Col. 4: 10; 2 Tim. 4: 11). Silas, already, after Luke's manner, introduced (15: 22, 32, 34), was there to take Barnabas' place.

Entering Cilicia by way of the gorge of the Amanus, the two evangelists spent some time in territory not of the kind where Paul exercised his most characteristic ministry, and Luke hurries on (41). Leaving the coast, they made

for the high country, traversing the Taurus Range by the Cilician Gates, and coming first to Derbe and Lystra, a single administrative area (14: 6), as Luke knew—better than some of his early critics. Geographically the region was united with Iconium (2). Vv. 3 and 4, and the circumcision of Timothy there described, imply that, needlessly sensitive about the opinions of the Pharisees, Paul went further than the provisions of the decree he carried (4).

An important section follows (6–10). They traversed 'the Phrygian region of Galatia'. It is a notable fact that Luke's casual reference to Galatia show that he moves with easy accuracy in an area complex in its ethnic, geographical and political pattern. Only a first-century historian could have so confidently handled the facts. His narrative has been abundantly authenticated by archaeology and epigraphy. The party crossed into the Roman province of Asia, found no opportunity to preach, passed into Mysia, and turned north with Bithynia in mind. Some compulsion checked Paul, and the party found itself in Troas, a Roman colony on the Aegean, a few miles from the ruins of ancient Troy, of the famous Greek siege. It is curious that, traversing the great east-west highway of Asia Minor, Paul and Silas found themselves unable to fulfil their intentions (6–8).

The vision at Troas (9) made it all plain. It was a section of Paul's life personally, as well as historically important to Luke. At Troas, Luke himself joined the party (note 'we' in v. 10). Luke was a physician, and Philippi had a medical school. Paul in his dream saw 'a certain man from Macedonia'. How did he know him, unless he was already acquainted? The dress was not distinctive. The Dardanelles strait did not divide cultures as it does today. Luke's proud description of Philippi (12), and his familiarity with the Jews' gathering place (13) suggests personal acquaintance. They proceed straight to Philippi by the old Via Egnatia as though under a guide. Luke, having met Paul at Troas, was taking him home.

Philippi, four centuries old, a military foundation of Philip II, father of Alexander the Great, was a Roman colony and a Roman strongpoint. To found a church there would be in accordance with Paul's emerging strategy of planting his Christian communities at nodal points. The Jews and their proselytes met by a river, when they had no synagogues, as they had done in Babylonian exile (Ps. 137). Lydia, a business woman from Thyatira, 600 miles away, was selling the dye of the madder root (Turkey red) or cloth dyed from that preparation, and became the first convert in Europe (15, 16). The slave girl, held in some hypnotic bondage by cruel owners (16–19), was emancipated from her mental servitude, and the loss to the slavers led to arrest by the praetors. The title for the magistrates is epigraphically attested. There was a tumultuous trial (22) and imprisonment from which the evangelists were strangely freed. Ramsay explains vividly how easily, in such a structure, a seismic ground

wave could produce the result described (26).

The gaoler is rapidly sketched— his stern devotion to duty (27), his rapid recognition of Paul's leadership (28–30). Take vv. 31–34 together. The household 'believed'. They did not simply follow the father. Luke's writing shows all the marks of an eyewitness. Discovering that they had dealt summarily with a Roman citizen, a misdemeanour of the highest gravity, the praetors try to rid themselves, without loss of face, of their embarrassing prisoners (35). The gaoler softens the message politely (36). Paul dealt with the petty tyrants with dignity (39). At their own good time Paul and Silas depart (40). Luke stayed in Philippi. 'They' resumes. 'We' is dropped.

Thessalonica to Athens
(Acts 17: 1–34)

THE party followed the Via Egnatia through Amphipolis and Apollonia to Thessalonica at the head of its gulf, a busy sea-port as its prolific coinage shows. The synagogue had penetrated society deeply. There were Greek proselytes, and a number of women of standing (4). The theme of Paul's ministry is summed up in verse 3. Trouble came from a familiar source (1 Thess. 2: 14–16). The idle of the market place (Matt. 20: 3), were ready fuel for the rabble-rousers. 'Bad characters from among the market people' (5), staged a demonstration round the house of Jason, and the 'politarchs' (8) took notice. The term used for the city authorities was once thought a mistake of Luke. There are now seventeen examples known in inscriptions. The bond taken from Jason (another practice papyrologically authenticated) was a subtle means of ensuring Paul's withdrawal (1 Thess. 2: 18). Local persecution seems to have continued (1 Thess. 2: 13, 14; 3: 3). The first converts stood firm (1 Thess. 1: 8, 9). Paul may have spent the first four or five months of A.D. 51 among them.

There was a better reception in the quieter atmosphere of Berea (11). The Jews were a more cultured community than in the brash seaport. The word (KJV, 'noble'; Gspd, 'high-minded'; NEB 'liberal-minded' etc.) implies this. Such finer spirits were equally rare in the not dissimilar port of Corinth (1 Cor. 1: 26). The sequence of events now seems to be that Paul left Berea and went on to Athens (14, 15), whence he sent to Silas and Timothy asking them to join him. He was anxious originally to return to Thessalonica (1 Thess. 2: 17, 18), and had left his friends in Berea to find out the attitude of incoming magistrates at Thessalonica. Athens, however, showed new opportunity. Hence the drawing of the team together again. He sent Timothy back to Thessalonica (1 Thess. 3: 1, 2) and Silas, probably, to Philippi (18: 5). Paul went on to Corinth (18: 1) where Silas and Timothy rejoined him (18: 5; 1 Thess. 3: 6). (Luke's brevity can be disturbing.)

Paul found Athens, a great city in the afternoon of its greatness, and living on its past, disturbing. The vast assembly of Athens'

superb pagan works of art, the glorious Parthenon itself, the phallic herms at the house doors, all tried the spirit of a Jew, revolted by idolatry (16). With the versatility which was one of his characteristics, Paul adopted the Socratic method, and taught and debated in the agora, an expanse excavated comparatively recently under the Acropolis (17). Athens was the resort of numberless would-be teachers, over whose activities the senior court of the city, the Areopagus, seems to have exercised some supervision. It was an assembly recruited from recognised members of the two rival schools, the Epicureans and Stoics. 'What', they said, using a word of sophisticated slang, 'does this seed-picker say?' It was a term used of the hopping birds of street and ploughland, collecting oddments here and there, and a fair description of many who sought easy money in Athens. Hence a courteous request to meet the court (18–20). Luke's ironical word of v. 21 was true, and may be documented from four centuries of literature.

Paul's address is a remarkable piece of pleading. Even in the précis of Luke, a practised eye can distinguish five allusions to Greek literature. Standing, as he most probably did, on the rock outcrop beneath the great platform of the Acropolis, Paul could see the three temples above him, and the mighty statue of Athene Promachos, when, with truly Athenian irony, he remarked: 'I observe that you are an uncommonly religious people.' Then, attaching his words, after Christ's fashion, to a fragment of reality, he spoke of the altars to 'unknown gods', some of which are known. The singular of his words, 'an (or the) unknown god', could have been as common, and have touched an old legend of a Cretan prophet in Athens. Paul proceeded to fundamental theism (24–28), quoting two Stoic poets. Indeed, bypassing the virtually atheist Epicureans, he spoke directly to the Stoics. Vv. 24, 28, and 29 are strongly Stoic. V. 29, with the two great statues of Athene a few hundred yards away, was amazingly bold. Having made his point in the context of the thought of his audience, Paul proceeds to his appeal. God has overlooked past ignorance, but has now spoken his final word (30) and authenticated his command by Christ's resurrection (31). At this claim the Epicureans laughed, and the Stoics gravely and politely dismissed him (32). The speech was not a failure. Observe two notable converts (34).

Corinth

(Acts 18: 1–18)

P AUL's developing strategy has been observed—to plant his Christian cells at vital points of diffusion through the empire. Corinth was ideal for such a purpose. It was a nodal point of Mediterranean communications, a staging post for the legions, a crossroads of trade, swarming with a cosmopolitan throng, multilingual, and evil as any seaport town.

Paul came to Corinth in some distress, perhaps a recurrence of his periodic illness (1 Cor. 2: 3; 1 Thess. 3: 7). He found a new friendship

(2, 3) with the much-travelled Aquila and Priscilla (18, 26; Rom. 16: 3; 1 Cor. 16: 19; 2 Tim. 4: 19). Paul, as was customary for all Jews, had the rudiments of a trade. Cilicia, Paul's home province, was known for its goat-hair cloth, and it was in the working of such material, chiefly used in tents, that Paul and his hosts were proficient (3).

Back in a Jewish context he resorted to the type of scriptural ministry he pursued in the synagogues (4), with division in the congregation as a result. A fragment of the lintel of the synagogue exists, a memorial to Paul's confrontation with the Jews. He was aided now by the two other members of his party (5, 6). A church, fed and fostered over a year and a half, began (7–11), conspicuous for its variety, its activity and divisions. It contained Gentiles and Jews, and a whole cross-section of the population (1 Cor. 1: 4–8, 12, 26; 7: 18; 12: 13—Rom. 16: 23).

The familiar pattern of events followed, but this time the persecutors of the Christian group struck an unusual magistrate, again, with Luke's usual accuracy, called 'the deputy' of Achaia—KJV's archaic, but correct rendering of 'proconsul'. The incident before the '*bema*' a structure of stone still to be seen at the far end of Corinth's agora, is an interesting exhibition of Rome in action. Her government was a rough-hewn art, not a science based on text-book rules, and as yet, in A.D. 52, no guidelines were laid down for the suppression of Christianity. Ephesus, scene of the next disturbance, was a sensitive point in the imperial network, but there were other corners of the Empire where Rome could afford to overlook some measure of disorder, especially where local and responsible diagnosis could judge its incidence as harmless or even salutary. Hence the historical significance of this story of Gallio, Seneca's genial and polished brother, and his judging of the Jewish tumult in Corinth. In that cosmopolitan city the Jewish minority presented no peril, as it did in Alexandria, and a magistrate could afford an exhibition of Rome's liberal disregard of other laws than her own (14, 15). Claudius edict of expulsion (2) was also a recent memory, and the ghetto, swollen by immigrant malcontents, may have been due for an official rebuke. With a breath of antisemitism in the air, Gallio judged it wise to allow a brief outlet for emotion, as long as it was in full view and under remote control. Corinth was an important centre, and it required a cool man, sure of support from Rome, to manage a riotous occasion with such skill (16, 17).

Luke becomes hurried again as he hastens on to Ephesus (18–23). Phoebe, a rich Corinthian, who lived by the sea on the Saronic Gulf at Cenchrea, apparently looked after him (Rom. 16: 1, 2). Perhaps, too, Luke was not happy about the Nazirite vow (18). Dr. Scofield's tart heading runs: 'The author of Rom. 6: 14; 2 Cor. 3: 7–14; Gal. 3: 23–28, takes a Jewish vow.'

Ephesus
(Acts 18: 19—19: 41)

EPHESUS was a deliberate port of call. Generally the shipping lines bypassed it as Paul's ship did in A.D. 57 (20: 16). It was part of the great city's decay that her once fine harbour was silting, choked by the topsoil from the eroding hinterland of Asia. It was an ancient Ionian colony, dedicated to the worship of Artemis (Diana to the Romans), whose great temple, one of the wonders of the world, stood there. It contained the Diopet, the 'thing which fell from heaven' (35)— probably a piece of meteoric iron.

Paul made a rapid visit to Jerusalem and Antioch for a purpose undisclosed (21, 22), made a return journey via the Galatian churches (23), and came to Ephesus (19: 1), to fulfil a promise (20, 21), and build on the work with which Priscilla and Aquila must have been entrusted (18, 19). He found with them the Alexandrian Jew, Apollos, a man instructed by the faithful couple (26), and now, after a mission in Achaia (27, 28), in Ephesus on the invitation of Aquila and Priscilla. (Observe that the order of their names varies. If the lady's name is indication, Priscilla could have been a member of one of Rome's ancient and noble families.)

The small group of John's disciples whom Paul met in Ephesus (19: 1–7) could have been a remnant of Apollos' less mature ministry (18: 24–26). Luke, pursuing his theme of Paul's global evangelism, may have thought it necessary to show a group, less profoundly instructed, who gladly accepted the wider gospel as soon as it was proclaimed. Apollos always had a following (1 Cor. 3: 4). The doctrine of the group is elusive. As disciples of John they must have known of the Holy Spirit (John 1: 33). Perhaps their notions of sin and repentance lacked some finality, and the quiet assurance brought by the presence of the Comforter.

The same sequence of events followed—the synagogue (8), rejection (9), and a long ministry in hired premises (10). There was an outbreak of superstition (11, 12), and an intrusion by charlatans into the church and its ministry (13–16), followed by a city-wide movement (18–20). As Paul made arrangements for another circuit through Greece, a great riot took shape. The story is told like a press report, in Luke's best style. W. M. Ramsay calls it 'the most instructive picture of society in an ancient city which has come down to us ... We are taken direct into the artisan life of Ephesus, and all is so true to common life, and so unlike what would occur to anyone writing at a distance, that the conclusion is inevitable: we have a picture drawn from nature.'

The facets of life and history which glint in the story are worth examination. The characters stand out—the two Macedonians (29), recognised as friends of Paul, and hustled down the great central street on the wave of the moving horde; Paul, cool as ever in a crisis (30); the provincial custodians of the Caesar-cult (31), not sorry to see some damage to the religion of Artemis; Alexander, probably a

Hellenistic Jew anxious not to be exposed to unpopularity or pogrom because of the conduct of a splinter-sect (33). Observe too, the germs of coming conflict with the proletariat, which the Roman writers Tacitus and Pliny note in their first secular accounts of Christianity. The metrical chant is almost audible (34), as it takes the place of reason in the collective mind of an eastern mob, which Luke describes with a phrase of classic irony (32).

Note, too, the sure touch of Luke's plural (38), which slips, a sharply remembered phrase, into his report of the city official's clever and politic speech. 'There are proconsuls,' he reminds the promoters of the tumult. See this in the context of the speaker's anxiety over the privileged standing of his city with the watchful imperial authorities (40), and another of those small convincing marks of historicity emerges. The plural could grammatically be 'generalising', but it is much more likely to convey a touch of obsequious respect for the two imperial stewards, who, having murdered the proconsul of Asia, M. Junius Silanus, the great-grandson of Augustus, must have been left with the administration of the province on their hands pending the appointment of a successor. The crime was of Agrippina's devising, shortly after Nero's accession in the autumn of A.D. 54. The tactful plural in the obsequious official's speech is evidence in a syllable of the aftermath of political assassination, and of Luke's clear recollection.

Last Journey
(Acts 20: 1-38)

LUKE omits the whole of a circuit through Macedonia. The purpose was probably subsidiary to the visit to Jerusalem. In a rather sad attempt to placate the Jerusalem church, which was growing more and more remote, Paul had conceived the idea of a Gentile collection for Jerusalem. His journey to Greece had, at least, the secondary purpose of fund-raising (1-5). It is significant that Paul was forced to change his travel plans because of a plot against him hatched by the Achaean Jews (3). The Corinthian Jews were no doubt still smarting over the incident in Gallio's court. The coherence of international Jewry, expressed and evident in more than one eastern Mediterranean city in the uprisings of both A.D. 66 and 132, is, however, also visible in the incident. A man who openly declared a Roman citizenship was marked down as a renegade, and faced mortal peril all through the cities where Jews were settled, and old tides of national consciousness were again flowing. Claudius' expulsion of the whole Roman colony in A.D. 49 (18: 2) may have had some valid and weighty reasons, in the mind of the ruler who wrote so sternly to the Alexandrian Jews in A.D. 42 about what appears to have been anti-Christian rioting.

Perhaps the journey into Illyricum mentioned in Romans 15: 19 took place while Paul was in northern Greece. The three months in Corinth with Gaius (3. Rom. 16: 23; 1 Cor. 16: 6) gave time for the writing of the letter to the Romans. Paul knew of the peril he faced (Rom. 15: 30, 31) and the Gentile Christians warned him everywhere (23).

Vv. 6-9 gives a glimpse of a Christian Lord's Day (1 Cor. 16: 2). A common meal in an upper room, and a considerable sermon seems to have been the custom. Luke passes rapidly over historic territory. The Troy of legend lay eight miles away. He walked an old Roman road to Assos, heavy with his own forebodings (13). Reunited with the Macedonian party, he met the Ephesian elders on the beach. Luke reports in this moving passage the only speech of Paul in his book which it is certain he actually heard. Usually he reports in outline, probably from Paul's description or Paul's notes. Here he is setting down words which he actually heard, and it is interesting to note how he uses Pauline expressions found in the letters. In consequence the speech authenticates the epistles and the epistles the speech. (See Rom. 1: 1; Phil. 1: 1; Tit. 1: 1; 2 Cor. 2: 4; 1 Cor. 10: 33; 2 Tim. 4: 7; 1 Tim. 1: 12; 1 Cor. 11: 23; 2 Cor. 7: 2; Col. 4: 17; Tim. 4: 16; Eph. 1: 14; 2 Tim. 4: 5; Col. 1: 12, 28.)

There is a clear picture of the three years in Ephesus. Paul sought no cheap popularity. He did his duty with zeal and consistent testimony. Note his tireless evangelism. Publicly and from house to house he had preached the gospel and founded Christian communities, not only in Ephesus but in the inland valley towns of Thyatira, Pergamum, Laodicea, Sardis, Philadelphia, Colossae and Hierapolis, as well as in the port of Smyrna. He lived in sturdy independence, earning his own bread. With clear foresight he saw the shape of the troubles which John's letters (Rev. 2 and 3) show truly came. He left the church efficiently organised and he left constituted leaders, duly warned and strengthened against subversion, to meet and solve problems yet to be.

It seems clear that Paul no longer had access to the city. The sailing programme of the ship may have precluded a visit but it is as likely that the Asiarchs had suggested that abstention from future intrusion might add to his safety and minimise their own problems.

Disaster in Jerusalem
(Acts 21: 1—22: 29)

IT is interesting to follow the course of the ship on a map (1-3). It was a frequented sea-lane, which was determined by the direction of daytime winds, a meteorological pattern itself dictated by the contours of the great land mass of Asia Minor and the contiguous sea. It took a week to unload at Tyre, and when Paul found the Christian group he was again warned not to go to Jerusalem (4, 5). It seems difficult to avoid the conclusion that Paul was moving against the revealed will of God in his determination to carry the monetary evidence of the Gentile Christians' goodwill to the Jerusalem church. Great and good men, in the grip of a fixed idea, can err.

The great galley unloaded (7),

and moved on to Akko (Ptolemais), and the large Herodian port of Caesarea, where Philip had long been in residence. It must have been on this occasion that Luke talked with the evangelist (8), and heard the story of Candace's officer. Always interested in the part women played in the church, he noted the fact that Philip had three unmarried daughters active in Christian preaching (9). (To 'prophesy' is to preach. Jeremy Taylor's work on 'The Liberty of Prophesying' was written, not to uphold the liberty of prediction, but freedom to preach the gospel.)

Into the household at Caesarea where Paul found refuge, came the strange person first mentioned in chapter 11: 27, 28. The three greatest O.T. writing prophets used symbolism and object-lesson to drive home spiritual truth, and Agabus carried a warning which must have had a strong impact on a man of Paul's training (10-13).

It convinced the congregation at Caesarea (12), who were loud in their entreaties. Apart from the alarming character of Agabus' warning, he knew Jerusalem and its tense atmosphere, for the passions which a few years later broke into the conflagration of the great rebellion of Jewry, were already hot in the air. Paul was known as a declared Roman citizen. His work among the Gentiles was considered by some a betrayal. A plot against his life had already been foiled. Luke himself added his plea ('we' in v. 14 show that he supported the general warning).

Paul's determination to persist in the course of danger is puzzling.

Perhaps he sought to follow the steps of Christ's passion and his 'setting his face steadfastly to go to Jerusalem' (Luke 9: 51). Some deep inner compulsion moved him. On the face of it, Paul seems to have moved on against unanimous, wise, loving and sincere advice, and commonly such counsel can be regarded as a major factor in the guidance of God. It is difficult to believe that Luke did not deplore his friend's determination. It is quite certain that a mighty ministry was to be tragically abbreviated by the events which the visit to Jerusalem precipitated. On the other hand, the custody of Paul produced the work of Luke (14-16).

The Jerusalem church welcomed the party (17), heard the report (18), and no doubt received the considerable Gentile contributions. It may be to misread Luke's brevity, but the impression lingers that the Jerusalem church was anxious about their primacy in face of the vast growth of Gentile Christianity, and that James found his colleagues moving from the liberal stance of chapter 15, and embarrassed by Paul's reputation (20, 21).

The Jewish tide was rising. Hence the suggestion, almost an order, from James. The Gentiles, he hints, had won a great concession. Why should Paul not yield a little, and demonstrate that his now famous ministry among the Gentiles had not destroyed old Jewish loyalties. Had they not heard that he himself had made such a vow in Cenchrea, and had he not written of his willingness to be 'all things to all men if by any means he might win some' (22-26)?

Paul, anxious to win his old associates, conceded the point and made a disastrous mistake. The report of the riot in the temple court is obviously narrative of an eyewitness. Paul's old enemies from Asia had been overlooked in the apostle's eagerness to meet the wishes of the Christian Pharisees. Ephesus had already demonstrated the possibilities of mob violence, and the peculiarities of crowd psychology. It appeared again (27).

Crying havoc against Paul (28-30), the Ephesian group stirred such a tumult that the garrison, stationed in the Tower of Antonia overlooking the area, was alerted and driven to intervention (32-35). A strong patrol descended one of the two stairways which led to the area, and drove violently through the crowd to the rescue. The impression was that a Jew from Egypt, a member probably of the notorious Alexandrian ghetto, was rabble-rousing in the capital. The old cry of the Pavement rose again (36. John 19: 15).

The tribune in charge of the garrison, Claudius Lysias, appears to have been one of the career men frequently met in the days of Claudius. He was a Greek, as his second name indicates, and his first name was acquired when, at the price of a considerable bribe, a piece of corruption common enough, he was granted the coveted Roman citizenship. On the other hand Lysias seems to have been a capable soldier, with good relations with his staff (26). The centurion is at ease with his commander. Paul made a strong impression on the officer (37-40). He did not reveal his Roman citizenship until after the second outburst of mob rage, and it says much for the commanding personality of the prisoner that a senior officer paused in the midst of a tense operation, and allowed an unidentified prisoner, just snatched from the hands of an excited mob, to stand on the stairs which led to the security of the tower, and, over the narrow barri-. cade of the soldiers' spears, address the angry crowd below (22: 1-22). It was on Paul's part a remarkable exhibition of cool courage and self-control. He had just been saved from lynching by the intervention of a rough detachment of soldiery, men who probably took little care to be gentle with the person at the centre of the disturbance. Most people would be too shaken to speak coherently. Paul clearly did, and momentarily calmed the crowd. At v. 15 he even modified Christ's own words to do so. But at the one word 'Gentiles' (21) the mob erupted again (22). It is a frightening portent of what was happening as Palestine moved on to revolution.

Paul spoke in 'Hebrew' (probably Aramaic) and Lysias did not follow the drift of events and with some anger brought him into the guardroom (24, 25).

The Sanhedrin Investigates
(Acts 22: 30—23: 22)

PAUL was now in Roman custody. He was to remain there for five years. Lysias had been well briefed in his relations with the difficult Jews, so set Paul before the Sanhedrin in search of specific charges (30). It was the fifth time on which the supreme court of Jewry was to investigate the Christian church. Paul's dexterous conduct must have astonished Lysias. The atrocious action of the high priest (2), in such contrast to the disciplined attitude of the Romans, enraged Paul (3). How it was that he failed to recognise the high priest is difficult to explain (5). He had been long absent from Jerusalem, and if his reaction contrasted with that of Christ on a like occasion (John 18: 22, 23), it conformed to common norms of human conduct which most people will readily recognise.

Paul could see that constructive argument would be fruitless (6-9), and appealed to his own class, the Pharisees, with whom he at least had a point of contact. The worldly, venal, heretical Sadducees were, in any case, beyond all argument of piety or reason. The Pharisees should have been with him on the vital doctrine of the resurrection. He spoke, therefore, to the Pharisees, as, with equal insight, he had addressed himself to the Stoics at Athens. He passed by both Sadducees and Epicureans. In the end Lysias rescued him a second time (10).

The plot which followed (12-15) throws unexpected light on Paul's family. He had probably been cast off by them, and perhaps by a wife, at the time of his conversion, and it is interesting to observe a sister's and a nephew's loyalty. The deference with which Lysias treats the boy is also indicative of the family's standing (16-22). Paul was snatched away. It may be confidently concluded that the plotters did not starve (14). The Pharisaic dexterity with the law could have provided more than one avenue of perfectly legal escape.

Felix Investigates
(Acts 23: 23—24: 1-26)

IT is indicative of the tense and dangerous situation in Palestine that it required an escort of 470 men to ensure the safety of one political prisoner travelling down to Caesarea (23). The tribune's report takes a slight liberty with truth in advancing the hour of Paul's revelation of his citizenship (26, 27). Paul was safely delivered at the garrison headquarters (28-35) where Felix, the corrupt creature who was brother of Claudius' equally base freedman Pallas, was competent to judge the case. Since the legate of Syria was the procurator's immediate superior, and since Cilicia (34) was under his jurisdiction, Felix could try the case. Felix seems to have been at least four, possibly six years in office (24: 10).

Tertullus (24: 1, 2) was no great orator. Felix, scoundrel though he was, seems to have been quite unimpressed by the suggestion that a case of treason was on his hands. The prosecution made a serious mistake in directing a side-blow against the capable commander of the Jerusalem garrison (7). Felix knew that his corrupt rule depended on the efficiency of such officers. In oratory the greatest art is to conceal art, and Luke seems to take a subtle pleasure in reporting the prosecutor's too obviously elabor-

ate flatteries (3, 4), an obsequious approach no doubt somewhat dimmed by the presence of the high priest in the court.

Paul ascribed to the oratorical courtesies of the occasion with becoming brevity (10), and dealt cogently with the vague charge of vagrancy (5. 11-13). 'The way' was no sect (14), and with devastating sincerity Paul demonstrated his innocence, obviously to Felix' satisfaction (15-22). His only problem was procedural (23). But something eluded him. Hence the introduction of his wife (24, 25). Drusa (Drusilla is a pet-name as Priscilla is of Prisca) was one of the daughters of Agrippa I. She married, probably about A.D. 53, Aziz of Emesa, a principality in the north of Syria. In the following year, still only about sixteen years of age, she was seduced by Felix, and became his third wife, a situation which provoked contempt even in Rome. Drusilla must have had some knowledge of her father's relations with the Christians, and now had the immense privilege of hearing a direct appeal from the most famous Christian of her day. She heard Paul preach of 'righteousness, self-control and judgment to come' (25). It is intriguing to imagine what she may have remembered of words in that distant courtroom when Vesuvius, on August 25 A.D. 79, destroyed the city of Pompeii where she is said to have lived.

Felix was tangled, like his predecessor Pilate, in a web of his own weaving (26). As with Pilate, it would have taken a mighty act of the will to cut himself free. He was unable to make that painful reappraisement and died as he had lived.

Festus Investigates
(Acts 24: 27—25: 12)

PORCIUS Festus succeeded to the procuratorship in A.D. 57 or 58 (1), and we have another glimpse of a Roman governor at work in a difficult situation. Festus had inherited from Felix a load of trouble. There was lawlessness in the countryside (2, 3), and armed rivalry between the factions of the hierarchy. Events were in full flow for the disaster of eight years later. Festus could not afford to alienate collaborators, and the determination of the priests to make away with an innocent man was a problem which required careful handling. It was the situation of thirty years before, repeated on another stage. Festus was a luckier man than Pilate. He found a way of escape through the prisoner's own action. He offered Paul an acquittal on the charge of sedition, and added the proposal, not unreasonable from his point of view, that the ex-Pharisee should face a religious investigation before his own highest tribunal (7-9).

For Paul it was a crisis. He knew the perils of Jerusalem, and understood the growing tension better than the procurator himself. If Festus found himself inhibited by official policy from frustrating the Jerusalem hierarchy, Paul proposed to save himself, and free the governor from embarrassment, by exercising a Roman citizen's right of appeal to the emperor (10, 11).

The process to which Paul had recourse was the act by which a litigant disputes a judgment, so that the case is referred to a higher court, normally that of the authority who had originally appointed the magistrate of the court from which the appeal originated. Caesar had appointed Festus. Festus was obliged to accept the appeal (12), and refer it on, accompanied by relevant documents and a personal report, which must have presented some difficulty. He saw no fault in Paul by any standards of law familiar to him, but Jewish law and religion were both unfamiliar to him. Festus had his career to make. His difficult province was a hard testing-ground, and the correct terminology of a document over his signature in a court so exalted as that of Caesar himself must have been a matter of anxious concern. Hence the alacrity with which he availed himself of the help of Agrippa II.

The Jews had no complaints to level against Festus. He was possibly the best of the procurators. It is a pity that he died two years or thereabouts later.

Agrippa Investigates
(Acts 25: 13—26: 32)

AGRIPPA was a man of ability, of wide knowledge of Judaism, and of more than a casual acquaintance with Christianity. He was, in fact, the best of the Herods, and eight years later risked his life in an attempt to stop the plunge into revolution. Paul's attitude and careful apologia show that he valued the opportunity to defend himself (2, 3). It was of prime importance to the prisoner, as well as to the procurator, that the report to Rome should be accurately phrased and properly supplied with detail (25: 14–27). The Herodian taste for showmanship is noticeable (12: 21). It is an interesting situation. The careful governor, obviously anxious not to make a false step amid the growing perils of the province; the care of Rome's representative to honour the client-king (23), so true to official policy as old as Augustus; Paul's battle for justice, so often to be repeated; the background of menace outside the safety of the garrison town—nowhere else in ancient literature is so authentic a document of the Empire in action to be found.

It seems clear that Luke was present. The Herods loved large gatherings, and the story is told with that authentic touch which marks the eyewitness. Observe Paul's characteristic gesture (1), his courteous exordium (2, 3) redolent of a Greek rhetorical training. It was a most important state occasion, and vital to the theme which Luke, among other objects, was developing—that Christianity was not subversive.

Paul was heard with patience until he mentioned the resurrection (23). It was the reaction of the Athenians repeated (17: 32). Festus marred his record for correct bearing with an irritable remark (24). Paul answered with courtesy (25), and the gentlest hint that Agrippa was in charge at the moment (26). The direct appeal to Agrippa was bold (27), and met by

a frequently misunderstood reply (28). The phrase translated 'almost' in KJV is literally 'in a little'. In Ephesians 3: 3 it is rendered 'in a few words' or 'in brief', while common Greek usage attaches the expression to time. Agrippa seems to rebuke the presumption of one who, in one public speech of no great duration, sought to make him a Christian. The word 'Christian' seems, at this time, to have been accepted. 'With a few words, you are trying to make me, Agrippa, a Christian.' 'Whether with few words or many,' Paul replied (29), 'I could pray that not only you but all my audience were as I am—except, of course, for these bonds' (ruefully holding up his hands). Some ms contain two small variants which could produce the meaning: 'With but little you are persuading yourself that you can make me a Christian.' It is no improvement, but the variants suggest that the early church found Agrippa's words as puzzling as we do. Perhaps his Greek was not good.

The pompous exit and the brief conference are told with an air of reality. Luke thought the common verdict important—as it was (30–32).

By Ship to Rome
(Acts 27: 1–44)

THE centurion Julius, a man of quiet decency and manliness (3, 43) was an officer of a special corps, detached for important and confidential duties (1). He shipped his party in a vessel from Adramyttium, the likeliest craft to put the company into the stream of east-west trade, for Adramyttium lies on the Aegean opposite Lesbos. The vessel had beaten north along the Palestinian coast, cut between Cyprus and the mainland, as the seasonal winds demanded, and then worked west along the Asia Minor Coast to Myra, at the extreme southern point of the peninsula (5). Here the party transferred to an Alexandrian cornship, which had perhaps chosen this northern route because of the lateness of the season. The shipmaster made for Cnidus, a port on the south-west extremity of Asia Minor (7). He was unable to make the harbour, for a wind off shore drove the galley south, and the shipmaster took refuge from the gale under the lee of the 140-mile long island of Crete (7). Halfway along lies Fair Havens, the port where Paul besought them to stay for the winter—the common practice of ancient mariners (9–11). The shipmaster decided to try for another anchorage (12, 13).

The eastern half of Crete is low, the western rises in terraces to form a group of lofty snow-capped mountains. The north-east wind, funnelled down through these highlands, now found them again and drove them off shore round the island of Clauda (14, 16). The passengers were called in to aid the crew, for Luke remembered vividly the struggle to haul in the ship's boat (16). The nor'easter had the cornship in charge. Far to the south, off the African coast, lay the Syrtes, a graveyard of ships, as underwater archaeology has revealed. Hence the battle to hold a westerly course, aided by a veering

of the wind to the east, as the cyclonic disturbance shifted.

The tremendous leadership of Paul emerged at the crisis (21–25). His advice at Fair Havens had been rejected, and he was human enough to mention the fact, but it is clear that Paul, not the centurion, nor the captain, was the one who stiffened the morale of the company. They were at the end of human resources. They had looped tautened cables round the hull to bind the straining timbers against the stress of the seas, and the leverage of the mast (17); they had cut loose and jettisoned all dispensable tackle and gear (18, 19), and it was all under a murky heaven, with the spray and driving cloud blotting out the stars, and the galley lurching west at nearly forty miles a day (20).

The end came. Hearing the sound of distant surf, the sailors suspected land or shoals ahead (27). The lead showed a shelving seabed, so the hulk was hove to for the night with anchors out astern (28, 29). This arrangement kept the ship heading in the right direction before the pressure of the wind. It was on the fairly transparent pretext of similarly anchoring the bow, that the crew proposed to launch the boat and escape (30), a plot frustrated by the alert Paul (31), and a few swordcuts on the ropes at the centurion's orders (32).

At this point the centurion or the captain seems to have numbered the ship's complement (37), a sensible measure before the abandonment of the vessel. They spent the night heaving overboard the cargo of Egyptian wheat (38), and with the dawn saw an unknown coast, a beach, and a practicable bay (39). A bar, due to a cross-current, frustrated the attempt to beach the ship which probably drew eighteen feet of water, and it was at this point that the escort, who were responsible for their charges, pro-posed to kill the prisoners (42). The centurion's admiration for Paul is apparent in the refusal (43). There was a struggle through the breakers and the whole ship's company reached the beach (43). It was a triumph for Paul's faith and no small tribute to his dynamic personality.

It is a magnificent story of ship-wreck, the best from all ancient literature, and marks the worth of Luke as a writer.

Interlude on Malta
(Acts 28: 1–14)

THE islanders were waiting. From the beach they had watched the galley lurching through the surf. The Greek 'barbaros' simply means those who speak another language than Greek—whose speech, in short, sounds to Greek ears as in-telligible as a lamb's bleating (bar-bar). The Greeks called their Persian foes 'barbaroi', while most freely admitting the material superi-ority of Persian civilisation. The 'barbarous' people were the Mal-tese (2). The island had been colon-ised by Phoenicians ten centuries before Christ, and the peasantry continued to speak in their native Phoenician, a Semitic tongue, as closely allied to Hebrew and Ara-maic as Arabic is to modern Israeli.

It is not impossible that Paul could make some sense of what they said. Hence the knowledge of what the bystanders thought when Paul, ready as ever to lend a hand at humble work, shook the torpid snake into the fire (5, 6).

The country estate of the 'first man' was not far away (7). As ever, the meticulous historian uses the correct term which has been epi-graphically attested. Villas, such as that of Publius, were large, self-contained establishments, and could well cope with the large addition to the community.

Three months later another Alex-andrian grain ship which had wintered at Valetta, took Julius and his company aboard. It was named after the patron deities of sailormen (11). They landed at Puteoli, modern Pozzuoli, a few miles from Herculaneum, destined to be des-troyed, seventeen or eighteen years later, along with Pompeii, when Vesuvius overwhelmed the coast. Was the house, still to be seen, with the Christian 'upper room', marked by a charred cross on the wall, the place where Paul was a guest for a week? It is remarkable that the Christians were so promptly to be found, and that communication between the Christian groups in the Empire was such that the Christians of the port were aware of the com-ing of Paul on such and such a ship. Paul must have been supremely trusted. Julius took a considerable risk for him. The port was big and cosmopolitan. It was full of hiding-places. The Christians were obvi-ously in touch with their brethren in Rome. Rome with its population of a million people was a great warren into which any man could disappear as Onesimus was soon to do. Paul could have been spirited away up the Via Appia with the greatest ease. It shows courage, acute judgment, and even friendly regard on the part of the senior soldier.

To be trustworthy as a citizen was a lesson Paul taught. Writing soon afterwards to Philippi, he besought the church to 'live as citizens worthily of the gospel of Christ' (Phil. 1: 27). He was himself a prime example. He had appealed to Rome. He was ready to go there. The centurion duly delivered him to the prefect of the praetorian guards. This was the able soldier Burrus, who had only two years to live.

And So to Rome

(Acts 28: 15–31)

ROME'S powerful household troops, the praetorian guard, took charge of Paul in his house confinement, probably in the Transtiber section of the city. They provided Paul with an unexpected sphere of evangelism (16. Phil. 1: 13). With the changing of the guard, over the space of two years (30), half of the 4,500 troops must have had contact with the prisoner. Half of them had only a few years to live, for the street-fighting of the terrible year A.D. 69 decimated the corps.

The Jews, according to Paul's consistent policy, had the first chance (17). They were back in Rome, and obviously Claudius' decree of banishment (18: 2) must have been rescinded. Nero had succeeded Claudius, and during the first five years of his principate, that pleasure-loving youth left affairs largely in the hands of the competent Burrus and the wise Seneca. If one or both of these men was instrumental in allowing the Jews to return, it would have been on condition that they keep the peace. The rabbis were therefore in a difficult position. A phrase in Suetonius seems to make it certain that it was because of disturbance over the Christians that Claudius moved against the Jews in A.D. 49.

And now a notoriously controversial figure had arrived, one whose path through the eastern and central lands of the Mediterranean had been strewn with riot and disorder. Or so, at least, the career of Paul could be represented by the cautious, not to mention the hostile. No Jew cared to have his hard-pressed community wantonly disrupted. Reception, in consequence, was mixed (24), and Paul set before them the honoured words of Isaiah (Isa. 6: 9, 10). The book ends with the last interview when, with some severity, the apostle announces again his 'turning to the Gentiles' (28).

THE EPISTLE OF PAUL
TO THE ROMANS

Rome as Paul Saw it
(Romans 1: 1–32)

PAUL had not yet visited Rome (11, 13, 15) but a church was already there (Acts 28:15). Paul had early formed the intention of visiting it (Acts 19: 21) and now writes to make his doctrine clear. It was A.D. 56 or 57. Paul introduces himself, commissioned by the church (Acts 13: 2) and God himself (Gal. 1: 15) for Gentile evangelism (1). His task was to summon men to 'the obedience of faith' (5. Acts 6: 7). 'Jesus Christ', that is 'Jesus the Messiah', is mentioned five times in eight verses. Christ's deity, saviourhood and eternal office were to be jealously guarded and assiduously preached. Rome was essential in Paul's theory of dissemination of the gospel from vitally placed strategic cells. He owed a debt to Greeks and non-Greeks (14. Acts 28: 2) but was keenly aware that the Roman church was not his foundation. Hence the humble and gracious approach (8–17 and especially 9–12).

Paul's picture of a godless society may be illustrated from the meagre remains of contemporary literature. The elegant Petronius was writing his *Satyricon*, the only novel from Rome of which fragments remain, and its bawdy pages show a society worthy of the young profligate Nero, who was emperor at the time. Too much of Paul's description is sombrely relevant in the 'permissive' society of today (18–32).

There was no excuse, for natural theology is apparent to all thinking men (19–21) and had its challenge unless it was blurred and corrupted by philosophy (22) or foolish idolatry (23). Paul had based his approach to the pagan Lystrans on this argument (Acts 14: 15–17) and to the clever Athenians (Acts 17: 24–29). He maintained that God was not beyond discovery (21. Acts 17: 27). By the old folly of carnal man they commonly missed the message (25. Ps. 150: 21).

At v. 27 Paul falls into a description of human corruption such as he was to repeat on the spot a decade later (2 Tim. 3: 1–9). On such societies judgment falls (38). He never toned down sin, never conceded that man, created a moral and a responsible being, was in any way to be excused for sin, and he never hid the truth of ultimate judgment. It is a trenchant preface to the great letter which follows.

The Law in the Heart

(Romans 2: 1–29)

JEW and Gentile both fell under judgment by their wilfully falling short of what conscience showed was right. Paul envisages good pagans (11–16). Seneca, doomed, like many Christians, to die at Nero's hands, was writing at this very time, and Seneca's view of evil was such that Tertullian said that he was 'one of us'. And yet, in his tutelage of Nero, Seneca often fell into compromise which betrayed his noblest thought.

Jew and Gentile therefore faced the final test of conduct (14, 22, 23). Paul and James thus agree. Man's responsibility is an awesome load to bear (4–6) and there is no covenant of indulgence for those whose opportunity has been cast aside (7, 8). Jew and Gentile, both errant humans, faced a similar judgment, with the Jew, if possible, with less excuse (9–11). Paul was well aware of the common sophistries of the niggling debates whereby the Jews mocked their privilege. Exodus 15: 26 spoke of 'diligently hearkening' (13), and there were those who argued that mere listening was of more importance than doing. Paul's sect, the Pharisees, were not guilty of this.

But observe how dexterously Paul moves from the contentiousness (8) of rabbinical debate to Stoicism. The Stoics had a doctrine of a 'law written on the heart', and they were the first Greeks to use the word 'conscience' in the Christian sense (15).

Irony is the note of the rhetorical address to the Jew (17–29). The Jew

is 'aware of moral distinctions' (18, NEB). Literally, he is equipped to 'test out things which differ' (Phil. 1: 9, 10). True, he could have been a guide, a beacon, and a teacher (19, 20). A missionary people had been the old vision of the Covenant (Gen. 18: 18; 22: 18; 26: 4; 28: 14) and of Isaiah (45: 22; 52: 10). They had a noble testimony to maintain before a watching world (21–24. Gen. 13: 7–9; Ezra 8: 22). And all their misplaced pride melted if their privilege was belied by less than pagan morals (25). A sign in the body was nothing, if a pagan, without such sign, lived a better life as the law would judge it. And nowhere, perhaps, was Jewish living more under such scrutiny than in the capital of empire. It was not a matter of outward but of inward demonstration. 'He is a Jew who is one in his secret soul; and his is the true circumcision—that of the heart, consisting in the Spirit's presence, not in the observance of the written letter. Men have no praise for such a man—God has' (29. A. S. Way).

The Law does not Save

(Romans 3: 1–31)

PAUL was a Jew (Phil. 3: 4–6) and naturally sees the Jews' bewilderment. What advantage have the Jews? Apart from advantages he will list from 9: 4, they are the custodians of God's oracles. This point made, he resumes the theme broken after 2: 17–29. The Jews had used their privilege ill. Some failed to see that special choice meant special duty. Some did not believe (3). To set up an antagonist was a Stoic device. The Stoics invented the sermon and Cilicia played a part in the origins of that school (Acts 21: 39).

Paul attacks the typically sophistic argument which some were advancing—that sin actually exalts God's righteousness, as darkness enhances light, and therefore why should a sinner be condemned (5–8)? The answer to such folly is that God would, in such case, be impotent and in no position to be judge. The argument is not completely 'remote from modern 'permissiveness', and the tampering with the absolute standards of truth and righteousness found in 'situation ethics'.

Jew and Gentile are 'under the power of sin' (9. RSV). In rabbinical style Paul begins a 'catena' or 'chain' of O.T. quotations (10–18), not dissimilar from the style of Hebrews. Context was not important (10–12. Ps. 14: 1–3). Quotation could be exact (13. Ps. 5: 9), free (14. Ps. 10: 7), or selectively extracted (15–17. Isa. 59: 7, 8). He is challenging Jews, who held the oracles of God, to apply them, and Jews would have found the 'catena' a devastating assault on the causes of human ruin, misery and damnation in speech and conduct.

The law, evoked in this epistle some seventy times, and in four different senses, is here (19, 20) used for the whole O.T. revelation, and the argument is that, if those who hold the O.T. revelation are condemned by it, how can anyone claim righteousness? Hence a daunting thought (20). Most Jews thought that the mere keeping of

the law made a man righteous (Luke 18: 18–27). Paul had faced the fact that the rich young man could not face (Phil. 3: 4–7). He found no peace, and in sudden clarity saw that the law merely revealed how far man fell short of the holiness of God. And therefore all, Jew and Gentile, stood condemned. For the Jew that grim revelation should have been more sharply apparent. What was sin (22, 23) but falling short of 'the glory of God'? (Ps. 4: 4; Isa. 43: 7).

Justification, that act of free grace by which God pardons sin and counts the pardoned righteous in his sight, can begin at this point of revelation, and nowhere else (24). Redemption is the act of buying out of bondage (Deut. 7: 8; Isa. 51: 11; Gal. 3: 23—4: 7). Christ becomes our 'propitiation', a word meaning expiation. To 'expiate' a sin is to annul guilt by some process of sacrifice, or securing, by payment or proper ritual, the satisfaction demanded. Christ paid all in his death 'the just for the unjust'. See remarks on 1 John 1: 9. 'Therefore we conclude . . .' (28. KJV is correct), that Christ is all and the law has its place. The chapter's whole argument is, in its Jewish context, an astounding reappraisal.

Father of the Faithful
(Romans 4: 1–25)

GENESIS 12–25, Galatians 3, and Hebrews 11: 8–19 are obligatory background reading. It was natural to evoke the great father of the race (Matt. 3: 9) as a test case (1–8). Abraham had, without compulsion, heard God's voice and obeyed. It was faith which moved him (Gen. 15: 6). The deeper thinkers of the O.T. had grasped the truth (6–8. Ps. 32: 1, 2). Paul is staging the sort of Jewish debate he knew well (Acts 17: 2; 28: 23). The imaginary opponent concedes the point. But Abraham was the father of the Jews (John 8: 33). What of the Gentiles of whom he has been speaking? Paul answers like a rabbi. In Galatians he pointed out that Abraham antedated the law by more than four centuries. Now he points out that the distinguishing sign in the flesh came *after* the covenant (Gen. 17: 9–14). Paul goes on to insist on the global nature of the promise (13–16. Gen. 12: 3; 18: 18; 22: 18). The national promise had been closely defined geographically (Gen. 13: 14, 15; 15: 18–21; Josh. 1: 2–4), but Paul stresses the wider meaning (Gal. 3: 16, 29; Heb. 11: 10). Abraham was to have wide and varied posterity (17), and his acceptance of this vast promise was by faith, sternly tried (18). All evidence was discouraging (19) but 'no distrust made him waver' (20). Thus he 'gave glory to God' (21). 'Faith', said James Denney, 'is the spiritual attitude of a man who is conscious that in himself he has no strength and no hope of a future, but who nevertheless casts himself on, and lives by, the word of God which assures him of a future . . . this is the attitude of Abraham and of all sinners who believe in God through Christ . . . The gospel does not subvert the religious order under which Abraham lived; it illustrates, extends and confirms it' (22, 23). Paul ends (24, 25) with a

re-affirmation of the faith which reads rhythmically like a credal statement. In v. 25, RSV obscures the origin of the O.T. language. KJV is nearer with its 'delivered for our offences'. In Isaiah 53: 6, 12 the Septuagint uses the word used here.

Paul's Peace

(Romans 5: 1–21)

REBELLION is over. Justification brings peace. Reconciliation is won (1. Col. 1: 20). God is available (2). Nothing bars the way or alienates (1 John 2: 28); and faith becomes, not only the act of appropriating salvation, but a daily pattern of life. Hence victory over anything life can do (8: 28). Paul never said that Christianity is easy. No one had a more trouble-strewn path than he. But trial and tribulation, he had found, committed in faith to the wise, transforming hand of the Almighty, produced rare qualities of character (3). Endurance, must be seen in the context of his whole life. It is no crouching under the shield of faith while adversity hurls clanging down every missile in its armoury. The shield could be a weapon of offence, and Paul's endurance was active. Hence character (4). No sturdiness forms in a hothouse. A Christian lives in hope. The Holy Spirit indwells him and the new-given life seeps out to colour all thought and action (5).

Paul, after the fashion which produces some of his finest writing, now breaks into a lyric passage on the love of God, a theme which

always called forth wonder (6–8. 1
John 3: 1; 1 Pet. 1: 3, 4). In v. 7 a
definite article is used—'the Good
Man'. To substitute an indefinite
article is a not uncommon fault of
the KJV (Luke 18: 13; John 3: 10).
The Stoics spoke of 'the Wise Man'
and Plato spoke of 'the Good
Man', who, he said, should he ever
appear, 'will be scourged, thrown
into prison, and after enduring
every pain will be crucified'
(*Republic* 361 E). Christ died, not
for 'the Good Man', but for sinners,
himself sinless (8). Thus God
'presents' his love. That assurance
removes the major difficulty. He
died, he lives. Can we ask more for
life (9, 10), more fulfilment? (11).

A tract of argument has run from
3: 21 to 5: 11. Paul now expounds
the theology. Adam admitted a
force of death into the close-knit
family of men (12). A parenthesis
runs from v. 13 to v. 17. The
sentence of Genesis 2: 17 fell on the
race (13), and sin was doing its work
before the commandments of the
law came to point and define it (14).
In vv. 15 and 18 read 'the many', an
echo of Isaiah 53: 11. Paul is intent
to show that Christ balanced Adam
in contravening death by life, a
glorious exchange, in which he sees
the mystic pattern which gripped
his mind (16–19). The law 'intruded
into this process' (20. NEB), 'to
make wrongdoing a legal offence'
(Gal. 3: 19 NEB). V. 20 uses a vivid
word: 'the law came sideways in'.
Grace, with this sudden stern invasion of moral rule, became a
desperate need. 'Grace reigns',
were the last words of Mr. Honest
in Bunyan's allegory. So Paul,
whom Mr. Honest had read.

Paul the Rhetorician
(Romans 6: 1-23)

A temptation for the theologian
is the verbal quibble, and Paul
imagines some such quibbler saying: 'The more we sin, the greater
the grace bestowed' (1). Using the
symbolism of baptism, which in
Jewish practice was immersion,
Paul speaks of rising to newness of
life (2–5). He who has 'died in
Christ' is freed from a servitude (6),
and released, as death always re-
leases, from the bondage of life (7).
There is a new freedom, a new life,
a new beginning, but it is a freedom
to be laid hold of, a life to live in
conscious realisation (8–10). Such is
the experience of Paul and of any
one of us, that such a condition
demanded the unbroken nurturing
of faith. The 'old man', a brilliantly
imaginative conception of Paul,
was alive, and struggling for dominance against the 'new man',
brought to birth by faith. It requires
daily exercise of faith to 'reckon'
old urges dead (11), and to promote
and further every thrust and aspiration of the soul towards good and
God, by the continual infusion of
trust and ready belief. It is a re-
orientation of all thinking and
desire.

A tyranny is broken (12). Our
bodies are not mere tools and
weapons (the Greek word means
both) to be used by an evil overlord
to destroy and be destroyed (13),
but living members of Christ. V. 14
repeats, like a refrain, the freedom
cry of v. 12. The objector of v. 1 has
his complete answer (15). No man
can serve two masters, and the
Christian has made his choice (16–

18. Matt. 6: 24). One servitude is a heavy burden and its end is death. The other yoke is easy (Matt. 11: 30). And those to whom he sends his words, says Paul with characteristic warmth, know and experience all this (17). 'I am simply using a human figure of speech,' he says, 'so that you will understand' (19. See 3: 5 and Gal. 3: 15 for similar apologies for points of style). In rhetorical fashion he proceeds to show that those who served sin 'owed no duty to righteousness' (20), a ruinous servitude the end of which was death (21). But 'now' (opposing 'then' of 21), now there was life unbounded (22). V. 23 is the fine climax of a piece of polished argument which interweaves rabinnical dialectic with Greek rhetoric, for Paul was a man of both worlds. In himself he fused two cultures.

Paul's Battle
(Romans 7: 1–25)

BOLDLY, too boldly for many Jews, Paul continues. There was bondage other than that of sin. The law, though given of God to convict of sin, was a bondage from which emancipation was due. Death frees a person from more than a few human legal obligations. The Christian is freed from the law by a sort of death (1–4) and should so 'reckon himself' (6: 11). The law can convict, but cannot save (5). The Christian is a freedman, no longer convicted, the dweller in another age. Christ can save (6).

But had there been no law, there would have been no urge to cry out for salvation (7, 8). It spelt death

for it could not be obeyed (9, 10). V. 11 contains a subtle touch of psychology. A commandment or a prohibition can become, by the touch of evil, a temptation (Gen. 3: 13). All this seems like personal testimony. He moved with deceptive moral rectitude until the law, rising from ambush by one commandment demonstrated the reality of evil (7, 8). He discovered the law and with it death (9). He was dismayed (10) and struck down (11). Hence the desperation apparent between the death of Stephen and the surrender on the Damascus road. It was not the fault of God's demands (12, 13), but of man's weakness.

The passage which follows is not a confession of hopeless defeat. It is common experience. The Bible sets no limits to the Christian's victory over his baser self, but it can lead to nothing but frustration and despair to suggest to those who come to Christ that all sinlessness lies effortlessly within reach, and to give the impression that there is no strife, no temptation, no chance of defeat save in unbelief. Paul never taught this, for he knew better. His words (15–25) are no mere recollection of unregenerate days. They arose from his daily battling with sin. Those who claim unbroken victory 'deceive themselves' (1 John 1: 8). The exclamation of thanksgiving in v. 25 shows, however, is no postponed consummation to be granted in another life. It is at hand. The military metaphor of v. 23 shows that the battle is now, but it is no stalemate or defeat. The conflict moves towards victory. Paul is to be thanked for his frankness.

Like the Psalms, the book is a record of the soul.

The Path to Victory
(Romans 8: 1-39)

THE chapter opens with one of Paul's great triumphant passages. The negative in v. 1 is emphatic—'no condemnation at all...' To be 'in Christ Jesus' means to live in utter committal to Christ (12: 1, 2). To 'walk according to the flesh' means to follow the body's lusts (Gal. 5: 19–21). To 'walk according to the Spirit' means to hold the conviction of God's emancipating power (2), made clear by God's self-revealing in Christ (3). So only can God count us righteous (4). There are two kinds of life, one which ends in death, introverted, self-centred, satisfied to follow the desires of the body (Luke 12: 15–23) and the other, as different as life is from death (Eph. 2: 1–6), John's 'eternal life', which seeks God's will, an outgoing life, free, conscious of God's presence and available by faith (5–14). Those who choose such life are the sons of God, his in Christ (15–17. Matt. 25: 34).

The adopted son can face the hostile world, live in this alien and polluted environment, conscious that he is a citizen of another world. The globe itself is 'polluted' under the feet of rebellious man (Isa. 24: 1–6), and not to be healed until God's day of consummation. It is an immense demonstration of Paul's insight into the man-made problems of this ravaged, damaged planet (18–23). The Christian can face life, face the clutter of human sin, outface evil because of hope (24, 25), sharpened by the first taste of ultimate reality (23).

A gem of Scripture follows (26, 27). Our words do not matter. God interprets our 'heart's desire' (Ps. 37: 5). Utter committal is, as the psalm says, all that matters. Perfect Wisdom allied to Perfect Love must produce a Perfect Plan (Eph. 3: 20, 21). The next verses (29, 30) touch 'predestination' which eludes comprehension. From Augustine to Calvin theologians have sought to reduce to logical synthesis God's foreknowledge and man's freedom. It cannot be done without raising more problems than it solves, and posing questions about the nature of God which challenge Scripture. Suffice it to say that those who look back over a tract of life in Christ are conscious of both their own choosing and a mystic compulsion. It is a theme for exultation and that is what the lyric passage is which closes the chapter. What can harm those who march with Christ safe from real harm, here, hereafter (31–39).

The Problem of Jewry
(Romans 9: 1-29)

CHAPTERS 9–11 are the sort of sermon Paul preached in the synagogues, and the probability is that the Roman church contained a large proportion of Christian Jews, accustomed to the language and thought forms of the O.T. Paul, like his compatriots, found the wide rejection of the gospel by a people divinely prepared to receive it an agonising problem. Their minds were torn between a life-long habit of thought which saw their race as God's privileged recipients of truth, and the Christian concept of salvation by faith open to all who believed.

Paul begins with frank expression of his pain (1–5), and passes to the sombre thought that God chose the forefathers of the race with no regard to their personal merit (7–13). His argument as always is notably single-minded in its drive. That is why problems emerge when his words are torn from the immediate Jewish context and more generally applied. Glance at several points which jar the Christian and the Western mind. Note: 'hated' (13) is a Hebraism and a relative term (Luke 14: 26); vv. 15 and 16 do not mean that one who with the passion and purpose of an athlete seeks salvation can be arbitrarily denied it by God. He does not create to destroy (Jer. 29: 13; Matt. 11: 28; John 6: 37). So too with Pharaoh. He hardened his own heart, but by the ellipses of Hebrew thought God hardened it in that he made the laws of mind and heart which Pharaoh violated (17. Exod. 9: 16). And this, the beginning of the argument, must be read along with the end (11: 25–32). Nor does the imagery of the pot (21–23) imply that God looks on men as things to shatter. He suffered in Christ for men. They are not insentient and irresponsible clay.

Israel was truly chosen. But Israel has too often denied its privilege. The prophets found it so, Hosea (25, 26), Isaiah (27–29). It had always been a 'remnant' which

had grasped the truth. Some had always wilfully rejected it, and as the O.T., now alive with new life in Paul's mind, had foreseen, those without the Jews' vast privilege, were entering into the heritage, a new Israel, as old as the covenant with Abraham.

Paul's Pleading
(Romans 9: 30—10: 21)

PETER knew this letter well. He probably heard it read in Rome, and the last four verses of ch. 9 made a deep impression on him (1 Pet. 2: 4–8). They preface a new cry of concern. The whole of the law, to which they clung with fervour, ended in Christ, and in self-will they halted short of the consummation (1–4). With a tissue of quotation Paul continues his pleading. Leviticus 18: 5, which he cites first (5), seems to contradict his argument. The Jew would reply that he was taking Moses precisely at his word. Paul meets the objection by turning Deuteronomy 30: 11–14 into a prophecy of Christ. 'Keep the law and live', is met by the contention: 'The law cannot be kept' (Gal. 3: 10–12), for can anyone love God to the extinction of all sin? Righteousness has not to be achieved but appropriated. It lies near, in Christ (7). Vv. 8 and 9, picking up the words of Deut. 30 in reverse order ('mouth', 'heart'), become a great evangelical proclamation. The Corinthian (and modern) heresy, that the resurrection is a symbol (1 Cor. 15: 1–19), is ruled firmly out (10). V. 11 quotes Isaiah 28: 16. Isaiah makes no reference to the law, nor to the exclusive privilege of the Jew. Those who believe will know no disillusionment. Observe the ease with which the O.T. Jehovah becomes the Christ of Paul (Acts 10: 36; Phil. 2: 10, 11). The phrase 'call upon the name of the Lord' is borrowed (Joel 2: 32). There is no distinction between Christ and God. Nor can there be distinction between Jew and Gentile (12, 13).

The digression which begins with v. 14 is obscure. Perhaps Paul is defending his own evangelistic rôle, and the need for his journey to Rome which his forward communication envisaged. If there is unbelief, hesitation, searching, there are those who need the gospel (15–17). The closing verses, with repeated insistence, show that Gentiles as well as Jews are included in the need, the proclamation and the response. Isaiah 52: 7 and 53: 1, Psalm 19: 4, Deuteronomy 32: 21 reinforce Paul's points, and it is interesting to see how rapidly the O.T. was being absorbed into the thinking of the church. In v. 21 Paul turns back to Israel. If Gentiles, so disadvantaged, believe, how overwhelmingly sad, and sad to God himself, is Israel's stubbornness. Vv. 14 to 21 seem to refer to some question, problem or challenge emanating from the Roman church. It is well to remember that communication was common and letters no rarity.

The Remnant
(Romans 11: 1–36)

RETURNING to the status of Israel, Paul recalls Elijah. Broken-hearted by the shallow conversion of the nation on Carmel, Elijah fled (1 Kings 18 and 19). In God's reply to his cry of despair (1 Kings 19: 18) the thought of the Remnant, the true Israel was born (Amos 9: 8–10; Mic. 2: 12, 5: 3; Zeph. 3: 12, 13; Jer, 23: 3; John 1: 47). God has not cast off the people who are really his but consolidated them in Christ along with the mighty reinforcement of redeemed Gentiles, as the prophets had foretold, saved by grace (1–6).

But why such a fate for a race so privileged? Paul can regard it only as a judgment on wilful sin (Isa. 6: 9, 10; 29: 10). This was a common Christian conclusion (Matt. 13: 14, 15; Mark 4: 12; Luke 8: 10; John 12: 40; Acts 28: 26, 27). The argument of the next verses (7–12) is Jewish and compact. Jews have treated their vast blessing with contempt, but a new Israel, Jews and Gentiles, is in the making, and Paul indulges the hope that Jewish obstinacy and apostasy will spur the Gentiles to awareness, and that the process may be then reversed with Israel streaming to Christ (13, 14). Let the Gentiles, indeed, beware lest they fall short like the Jews, and let them not hold the rebellious Jews in contempt.

Israel's failure has been the Gentiles' opportunity and Paul's own ministry was illustration (Acts 13: 46–48; 18: 6; 28: 25–28). Alluding to the ritual of the consecration of the dough in bread-making (Num.

15: 17–21) he points out that the race was of old renown, and God still remembered the consecration of their beginnings. So v. 16 seems to mean, but some application eludes. Does the figure mean that the first Christians were Jews? At any rate, it is obvious that the Christians of Rome must have been uncommonly well-taught in the Jewish scriptures.

If an olive was deteriorating, a graft of wild olive was thought to rejuvenate it. Dead branches were lopped and, in the graft, the tree resumed vigour and new fruitfulness. So Paul hoped to see the church bring Jewry back to life (17). Let the graft not, therefore, presume (18). The new branches took the place of those cut off (19) but the process can continue (20). God's goodness is not soft indulgence (21–25). Antisemitism, which has sometimes stained the church, is thus cut at the root.

The concluding verses contain difficulties (26–36). Observe that Paul cannot mean that all Jews, regardless of rebellion, will be saved. A mind so powerful would not thus contradict itself. He must mean the 'new Israel', the sum of the redeemed. Otherwise the argument of the whole epistle falls apart. Let v. 26 mean the Spiritual Israel, and the whole pattern of doctrine works to a proper conclusion.

The Committed Christian

(Romans 12: 1–21)

THERE was no contradiction between Paul and James. Hence vv. 1, 2. No commentator or trans-lator seems to note that the opening word 'parakalô' (I beg) is the modern Greek for 'please' and could have meant that when Paul used it. Giving due weight to moods and tenses translate therefore: 'Please, my brothers, considering all that God in his mercy has done, offer him your persons, no dead sacrifice, but alive, holy, something God can accept, and the only service you can really render. Stop trying to adapt yourselves to the society you live in, but carry on the transformation which began with the new life in your minds, so that you can try out for yourselves how good, satisfying, perfect God's will for you is . . .'

And v. 3 . . . 'but cultivate a balanced soundness of mind according as God has given every man faith as a measure'. Faith is the measuring instrument (Rev. 21: 15) by which a man can sanely measure the balance of his religion, and judge his attitudes and obligations. The notion of an articulated body is found in Plato and could reflect conversations with Luke (1 Cor. 12; Col. 1: 18; Eph. 4: 15, 16). A rich metaphor, if followed through (4). The body of Christ functions well only as each member does what is properly his function to do (5, 6). Prophesy is informed exposition of the meaning of the faith of prime importance while the canon was being formed, but was then to cease (1 Cor. 13: 8). It was historically transient. Teaching (7) expounded revealed truth. Service (7. 'ministry' KJV) is to be interpreted, no doubt, widely. It is special work in the name of Christ. 'Exhortation' (8) flows from an ardent personality. Giving must be natural, not forced. A leader must zealously, not timidly lead. Observe the out-working of 'balanced soundness of mind' (3).

In the same spirit love, utterly sincere, must not condone evil (9). Brotherly love must not, likewise, issue in a crude egalitarianism. Rank must breed no self-esteem, merits respect, but by no means servility (10). The word 'zeal' occurs twelve times in the N.T. and is translated seven different ways. It means earnestness and alertness (11. Acts 18: 25). Hope is not tense. It is a happy expectation (12), a stay on dark days, sustained by prayer. 'Pursue hospitality,' he continues (13) and the verb is used in 9: 30, 31; 14: 19; 1 Corinthians 14: 1; 1 Thessalonians 5: 15. 'Hos-pitality' is 'love of strangers'.

The curse is the formal commi-nation, the weapon used by the Jews when peril closed in by the river, as the tiny drama of Psalm 137 shows it (14). Observe the 'balanced soundness' (3) illustrated in v. 15. The Christlike sympathy of v. 15 calls for understanding, a quality never found in the self-centred. Hence v. 16: 'Try and share in the thoughts and desires of others.' True eminence is not self-conscious—nor conceited (16). Ab-staining from evil is passive. Do not stop there—do good (17). Observe the opening of v. 18. If there be strife, do not begin it. 'Leave room for God's wrath' (19. Ps. 37: 7; Isa. 54: 17)—but not passively (20. Prov. 25: 21, 22)—not a subtle form of vengeance, but a mode of witness (21).

Paul the Citizen
(Romans 13: 1-14)

PAUL's vision of the Empire for Christ had not yet faded. He had learned in Gallio's court (Acts 18: 12-16), and he was to learn again in riotous Jerusalem (Acts 21: 27-39) that Roman discipline and justice, rough though it sometimes was, and corrupt though it could be in such vicious hands as those of Felix, was a protection and a shield. Moreover, the Jews were restive throughout the world. The mood of the Empire's most difficult people was heading towards the tragic explosion of A.D. 66, and that event had world-wide repercussions. As Paul found when seeking a passage from Corinth to Jerusalem (Acts 20: 3), and again in Jeru-salem itself (Acts 23: 12-22), a collaborating Jew, as he was con-sidered to be, and a Jew who held and exercised his native Roman citizenship, stood in dire peril.

He did not wish to have the church branded as a dissident group, the position into which the Empire drove the church a decade later. At this time too it is a fact that, under the principate of the youthful Nero, whose vice and profligacy became legendary, the provinces enjoyed such quietness and stability that 'Nero's Five Years', the quinquennium during which government was controlled by the wise Seneca, and the soldierly Burrus, became a legend for just administration throughout the world (1-7. 1 Tim. 2: 1, 2; Tit. 3: 1; 1 Pet. 2: 13-17).

In v. 7 Paul is remembering a famous saying (Matt. 22: 21) and in the following verses the incident recorded in Matt. 22: 35-40. It is interesting to observe the oral tradition in action for Matthew's book was not yet written. He also remembers the story Luke told of the rich youth (Luke 18: 20) and lists the commandments in an order which reflects Luke and not Exodus 20.

A touch of poetry closes the chapter (11-14). 'Let us be Christ's men from head to foot, and give no chances to the flesh to have its fling' (14. JBP).

The Weaker Brethren

(Romans 14: 1—15: 13)

PAUL, the humane leader and concerned Christian appears in these closing chapters. If theology does not issue in such personal quality and concern, it fails in its impact. Some reported problem prompts this digression and its wise advice. The Christian with deviant convictions is often a problem—the sectaries of Corinth, the 'foolish Galatians', the superstitious Colossians. The oral tradition preserved the teaching of Christ and there are echoes in this chapter (e.g. Matt. 5: 6; 6: 31; Mark 7: 20-23), but little was yet written and in the hands of the church.

Paul points out that we are truly our brothers' keepers. 'No man is an island.' 'Neither in life nor in death are we self-contained units. Through all life, and when we die, we are in Christ's presence' (7, 8). A few scruples about food or holy days are not enough to entitle us to be another's conscience (9, 10). We should look to our own integrity

(11, 12). More—a strong personality pressing his views on another can make that person do what he considers wrong, and so to sin (14-16). Indeed, it is the obligation of the 'emancipated' to abstain for another's sake (21. 1 Cor. 8: 13). 'We who have strong faith ought to shoulder the burden of the doubts and qualms of others, and not just go our own sweet way' (15: 3 JBP). Those who are actively at one with Christ are naturally at one with each other (15: 5), and so we honour God (6).

Perhaps vv. 7 and 8 reveal what was dividing the Roman church. It may have been so predominantly Jewish that Gentiles were finding Jewish habits inhibiting. Let all remember that the mingling of both groups was foretold (8-12. Ps. 18: 49; Deut. 32: 43; Ps. 117: 1; Isa. 11: 10). From the last quotation, with quite exquisite tact, Paul picks one word—'hope' (13).

Future Plans

(Romans 15: 14-33)

'THE grace of God is in courtesy', and Paul, so often on the strength of two incidents (Acts 15: 39; Gal. 2: 11) thought to be a hard man, really appears in his own writings as gentle, thoughtful and tactful (14-20). The Roman church clearly needed the careful instruction in vital doctrine which has filled the letter, but, with that duty faithfully discharged with some of the most intense argument in the Bible, he turns with warmth and feeling to matters more personal (28-30, 32).

He quietly reminds them of his God-given office (16-19), and how he has worked to fulfil its obligations. The unreported ministry in Illyricum completes an arc of Gentile territory curving from Cyprus (19), and on, he hopes, to Rome and Spain. It was sure insight. Seneca and Lucan, the philosopher and poet, uncle and nephew, were active in Rome at this very time. Spain was to give Rome her greatest emperors, Trajan and Hadrian. Whether Paul reached Spain is not known. The hazardous journey to Jerusalem (25, 31), to carry the Greek goodwill offering to the church (26, 27), ended unexpectedly in Rome (Acts 21-23). If the Spanish journey took place it was after Paul's presumed acquittal.

Final Greetings

(Romans 16: 1-21)

THIS chapter gives deep insight into the social structure of the church. There was Phoebe, called a 'deacon' of the church for her services to Paul, and the bearer of the letter (1, 2), a rich woman travelling on business. Prisca (Priscilla) and her husband, Aquila, a much travelled pair, were back in Rome, with Claudius' edict now a dead letter (Acts 18: 2, 18, 14-26; 1 Cor. 16: 19; 2 Tim. 4: 19). They left Christian cells in Ephesus and Corinth.

The Roman Christians mentioned number twenty-six, several of them women. Thirteen of the names actually occur in documents and inscriptions referring to the imperial civil service ('Caesar's household'—Phil. 4: 22). Narcissus was the notorious senior officer of Claudius (11) and although Nero killed him, his 'household', or staff, was probably retained as a functioning unit in the civil service. Aristobulus was probably grandson of Herod, 'the Great' (10). He was educated in Rome, and when he died his 'household' was also probably kept intact. It may have constituted a Jewish group in both synagogue and church. Tryphaena and Tryphosa 'laboured to exhaustion' (12). Paul is writing with affectionate humour, for the names mean 'Dainty' and 'Delicate'. Is Rufus (13), the son of Simon (Mark 15: 21), a migrant to Rome by way of Antioch (Acts 11: 20)? One Nereus was chamberlain to Domitilla, a niece of Domitian. Is this the man (15)? Paul's circle send greetings (Acts 13: 1; 17: 5-9; 20: 4; 1 Cor. 1: 14; Phil. 2: 19, 20).

A doxology (25-27), containing all the chief ideas of the latter, closes this great document of Christianity. It has demanded hard thinking and searching of the heart.

THE FIRST EPISTLE OF PAUL
TO THE CORINTHIANS

Paul and the Corinthians
(1 Corinthians 1: 1–31)

WE learn little of Corinth from Acts 18: 1–18, where Luke summarises eighteen months' ministry. His main preoccupation was Gallio's judgment, that the Christians were no peril to Rome. This letter, on the other hand, written from Ephesus in A.D. 55 or 56, three or four years after the end of the Corinthian ministry, late in 52, teaches us much.

Corinth was important in Paul's strategy. It had once been one of the chief city states of Greece, a naval power, and a foe of Athens. Lucius Memmius the Roman commander had destroyed the isthmus town in 146 B.C., because of its strategic significance, and for the same reason Julius Caesar rebuilt it in 46 B.C. Now a century old, it was a nodal point of Mediterranean trade, a gateway between East and West, a cosmopolitan port where the languages and peoples of the world mingled. Like all great ports it was a vicious place, further corrupted by the carnal worship of Aphrodite on the Acrocorinthus, the 2,000 foot crag above the town.

It was a triumph to found a church there, and Corinth was reflected in its congregation. There were orthodox Jews who clung to Peter, Hellenistic Jews who may have been Apollos' following or Paul's, mistakenly dividing into factions (12, 13). There were rich folk like Phoebe, who lived on the Saronic Gulf, and perhaps Chloe (26, 11), leading men like the treasurer Erastus (Rom. 16: 23) and Crispus (14. Acts 18: 5–8), Sosthenes (1) and Stephanas (16. 16: 15). The spirit of a city can penetrate a congregation and faction was an old Greek vice (11).

There was also abroad a shallow intellectualism which Paul scorned, determined not 'to preach the gospel in philosophic terms' (17). This was no repudiation of the Areopagus address, but a demonstration of Paul's awareness of the philosophic pretensions of Corinth's very different audience. Vv. 18 to 25 are a polished sample of Paul's Greek irony which infuses four chapters. He was philosophically educated better than all of them, but was determined not to reduce Christ to a code of ethics, or to allow the resurrection to be attenuated to metaphor (11. 6: 9–20; 15: 12).

Christ, himself the Truth and the Way (John 14: 6) was his wisdom (30. 20–25), righteousness (Rom. 3: 24), sanctification (Heb. 10: 10), and redemption (Rom. 8: 23; Eph. 1: 14; 4: 30).

The Natural Man
(1 Corinthians 2: 1-16)

'NOR did I come to you', says Paul, 'with parade of speech and wisdom' (1). He came, he claims, with plain and simple language, bearing witness, not to himself but to Christ. (No man can do both at one and the same time.) He sought to be one through whom Christ spoke (1: 23). He came to Corinth a shaken man, from experiences of persecution (1 Thess. 2: 14-16; Acts 17: 5-15). Athens had also dispirited him, and his health was a problem (3. 1 Thess. 3: 7). The consequence had been some heartless hostility (1 Cor. 4: 10; 2 Cor. 10: 1-11; 12: 5), and the friendship of Aquila and Priscilla had been necessary therapy (Acts 18: 2, 3; Rom. 16: 3, 4). The return of Silas and Timothy also, with good news from Macedonia, had nerved a sensitive and discouraged man to launch into the Corinthian ministry (Acts 18: 5; 1 Thess. 3: 6-9). By this time he had marked the Corinthian taste for a gospel conformable to their pretensions (2 Tim. 4: 3), and determined on a ministry of single-minded simplicity (4, 5) with none of the sophist's and the rhetorician's arts. Those who sought such an approach revealed a simple view of 'wisdom' (6), a naïveté destined like all whims to pass. The wisdom hidden in the gospel eluded the world (7, 8), the godless (9, 14), and indeed, all those who, in all ages, have sought for truth without accepting the transforming and enlightening fact that God exists and that 'in the beginning was an Intelligence which expressed itself in Christ' (John 1: 1, 14). In folly the politicians set up the cross of Christ (8), in folly the philosophers were blind to its meaning. In both groups those deemed powerful and wise were proved fools (1: 27, 28). The Spirit of God links man with God in understanding (12, 13), and gives a sharpened apprehension which lifts man above carnality, and the confined and cabined thought, which philosophy's self-imposed restrictions, and man's dulled apprehensions, impose on the 'natural man'. There is 'something far more deeply interfused' which only those emancipated from the limitations of physical sense can grasp and enjoy (9, 10). The 'natural man' of v. 14 is unregenerate humanity at its best, and that man lacks a dimension of understanding granted to those who live by faith (Rom. 8: 5; John 15: 18-21; 1 John 4: 5). In v. 15 Paul subtly shows that he is aware of the Stoic doctrine of 'the Wise Man' —the one who understands. The Christian is such a one. He has 'the mind of Christ'.

No Other Foundation
(1 Corinthians 3: 1-23)

INDEED, Paul continues, still gently ironical, he had not been able to lead the rather opinionated Corinthians deeply into truth. He had treated them as babes in understanding (1, 2). Were they not illustrating their immaturity by their very sectarianism? (3, 4). Their teachers, as teachers do, emphasised different areas of truth but it was truth which mattered, not the nature of its sowing and its cultivation. The miracle of budding life was God's doing. The teachers were God's team of husbandmen, one in him (5–10).

Three dynamic leaders had ministered. Paul had stressed his doctrine of liberty, emancipated, as he had been from the harsh bondage of Pharisaism, and had sometimes been misrepresented (2 Pet. 3: 16). Peter's path out of Judaism had been difficult (Gal. 2: 11–14). Apollos, the Alexandrian Jew, perhaps brought to his preaching the practice of allegorising the O.T. which became a feature of Alexandrian teaching, and of which Hebrews could possibly provide a conservative example. Paul, remembering words spoken at Sychar (John 4: 36–38), is seeking to show that the divine husbandry needs many hands.

The church is like a building. Perhaps, writing to Corinth, he remembers Athens where the lovely Parthenon stood on the rock foundation of the Acropolis. On such a base, like another Ictinos, Paul had built a church. Christ held it firm (10, 11). And, perhaps remembering the myth of Philemon and Baucis, which had almost cost him his life at Lystra, and the rich temple of marble and gold which had sprung from the old couple's wattled hut, he spoke of building, divine and human, worthy and unworthy, which man can build on such firm foundation (12–15).

Corinth was conscious of its own temple. On the ridge above the agora, with a fine view down the Gulf of Corinth, stood (eight columns still stand) a temple to Apollo, the one building the Romans spared in 146 B.C. When, on the one occasion in his life Paul was checked as he began to speak (Acts 18: 14), and turned scarce believing from Gallio's bema, he saw that temple, high against the sky. Does he picture it as he writes vv. 16, 17? It was clean, prominent, dedicated to one deity. It was worthily and richly built of solid stone. Corinth too commonly built out of the rough and ephemeral notions of conceited men (18–21). V. 19 neatly quotes Job 5: 13 and any well-read Corinthian would see in v. 20 a whimsical saying of Socrates. The Delphic oracle rightly pronounced him the wisest man, not for his wisdom but because he was the only man prepared to admit that his 'wisdom' was nothing. It is the vice of shallow philosophy that it breeds pride. Humility is the prerequisite of all virtue (21–23).

The Nicolaitans Appear
(1 Corinthians 4: 1–20)

THE theme continues. The apostles were simple servants of Christ, responsible only to God for passing on the inner truths of Christ ('mysteries'). God only was their judge (1–3). His own conscience is clear, but it is God who passes the final verdict (4) and certainly no self-appointed and premature Corinthian tribunal (5). The last court awaits.

With sad irony Paul turns to the

Corinthians' woeful overestimation of their own attainments (Rev. 3: 17). The imagery of wealth and royalty was familiar among the Stoics ever since the philosopher Diogenes, whose tomb was in Corinth, had taught them to say: 'I am rich, I am a king' (7, 8). The Stoics claimed in their arrogance, to provide a watching heaven with a 'spectacle' of virtue. Spectacle, indeed, says Paul, such as we apostles provide, men led to death at the rear of some pagan triumphal procession.

The immensely learned Paul endured for Christ's sake to be called a fool (Acts 17: 32; 26: 24). But they, forsooth, were 'men of sense' (KJV 'wise' 10. It is the word of 2 Cor. 11: 19), who, by their adaptations of Christianity to suit the pagan thinking of the world, escaped the offence of the cross (Gal. 5: 11). We are probably meeting the forerunners of 'the Nicolaitans'. (Rev. 2: 6. Cf. 2 Pet. 2: 12–22; Jude 8–9). Such was the daily lot of good men for Christ's sake, deprived (11), overworked and scorned (12), 'the dirt and the dross, and the dust and the scum of the earth' (13).

Irony done, Paul softens and appeals. Like Greek children, they had their 'pedagogues', those household slaves who took boys back and forth to school, and they were acting like wayward children who prefer such menials to parents (14, 15. Gal. 3: 24, 25). He begs them to return to love (16). He probably intended Timothy and Erastus (probably a Corinthian, Rom. 16: 23) to visit Corinth after Macedonia (17. Acts 19: 22). And he, too, was fully intending to come and have

certain questions out, face to face (18–20).

Scandal in the Church
(1 Corinthians 4: 21—5: 13)

CALVIN rightly said that 4: 21 should belong to 5. There was notorious scandal in Corinth, which not only the O.T. (Lev. 18: 7, 8) but moral pagans scorned (1)—and this grave tolerance lived amid the pretensions of their false philosophy (2). It called for action, on grounds already made clear (9), and Paul could judge the case out of hand, with no further enquiry (3). Such a sinner could only be excommunicated. The unrepentant sinner is to return to the realm of Satan, outside the church, where death reigns, and in the hope that the shock of disgrace, and the natural consequences of such flagrant sin, might ultimately save the man's soul through repentance (5). No more can be made of v. 5.

Evil is contagious, and Corinth's complacency shocking (6). Sin so virulent could permeate the mass. Cleanse it out, therefore, leaving the whole church clean, as was the house after the pre-paschal purging (Exod. 12: 15; 13: 7). Paul develops the imagery of the symbolic Jewish Passover (7). Christ is now the lamb, and in the face of his sacrifice all the old creeping corruption, the leaven of the new covenant must be purged (8). The company of evil men cannot be avoided without avoiding the multitude of humankind (10). Such corruption, however, can and must be removed from the brotherhood of Christ (11).

God will judge the pagan. But let the church judge and expel those who presume to belong to it, but live in ungodliness (12, 13).

The Church in the World
(1 Corinthians 6: 1-20)

THE world had too deeply infiltrated the church in Corinth. The old Greek vice of 'stasis' or 'faction', which had bedevilled Greek politics all through history had appeared in Corinth, a community perilously conditioned for it (ch. 3). Speculation, another habit of the Greek mind, was corrupting truth (ch. 4). Moral looseness, indigenous to the city of Aphrodite, was a scandal (ch. 5). And now the Greek proneness to litigiousness was making Christians an object of shame, Christians destined to judge the fallen angels (2, 3). Surely such men of wisdom as they claimed to be, could keep the differences of Christians within the enlightened arbitration of their own community (4, 5) and avoid the shame of strife in court before the watching world (6). Even Plato (Rep. 3) refers in scorn to men who go to court over money or property, matters unworthy of a free, good man. Better suffer loss than such reproach (7, 8).

Corinth was notoriously immoral. The name of the town had become a prurient parable in the first century. Paul must have found the evil reputation of the place well-merited, for it was from Corinth that he wrote two of his most searing descriptions of the contemporary scene (1 Thess. 4: 3-7; Rom. 1: 18-32). They, the members of

Corinth's divided, contentious, pretentious, morally damaged church, were brands plucked from such burning (9-11). It remained to walk worthily of the new life (19. 2: 12; 3: 16; Rom. 5: 5; 8: 2, 9). The teaching of the libertines (Rev. 2: 20-22) was also lifting its sinister head, the pernicious notion that sin on the carnal level and the indulgence of the body's appetites could not mar the purity of the redeemed soul. Stoicism, at one low level, had encouraged such heresy (13).

It provokes Paul to one of his great utterances. The body was made sacred in Christ (14) and through the indwelling of God's spirit. He remembers again the haunting sight, familiar to every Corinthian, of the clean temple on the ridge above the town. The divine guest is dishonoured in the body's misuse (15, 16). The daily temptation of every man must be resisted (18). The body is not a tool but a vital part of us. Immorality was sacrilege (19). Like emancipated slaves Christ has bought us (20). Our bodies are his to use as he will (Rom. 6: 11-13). Part of the Corinthian sin was acceptance and elaboration of the Greek view, that the body was the perishable container of the immortal spirit. Paul propounds the Christian view that the body is the abiding vehicle of the spirit.

Marriage
(1 Corinthians 7: 1-40)

PAUL now turns to specific questions addressed to him by the Corinthians (1). The first concerned marriage, and, at the opposite pole from the libertines of the last chapter, was an ascetic group, probably those who said: 'I am of Christ' (1: 12), who were teaching that marriage was sin. First observing that celibacy is not wrong (1), Paul recognises the strength of bodily instincts and desires, and lays down some rules for happy and balanced physical relationships within marriage (2–5). This advice, he maintains, is his own Christian view. He had found no clear directions in the oral tradition (6), as he did in the case of divorce and separation (10). No man, naturally eager for marriage, should coerce himself into celibacy on the principles of asceticism (7). He himself felt able to carry on unmarried, and thus found, perhaps, freedom to concentrate on his task (33), and perhaps less of a load of responsibility in coming trials (26). Some, unmarried or widowed, may be able to take the same course (8), but if it was physically burdensome, marriage was a remedy (9). All this is clearly stated.

The Lord had not specifically commanded any firm course of action in cases where Christians found themselves bound by marriage to non-Christians. That is why Paul specifically limits the command he lays down to his own personal authority. He is in no way disclaiming inspiration, nor betraying doubt of his competence to legislate. The gospels were not yet written, and he is merely underlining the fact that he is speaking outside the oral tradition of Christ's remembered words. The rules (10–16) are eminently sensible. If a harmonious marriage exists, let it continue.

This leads to general advice (17–24). Paul deprecates social disruption. Let converts accept the pattern of society as they find it, add no ordinances to the practice of their faith (18, 19), and accept servitude or emancipation as their lot might be (20, 21). For the slaves, Paul gives a Christian tinge to doctrines of spiritual freedom already promulgated by the Stoics (22, 23). Epictetus, a Stoic born about the time Paul was writing, was to say much about physical and spiritual slavery. Such discussion was already in the air.

Vv. 25 to 40 read differently in KJV and NEB. From the former the impression is that 'virgins' are daughters of the household. What should a man do? Give them in marriage or keep them unmarried? In view of apocalyptic disaster against which the Lord had warned, and in view of catastrophic change which perceptive minds could see looming, might not the fewest worldly trammels be best? NEB seems to envisage a man and woman living in celibate partnership (36, NEB), an impracticable and unnecessary practice for which there is some evidence from the early church. Paul envisages the breakdown of such ascetic vows, and absolves those who abandon them from sin. The KJV is probably the truer rendering, though it must be admitted that 'daughters' instead of 'virgins' in v. 25 might have removed all doubt. Corinth, to be sure, was a place of odd practices. But for Paul's letter we should have had no knowledge of baptism 'for the dead', for the formalities of the Lord's Supper, or concerning the ecstatic phenomenon of glossolalia or 'speaking in tongues', apparently the emotional release discovered by the self-repressed ascetic sect.

Idol-meat

(1 Corinthians 8 and 10: 23–33)

THE second question concerned the propriety of eating meat from the pagan altars, a perquisite of the priests and the chief supply for 'the shambles', the butchers' shops (10: 25), the ruins of which may still be seen in the agora of Corinth. The Jerusalem circular had caused a Christian problem here (Acts 15: 20), for Christians were normal men and women and shrank from unnecessary rigour in social intercourse, and continual confrontation with the secular world around them.

The Corinthians who believed in liberty had been, it seems, irritatingly dogmatic. Paul does not like 'puffed up' people. He is the only N.T. writer to use this word, and save for one context (Col. 2: 18) he applies it only to Corinthians. Love does not produce an arrogant contempt for the less emancipated (1–3). Paul admitted that the question was decided in principle by the fundamental truth that God was one, and that the Corinthian 'idols' had neither existence nor meaning. And so, sacrifice to such creatures of myth and superstition was without validity for good or ill (4–6. 10: 19, 26). The meat contained no peril, and suffered no change. On the other hand there were those who could not lay clear hold on such emancipation. There was

lurking fear. Conscience, in such brethren, was active, and to violate conscience is a sin (7. 10: 23–30). For the sake of such 'weaker' brethren, those who genuinely see no harm in such meat should unselfishly restrict their liberty (8, 9). For such reasons Paul has restricted his own liberty (9: 1–22; 10: 33—11: 1). 'Is a weaker brother to be ruined,' he asks, 'because you claim insight?' (10–12). This would be sin indeed (12, 13). The final verse is an inviolable principle which, if honestly and unselfishly regarded in modern society, might give strength to the church. The Corinthian problem is continually with us.

As for buying meat in the market, or when dining at an unbeliever's table, the Christian need not enquire concerning the origin of the meat, but, if the fact is pointedly brought to his notice, a challenge emerges, and the Christian must make his stand (10: 25–30).

Paul's Apostleship

(1 Corinthians 9: 1–27)

THE question of idol-meat appears to have been bound up with a doubt about Paul's authority, perhaps among those who, certainly without that apostle's sanction, regarded themselves as 'Peter's party' (1: 12; 2 Pet. 3: 16). The arguments aimed at diminishing his apostolic standing may perhaps have pointed to his liberal attitude about idol-meat (4), his celibacy (5), and his abstention from the right to maintenance as an apostle, a sacrifice he shared with Barnabas (6). The right to maintenance was embedded in Scripture. It was, says Paul, natural law that a man be kept by those he serves (7–10). It is intrinsic justice (11). It was Levitical practice (13). It was Christ's command (14) implicit in the appointment of the apostles (Matt. 10: 9–13). Paul had simply refrained from claiming this privilege (12, 15). He had his reasons, perhaps related to the critical environment and the hostile scrutiny of Corinth (Acts 18: 3). He applied the same principle in Ephesus (Acts 20: 33–35). He varied the practice at Philippi (Phil. 4: 15). It was his business, his right, to accept or to refuse. It in no way diminished his authority, whatever he chose to do (18). He adapted his freedom to the environment, acting socially, and proclaiming the truth in a manner best adapted to those he sought to win (19–23). His sermons at Lystra and in Athens, his judgments on marriage and idolmeat, Romans 9 to 11, equally with his speeches in court, all variously illustrate vv. 20–22. Most resolute of men (Phil. 3: 7–14), he became 'for the gospel's sake' (23) the most versatile. He was human, and on two occasions his versatility may have betrayed him into inconsistency (Acts 16: 3 and 7: 18, 19 above) and catastrophe (Acts 21: 20–28).

The Corinthians hosted the Isthmian games, one of the four athletic festivals. They knew the rigorous rules which governed participation—the regimen of training, its austerities and prohibitions. It was stern discipline, and can a man do less for Christ than an athlete did for a crown of parsley? (25). 'Castaway' (27. KJV) is misleading.

'The fire shall try every man's work,' says 3: 13. Here a negative adjective from the same verb is used—'lest I should myself be tried and found wanting'.

The Christian among Pagans
(1 Corinthians 10: 1–22)

PAUL now turns to a typically rabbinical illustration. Perhaps he is showing his goodwill to the 'party of Apollos', who, tutored by an Alexandrian, may have found such allegorical exposition of the O.T. satisfying. Sacraments, he is saying, are no safeguard if life is inconsistent (1). He finds a parallel in Israel, symbolically baptised at the Red Sea (2), fed with manna and God-given water, as Christians, at the Lord's table, ate the symbols of Christ crucified (3, 4), Israel, who yet sinned, and were punished (5–8). 'All' is repeated five times (1–4), yet how few qualified for the Promised Land. It is the figure of 9: 24–27, transferred to a Hebrew context. Paul again identifies the church with Israel (Rom. 4: 1; 11–18; 11: 17–25; Gal. 3: 7, 29; Phil. 3: 3). What happened in one historical context can happen in another (9–11). The fall of Israel was due to the very temptations which faced Corinth—idolatry and immorality, daily experiences not to be treated with overconfidence (12), but with trust in God, able, in all circumstances, to save (13). But, like Joseph, let men avoid the time and the occasion (14. Gen. 39: 1–13).

Having mentioned the Lord's Supper (3, 4) Paul is prompted to speak of the guild feasts. The trade guilds of the ancient world were not trade-unions, but societies of craftsmen, employers and employees (Acts 19: 24, 25). The custom was to meet periodically in the shrine of some patron deity and it was no doubt economically disadvantageous for a Christian tradesman to sever fellowship with those of his calling. This was an agonising dilemma for Christians. And yet, says Paul, how could they compromise, both because of the 'weaker brother' (8: 10) and because attendance at the guild feast meant passive participation in the worship of the pagan deity involved. To 'flee from idolatry' (14), demanded abstinence. It was to 'provoke the Lord' (22) to drink his cup, and take part in idol worship. The Nicolaitan group apparently did so (Rev. 2: 20) forty years after Paul wrote, thirty years after Peter and Jude had reinforced his words with vigour (2 Pet. 2: 1–22; Jude 4, 12, 13).

Propriety in Worship
(1 Corinthians 11: 1–34)

PAUL'S authority rested, he readily testifies, only on his own loyalty to Christ. A Roman Cynic philosopher who was in Corinth around this time, one Demetrius of Sounion, is described by his friend Seneca as being 'not only a teacher of the truth, but a witness to it'. So Paul sought to be (1). With this word of exhortation and of thanks (2) Paul proceeds to another matter —etiquette in worship.

Plutarch says 'usually women cover their heads and men uncover them when they go into a house'. Valerius Maximus speaks strongly of the impropriety of women out of doors with uncovered head. Vv. 4 and 5 seem to relate to these customs. Custom must be observed when taking part in worship (6). A head uncovered is as shocking, he says, as a close-cropped head, in a woman. One of the comedies of Menander, of which the scene is set in Corinth, has for plot an outrage done to a girl by a jealous lover. He cut her hair. The priestesses, courtesan attendants of Aphrodite, went bare headed into the streets of Corinth. Some of the women in the church were converts from among them. It behoved them to show that they were changed. The Jews in the congregation had also to be considered, on the principles already enunciated, and in their opinion, based on the priority of creation, women were required to demonstrate their dependent position by covered head, and to show this in the sight of God ('because of the angels' (10) is probably a euphemistic way of saying this). The covering veil recognised man's 'power' or 'authority' (7–10). Vv. 11 and 12 reassert the Christian position. Paul to this point is reinforcing Jewish custom for the sake of unity in the church. The Gentiles must, in respect for Jewish conviction, conform. Vv. 14, 15 are difficult to interpret without wider knowledge of contemporary Corinthian custom. Greek men were not averse to long hair generally, but it may have been a sign of effeminacy in that place and time for a man to go long-haired, and equally of masculinity in a woman to be shorn. 'If anyone wishes to dispute this ruling,' Paul concludes brusquely, 'I can only say that nowhere do we observe this custom' (16).

He turns now in consternation and rebuke to what he has heard of the common meal. The Christians met to share the fellowship of a meal, as part of which bread was broken and wine taken in memory of Christ. A disgraceful situation had developed. Groups sat apart. Perhaps the groups of 1: 12 preferred their own company. Perhaps, in the formidable mixture of the Corinthian church, rich despised poor (18). 'Heresies' (19. KJV) must mean the 'divisions' (18. KJV)—and both mean 'cliques'. 'I suppose it is inevitable,' he continues ironically, 'if only to separate good from bad' (19). Such a gathering cannot eat the Lord's supper (20). There was no waiting for the poorer or less well-provided (slaves and workmen) to arrive. The first comers went to work (21, 33) and drunkenness was not unknown. Let such impatient people eat at home, and honour the fellowship meal (22). The essential part of the meal was the holy celebration, and Paul quotes the oral tradition (23–26). Familiarity had bred contempt. Disorder, crudity and discourtesy at the common meal made participants unfit to handle sacred things, respect holy memories or reverently to treat the symbols of the Lord's death. That is why the two meals were later separated. To bring carnality to such a moment was dire sin (27). Let a man cleanse his heart (28), or he will demonstrate that he knows not Christ (29). Paul

appears to have discerned some difference in physical health between disciplined Christians and the less self-controlled who crassly offended in spiritual matters (30). Let such affliction lead to self appraisement (31) and recognition of divine chastisement (32).

The Body of the Church
(1 Corinthians 12: 1–31)

THE Corinthian church was a frighteningly mingled group, ascetics, self-styled philosophers, disciplined Jews, undisciplined Greeks, liberal thinkers, anxious conservatives, of every social stratum, perhaps of many nations. How was such a diverse congregation to be brought, understandingly, efficiently to function as a whole. Paul recalls his metaphor of the body (Rom. 12: 4, 5) and expands it lucidly. He may have known Plato's use of the same imagery for the ideally articulated state in his *Republic* (5: 462), where v. 26 especially is anticipated. A famous incident in Roman history, the speech of Menenius Agrippa in 494 B.C. to the dissident plebeians, and known in English literature by a fine rendering in Shakespeare's *Coriolanus*, could also have been known in Corinth.

Paul wanted corporate unity among the social, ethnic and sectarian groups in the divided, troubled church. To be sure, their gifts were as varied as the diverse functions of the body's organs (4–11. 12: 31). A body functions healthily when all its parts, visible and invisible, function sufficiently, and not excessively, in harmony, and not discord, each fulfilling its purpose in prominence or in obscurity, each essential in its rôle, each vital. Any close consideration of the body's functioning, of the pathology of disease and the bases of health, will show how rich this imagery is. We are Christ's members, his hands and feet, his voice ... and each single Christian has his part to play. All have one gift or another. The absurdity of specialised members of the body invading alien roles is too often reproduced in the corporate functioning of the church.

Two matters call for attention. The whole subject arises from some comment from Corinth. As pagans some had known the frenzied cries of various Dionysiac cults (2). Perhaps they had heard shouts of blasphemy from the synagogue next door (Acts 18: 7), such denials as Paul had, in his rôle as a persecutor forced Christians to utter (Acts 26: 11). It is even possible that some, given to the ecstatic phenomenon of 'speaking in tongues', had dishonoured Christ by their words. Paul gives a simple test (4).

This leads to the question of the nature of 'tongues'. The problem is obscure. The Corinthian phenomenon is not that of Pentecost, itself not clear (see comments on Acts 2). Rarely, in Luke's story, the phenomenon of ecstatic speech is associated with conversion. In Corinth some groups seem to have found emotional release by such unintelligible speech—a phenomenon to be widely paralleled in the records of religious experience, Christian and pagan. The community was multilingual. All the languages of the Mediterranean were spoken in Corinth. Perhaps, in that undisciplined church, some were seeking to lead devotions in the tongue of their first religious utterance. Certain it is that Paul, not thinking it wise to repress the phenomenon, goes far to derate it. It is last of the 'gifts' (10, 28), confined (30), ephemeral (13: 8), not useful (14: 2–22). And it is worth noting, in view of the unnatural and unscriptural importance given to certain phenomena of similar nature today, that 'tongues' are not found in the gospels or in the circle of Christ, not in most of Acts, in no other epistle of Paul but the first letter to Corinth, in the writings of no other Apostle or the three other contributors to the N.T.—James, Jude, and the author of Hebrews. And finally, says Paul, set all this aside and I will show you 'a way of excellence', a path to unity, peace, tolerance, by-passing all trivialities, heresies, schisms, all else which troubled and divided.

'Ah, Love, could you and I with Him conspire . . .'

(1 Corinthians 13)

A way of excellence! Could all argument but be cast aside, and Corinth fused, mankind be fused to unity in that one Christlike glow, how much would vanish which divides, afflicts, torments and baffles. Indeed, without love, what are we? All we say, proclaim, demand, is in God's ears like the blaring brass and the clashing cymbals of some Eastern cult, the priests of Cybele or Isis cavorting down the street (1).

To see deep into the meaning of God's truth, to know the Word from end to end, even sturdily to trust (2), to dole out substance for the dispossessed, to face the very fire, what are all these without the gentleness of Christ's pity, the warmth of his concern, the godlike treasure—Love?

'Love is long-tempered, kind, not envious, no braggart, not swelled with conceit, not unmannerly (4, 5). Love is no stickler for her rights, not sharp-tempered, not mindful of evil (5). Love does not rejoice over wrongdoing and shares in the joy of the truth (6), is always tolerant, always trustful, always hopeful, always patient (7). Love never stumbles. Inspired teaching, ecstatic utterance, doctrine—these shall pass (8), for knowledge and teaching are both imperfect (9), and imperfection shall give way to perfection (10), as immaturity vanishes as we grow (11). It is like looking in the polished bronze of those mirrors, for which Corinth was well known. The image is not like the reality (12). We know partially but shall know indeed, even as we have always been known. Faith, hope, love, to be sure these stand firm. But the greatest is love.'

There is no need to say more. Consider the clutter of Corinth's faults exposed to light so luminous.

Tongues

(1 Corinthians 14: 1-40)

THE very small place the Corinthian phenomenon of tongues occupy in the N.T. has already been mentioned in comments on ch. 12.

After love, says Paul, those gifts should be sought which uplift the church, notably the inspired preaching called prophecy which communicated divine truth before the N.T. took shape (1)—a gift so much more worthy of sanctified ambition than 'the language of ecstasy' (NEB), which, while giving the speaker emotional satisfaction, did nothing for the church.

In rabbinical fashion adapting the words of Isaiah 28: 11, 12 ('In strange language, by the lips of foreigners, I will speak to this people'), Paul leaves unsolved the mystery of what 'tongues' actually were. It could have been some rapturous soliloquy, after the manner of the oracle of Delphi, whose incoherent cries the priests professed to interpret. That phenomenon is common through all the history of religion, pagan and Christian. It occurred among the Huguenots and many other sects. Strange and meaningless second and third century papyri seem to contain examples. Or was it, as v. 21 might indicate, the intrusion into worship of one of the many languages common in cosmopolitan Corinth. No discipline controlled participants in that disordered church (23, 26, 40). Perhaps the phenomenon was not homogeneous including both the language of emotional rapture, and the wilful use of a less commonly known language.

To what purpose? What use, Paul asks, would he have been had he come to preach without lucid and intelligible speech—like an inexpert bugler, unable to sound the notes his cohort would understand (6–9)? For proper communication one must not speak like a foreigner (10–17. 'Barbarian' is 'foreigner'. Acts 28: 2). V. 18 could mean simply that Paul was an accomplished linguist—the popular Aramaic to the crowd in the temple court, classical Hebrew to the Sanhedrin, competent Greek laced with quotation to the Areopagus, Latin to the centurion and before Caesar. In a dangerous situation, no miraculous gift of Lycaonian Gallic was granted him (Acts 14: 11). Nor need v. 19 suggest more than that, in private prayer, he used those abbreviations and ejaculations mentioned in Romans 8: 26—'agonised longings which cannot find words' (JBP).

Along with a vehement mysticism, Paul's mind, as Gilbert Murray put it, had 'a clean antiseptic quality'. Some had obviously asked him to suppress the 'tongues', but he hesitated to divide further that sadly riven congregation. He gently steers then to more worthy desires (39), and is concerned lest the chance outsider, witnessing the disorderly scene, should think the Christians mad (23)—while the same visitor, his attention caught by the penetrating words of prophecy (25, 26), might come to faith. If, then, there must be unintelligible speech, let it be limited (27), and not even used, if there is no one, either familiar with the language or the user's mind, to translate (28). 'Have only two or three speakers while the rest weigh what is said' (29). There must be courtesy, order, self-control (30), taking proper turns (31). 'The spirit of a true preacher is under his control' (32).

God is honoured by order, dishonoured by indecent confusion (33, 40). Vv. 34, 35 set in sequence and context suggest that it was the women in Corinth, some of sombre and uncultured background, who were causing some confusion. Paul's ruling on these matters had been challenged. Hence the sharp rebuke (36. 'You challenge this rule? Pray, did God's word start from you?' Moff).

Risen Indeed
(1 Corinthians 15: 1–58)

SUMMING up, Paul repeats his message. It was the gospel he had received, committed to the church (1–4). He stresses the historic fact of the resurrection which some in Corinth, with their philosophical pretensions, were turning into metaphor (5–12). A philosophy, no doubt, can arise out of a theology, but sound theology is born of revelation, not philosophy.

The passage (5–8) which stresses the physical fact of Christ's resurrection, is the first account of the resurrection to be written, antedating the gospel narratives, and containing material not recorded by the evangelists. Peter never described his private meeting with the Lord (5), nor has the larger gathering of witnesses been elsewhere described (6). Paul had, however, heard their testimony. Some were still alive.

Then, in a passionately emphasised statement, he stressed the vital place of the resurrection in Christian belief (12–19). Without that certainty there is no assurance of survival (20–23). Wretched, indeed, is man if this tiny experience in place and time betrays all his aspirations and makes a mock of faith (19). The last enemy must die (26), and the consummation in Christ, now held by faith (21-25), must become historic reality (27, 28). Why otherwise endure what he and his endured? (2 Cor. 1: 8-9; Acts 20: 19). People like the group who undermined such essential truth are to be avoided. They contaminate, says Paul, quoting the Greek comedian, Menander (33. 'Bad company - ruins a good character'). Wake up, shun sin, show sense (34).

True, some might wonder how the resurrection can take place. He remembers the symbolism of Eleusis to which the Lord refers, speaking to Greeks (John 12: 24), the grain of wheat which dies and is transformed. He passed through Eleusis on his way to Corinth. The memory is alive, as he writes, and the Lord's words, not to be written down for almost forty years, come into his mind. They were part of the church's tradition. It was, he says, something like the miracle of the springing corn (35-50). In apocalyptic language, he then seeks to grapple with the problem of those still alive at the moment of consummation, the coming of the Lord (51-53). And in lyrical conclusion, he triumphs over defeated death (54-57).

Concluding Words

(1 Corinthians 16: 1-24)

CONCLUDING, Paul turns to the collection for the impoverished Jerusalem church on which he had set his heart. It was to be a demonstration to that conservative group of Gentile benevolence (1). He establishes a mode of giving (2). The N.T., in fact, gives few specific directions on giving. God owns all. Christians are bought with a price (6: 20; 7: 23), and their generosity or sacrifice is not ordered, prescribed or reduced to law. Tithing is not a regulation, save it be adopted by those who so desire, as a chosen method. The guiding principle is in v. 2—'as God has prospered'. The rest is governed by love, liberty and responsibility. Paul proposed to provide an escort for the gift (3) and if necessary accompany it (5). He outlines his plans. Opportunity is wide (6–9. 2 Cor. 2: 12; Col. 4: 3; Rev. 3: 8).

There are pleasant glimpses of Timothy, who stood in need of support, a young man, gentle and not over confident (10, 11), and Apollos, with whom Paul sensed no rivalry or difference (12). He hints that Stephanas, who had filled in gaps in Paul's knowledge of the Corinthian church (17), and mightily encouraged him (18), might well be recognised as leader (16). Greetings follow (19, 20), including the salutation which the church later abandoned (20. Rom. 16: 16; 1 Pet. 5: 14). With a flush of indignation Paul remembers the reported blasphemy, either shockingly within the church, or from the synagogue hard by, and commits the sinners to judgment—'anathema' (12: 3; Rom. 9: 3; Gal. 1: 8, 9). And then, as though gently touching the 'tongues' phenomenon with one word, he adds in Aramaic: 'Maranatha'—'Our Lord, come' (RSV).

THE SECOND EPISTLE OF PAUL TO THE CORINTHIANS

To Corinth Again
(2 Corinthians 1: 1-24)

THE letter contains more autobiographical material than any other letter of Paul, but it is difficult to fit it all into the recorded pattern. Luke can abbreviate ruthlessly. Acts 20: 3 implies a three months' stay in Corinth (12: 14 and 13: 1) but some believe that this second disciplinary visit was made during Paul's long stay in Ephesus. Corinth was little more than a week's sail away. Paul's apostolic authority had been questioned immediately on his departure (1 Cor. 9: 1-3), possibly by the 'Petrine' party, and the challenge was not quenched. This and the moral problems of the church occasioned the second visit, which itself seems not to have stabilised the situation.

Hence perhaps a lost letter, mentioned in 1 Corinthians 5: 9. At this point, Titus may have exercised a healing ministry for he returned to Paul with news of progress. Whether Titus' report produced this letter (2 Corinthians) cannot be said. Nor is it clear whether the letter of 2: 3, 4, 9 and 7: 12 is the lost letter, the first epistle, or even the second letter, or chapters 10 to 13 of the second letter. Several dogmatic cases have been made on all these arguments. The only solid evidence is that manuscript tradition implies the unity of the second letter to Corinth, and that, allowing for changes of mood, or improved reports modifying the approach, the letter can be read as a unity.

Timothy's visit (1 Cor. 16: 10, 11) had possibly not produced results, and this may have made Paul's brief disciplinary visit necessary. Hence the association of Timothy with himself (1). 'Apostles' included more than the immediate Twelve (1 Thess. 2: 6; 2 Cor. 8: 23). In vv. 2-7 Paul's vital and absorbing beliefs emerge to colour and reanimate the conventional greetings with which an ancient letter began. Christian convictions have a way of penetrating the commonest things of life.

In vv. 5 and 6 Paul touches the deep truth of Colossians 1: 24. He saw the burden of his pain and sorrow as something akin to the passion of Christ. It was an honour to be accepted (Mark 10: 39; Gal. 2: 20; Phil. 3: 10). Christ's suffering was, none the less, different from the Christian's pain (1 Cor. 1: 13). Paul's own trials (8, 9) are probably hidden in the list of 11: 23-27. Or perhaps it is contained in 1 Corinthians 15: 32 which probably does not refer to Acts 19. He had been wondrously rescued (9–11), the fruit of prayer (12).

Paul claims that he has always approached the Corinthians with simple sincerity. He had no mask. No one need 'read between the lines' in his letters (13. Moff.). He wrote to be understood. Nor was he fickle (17). He had reasons under God for not visiting Corinth on his way to Macedonia and for postponing his visit until his return from the north (1 Cor. 16: 5). 'God is faithful. His message I passed on, not a message of ambiguity (18). The Christ we have preached was not ambiguous. He was God's affirmation (19), like all that which God offers in him (20), God who has given us security (21), and guaranteed us (22). I assure you, I did not bypass Corinth to spare you (23)—not that I seek to override you and your faith. Your happiness I would promote' (24).

Paul's Tenderness

(2 Corinthians 2: 1–17)

THERE is much of Paul's gentleness and compassion in this chapter. His special visit to Corinth and his letter of rebuke had cost him much mental suffering, and he wanted, if he had to visit them again, to do so under happier circumstances. Only his love for them had imposed the duty of rebuke, and such words, between those who should only give each other joy, were painful indeed (1–4).

The KJV makes heavy weather of this epistle, and a modern version should be used. Consider v. 5 which

KJV obscures badly. 'If the behaviour of a certain person has caused you distress, it does not mean so much that he has injured me, but to some extent (I do not wish to exaggerate) he has injured all of you' (JBP). This person was either the offender of 1 Corinthians 5: 1–5, or a ringleader of an anti-Pauline faction.

Paul had insisted on punishment, but in such a way that it should not preclude repentance and readmission to fellowship. The discipline demanded was a test of their obedience (9) but punishment was not vengeance but correction, and Paul now urges them to cherish and forgive the penitent offender. He had required him to be given over to Satan (1 Cor. 5: 5) but not for the destruction of his soul (11). If they should forgive, he too forgave (10). Here is the 'binding' and 'loosing' of Matthew 18: 18.

So anxious was he over this that he left demanding opportunities in Troas, and went to meet Titus in Macedonia to hear his report a few days earlier. Titus' route to Troas would take him north from Corinth to Philippi and down the Via Egnatia to Neapolis, and then by ship to Troas (Acts 16: 11, 12). He was now relieved and triumphed with Christ, who 'uses us to spread the perfume of his knowledge' (that is 'the knowledge of him'). This is not a tangled metaphor as some make it. Christ has won a victory and rides like a commander. His faithful share it all. The incense of his presence pervades. To God Christians are a sweet presence, as also to their fellows. If the savour revolts the world they are like

Goethe's Mephistopheles, who found the angels' song 'intolerable jangling'.

The Splendour of God
(2 Corinthians 3: 1–18)

THE letter of commendation was a common custom in both pagan and Christian circles in the ancient world. Romans 16 is an example, introducing Phoebe. The last verses of the preceding chapter (15–17), Paul says, looked like such a testimonial (1). He needed no such introduction to Corinth (1–4). Their own changed lives were Paul's commendation to Corinth. And Christ's commendation is written on the living hearts of men (3).

Lest any should still interpret his words as self-praising, he hastens to add that he was not confident in his own resources (5). God had made him minister of Christ's new covenant (1 Cor. 11: 25), that contract between God and man first sealed in the Mosaic law, and renewed in Christ. The old covenant was a written document (Exod. 24: 1–8), rules and regulations, not a living spirit in the heart (6). The law was an instrument of death (Rom. 5: 20; 7: 9; 8: 2) for it engendered a sense of sin, a force which killed and condemned. Christ made alive. He came not to destroy, but to fulfil. It would seem that Paul was anxious over an intrusion of Judaism into the Corinthian church.

Yet the glory of God was in the law, with its historic asservations of sin and of righteousness. It enlivened Moses' face (Exod. 34: 30),

a transient splendour like that of a lamp before the rising of the sun. It is human, and not always wrong, to cling to the old and reject the new. When God reveals a greater good such conservatism is folly (1 Cor. 13: 12). If the covenant which condemns was glorious, how much more glorious the relationship which acquits (7–11).

With utter frankness then let such splendour be revealed. Moses veiled his face, and in rabbinical fashion Paul suggests that such a veiling hides the true meaning of the law from the Jew (12–15). In Christ we see God unveiled (16), receive with forgiveness liberty (17), and a new life in him, not bound by regulation but constrained by love. And we are mirrors which reflect the glory of the Lord (18). The difficulty of the passage arises from Paul's sustaining of the imagery of God's splendour, in the law, on Moses' face, in Christ, in Christians.

The Invincible Spirit
(2 Corinthians 4: 1–18)

PAUL insists that he has a God-given ministry (1), not countenancing licence as some, twisting his doctrine of liberty, alleged (2. 2 Pet. 3: 16), nor using Scripture with subtle manipulation. Only self-willed rejection of Christ's good news hides or obscures the truth he speaks (3). To cherish evil, and follow Satan, dims the understanding. Truth comes to those only who diligently seek it; a self-chosen judgment (4. Acts 28: 25–27) lies on those who wilfully shut the mind. Paul uses a phrase of Christ, not yet recorded (John 12:31; 14:30; 16:11). He uses it again in Ephesians 2:2. It is probable that 'Deliver us from the evil one' is the correct translation of Matthew 6:13.

V. 5 is one to be solemnly remembered. No man can exalt Christ and himself at the same time. He based his gospel not on the blaze of light on the Damascus road (6) but, picking up a theme from the last chapter (3:7), on God envisaged in the splendour of Christ. He, Paul, carried the treasure of such knowledge in a frail and ravaged body (10:1, 10; 11:6; 12:7), like the earthern jars in which precious treasures were hidden. A decade later, down by the Dead Sea, a community of Jews were so to conceal their scrolls.

Hence his unconquerable soul. Life and evil could not harm the immortal part of him. (8-11. 1 Col. 24). 'We are always facing death, but this means you know more and more of life' (12. JBP). Our faith is like that mentioned in the Psalms (106:10). 'I so speak because I believe it to be true, and know that since Christ rose from death, so shall we (13, 14). I suffer this for you, so that as God's abundant grace spreads more widely, so too may spread the gratitude of those who receive it (15). That is why we battle on, physically bearing the marks of the conflict, but eternally renewed in spirit (16). Our present troubles are shortlived, but build up eternal blessedness.' His language becomes rhythmical as he seeks to turn the readers' attention to the true realities of the unseen world, and away from the transient, the passing – the things of what C. S. Lewis calls 'the Shadowlands'. The thought is Platonic.

God was in Christ
(2 Corinthians 5:1–21)

LAUNCHED on the theme of the transience of life and the body's fragility, Paul speaks of the taking down of the earthly tent (1). The tent was a Hebrew symbol for the passing and the temporary (John 1:14, where the phrase means 'camped among us'; Heb. 11:9; 2 Pet. 1:14). The Pythagorean philosophers used the same figure—'the tenement house', 'the earthen jar' (4:7). The body, he felt, was too narrow a habitation for the illimitable aspirations of the soul, the vast outreaching, the wide desires which the weakness of the body mocks by its limitations. He wants to be clothed, he continues, changing the metaphor from tent to robe, with his 'resurrection body', the heavenly reality he sought to explain in 1 Corinthians 15. It is not the nakedness of death the Christian seeks, but the robing of another life, when the personality, irked by its outworn garment, shall have that which more fittingly allows life and expression (1–5), a desire begotten in us by God, a natural longing sustained by faith (6, 7). He senses the dilemma of Philippians 1:21. 'In this confidence we would gladly leave our home in the body and make our home with the Lord' (8. The tent metaphor reappears). 'And so my consuming desire is, at home or absent, to satisfy him' (9). 'Indeed, on this matter we must face his judgment' (10).

In no part of Paul's writings is the absence of the letter or the information which he is answering so to be deplored as in parts of this epistle. He is writing, too, in staccato phrases, under the stress of deep emotion. Corinth has hurt him and he replies, determined to deal with slander, but in no way to diminish Christ. Moffatt, assuming that he quotes what has been said to or of him, gets close to the meaning. The rapid, abbreviated Greek quite baffles the KJV translators. 'If I "appeal to the interests of men", then it is with the fear of the Lord before my mind. What I am is plain to God without disguise, plain also, I trust, to your own conscience. This is not "recommending myself to you again"; it is giving you an incentive to be proud of me, which you can use against men who are proud of externals instead of the inward reality. "I am beside myself", am I? Well, that is between myself and God. I am "sane", am I? Well this is in your interests ...' (11–13 Moff.).

The passionate sentence sparks some great theological statements. Paul had found the truth of Christ's hideous death, and found it only where it must be found, in the sublime words of vv. 14 and 19, that God suffered in him to reveal his involvement in human sin; that such a shattering truth must be open to all men's apprehending so that their death should be made life (14, 15), life transformed by the overwhelming realisation of what Christ did, and God in Christ. V. 19 is the most comprehensive picture of the atonement in the N.T. Only thus can God 'justly' forgive (1 John 1:

9). Vv. 17, 20, 21 fly blazing from the same hot heart. V. 16 is a parenthesis. The Jesus of Paul is never seen save in his risen person, the Lord who died and rose again, and met Paul on the road to Damascus. That is why the 'Jesus of history' must always be 'the Christ of faith'. They cannot be separated, as John was to show over thirty years later. The Jesus of the gospels is already the divine saviour (Matt. 26: 28; Mark 10: 45).

The Enduring Servant

(2 Corinthians 6: 1–18)

THE passionate oratory continues, merging into the balanced cadences of a psalm. He is God's ambassador (5: 20) bearing the terms of peace to a rebel world. He works with God (1. 1 Cor. 3: 9. Cf. Acts 15: 4) to implore men (Rom. 12: 1) to accept the proffered gift. It is vain giving if faith and obedience do not follow to receive. It is urgent. It may be later than any think (2. Isa. 49: 8). And according to Paul the ambassador brings more than words. He must be the worthy envoy of his sovereign (3), upholding in bearing and in person the truth of the message he bears.

The world, still hostile, makes the path difficult for the one who brings the terms of peace. Four words spring to life from Paul's experience (4). He needed endurance, for he met sufferings (Acts 9: 16), hardships, dire pressures. The last two words (KJV's 'necessities, distresses') are loaded with the idea of stress and confining pain. He faced physical assault, loss of liberty, rioting, overwork, sleepless nights, lack of proper food (5). And by God's grace he faced them with the qualities of Christ (6), with the gospel and the righteousness which the gospel gave (7), and this through honour and ignominy, whether men spoke good or ill, holding truth though slandered as an impostor (9. 1 Pet. 4:4, 5). Amid sorrow, poverty, indigence—yes, but rejoicing (Matt. 5: 12), rich beyond the imagination of the Stoic paradox, heirs of God's wealth (10).

'My heart is open to you, friends of Corinth. Why not open yours to me? Grant me your love, me, your father in God' (11–13). By a leap of thought Paul then fixes his challenge on the barrier between them. They trifled with the pagan world around them, held compromising fellowship with its servants, soiled testimony by association with the pervading heathenism. To be separate, uncontaminated, as Paul demanded, must have demanded much of Corinth's Christians. Their membership of their trade-guilds called for recognition in the guild meals and business gatherings of the patron deity. We have met the difficulty of 'idol meat', but that was one only of the dilemmas which plagued the Christian in pagan society. Yet no other course was possible in loyalty. The Christian's person was, and is, a shrine not to be shared. In one surge of passionate pleading Paul lays down principles which still apply. Contexts, situations, confrontations change. God's word does not (14–18).

Paul the Pastor
(2 Corinthians 7: 1–16)

THE chapter should be read as a unit and in a contemporary translation. It reveals Paul, the pastor, as no other passage in his writings does. It needs small comment for the words burn with a soul's sincerity, lucid, dexterously woven. The style is the man. In desperate anxiety, he had journeyed to Macedonia to meet Titus. He was in agony of mind lest he should have spoken too harshly in his letter— and yet he could do no other than write as he did. Titus brought glad news of his own reception and the repentance of the church. Even then Paul felt pain that he had so pained them, fruitful in good though their pain was. His perceptive mind, his fervent heart vibrate in his words. Paul is a living illustration of what he had written about love in his first epistle.

The Collection
(2 Corinthians 8: 1–24)

CHAPTERS 8 and 9 return to the theme of 1 Corinthians 16: 1–4. The strain between Paul and the church is over and he can raise the matter close to his heart—the Gentile relief fund for the poor of Jerusalem (Acts 24: 17; Rom. 15: 25). Philippi, Thessalonica and Berea had responded well. The area was depressed, for the Romans had sequestered Macedonia's mineral and timber resources. In spite of this, they had given generously, a reflection of their committal to Christ (5). There is no other real basis for Christian giving (9). Corinth, perhaps, required a little urging and how tactfully this is done (10, 11). Some day, in such a world, they may need from Jerusalem what, at the moment, Jerusalem needs from them (14). Paul is despatching collectors and supplies a 'letter of commendation' (cf. 3: 1). Luke, probably a Philippian (Acts 16: 10; 17: 1), is likely to have been the unknown brother of standing (18) who went with Titus.

The Theme Continued
(2 Corinthians 9: 1–15)

PRESSING his case, Paul reminds the Corinthians that he has boasted about their earlier readiness to give to the Christians of Macedonia (1–5). The word translated 'service' in v. 4 (KJV) is one used once or twice by Paul. It is *'leitourgia'*, and was used in Athens for a compulsory tax levied on the rich for a special task, the fitting out of a naval vessel, for example. The Christian is under no compulsion. He must think, and deliberately choose (7). He wants no glum or resentful giving. Nor do vv. 8–11 imply that giving is a good investment. It is a service rich in joy, a token of remembrance of God's great gift (15), a buying of prayer, that rich consciousness of fellowship (14).

The Critics Answered
(2 Corinthians 10: 1–18)

IT must be admitted that 10: 1 to 13: 10 seem to resume the argument of the earlier chapters. The

letter appeared appropriately to end at 9: 15. It has been stated in the opening notes that the letter can be read as a unit, but that fact does not preclude the possibility that the greater part of the four concluding chapters could have been displaced. The letters were no doubt kept in the archives of the Corinthian church, and multiplied in sections by the hands of various copyists. It is easy to see how a section could become displaced, and how the disarrangement could perpetuate itself when, perhaps forty years later, Paul's letters were collected to be a possession of the church.

Paul is addressing again the rebellious group which had grievously slandered him, and questioned his authority. He speaks with 'the gentleness and courtesy of Christ' (Knox). Christ was 'meek', gentle, that is, submissive in God's hands (Matt. 11: 29), but such a virtue does not preclude firm words and vigorous handling of sin. Some had criticised him for his gentleness among them, and the stern strength of his written rebuke (10). Such variety was not inconsistency, and he begs that he may not have to demonstrate the fact in person (1, 2, 11). He soldiers for Christ (3), equipped like any warrior, but with the arms of God (Eph. 6: 12–17; 2 Tim. 2: 3), to assault evil at its base and in the fortress of the soul (5), putting down rebellion (6). 'Let them look facts in the face (7). Yes, my critic says he belongs to Christ (1 Cor. 1: 12). So do I (7). I also possess authority, though I do not press the point. Such authority is for the benefit of the church (8) ...' Such is the drift of the argument.

More cannot be said without the report or the letter from Corinth which contained the substance of the criticisms answered. Vv. 12 to 18 cannot be adequately explained without this lost material. The Corinthian sectaries appear to have been arrogant and boastful over some spurious success (12). Boasting he despises. He knows how he falls short of his ideals (13). In real fact the trouble at Corinth was hampering his desire to reach beyond them into untouched fields (14–17).

Paul's Record

(2 Corinthians 11: 1–33)

THE difficulties of exegesis in the absence of a frame of reference continue. We listen to one side only of a tense debate. The difficulty is increased by the passionate and staccato style, intermingled with an irony sometimes hard to detect. The KJV translator was baffled by it, and is not to be too severely blamed for his obscure English. The best approach for those who seek Paul's mind is some modern translation.

Certain facts seem to emerge. Paul has been called a fool. Very well then let them listen to a fool (1) who yearned over them, desired their unsullied purity, and hoped to hand them, a virgin bride, to Christ (2)—an O.T. concept (Isa. 54: 5, 6; Jer. 3: 1; Hos. 2: 19, 20). Hence his anxiety over folly as old as the race (3). Some new teacher had seduced them, and Paul's warning assumes the edge it does in the Galatian letter (4. Gal. 1: 6–12). The intruder donned apostolic authority (5),

spoke with the polish of a wandering sophist of the sort common in the Greek world (6), and, like such people, assumed dignity, and expected money. He himself had been humble, and had earned his own living (7. Acts 18: 3). Other churches had supported him (8–10). The sectaries, criticising this very self-sacrifice, were no less than agents of the devil (11–15).

An ironic interlude follows (16–21). 'A fool, am I?' he says. 'But what fools are you, duped, over-ridden, exploited by a man whose hollowness you cannot see?' (19, 20). Let his own record be considered. The moving autobiographical passage which follows, reveals how meagre the written records are. Pursuing his apologetic purpose determinedly, Luke omits so much it would be good to know. There were hidden and silent tracts in Paul's life, and here is fitful light on some of those unwritten pages in a toilsome and heroic story (22–33). It is a record of bravery, unremitting labour and the love of Christ.

Suffering Servant

(2 Corinthians 12: 1–21)

THE autobiographical theme continues. The Corinthian sectaries were boasting of mystic spiritual experience and miraculously answered prayer. As for the former, he himself had known a wondrously ecstatic moment. It is impossible to identify the occasion. It may have been when he was set aside with Barnabas for special work, during which he perhaps relived in overwhelming vividness the noon hour on the Damascus road (Acts 9: 6; 13: 2). It could have been at the time of his brush with death at Lystra (Acts 14: 9). Such matters were not for boasting (1–6). God had, indeed, left him with a persistent infirmity, and an experience of unanswered prayer. The malady, Ramsay thought, could have been malaria, of the sort endemic on the Asia Minor coastal strip. God chose rather to teach Paul how to transform a physical malady into a spiritual blessing—the answer Paul would have chosen in his heart of hearts, had the alternatives been presented (7–10).

Vv. 11–13 must be read as deep irony. The self-styled apostles who had bred the mischief in Corinth, made much of signs and wonders. Their founder, he, Paul, their parent in God, had only one remarkable attribute—he did not take their money. 'Pardon me this wrong,' he says. Indeed, as their parent, he was responsible for the children's welfare (14).

But away with such playing with words, he seems to say. It is your love, Corinthians that I covet, and he was desperately afraid of finding, on a third visit, the appalling state of affairs described in vv. 20, 21. The whole chapter is another moving insight into the reality and sincerity of the man who wrote 1 Corinthians 13.

Last Words

(2 Corinthians 13: 1–14)

LOVE, nevertheless, cannot be weak. Sin must be judged, and seen to be judged (1 Deut. 19: 15).

This will prove to them that he speaks for Christ, a spectacle of what men call weakness on the cross but risen and living by the power of God (3). There is time for the offenders to examine afresh the very basis of their faith (5). Moffatt catches the force of the word which KJV's dated 'reprobate' misses: 'Otherwise you must be failures (5. end). But I trust you will find I am no failure (6), and I pray to God that you may not go wrong—not to prove that I am a success, that is not the point, but that you should come right, even if I should seem to be a failure (7). Fail or succeed, I cannot work against the truth but for it (8) . . .'

Some maintain, with some plausibility, that vv. 11–14 are the conclusion of a letter ended at 9: 15. The suggestion made above about a possible misplacement of a section in the transmission of the letter, through the archives of the Corinthian church to the final collected corpus of Paul's correspondence, could accommodate some such theory of faulty editing.

The greeting ends with a well-used benediction. And how significant that, a little longer than a generation after his death, the name of Jesus, honoured with two divine titles, should quite naturally accompany the names of the Father and the Spirit in such an utterance – and from the pen of a great man of supreme intelligence, who had once hated the man Jesus as an impostor.

THE EPISTLE OF PAUL TO THE GALATIANS

No Other Gospel
(Galatians 1: 1–24)

ANYONE conscious of the pattern of Paul's imperial evangelism and the contemporary tensions between the two wings of the Christian church, must accept that the 'Galatians', to whom this epistle is addressed, were the preponderantly Gentile (3: 28; 4: 8) congregations of Pisidian Antioch, Iconium, Lystra and Derbe, all founded by Paul in the period described in Acts 13 and 14 (1: 8–11; 3: 1–3; 4: 13, 14, 19, 20). It was here and then that Paul had made his historic approach to the Gentiles, and this sensitive and challenging area was the most likely target of attack by those who sought to impose Mosaic legalities and circumcision on the congregations which had been formed of largely Gentile segments of the southern regions of Galatia. These people had received Paul gladly (4: 12–15). They had been steadfast (3: 4) and he had left them 'running well' (5: 7). Many of the Greeks among them were Jewish proselytes. Paul assumes their knowledge of the O.T., and that perhaps made them peculiarly vulnerable to the inroads of the Judaistic element in the church. The attempt by the Jeru-

salem Council (Acts 15) to deal with these controversial issues had been reported to the Galatian churches on the second visit of Paul to the area, when there seems to have been no hint of disturbance. That is why a date round A.D. 52 seems likely and the place of writing Corinth.

With firm asseveration of his apostolic authority (1) and its acceptance (2), Paul expresses, in the strongest language, his alarm that his gospel had been tampered with (6–9). The churches of Galatia, unlike the seven congregations of Revelation 2 and 3, were linked by a great imperial road, and had suffered together the rush of the Pharisaic wave which ran through the area. The pressure was heavy and persuasive. They were 'removing themselves' (6. Not 'are removed' of KJV) from the gospel's simplicity.

Paul's unnecessary concession to Judaism over Timothy (Acts 16: 3), and his promotion of the Jerusalem circular (Acts 16: 4) had not produced goodwill, but had given opportunity to those who called him a time-server (10). He had wrestled through to the gospel he preached, by no human agency (11, 12). He had been a Jew indeed (13, 14; Phil. 3: 4–7), but God had laid hold of him for a purpose (15), had taken him apart like another Moses (16,

17). Only then, his gospel already shaped by such fellowship, did he make contact with the senior apostle (18), and no other save James (19). Vv. 21 to 23 pass over ten years of Paul's life between his flight from Jerusalem to Tarsus, and his return thither for the Council. There was one visit to Jerusalem with Barnabas to deliver famine relief (Acts 11: 30), but it was uneventful, and not theologically significant. During this time he 'was becoming unknown' (22) to the Judaean brethren.

Confrontation
(Galatians 2: 1–21)

A RAPID survey of thirteen years has underlined Paul's claim to preach a gospel shaped in his mind by God, and taught by no man. He goes on to detail the negotiations in Jerusalem in the fourteenth year after his conversion. He and Barnabas went to Jerusalem specifically to plead the cause of Christian liberty for the Gentile converts. James, Peter and John welcomed them. In Acts 15: 1–29 is recorded a protest at Antioch against Paul's and Barnabas' policy of exempting Gentiles from circumcision. Hence the visit to Jerusalem, and the vindication of the two envoys to the Gentiles. Some, in that search for damaging contradiction which seems endemic among N.T. critics, and so alien to the classical critics, have imagined discrepancies between Galatians and Acts. It is well to remember that Luke and Paul wrote with differing purpose, that Luke wrote a decade or more later than Paul, that Luke

had his facts from Paul, that both wrote as briefly as their aim allowed, and that, if there are details difficult to harmonise, two or three scraps of further information would no doubt eliminate all uncertainty.

In Jerusalem Paul had clearly silenced his opponents, and met brotherly acceptance from those who mattered (1–10). Then, unbelievably, says, Paul, Peter and Barnabas, abashed by Jewish visitors from Jerusalem to Antioch, lacked the moral courage to continue full fellowship with Gentile Christians, and earned Paul's rebuke—a passing incident, and therefore not mentioned in Acts. Some years later Paul thought it not worth mentioning to Luke (11–14). The incident, none the less, demonstrates the power and the influence which the Jewish wing of the church could bring to bear against Paul's global gospel.

At v. 15 Paul passes to doctrine. Did the Judaistic approach ever aid or amplify the gospel? Did Judaism justify with God? Objection to the doctrine of God's free grace to the guilty alleged that it offered licence to sin by removing the restraints of the law. The fallacy is dismissed with scorn, as it is more fully refuted in Romans 6. 'If, indeed,' he continues, 'I re-establish the authority of the law over Christian life, it becomes true that Christ did lead me into transgression' (17, 18). He 'died' under the law, was therefore dead to the law's demands, and dead that he might live for God (19). Knox lucidly renders vv. 20 and 21: 'With Christ I hang on the cross and yet I am alive; or rather not I; it is Christ that lives in me. True I am living here and now this mortal life; but my real life is the faith I have in the Son of God, who loved me and gave himself for me. I do not spurn the grace of God. If we can be justified through the law, then Christ's death was needless.'

The Pedagogue

(Galatians 3: 1-29)

PAUL'S exposition of the Abrahamic covenant in Romans 4 should be read again. In this chapter he repeats the substance of the argument. 'Evidently set forth' (1. Variously: 'depicted' [TCNT], 'exposed to view' [Moff,] 'displayed' [NEB], 'publicly portrayed' [RSV]), means 'previously written about'. All versions seem to miss this point, but Paul uses the word in Romans 15: 4 and Ephesans 3: 3, both times of an earlier communication. Paul means that Christ was 'set plainly before them' in a written communication, probably a statement of doctrine left in their hands. It is clear from 2 Thessalonians 3: 17 that such apostolic statements were lodged (1). The confidence in Christ thus born within them was no gift of the challenging, powerless law (2). It was a fruit of faith. Beginning and consummation are expressed in the same words (3) in Philippians 1: 6. The Galatians, too, had suffered at the hands of the bitter Jews (4). Was it to no purpose that they had provoked such sectarian hostility? The word 'minister' of v. 5 is the word of 2 Corinthians 9: 10. It implies a generous, free giving.

Paul repeats Genesis 15: 6, his

basic passage for Abraham's faith. In Romans 4: 3 Paul uses it to show that God imputes righteousness on the grounds of faith, and James (2: 17-23) guards the passage against representation by those who degraded faith into a barren assent of the intellect. Since faith was the ground of Abraham's justification, so those who inherit his faith are his true sons (7), and in the Genesis story there is anticipation of Paul's doctrine that such blessing is for all on earth (8, 9. Rom. 4: 10-12).

The rival doctrine of the Judaisers claimed special blessing for those who observed the law. Rather, says Paul, it placed them under the sanctions of the law, for none could obey it (2: 16). Paul sums up Deuteronomy 27: 15-26 under the brief sentence of v. 10. The failure of the law to justify is further established by two statements: Leviticus 18: 5 shows the Spirit of the law. It calls for obedience, as a necessary condition for God's gift of life (Rom. 10: 5), while Habakkuk 2: 4 makes the gift of life depend on faith (11, 12). To be sure, the law set forth a blessing and a curse, but such was human frailty, that only the curse was operative (13). It was this fate from which Christ redeemed man, extending the blessing to all, and giving his Spirit to indwell, re-animate and regenerate (14).

And so an illustration from everyday life: even a human contract, once ratified, stands (15). A promise was made to Abraham's offspring— singular—one who should spring from Abraham—Christ (16). That contract preceded the law by centuries, and was not superseded by it (17). If the law, then, were to be set down as binding, that would, in fact, disannul the contract with Abraham (18). The law, as a subsequent arrangement, is to awaken men to their sin (19). God is one, and there is no second party to his promises (20). That is why the law does not disannul the older contract. It could not itself justify (21). It merely stressed sin (22), and so brought us, like a child's attendant, to Christ (23, 24). And like a child, brought safely to school, we need the attendant no longer (25). For children of God we are indeed, in Christ (26), in his family likeness (27), no matter what our earthly race (28), made children of faith's great forefather (29).

Come of Age
(Galatians 4: 1-31)

WITH the thought of school-child and attendant (the *paidagogos*) still in mind, Paul elaborates the theme of coming of age, which might have ended at 3: 29. He goes on to point out that tutelage and immaturity mean ultimate emancipation and maturity. Ramsay suggests that, writing to Greek Galatians, Paul has in mind, not Roman law, but a Seleucid system of Greek law, with a guardian and trustee appointed by a father for the supervision of minors. This is not clear, and is of small importance. The main point is obvious. The child is not free of control until maturity. The 'elements of the world' (3. KJV) is also an obscure phrase. Most translators take it to mean elementary tuition—'our childhood's lessons of outward or-

dinances' (Conybeare), 'slaves to the puerile teachings of this world' (TCNT). Some others assume a mystical meaning, which would itself be difficult to explain—'the elemental spirits of the universe' (NEB and similarly Moffatt). In any case, the total meaning of vv. 1-7 is obvious—the law was a tutelage, a bondage, and with Christ came emancipation and adulthood. To go back to legality is to abjure the inheritance, and abandon maturity. To go back to the legalistic observations of Judaism was precisely such regression (8-11).

They had so tragically changed. Paul reminds them of his earlier visit (11-13). He was ill. Perhaps it was his 'thorn in the flesh' (2 Cor. 12: 7), which could have been malaria. Perhaps it was ophthalmia, damaging both to sight and physical appearance (14, 15). 'You treated me as your close friend. I feel still towards you as you felt towards me, but I am duty bound to speak the truth to you' (15, 16). 'Those people are very keen to win you over. They want to shut you off (from me? from the inheritance of which I speak?), not honourably but to make you dependent on them.' (The Greek is not lucid and probably contains allusion or quotation from a Galatian source) 'I am not jealous,' he implies. 'It is good for people to court you, provided it is for an honourable end, whether I am there to watch or not' (18, 19).

The closing words of v. 19 break into a fervent appeal. How much easier it would be to speak rather than write, that his tone might mitigate severity of word (19, 20). They want then the law? Very well, let them listen to the law (21). Then with a rabbinical argument, typical especially of the Alexandrian expositors, Paul speaks of Sarah and Hagar, and the two sons of Abraham, one typifying freedom, one bondage (22–24). Hagar's son suggested Sinai and the earthly Jerusalem, the fountain of Judaism (25). There is, however, another Jerusalem, metropolis of freedom (26). Let us be its citizens, and cast out the slavery of the law (27–31). The argument is very remote from our thinking, but was potent exegesis in Paul's day. The curious fact is worth noting, that Paul's Greek Christians, many, no doubt, once adherents of the Galatian synagogues, understood it.

Liberty

(Galatians 5: 1–26)

V.1 CARRIES on the thought of 4: 31. The chapter break is not happy. Why go back to bondage? V. 2 shows the subtle approach of the Jewish faction. They made an issue of the Jewish rite. It was necessary, they maintained, if they were to become truly 'Abraham's children'. Paul regarded the 'sign in the flesh' as a symbol of surrender for Gentiles, and a logical acceptance of the whole, enslaving law (2: 21). It placed the sinner back where he began (3). The two systems could not coexist, so to accept the law was to separate from Christ (4). 'For to us, the hope of attaining that righteousness which we eagerly await, is the work of the Spirit through faith' (5. NEB). Faith, expressing itself through love, no outdated ordinance, is all that matters (6). 'You were running well. Who put obstacles in your path?' (7). The pressure certainly came not from the God, who had called them (8). Leaven became a symbol of moral and spiritual corruption because of the permeating fermentation which comes from it. Hence this proverb (9. 1 Cor. 5: 6). Some strong personality is hinted at both in v. 8 and v. 10. V. 11 indicates that Paul's perhaps mistaken act in circumcising a Galatian convert, because he was half-Jewish, had been used against him (Acts 16: 1–3). Why, he asks, do the Jews persecute him, if this act was a surrender of principle? They stir his ardent anger (12). The verb is probably correctly rendered by JBP: 'I wish those who were so eager to cut your bodies would cut themselves off from you altogether', rather than NEB's '. . . had better go the whole way and make eunuchs of themselves'.

Let them not use liberty as a base of operations for corruption (13). The word translated by KJV as 'occasion', is a military word, for a base or bridgehead (Rom. 7: 8, 11; 2 Cor. 11: 12). There is a paradox. Christians are freed from the old law, not to please themselves, but to accept the bonds of love, and mutual contention is no sign of love (14–16). There are conflicting forces, spirit and flesh (17. Rom. 8: 6, 7). The Spirit, God's spirit, woven with the surrendered will, must prevail. It is like Plato's concept of the two horses, the black pulling down, the white pulling up. The soul, the charioteer, must make the black pull with the white. The psychologist calls the process 'sublimation' (18). It will be profitable to look at the listed vices and virtues in various translations (19–22). Law can have no relevance for those who monitor their actions in the partnership of an indwelling, governing, prompting Spirit (23). As Paul said in Romans 6: 11, life is a conscious exercise of counting sinful urges dead, and promoting every. movement of life (24, 25).

Conclusion

(Galatians 6: 1–18)

THE closing verse of the last chapter protested against unbrotherly strife. Hence v. 1, presenting the claims of brotherly love, even in cases of wrongdoing. 'Overtaken' suggests sudden temptation, but also the realisation of guilt. 'Restore' means repair, put together again after breaking (Matt. 4: 21). 'Gentleness' (KJV 'meekness') is love in action.

The next verses illustrate. Lend a hand when the load is heavy (2). Conceit is delusion (3). Honest self-appraisement before God is the way of peace (4). The 'burden' of v. 5 is the soldier's pack, which he needs must carry (Matt. 11: 30 has the same word). The 'burdens' of v. 2 are the heavy loads our life puts on us. 'Help one another to carry the heavy loads, but shoulder your own pack' (2, 5). V. 6 seems certainly to mean: 'The man under Christian instruction should be willing to contribute towards the livelihood of his teacher' (JBP). Acts 14: 23 tells

of the appointment of presbyters, and might suggest a group maintained, at least in part, by the church. Paul establishes elsewhere the right to proper maintenance (1 Cor. 9: 14–17), and suggests that such contributions acknowledged benefit received (1 Cor. 9: 11; Rom. 15: 27). It was showing 'fellowship in the gospel' (Phil. 1: 5). And all actions produce their like result. There is a moral law, woven into the universe, from which no living being is exempt. The result tarries but is exceeding sure (7–9).

Paul signs off, in a large hand. He wryly notes the contrast with the smaller letters of his amanuensis. He regularly dictated (Rom. 16: 22; 2 Thess. 3: 17), and the larger characters of this personal postscript would seem to indicate some degree of damaged sight (4: 15?). And it is in his own handwriting, as though to underline his argument again, that he attacks the insincerity and basic pride of those who sought to diminish his gospel (12, 13). There is one cause for 'boasting'— and that is the cross and what it meant, that supreme event which, when it touches with its full meaning and strength a human life, turns all else to dross (14. Phil. 3: 8). Before it all difference dies (15). Those dead to the world and born again are one family in the Crucified (2 Cor. 5: 17).

The benediction is peace (16. Num. 6: 26; Ps. 125: 5)—and peace upon 'the new Israel of God'. V. 17 probably refers touchingly to the wounds they knew—those of Lystra (Acts 14: 19).

THE EPISTLE OF PAUL TO THE EPHESIANS

Christ the Head
(Ephesians: 1: 1–23)

THE Epistle to the Ephesians is one of the most sublime of Paul's writings. Knox, Calvin and Coleridge are among its many eulogists. It has been variously called 'the Epistle of the Ascension', 'the Queen of the Epistles', 'the Christian's Sixty-Eighth Psalm'. It was written in prison (3: 1; 4: 1; 6: 20) and carried by Tychicus along with the letter to Colossae (Col. 4: 7; Eph. 6: 21). Over fifty verses are the same in both epistles. Although Paul spent longer in Ephesus than in any other one place (Acts 19:9, 10), and knew the people intimately (Acts 20: 17–35), there are no personal details in the letter and the destination is not, as is commonly Paul's habit, given at the beginning in the most ancient manuscripts. It is probable that the letter was written to all the Asian churches but that the Ephesian copy was the one which survived to be incorporated into the body of Paul's letters when they were collected. This theory would reconcile several differing critical views.

The key thought is the gathering of all things together in Christ. Only thus is the fragmented universe, the fragmented world, divided man, the riven soul, to find its unity and peace (9, 10). The rôle of the church is that of Christ's members. That is why, supremely, this letter is 'the Epistle for Today', a writing whose hour is come. It antedates the very gospels for it must be a work of the very early sixties. It is as relevant in this age as the letter to the Romans was in Luther's time.

Paul dictated chapter 1 with a fervour which overwhelmed his scribe. His thought outraced his words and syntax. Vv. 3–23 appear in the Greek text as two sentences, vv. 3–14 as only one. Barclay makes fifteen sentences out of KJV's five. NEB manages with ten.

It is because we are 'in Christ' (1, 3, 6, 7, 10, 11, 20), a favourite phrase of Paul, that our blessings are 'in heavenly places' (3)—'where Jesus is, is heaven there', and he is here, 'with us always' (Matt. 28: 20). Those who are Christ's have become part of a vast eternal plan (4, 5) adopted (5), accepted (6), redeemed, forgiven (7), made wise (8), given understanding of God's long-hidden purpose (9). Christians thus became part of the great plan revealed in God's good time to accomplish his final, unifying reconciliation in Christ (11), the reward of faith (12), confirming in the heart a vast conviction, itself born of God (13), sealed, authenticated, guaranteed (14). The Christian's past, present and future differ only in degree (John 3: 36). And so Paul prays that his children in God may grasp the wonder of God's plan (18), and what it means and shall mean to be a Christian with the very power which defeated death in Christ available to strengthen and enable (19, 20). He is the victor over all forces of evil. V. 21 is simply a rhetorical accumulation (3: 10; Col. 3: 16; Rom. 8: 38). Let the body so endowed be worthy of the head (22, 23).

'Amazing Grace ...'
(Ephesians 2: 1–22)

THE Christian, in Christ, has risen with Christ to a life which differs from the life of carnality and sin's bondage as what men call life differs from death. Paul has caught up John's yet unrecorded doctrine of 'eternal life'. This, too, was God's doing. It was all of grace. That beautiful word meant to the pagan Greek all that was polished and winning. It signified magnanimous and unmerited generosity. Paul packs it with fuller meaning. It was the facet of God's love which offers rebels restoration, the dead new life, the hostile peace—simply for receiving. The Christian is made whole in Christ, not as a reward for virtuous endeavour. Paul showed the Romans the futility of such striving. None can boast. All can accept and rejoice, and recognise a

transformation, a newly made personality (1–10), with a purpose. The Gentiles of Ephesus, like those of Rome, must have had special cause to be uncommonly aware of the Jews' nationalism and religious arrogance. Paul, in writing both these words and the letter to the Romans, accepts a divine purpose in God's choice of Israel, but forthwith demolishes any spirit or pride which the 'chosen people' cherished. That ancient purpose had been superseded in Christ, all barriers broken down, the old ordinances done away with. There was no division. All were brought near to God. There was no difference between Jew and Gentile, no room for class, caste, or arrogance of race. The Jew, like the Christian, should see no tribute to merit, for man can win no standing in God's eyes by being of this race or that, doing these deeds or those. It is all of grace (8, 9, 11–18).

The magnificent image of the edifice of God follows (19–22), its foundation, its binding cornerstone, its well-knit coherence, a temple for God's dwelling. It is easy to see how splendidly contemporary such teaching must be. An international religion was a new idea in Paul's world. Some great minds—Alexander the Great was one—had glimpsed some notion of the unity of all mankind, but in Christ the idea came to earth, rooted in the spirit, and beat down all denial. It has permeated the enlightened world even in an age which has lost its hold ruinously on other equally essential Christian concepts.

The Love of God

(Ephesians 3: 1–21)

Vv. 2–13 are a parenthesis. (Observe 'for this cause' [1], picked up when the theme resumes in v. 14.) Paul was, he says, a 'prisoner of Jesus Christ'. One might have supposed him a prisoner of Nero, but Paul saw nothing without purpose in the committed life (Rom. 8: 28). The 'prison epistles' were one fruit of his suffering. A vast secret of God had been made known to him—that God's plan embraced mankind (3–6). To be made aware of truth carries the obligation to proclaim it (7, 9), and such calling was wonder to his heart (8). It was through the church, Paul goes boldly on to say, that the unfallen beings of another realm would themselves be made aware of the many-sided wisdom of the God they purely served—the divine secret that in Christ all the purpose of Creation should be finally made clear. The church, and those that helped to build and nourish it, were, in a word, part of a cosmic purpose (11). To such a Christ can redeemed man boldly come (12). So let them not be baffled or afraid over the apparent disaster which had befallen their minister (13).

He, in fact, simply committed it to God (14), their father, his, and of all mankind (15), that they might have the strength that matters most, not the passing power of muscles and limbs, but the eternal, the indestructible fortitude of the Spirit, the strength which outfaces the devilry of evil, stands true though the corners of the world come in arms, and holds the fort till time's last trump (16). And whence such strength, save it be his who holds the stronghold, Christ held in the centre of the personality (17)? Only thus can love be root and foundation, and the mind begin the effort to comprehend the many-splendoured thing, the vast, surpassing love of God in Christ. Thus, and only thus, can this frail and human vehicle contain the very spirit of the almighty God. That is why prayer is not only real, but is answered beyond our poor specifications, or petty anticipations or anything aspiration or imagination can foresee (19, 20).

The True Christian

(Ephesians 4: 1–32)

As in other epistles the doctrinal statement is followed by the practical application. He begs them in humility and gentleness to be one in the peace of God (1–3). These were passive virtues repudiated by the world but which Christianity has glorified. There is an honesty of mind which leads to a true estimate of self, and a sense of our own moral inadequacy and demerit (Acts 20: 19; Phil. 2: 3; Col. 3: 12; 1 Pet. 5: 5). A quiet restraint in conduct is the path to unity and peace—but not without endeavour (3). Six times the word 'one' is repeated in vv. 4–6. Whence, then, the excuse for division?

In rabbinical language Paul returns to the transcendence, sovereignty and immanence of Christ (7–10). The 'descending' of v. 9 could mean either the descending to earth (Genitive of Definition) or to the grave. It does not matter. Paul is leading to v. 11, and the Corinthian theme of diversity of calling. There is no full stop after v. 11. Gifts are not for self-glory or for boasting. They are for the whole.

'Perfecting' means 'full-equipment' (12) and the final aim is a humanity perfected in Christ (12, 13), a process hampered and retarded while we act like children, unsteady as a storm-tossed ship (how well Paul knew this experience!), the victims of men's trickery (a metaphor from loaded dice) and the crafty ambush of deceivers. The hawkers of error were loose in Asia, and Colossae was not the only abode of dupes.

Picking up the metaphor of the body from 1 Corinthians 12, Paul speaks in vv. 15–17 of growing up, maturing, worthily of the head, every limb and organ harmoniously functioning. To such an end the bent ways and distortions of pagan living must be put aside. It lacks purpose (17), clarity of aim. As well it might, for pagans 'banish themselves' from the source of understanding, in ignorance and blindness (18). Lust, impurity, greed is the consequence of such dullness. Such creatures are automata without the tingling awareness which is life. They are bored, insensitive, destroyers of beauty, joy and zest for living. Christ offers a new life altogether (John 6: 68). 'Strip off such vestments (22. Rom. 13: 14). You are born again (23. Rom. 12: 2). Be clothed in Christ, abandoning the rags of an old life, deceitful (25), passionate (23. 'and' is 'but',

as not uncommonly in Greek). Do not court temptation (27). Disdain fraud. Work (28). Be clean in speech, using the tongue for good (29). Sin gives God pain (30) so away with animosity, acrimony, every passionate evil, self-assertiveness, railing, blasphemy and desire to harm (31)—but put i1 the empty place the virtues founJ in Christ, imitating him (32).'

The Christian's Walk

(Ephesians 5: 1–33)

How a person walks tells much of mood and personality. Hence the metaphor of v. 2. Christ must be the centre of life and character. The common preoccupation with the 'problems' of sex and marriage might well take thought of v. 3, frivolity the words of v. 4, and 'permissiveness' the stern statement of v. 5. There will be wordy intruders, Milton's false shepherds who 'creep, intrude, and climb into the fold' who, with words of this philosophy or that, will tempt to disobey (6). The children of light should have none of them (7, 8). Christ is light (John 9: 5) as God is (1 John 1: 5). Light reveals truth (John 3: 20, 21; 1 John 2: 9–11), uncovers beauty, promotes growth. Darkness is absence of light. Hence discernment (10). The mere presence of Christ shows what sin is. From sin we must separate as from contagion (11–13). 'Walking with Christ' is the safe path (14), and is wisdom (15). The word—akribôs ('circumspectly' of KJV), means 'with strict care'. In such days the most urgent need is to buy up opportunity (16), and to know the will of God (17), his Spirit interwoven with our thinking (18). Singing was especially needful in the early church for doctrine was embedded commonly in song— a measure by which to test our own hymns (19, 20). The N.T. was not fully available for another fifty years.

Paul now turns to family living, and finds the solution of all problems in the theme of the epistle— 'all things brought to unity in Christ'. To love and honour the Lord reflects the love and honour husband must show to wife, and for a wife's submission the pattern likewise stands. It is such submission as a human being gives to Christ. The demand such a standard makes on both man and woman is awesome. It destroys all arrogance, selfishness, tension, bitterness, irritation, strife. It quenches anger, tames the tongue, sweetens fellowship. The chapter is a supreme example of theology, in Pauline fashion, transformed into conduct (21–33).

The Warrior Armed

(Ephesians 6: 1–24)

OBEDIENCE to the Lord is the pattern for obedience to parents (1). Obedience is the duty enjoined, and honour (2) the disposition of which obedience is born. To obey is literally 'to listen to'. Honouring an elder involves understanding the tradition he seeks to transmit, an enormously important process in the preservation of a nation.

Hence the 'promise' given (3. Prov. 30: 17; Rom. 1: 30; 2 Tim. 3: 2). As with husband and wife, so between parent and child, there is a two-way movement of love. 'Do not chafe your children's tempers, but train them in such discipline and advice as is worthy of Christ' (4). Similarly Paul advises slaves. On the question of slavery see the comments given on the case of Onesimus in the letter to Philemon. For the phrase 'with fear and trembling' (5. KJV) see 1 Corinthians 2: 3; 2 Corinthians 7: 15; Philippians 2: 12. The words mean with respect and eagerness to please, without hypocrisy, such solicitude in service as might be rendered to Christ. V. 6 repeats the advice—'not serving them as though they were watching you' (6), but as servants of Christ, seeking to carry out the will of God. Service, whatever the context, is service, to be rendered in the wider context of duty to God (7, 8). But again, there is a framework of reciprocity. Masters are themselves servants (9). All relationships demand the transforming power of God to soften, sweeten, strengthen (10).

With the soldiers of the Praetorian Guard around him, Paul turned to the equipment of Christ's soldier (11). The battle is real, and to deny the force of spiritual evil is to close the eyes to the real evidence of sinister powers at work, to which man can basely surrender (12). Man needs the armour of God to withstand, and at the battle's end still to stand, perhaps battered, but unbowed (13). The shield of faith is as old as the word to Abraham

(Gen. 15: 1). The Psalms are full of the metaphor. The belt of truth holds the breastplate of Christ's righteousness firmly strapped (14). The gospel required hard marching, as Paul well knew, as he looked at the hobnailed caligae of the household troops who guarded him (15). And some of them could tell of the Parthian arrow flights, for Rome at that time was making yet another effort to seal her eastern frontier (16). God's salvation covers the very seat of thought, and the word of God arms the hand (17). Awareness of the forces ranged against him turns the Christian to seek God's reinforcement, not for self alone but for all the farflung battleline. Let them think of him as their representative in Rome, fearless anywhere to speak of his king (19, 20). The rest, the bearer of the letter will tell (21, 22).

THE EPISTLE OF PAUL TO THE PHILIPPIANS

Colony of Rome
(Philippians 1: 1–30)

PHILIPPI was four centuries old when Paul, in obedience to a vision, came up the Via Egnatia. It was a foundation of the dynamic Philip II of Macedon, the conqueror who had finally destroyed what was left of freedom in the disorderly complex of Greek city states. Here Alexander was born, he who was to carry Greek conquest, speech and culture to the ends of the known world. Here, in 42 B.C., the final clash of arms took place between Brutus and Cassius, the assassins of Julius Caesar, and Mark Antony and Octavian, later to be the great Augustus. Turn back to the comments on Acts 16: 8–40, for the story of how, in A.D. 49, Paul came to Troas, and was persuaded, probably by Luke himself, to venture into Europe. The church he founded in Philippi was dear to him, and now, in answer to a letter from them carried by the good Epaphroditos (2: 25–30), Paul writes from prison in Rome. It was about A.D. 61.

Timothy was with Paul (1) and shares the greeting to the whole church and their officers. Organisation was under way, and 'bishops' (literally 'overseers' [1 Pet. 2: 25]),

and 'deacons' are named. The overseers are probably the 'elders' of 1 Timothy 3: 2 and Titus 1: 7. The deacons go back to Acts 6. Philippi could have pioneered such organisation. It was a Roman colony, and accustomed to social order. Thanksgiving (3) commonly opened a Greek letter, and Paul had much to be grateful for in Philippi. Observe the care with which he stresses regard for 'all' of them (5, 7). He has a purpose in this. Some are to meet rebuke (4: 2), but not without the prior assurance of love. They were, after all, those in whom God had 'initiated a divine project' (6). A large, majestic term is used— the word of Galatians 3: 3. Affection again overflows in vv. 7 and 8 for 'all of them', from the slave girl and the gaoler to Epaphraditos. But let them be wise, see the apparent disaster of the great leader's imprisonment as an opportunity (7), and grow in moral awareness. V. 10 literally runs 'test out things which differ'. It is the verb of Romans 2: 2 ('prove, test for yourselves, how good the will of God is'). Things 'which differ' are ethical opposites. Christianity, Paul never ceases to insist, involves uprightness of life (11), it involves the whole person. The power of God in a redeemed life 'fills out the fruit of righteousness', like some ripening sap. So v. 11 literally. And now (12-20) some autobiography. Contrary to the anxiety in Philippi, (hence 'rather' [12]), good is coming from Paul's contact with the Roman city garrison—the Praetorian Guard ('palace', wrongly in KJV [13]). There were, sadly enough, some sectarians (15), perhaps members of the church already in Rome, who disliked the fuller Pauline theology, its freedom, its absence of Judaistic traits (16). Others accepted him (17) but in any case Christ became a theme of discussion (18). It was also becoming clear to those who were to try Paul, and to those who watched him undecided, that he was the victim of a plot (19), and every day that the trial was delayed, possibly for lack of witnesses or documents (20), chances of acquittal improved. Not that he would fear death (21, 22). Indeed he would like to 'slip the cable', as he had so often seen a galley do (Acts 27: 2, 4), leave toil behind (2 Cor. 11: 23-29), and be home. Still, they seemed to need him (24-26). Let them 'live as citizens worthily of Christ's gospel' (27). They were citizens of Rome, and in Philippi Paul had first claimed his Roman rights. But a Christian, Rome should realise, is a better Roman. So should it still be. Let them be united, 'striving like a team' against adversity (28), and, if need be, persecution (29). So they had seen him do (30. Acts 16: 19).

Mind of Christ
(Philippians 2: 1-30)

THE great Christological passage is loaded with meaning. Love welds and strife disintegrates. Pride poisons. Self-assertion spawns division. Paul fears such a trauma for beloved Philippi. And so 'if there be appeal in Christ, comfort in love, fellowship of the spirit, if pity means anything and compassion, fulfil my joy by a common aim, a mutual love, one goal before you. Do nothing in a spirit of faction or self-glory but with humility, each seeking another's advantage . . . (1-4)'. Let them be like the Lord (5) who abandoned divine glory (John 1: 14) to show man in human language what God is (6, 7). Perhaps vv. 5-11 are a Christian hymn, for many times it seems the early Christians sang their basic beliefs. The temptation of Christ best illustrates v. 6. Christ did not 'consider equality with God something to lay hold of, but emptied himself and took on the likeness of a slave . . .' His deity was no weapon or tool to use before all difficulty (Luke 4: 3, 4; John 4: 6; 18: 11). No Philippian citizen could be crucified on any charge. They were Romans.

An obligation follows. Having and holding the precious gift of God let them 'put it into effect with reverence and self distrust' (12), no impossibility with a power beyond measure working within (13). So shall the church make its impact, if a pagan world sees folk 'without reproach and sincere, God's blameless children in the midst of a bent and perverted race, beacons to show the Way . . .' (15). Paul echoes

Deuteronomy 32: 5 and Daniel 12: 3. Only in such Christians could Paul 'exult', feeling he had not lost the race or worked to no purpose (16). Greek and pagan would understand the figure which follows (17. Num. 28: 7). 'These laid the world away,' wrote Rupert Brooke in 1914, 'poured out the red, sweet wine of youth ...' The sudden change from the quiet joy of v. 18 to the outburst of v. 20 may follow news of disloyalty, which came perhaps in a break in the dictation. Some calculating persons in the Roman church (21) were a contrast to the faithful selfless boy (20, 22, 23).

Epaphroditos, recipient of the magnificent testimonial (25), had been ill, perhaps with malaria caught in the Pontine marshes which lay on the road from the south to Rome. He had nearly died (27, 30), but was chiefly anxious about concern at home (26). He 'set his life at stake', says v. 30, 'in his single-handed efforts to supply all deficiencies of service you were not here to render.' The same word is used in 1 Corinthians 16: 17: 'They have made up for the fact that I have not you'. Epaphroditos tried to represent all Philippi to the detriment of his health.

Racing for Christ

(Philippians 3: 1–21)

THE letter was not a treatise, and there is no evidence that this chapter begins another document accidentally or designedly conflated with what went before. Paul is answering a communication from Philippi point by point. Life too,

has its interruptions. The letter was not necessarily dictated at a sitting. The 'same things' (1), which Paul thinks it safe policy to repeat, are probably the stern injunctions to vigilance which follow (2, 3) concerning the proselyte-making Judaisers (Matt. 23: 15). The dog had a poor reputation in the ancient world, a figure for shamelessness, cunning, and predatory cruelty (Ps. 22: 16). The spiritualising of the Jewish 'sign in the flesh' goes back to Jeremiah (Jer. 4: 4), and is a common thought in Paul (Rom. 2: 28, 29; Col. 2: 11–13). Here with contempt, he says that, unless its religious significance is deep and spiritual, the covenant sign is a mere mutilation ('concision'. 2). In v. 3 render 'worship God in spirit' on the basis of John 4: 23, 24; Romans 1: 9. 'The flesh' equals self (Rom. 8: 9; Gal. 3: 3; 5: 19). The word includes all that is of man's effort, his unsanctified ambition, pride and self-assertion. It finds its ugliest illustration in the arrogance of caste. No one had thrown such grounds of pride away more firmly than Paul (4). He was of the Chosen People, of a loyal tribe, not circumcised on the thirteenth day, like some son of Ishmael (Gen. 17: 25). He belonged to the strictest sect (5) and had been fanatically loyal to it (6). He met Christ and saw all such advantage for the tawdry thing it was (7). He grows lyrical over the glory of such choice (8, 9), eager to live out in his own experience the self-surrender of his Lord, his own crucifying of the flesh and his personal resurrection to new life (i.e. 'bringing myself into conformity with his death'. 10). The goal lay ahead (11). The thought led to a figure from the Roman chariot race. Rome was obsessed in Nero's day with chariot racing, and Paul would hear the soldiers on guard talk of little else. He was like a charioteer flinging himself into one task—to lay hold of Christ who had grasped him, a sinner on the Damascus road (12), not daring to look behind, but leaning over the galloping team, careless of the roaring multitude (13), and with only the prize in view (14). So, he says, let us look on life (15). Perhaps his hearers have other views (16). So be it. But let them make a start. There are many moods in Christian living. Some race forward. Some 'wrestle on towards heaven' (16). V. 17 is not boasting. Paul was a new man in Christ. He had paid the price in suffering. There were not many Christians about, and they stood in stark contrast with the world. The N.T. was only just taking shape. Christ demanded uprightness, utter surrender. He was no new showman, but the living God (17, 18), who will tolerate no blasphemous caricature (19). They were citizens of another world, just as Philippians were citizens of Rome (20), immensely favoured people to whom their emperor will one day come to transform this thing of flesh and pain into his likeness (20, 21).

The Mind of the Christian

(Philippians 4: 1–23)

THE civic crown, a wreath of oak leaves, was the Roman soldier's Victoria Cross. Octavian had beaten down the army of Caesar's assassins at Philippi a century before, and when he became the emperor Augustus a golden civic crown hung over his door in Rome (1). And suddenly, after this warm word, Paul comes to the point he was postponing. Two women, listed alphabetically, deserved rebuke (2), and needed gracious help (3). The 'yoke-fellow' was Epaphroditos, taking down the letter and imagining an aside was part of the dictation. Praise follows to soften rebuke. This management of a remote church quarrel is a model of tact.

He proceeds to general directions. Happiness lies only in Christ (4). In the assurance of his presence a man can exercise gentle forbearance (5), the tolerance, magnanimity and nobility of outlook which commends Christ. And with the sense of that same presence sharp and clear, need a man be anxious (6. Matt. 6: 25, 27, 28, 31, 34)? Anxiety is an affliction, not a sin, but there is peace and quietness available according to the measure of faith (7). Such peace 'garrisons' heart and mind, as Philippi stood, ancient garrison of Greece. Conduct and character begin in the mind. A disciplined mind trains itself to think of good things, to have done with deception, to cherish 'honourable' (RV, RSV. 1 Tim. 3: 4; Tit. 2: 2 KJV) thought. The word precludes the trivial, the frivolous, the petty, and the foolish. It does not rule out gentle humour or fine imagination, but devastates many other preoccupations of the Roman and the modern world. So does a dedication to the pure, the lovely, the gracious and good in speech. Such are the realms in which the Christian's thought and conversation should move. 'Reckon these things as assets' (8). It is a grand picture of the Christian man.

Philippi had sent aid to Paul, as they had done once before (10). He had claimed none, having been schooled by life and faith to know Christ's all sufficiency. He had learned the virtue sought by Stoic and Epicurean to be superior to circumstance, complete in himself (11), and yet not unaided (12, 13). Still it was gracious of them to care for him, as no others had done (15).

Paul cherished independence (Acts. 18: 3; 1 Thess. 2: 9; 2 Cor. 9: 1, 2) and may actually have been a little embarrassed at a gift from Philippi. And yet he had the delicate task of concealing embarrassment under a gratitude which could not be construed as solicitation. Hence the bantering sustained metaphor from the world of finance (16–18). 'My receipt then for all things (18). I am well supplied. And out of his wealth Christ will make all good' (19. Rom. 2: 4; 9: 23; 10: 12; 11: 12, 33). 'Caesar's household' was the imperial civil service. The gospel was reaching high (22).

THE EPISTLE OF PAUL TO THE COLOSSIANS

Apostle's Appeal
(Colossians 1: 1–29)

COLOSSAE was a small town in the Lycus valley within walking distance of both Laodicea and Hierapolis (2: 1; 4: 13, 16). It was not a foundation of Paul, who had never visited the church (2: 1; 1: 4), a lack he proposed to remedy (Philem. 9, 22). Epaphras was probably the founding father of the church (1: 7) a man probably influenced deeply by the Ephesian ministry (Acts 19: 10) and the inspirer of Paul's letter, written after disturbing news of strange doctrine at Colossae, from Paul's confinement in Rome (Acts 28: 30) about A.D. 62 (4: 3, 18). Tychicus was the bearer (4: 7, 8).

There was heresy of some sort active, some doctrine of angelic mediators of whom Christ was but one, albeit pre-eminent among them. There were ascetic practices irrelevant to the gospel, rigorous observance of rules about fasts and feasts, all interwoven with some philosophy which diminished Christ. Whether the heresy was Jewish or Greek or both, and who propounded it, is not clear, but Paul countered it with a reaffirmation of Christ.

Hence the authoritative opening

(1). Writing with more personal intimacy to the Philippians and Thessalonians, Paul omits his apostolic standing. He writes to 'the faithful in Christ' (2), and it is significant that the messianic title occurs with uncommon frequency in this letter. There is a certain formality about the opening expressions of thankfulness (3–8), not without parallel in the papyri of the day. Paul does, however, in the same context, stress the integrity of the gospel, as he does in stronger terms to the Galatians (6. Gal. 1: 6–12). It is the apostle's prayer that the folk of Colossae be filled with deep knowledge, spiritual insight and understanding (9), amid active goodness, through a deeper comprehension of God's will (10), with that enabling fortitude of spirit which breeds endurance, patience and the joy both bring (11), joy from the deepening conviction of an empowering God, into whose plan and purpose a dedicated Christian is called through God's redeeming plan (12–14). Paul packs his whole gospel into a few clauses (Acts 26: 18). It was simple for him to slip from this point into a full description of Christ, the same positive affirmation as that with which John met error (15–22. John 1: 1–18). Only in Christ is the unknowable

God made known (15. 2 Cor. 3: 18). He has no rival in the universe (16), none pre-existent (17), the one redeemer (18), God's last revelation (19), the complete saviour (20). Paul speaks mainly to Gentiles, it seems (21—cf. 27; 2: 13; 3: 7). Therefore let Paul's gospel not be modified (23). The difficult v. 24 probably means that Paul thinks of his pain as shared by Christ ('No throb nor throe, that our heart can know . . .'). Christ's own suffering was complete atonement, but he suffers with his own, as they suffer for his 'body', the church.

The Completeness of Christ
(Colossians 2: 1-23)

IT was Paul's way, if he had correction or reproach in mind, to begin at some distance from the point at issue, and build a background of goodwill or understanding. The letter to Philippi is a prime example. Chapter 1 is also an illustration. He mentions casually his authority (1); he bestows gracious praise (2-8); he tells of his ambition for his friends (9-12); he exalts Christ (13-15). At v. 15 he develops this theme—the worth and sufficiency of Christ, himself the full answer to all evil, error and misconception (16-23). In the closing six verses he speaks of his own involvement with them and with their Lord. It is all a model of gracious self-control before pernicious error which he might have been tempted to flay with ruthless words. In chapter 2 he continues the theme which closes chapter 1. Laodicea appears to have shared the Colossian error

(1). Evil is difficult to isolate, in space or time. He urges again the truth that they have all 'wisdom' in Christ (3), he who was God's last word. Paul hints that some person whom he could name was distorting truth (4), distortion which those steadfast (5), and rooted, and built up in Christ, and grateful for such blessing (6, 7) could undoubtedly withstand. 'Beware lest someone be found to rob you, through the empty deceit of his philosophy, based on human tradition and the attitudes of the world—and not on Christ' (8). In Christ, who revealed God himself in such fulness as the mind could comprehend (9), they had all that God could give. He has no rival spiritual authority (10). The old Jewish rituals no longer had validity. Spiritually he fulfilled the old covenant (11). The death of the believer in Christ is death to sin (11, 12. Rom. 6: 10), to the law, and all ancient bondage (13-17). The battery of metaphor finds a climax in v. 14 which claims that Christ paid the debt, cancelled the written statement, nailing high in public exhibition the outdated document of obligation (14), and, like a Roman general on triumphant procession to the shrine of Capitoline Jupiter, he had led all oppressors chained and captive (15). Why, then, in folly fall again under the tyranny of their petty regulations (16), laws only framed to educate the uninformed until full truth should break on them in Christ (17)? And this freedom was a reward to hold. Let no petty theological despot, usurper, charlatan or concocter of strange doctrine cheat them of such treasure (18). The deceiver was in the church but failed to function as a part of that knit and active body (19). It was absurd for a member of Christ to function outside that unity (20), a slave to superseded rules and regulations (22).

The Christian Society
(Colossians 3: 1–25)

WITH the last verse of chapter 2, Paul reaches a climax of his argument. In a passage packed with allusion and metaphor, he has stressed the finality of Christ. The corpus of unnecessary rules and regulations which someone had persuaded them to follow, had, indeed, an appearance of deep teaching to feed their self-inspired devotion and the false humility of their ascetic practices, but it had no value, pandering as such doctrine did to base pride (2: 23). There was a more excellent way for those 'risen with Christ', new men (1), re-orientated (2), alive with a new life (3), and with a glorious destiny (4). An active concentration on that which belongs to the new life and the Christ which fills it, leaves no time or inclination for a religion built of petty taboos, superstitions and prohibitions. They belong to earth not heaven. So he bade: 'Put to death' (the tense of the imperative implies one decisive act. Rom. 8: 13) 'that part of the person which belongs to earth, its lusts, passions, evil desires and greed—itself idolatry' (5). All such sins are the marks of a doomed society 'from which you have broken free' (6, 7). In passionate revolt against such a world, Paul bids the little church have done

with all its marks and features—'its anger, rage, spite, godless and filthy talk (8), its mendacity—all part of the old dead life, sloughed off in Christ, the old self and all that went with it' (9). Observe that in these ten verses, almost every phrase is a familiar quotation. The passage is Pauline rhetoric, in full spate against evil, at its best. But Paul advocates no fierce repression, no garnished, swept vacuum for other evil presences to fill (Matt. 12: 44). As he had told the Roman church, there is a new life to put on like a clean garment (Rom. 6: 6; 13: 14), a daily growth in a transforming knowledge (10). There is no barrier of race (11). 'As God's own, consecrated, loved, put on like new clothes compassion, kindliness, humility, gentleness, sweet patience (12).Forbear,forgive, as Christ forgave (13). Be clothed in love, the last and finest garment' (14). Peace over all the mind's tumult victorious (15), peace fed by Christ's remembered words, real wisdom to be shared in speech and song (16), and translated into the doings of every day (17), into the relationships of home (18–21), into the work of the household (22) . . . For no action escapes the hand of Christ moving in a surrendered life (23). Fundamentally in all activity we serve him, no other, and he will requite (24, 25). Paul, like James, refused to recognise as faith that which did not produce lives, homes, and all else graced by the beauty of Christ. There was hard theology in chapter 2. In chapter 3 there appears the fruit of right believing.

Personal Remarks

(Colossians 4: 1–18)

PAUL had just written the letter to Philemon (see comments on this) who was a Colossian. The runaway slave Onesimus accompanied the bearer of the letters to the church and to the churchman. It is natural that Paul should have the problem of slavery in mind, and his precept here and in the private letter (15, 16), that Christian slaves were brothers in Christ, was the beginning of the salutary erosion by which Christianity was to destroy the hideous institution of servitude (1). He moves, as was his habit in closing a letter, to principles of life and conduct for healthy Christian living. Prayer is vital. Fail there, and the failure is fatal (2). It requires, none the less, discipline, controlled habit, and wakefulness in its wider sense. Irked by his house arrest, Paul begs them to pray for widening horizons (3). It is clear from the letter to Philemon (22) that he expected early release. The prosecution had probably defaulted. And let them pray not only for opportunity to speak, but that he may speak effectively, plainly, as was his duty to do (4). V. 5 should be more widely heeded by all Christians concerned for the witness of the church—'conduct yourselves with tact, prudence, wisdom before those outside the church'. The follower of Christ is watched. He is never off duty. He never ceases to bear witness. He should speak graciously, courteously, not with insipidity, but with words related to the enquirer's questions and need (1 Pet. 3: 15).

Tychicus also carried the Ephesian letter (Eph. 6: 21, 22). He was charged also with a verbal message (7, 8), and the safe conduct of Onesimus. Aristarchus (Acts 19: 29; 20: 4; 27: 2) was with Paul, but why he was a fellow-prisoner is not clear. He could have deliberately posed as Paul's slave. It is good to find Mark in fellowship again (10. Acts 13: 3, 5; 1 Pet. 5: 13; 2 Tim. 4: 11; Philem. 24). It is not known why Epaphras did not at this time return to the churches to whom he ministered (11, 12). V. 14 seems to make it clear that Luke was a Gentile. He is not included in the list of Jews which closes with the unknown Joshua, or Justus to give him his non-Jewish name (11). In v. 15 is seen the dawning realisation that the apostolic letters were forming an authoritative corpus, relevant to the whole church. The same verse throws light on the household meetings of Christians, who had no special buildings until Constantine's day. The touch of anxious warning to Archippus (17) may be a faint foreshadowing of Laodicean slackness so visible thirty years later (Rev. 3: 14–19). As he signs he sees his manacled wrists (18).

THE FIRST EPISTLE OF PAUL TO THE THESSALONIANS

Mission Accomplished
(1 Thessalonians 1: 1–10)

SEE comments on Thessalonica, the eastern anchor of the great Via Egnatia, at Acts 17. The church, mainly Greek (1: 7, 8) was founded in the summer of A.D. 50 by Paul, Silas and Timothy (Acts 17: 1–9) after a three weeks' synagogue mission, followed by a longer period in Jason's house. Driven out on false political charges, Paul continued his evangelism from the more hospitable Beroea fifty miles away (Acts 17: 10–14). Here he left Timothy and Silas who rejoined him in Corinth (Acts 18: 5) whence Timothy was sent back with a letter. Timothy could have collected the epistle on an intermediate visit to Paul while the apostle was still in Athens (3: 1, 2). On either count the letter must date from A.D. 51, the earliest of Paul's letters with the possible exception of Galatians.

Faith, hope, and love (3) are not passive concepts in Paul's thinking. They are active. Faith issues in work, for faith is the conviction that God is concerned with man and expects man's cooperation in the outworking of his purposes (James 2: 18). Love's natural product is labour, for God is love and he is 'working still' (John 5: 17), un-pausing, unceasing in benevolent self-expression. Hope, too, is active for it is built on faith. It breeds patience, no inert acceptance or sterile resignation, no mere waiting for evil to pass but steadfast alertness and waiting on orders. The apostles felt certain that God was at work (4) when they saw the effectiveness of their ministry (5) demonstrated in firm faith, steadfastness under persecution (6), visible through two important provinces (7) into which the Macedonian Christians penetrated. It has been remarked that Paul planted his Christian cells at points of dissemination, and a church on the great east–west road was an inevitable point of diffusion. The mobility of people (for example Aquila and Priscilla) is striking. Paul expected his churches to be propagating agencies (8). News of his own visit filtered back to Paul all down to Corinth (10), along with the abandonment of paganism which followed. It was a world ready for a dynamic faith and such gusts of acceptance were a phenomenon of a spiritual climate. The second advent, the resurrection and judgment were Paul's dominant themes (Acts 17: 31) at this time.

The Theme of Evangelism

(1 Thessalonians 2: 1–13)

PAUL had come from Philippi without illusions. As in Asia, so in Europe, the old patterns of the Lord's own ministry were to work out. In Thessalonica he was prepared for no less (1, 2). The gospel is a trust to those who are called to preach it (4). Its preaching must be without ulterior motive, self-seeking, or rhetorical trickery (3). The manner of exhortation must be stern and downright. No flattery of the audience can aid the appeal. Any thought of personal advantage takes away the evangelist's effectiveness. A critical world, alert for such sin, surrounds his witness (5). Paul went further: not only was he free from all pride, conceit, and self-advertisement, he refused even his just dues (6). He who was by nature so vehement, walked among them in winsome gentleness (7), seeking no adulation, no pre-eminence. He gave himself with his message (8), for indeed he was part of it, a living epistle, a sermon in deeds as well as in words. He worked, not only as a preacher, but as one who sought and won his daily bread (9). He guarded jealously his testimony in that critical Greek environment (10). He preached no facile gospel in the generalities of sermon and public exhortation. With a father's urgent care (11) he dealt personally and eagerly with those he sought to win, and set before them the fruits in life and in character which the faith he preached must generate (12).

It requires an effort of the imagination to realise that the church at Thessalonica rested on Paul's word alone (13). They had no N.T. Jews and Jewish adherents among the converts had their O.T. in Greek, but it was impossible for them to turn to a body of authoritative doctrine for study, confirmation and guidance. The fact that the little group stood firm in faith, endured persecution, and revealed the fruit of their belief in life and character, is a testimony to the evangelism Paul describes (3–8), to his genius as a preacher and teacher, and to the power of God which went with him. The compelling conviction which must have accompanied the preaching of the witnesses of the risen Christ is itself a powerful argument for the factual and overwhelming truth of Christ's resurrection.

Paul's Care

(1 Thessalonians 2: 14—3: 13)

PAUL found a certain sombre confirmation of his message when the spite and bitterness of the Jews of the Dispersion reproduced, in alien geographical and historical contexts, the attitudes of hostile metropolitan Jewry (2: 14–16). Paul had found the response at Thessalonica moving (17). He had desired most heartily to return (18). The compelling impediment ('Satan') may have been illness, the power of the politarchs over Jason (Acts 17: 9), or the pressing demands of Athens, and especially Corinth. He had, however, in his love for a cherished triumph of evangelism (19, 20) sent his most trusted helper when he could least spare him (3: 1, 2). Conversion, he remarks, is not the end of the process. A community must be 'established', with all that word contains of well-founded conviction and organisation. 'Comfort' (2) bears the meaning of 'making strong together'. There has been a weakening in the force of the English word. For a church so young the pressure of a hostile administration must have been difficult to bear (3), forewarned though the community had been (4). Hence a personal anxiety of Paul (5), mightily relieved by the fine report Timothy brought down to Corinth, a message containing, as a last full measure of encouragement, a word of love and remembrance for their evangelist himself (6). The touch of humanity is delightful. Their faith put new life into him (7–10). The phrase which opens v. 10 is a common formula from letters of the period which means: 'I am always remembering you in prayer.' These little touches show how truly the N.T. letters followed the forms and patterns of the correspondence of a literate age. The subject of his prayer fills the remaining four verses. He wants to fill in the details of their faith. There is still so much they should know and understand. May God give him the opportunity (11) and keep them united in love (12) against the coming of Christ.

'He'll find me pickin' cotton when he comes'

(1 Thessalonians 4: 1–5: 7)

PAUL is as insistent as Peter that the first front of a Christian's witness is the manner of his living, and the first utterance of the evangel is the fashion of life in the Christian community (1). He had set in contrast the stern obligations of Christian living and the life of a dissolute age (2). The age was decadent and sexual laxity a marked feature of society and the first firm stand a Greek Christian was called upon to make was against the carnal sin which, even under cover of religion, was practised around him (3). The twentieth century is drawing near in this manner to the first. A man must learn (note the word) to master his own body (4) in God's own pure way, not in a passion of lust (5) like a carnal world. Let him who is a Christian abstain from fast dealing in business (6). To overreach invites judgment. Such conduct is unclean (7). Despise this warning and it is God who is despised (8), he who is the fountain of all goodness (8) and aids all who seek it (7). Report convinced Paul that the spirit of the community was fine (10) and a matter of admiration. But this, let them remember, demanded unselfish industry. A brotherly community can be the hunting-ground of the dissolute and the slothful. The problem was emerging in an odd way (11). In expectation of the coming of Christ some had ceased to work. Such unnatural excitement has been known in other church contexts. Such attitudes were commented upon adversely by non-Christians (12).

Some Christians had died, and Paul seeks to deal with his readers' natural perplexity (13). He had preached that Christ would come again, but they had gained the impression that the coming was near, and that none of them should go the natural way of death. Paul bids them offset their grief with the thought of immortality (18), and then speaks, in the language of O.T. apocalyptic literature, of the end of the age. It is misleading to be literal, and idle to speculate, on the meaning of such phrases as 'the voice of the archangel and ... the trump of God' (16). It is part of that imagery whereby human language seeks to express truth beyond its reach. But always a clear point emerges if we are prepared to take it in simplicity. Paul is obvious enough when he thus indicates that the end of the era will be sharp and sudden, is not to be feared by those living to see it, and leads to blessed union with the Lord, and reunion with those 'loved long since and lost awhile'.

'We' in v. 15 does not commit to a date. Paul fixed no dates (5: 1–3), but wrote in terms applicable to Christians of all ages. Only audacious disregard of Scripture presumes to date the doings of God. Meanwhile a task awaits, and the best attitude for the Lord to find us in is at work, engaged about his business, and alert to his command.

The end of the age will come with sudden judgment. The suddenness of God is indeed a theme of Scripture. Man's arrogance goes on apparently unchecked. The heavens seem empty and unaware of pain and prayer. Then suddenly judgment descends. Our own age has seen apocalyptic judgment on vast wickedness, such as fell on the antediluvian world, on Nineveh, on Babylon, and Tyre. Pharaoh and Ahab knew its impact. Sodom and Kadesh-barnea illustrated the same sudden end and turning point. It is

part of the patience of God to wait, have mercy, and forbear, but such patience has no indecisive end. 'He who is often reproved, yet stiffens his neck,' says Proverbs 29: 1, 'will suddenly be broken beyond healing.' So in the final ending, 'as were the days of Noah, so will be the coming of the Son of man' (Matt. 24: 37). Evil shall see the sudden lightning of God's swift sword, and persistent rebellion find its last reward. But for those whose sin is already judged, for those for whom there remains no condemnation, such a day of final consummation holds no terrors. 'They shall be mine, says the Lord of hosts, my special possession on the day when I act, and I will spare them as a man spares his son who serves him' (Mal. 3: 17).

Holding True

(1 Thessalonians 5: 8–28)

WHILE he waits let the Christian stand to arms (8). Paul picks up a figure of speech he was later to develop in detail (Eph. 6: 12–17). Many a legion marched along the Egnatian Way. Paul saw their glinting armour, swinging swords, flashing helmets. The Christian holds a guarantee (9) of reinforcement and an ally (10). Therefore let him close ranks with his fellows (11), esteem the worthy (12), promote peace (13), be firm with the unworthy and the foolish (14), be merciful to all men and cultivate that most difficult and fragile of virtues, patience (14). He should despise revenge, both inside and outside the Christian community (15), cultivate cheerfulness (16), and maintain an alert sense of communion with God (17). He should develop an attitude of grateful dependence on his Lord (18), spiritually sensitive to the mind and will of God (19), reverently discerning God's will and message in the words of those with insight (20), discerning (21) and adamant once the good is clear (Phil. 1: 10; 1 John 4: 1, 2), and determined to maintain a worthy image before a critical world, even at some cost in unselfish conduct (22). God, whose whole presence is peace, reconciliation, love, will do his part, so that the fully surrendered will be found without blame (24). He, at any rate, will be true (25. Phil. 1: 6). Paul was conscious of his own need of support (26). The kiss was a social custom. It is not unknown in continental greeting today. Generally it is commoner than it once was. It can also be abused, and Clement of Alexandria (A.D. 150–215) said that it had become a reproach in the church, sneered at by non-Christians. (. . . 'with a handshake all round', says JBP boldly). It is Paul's personal greeting. The urgency of v. 27 is not significant. Paul was anxious that none should miss his message.

The picture of a Christian emerges, balanced, ardent, happy, sane, self-controlled, emancipated from spite, carnality and compromise. He is not the Stoic 'Wise Man', defying the world, and holding lesser beings in contempt. He is not the Epicurean, selfish, aloof. He is immersed in life, but armed against its evil. He is active, not passive. His God is near, not remote.

THE SECOND EPISTLE OF PAUL TO THE THESSALONIANS

Two Certainties

(2 Thessalonians 1: 1–12)

THE second letter probably followed a reply from the church to the first. Perhaps the little community deprecated the warmth of Paul's praise (3, 4). It also seems to have touched on the matter of persecution, which was sharpening in its intensity (4, 5), mentioned again the matter of the response of some members to the preaching of the Lord's return, and asked for clarification. The presence of the whole party (1) makes it certain that the letter was sent from Corinth.

The inevitability of persecution was part of the Lord's first recorded utterance (Matt. 5: 10–12), and the warning was more than once repeated. Good challenges evil, and through all the centuries evil has sought to dash the challenge aside. As clear in Scripture is the inevitability of judgment on the persecutor and, indeed, the doom of obstinate sin. 'If there is any truth in Scripture at all,' wrote Denney, 'this is true—that those who stubbornly refuse to submit to the gospel, and to love and obey Jesus Christ, incur at the Last Advent an infinite and irreparable loss.' The

N.T. has nothing more than that to say, and the persecution of Christians is the one demonstration above all others of that stubborn refusal to submit to God.

In general, Christians should be careful in passing judgment on the condition or state of other people in the eyes of God (Matt. 7: 1, 2). His are eyes which see deeper than ours. About the persecutor they can be dogmatic. Those who deliberately harm the good, proclaim and parade arrogant and deadly sin. Punishment is the other side of sin, and it is not out of place for the Christian to expect wrong to suffer retribution (8). 'Vengeance is mine, I will repay', says Hebrews 10: 30, echoing Deuteronomy 32: 35, 36. The Christian should not be surprised if God's arm descends. Meanwhile, endurance is the test (11, 12).

The Man of Sin

(2 Thessalonians 2: 1–12)

THIS is a difficult chapter interwoven with apocalyptic language, and perhaps intentionally, like the letters of Revelation 2 and 3, obscure to the 'uninitiated'. After all, the insane Caligula had planned, hardly ten years before, to set his image in the temple of Jerusalem, an act which would have most assuredly sparked off a Jewish war. All the forces which could find such an outlet of disaster were still at work. The folly of Caesar-worship contained a strong potential for evil, which, in A.D. 50 and 51, some power seemed to restrain (6, 7). The emperor, through this one dire policy, could at any moment become Antichrist (4, 5). The central teaching of this chapter is that Christ's coming will not take place before a portentous prophecy, already discussed in Thessalonica (5), is fulfilled. This fact is clear enough. Paul expected the emergence of a being of consummate sin before the Second Advent. John, in the final writing of the N.T., echoed this word. An 'Antichrist' is a being who reverses the characteristics of Christ, replaces love with hate, offers death instead of life, stands for rebellion towards God instead of service, and harms instead of heals. The Bible is clear enough about a final mustering of evil forces (Matt. 24: 10–26; 1 Tim. 4: 1–3; 2 Tim. 3: 1–9; 4: 3, 4; 2 Pet. 3; Rev. 13) John alone in his epistles (1. 2: 18, 22; 2. 1: 7) actually uses the word 'Antichrist' as the head and leader of the powers ranged against the church and its Christ. History has seen many such in the strutting tyrants of war, fear-ridden despots, preachers of class hatred, destroyers of happiness, life, and peace. History has seen the final madness of men seeking to be worshipped as gods, and that utter blasphemy was not confined to the ancient world or the emperors of Rome. Our own

century has known, and still knows, such megalomania. It is possible to envisage a personality of evil seizing control of a unified world, buying human adulation with a false gift of elusive peace, and using science to brainwash, dominate, and control a dehumanised mankind. The uncanny insights and foresight of the Bible are demonstrated afresh in each day's news. From man's ravaging of his earth to the horrors of new tyranny and audacious apostasy, the Bible's view of godlessness and its end is vindicated.

The church is called to awareness. A vast apostasy is envisaged as the prelude to the unveiling of the antichrist (3), a time when, as Yeats envisaged it in his apocalyptic poem (*The Second Coming*), 'the good lack all conviction and the bad are filled with passionate intensity'. It will be a time when the 'very elect' (Matt. 24: 24) can be deceived, when doctrine wavers (2 Tim. 4: 3), when standards collapse (2 Tim. 3: 2, 3), when the church itself loses loyalty, love and power (2 Tim. 3: 5; 2 Pet. 2: 1, 2). Hence the exhortation of v. 11. To accept deception is to plant it in the life with one inevitable result.

Final Exhortation
(2 Thessalonians 2: 13—3: 18)

PAUL realises that he has painted a grim and terrifying picture of the end of an era. Fear can paralyse and dismay. He does not wish to produce such maladies in the bewildered Thessalonian community. He has already pointed out that it is those who reject the truth who bring the darkness of the world's judgment upon them (12). Christ's own should rest secure in their faith, holding strongly to their trust that God had done a work in them (13, 14), bearing in mind the doctrine in which they had been carefully instructed (15), firm in hope (16). A great hope will not fit into a small soul. Hope is the antidote of fear. 'Hope', said the quaint Victorian Samuel Smiles, 'is like the sun, which as we journey onward towards it, casts the shadow of our burden behind us.'

Therefore, says Paul, 'may God comfort your hearts' (17). He must have known the Lord's own words, as yet unrecorded, in which he linked the promise of his coming with the same exhortation: 'Let not your hearts be troubled . . .' (John 14: 1–3). Besides, there was a task to hand. Paul had no illusions about the sources of his power. He was no proud and self-sufficient man. He knew that he stood in need of prayer, and that the persuasion and appeal of the gospel were mysteriously forwarded by the prayers of the humblest Christians (3: 1). So too was his own safety assured from 'bigoted and evil men' (2), of the sort not yet purged from the world. At v. 6, as though he had over-

looked some stern advice, Paul bids them exercise discipline in the community; for there were some, as we have seen, clinging to a false view of the Second Advent, and forgetting the example of Paul himself, who were living on their more active and energetic brethren (11). An idle and work-shy community is no commendation of the faith it professes—a fact which applies in more contexts than one. 'In the name of our Lord Jesus Christ,' says Paul, 'we appeal to such people— we command them—to settle down, to work, and earn their own living.' These people 'walked disorderly'. It is a military metaphor. They were 'out of step', had 'broken ranks'.

Then, in the anxiety of love, Paul bids his Christians not close their heart because some had been found to abuse generosity. And let even such necessary discipline be exercised by the church without rancour or bitterness (15), for redemption and peace is the aim. Rebuke loses all its moral meaning, if a taint of personal hostility invades it. An ancient rabbinical comment on Deuteronomy 25: 3 suggests that, after punishment, the offender should be expressly addressed as 'brother' or 'sister'. Paul obviously has the generous precept in mind.

THE FIRST EPISTLE OF PAUL
TO TIMOTHY

Charge to Timothy
(1 Timothy 1: 1–20)

IT was loyalty which Paul sought when he put young Timothy in Mark's place (Acts 15: 36–39) and from the N.T. emerges the picture of Timothy as a trustworthy, faithful and affectionate man (Rom. 16: 21; 1 Cor. 16: 10; Phil. 2: 19 ff.). Note Paul's stress on his apostolic authority (1). (See variants in Rom. 16: 26; 2 Cor. 7: 6; Tit. 1: 3.) 'Grace, mercy, peace' (2) a mingling of Greek, Christian and Hebrew salutation, occurs again in 2 Tim. 1: 2; 2 John 3; (Gal. 6: 16).

'Teach no other doctrine' (3) is one word, which occurs again at 6: 3. See Gal. 1: 6 and 2 Cor. 11: 4. Paul's foreboding was coming true (Acts 20: 29, 30). The heresies were a clutter of myths and genealogies (4). The writers of the N.T. knew quite well what myths were (2 Pet. 1: 16). 'Heart, conscience, faith' are a sound psychological progression. The springs of moral insight must be unpolluted (5. Matt. 5: 8; 2 Tim. 2: 22). For 'good' see 1: 19; 3: 9; 2: 1: 3 and for 'without hypocrisy' 2: 1: 5; Romans 12: 9; 2 Corinthians 6: 6.

The law, says Paul, and none knew better (Phil. 3: 6), was good in a proper context (7–10), both the Decalogue and the codes of men, but the gospel absorbed it, and included all in its 'sound doctrine' (10). Paul has the decalogue in mind in vv. 9 and 10. For 'sound doctrine' read 'healthy teaching' (see the collect for St. Luke's Day). The metaphor was Stoic and Platonic, another indication that Paul was familiar with the philosophers. He uses it five times in the pastorals (1: 6: 3; 2: 1: 13; Tit. 1: 13; 2: 2 and 8). The early church fathers often described salvation as 'healing'.

The mention of the 'glorious good news' (11) leads Paul into biography (12–14. 1 Cor. 15: 9; Eph. 3: 8) and lyric praise (15–17). 'Enabled' means 'made me equal to the task' (NEB). It is a word used only by Paul (2: 2: 1; 4: 17; Phil. 4: 13) save for Hebrews 11: 34 and Acts 9: 22 where it reflects a word of Paul. 'Faithful' is used eleven times in this letter. 'Ministry' is any form of service. It is 'diakonia' (whence 'deacon') and used in various forms (1 Cor. 3: 5; 2 Cor. 3: 6; 5: 8; 6: 3; Col. 1: 23; Eph. 3: 7). Humility is the common language of human piety (15). Contrast the unrepenting holiness of Christ. There are three doxologies (17) in the pastorals (1: 1: 17; 6: 16; 2: 4: 18). Perhaps these formulas of reverence and worship were established (Heb. 13:

21; 1 Pet. 4: 11; 5: 11; Rev. 7: 11, 12).

To such ministry Timothy was charged (18) 'according to the inspired words which pointed to him.' It was 'a good campaign' (2: 2: 3). The process of excommunication must have been corrective (1 Cor. 5: 5). KJV is wrongly ironic (20). Moffat sharpens this. Render 'that they may be disciplined not to speak lightly of holy things.' Some form of salutary exile is envisaged.

Christian Attitudes

(1 Timothy 2: 1-15)

FOUR words cover the nature of prayer (1). 'Supplications' are earnest requests implying a sense of indigence, helplessness and need. 'Prayers' are entreaties. The two words occur in reverse order in 5: 5; Ephesians 6: 18; Philippians 4: 6. 'Intercessions' imply a meeting of two, an interview with one in authority, a Christian privilege of entry (1 John 2: 28). 'Giving thanks' should accompany all prayer (Phil. 4: 6; Col. 4: 2). But Paul is making no difficult classification. This is rhetoric, not doctrine. The Lord's Prayer illustrates all four aspects.

Nero and Herod were included in prayer's beneficiaries (2). It is the business of authority to provide peace and security, the business of the church to cement the social structure by holy living, 'in full observance of religion and high standards of morality' (NEB). 'Honesty' (KJV) includes notions of dignity, seriousness and earnestness. It is seemliness and decorum in behaviour, a proper reserve which

avoids foolish speech or action. Prayer promotes such quiet self-control, and moulds the man of God (3).

Paul's vision of a global gospel (Tit. 2: 11) was embedded in the O.T. and can be illustrated from Isaiah's later prophecies and Psalms 95 to 100 (4.) Paul does not say 'wants to save' but 'wants to be saved' (cf. NEB, 'whose will it is that all men should find salvation'). There is room for rejection of the proffered grace. The word 'truth' occurs fourteen times in the pastorals (3: 15; 4: 3; 6: 5; 2: 2: 15, 18; 3: 8; 4: 4; Tit. 1: 14). V. 5 was levelled against both pagan polytheism and heresies such as those of Colossae. Observe the threefold emphasis on Christ's humanity, 'man ... men ... man.' This truth (4,–6) is to be preached and taught (7), a God-given task and privilege which the church dare not forget.

V. 8 prescribes no attitude. It was Hebrew custom (1 Kings 8: 22; Ps. 28: 2 etc.) Irritation of spirit, angry thoughts (Matt. 6: 14, 15; Mark 11: 25) inhibit prayer. Paul's directions to women (9–12) may be left to make their own impact, like Peter's (1 Pet. 3: 1–6).

The Expositor's Greek Testament has an ingenious note: 'Eve's reasoning faculty was overcome by the allegation of jealousy felt by God, an allegation plausible to a nature swayed by emotion rather than by reflection. The Tempter's statement seemed to be supported by the appearance of the fruit, as it was rendered attractive by hopes of vanity to be gratified. Adam's better judgment was overcome by personal influence (Gen. 3: 17); he was not deceived. But the intellectual superior who sins against light may be morally inferior to him who stumbles in the dusk.' The difficult phrase, 'she shall be saved in childbearing', remains. It is just possible that this could mean: 'She shall be saved by the childbearing'—a reference to Mary's gift of Christ and the words of Genesis 3: 15, a chapter fresh in Paul's mind as he wrote. Montgomery's translation, following RV, supports this. The simpler explanation is better—the thought that woman's noblest and finest fulfillment is motherhood and all that it implies. In the carrying out of this function she escapes much of the stress of temptation, the drag of society and its corruption, and the wear and damaging burden of public life.

The Leadership

(1 Timothy 3: 1-16)

CERTAIN differences between directions given to Timothy and Titus reflect the fact that the former ministered in an area where the church was well established, the latter in a more primitive community. The distinction between 'bishops' and 'deacons' is a matter of controversy but it probably reflects a division observed commonly today between elders and deacons, the former entrusted with spiritual problems, the latter absorbed more in administration. The church moved in a world of ordered government functioning at imperial, provincial, and municipal levels. It was habitual and instinctive to adopt some pattern of organisation. Paul was now convinced that the church was to function beyond the death of its first founders, and wisely, like a good Roman citizen, set to work.

He believed in the leadership of character. Desire for leadership, itself no unworthy ambition (1), was likely to be purged of pride by the daunting demands involved (2, 3). An 'overseer' (which *'episkopos'* literally means—'bishop' is a direct derivative) must be a man beyond charge of wrong-doing and of exemplary married life. Polygamy, concubinage and possibly celibacy (but see 1 Cor. 7: 17) are envisaged. A second marriage is permitted (1 Cor. 7: 39; 1 Tim. 5: 14). He must be 'sober'. This is one of the most difficult words in Greek to render accurately. It suggests the goodness which avoids all extremes, a quality which the Greeks cherished. Romans 12: 3 makes play with the corresponding verb. The word has two contributing roots, an adjective meaning 'safe', and a noun meaning 'mind'. The notion in Greek was an ideal balance of thought which never moved to extremes. There is much truth and worth in the idea. Courage stands balanced between the vice of cowardice and the vice of rashness. Moral purity preserves a balance between impurity and prudery. Virtue is always delicately poised. If it slips either way, it gravitates to vice, it errs either by excess or defect. Observe, then, how inadequate the translations 'sober' or 'temperate' are. 'Self-controlled' approaches it. 'A man of balanced virtue' is nearer the mark.

Good behaviour flows from the

other virtue. 'Orderly' or 'dignified' might render the word. Hospitality was a prime virtue in a world
where inns were dangerous and
places of immorality (5: 10; Rom.
12: 13; Heb. 13: 2; 1 Pet. 4: 9; 3
John 5). The leader must be able
to teach (2: 2: 24; Tit. 1: 9; Eph. 4:
11). He must not be a man of
violence, the common result of alco-
hol (3). In a world of slavery this
was most pertinent. No arrogant
bully can make a church leader. He
must not be money-hungry. If, by
some fault of character, he fails to
hold his own family in disciplined
loyalty (4, 5) he stands disqualified.
'Gravity' means dignity, decorum,
control, and if children rob a parent
of such reputation they bear the
burden of marring his testimony
and denying him honourable office.
The church is a household, like
Israel before it (Num. 12: 7; Hos.
8: 1; 1 Cor. 4: 1; Gal. 6: 10; Eph. 3:
9) 'Take care of' is the word used in
Luke 10: 34, 35 (twice, and nowhere else in the N.T.).

'Novice' (6) means a 'new shoot'
and is used in Psalm 144: 12 (Septuagint) for newly planted trees.
The verb 'lifted up with pride' is
found only here and at 6: 4 and 2:
3: 4. It is the vice of 1 Corinthians
13: 4. 'By that sin fell the angels',
(*Henry VIII.* 3: 1: 441). V. 7
returns to blamelessness, and Peter's
earnest preoccupation with the
watching world (1 Pet. 2: 15 etc.).

'Grave' (KJV 8), the Roman
'gravity', the Stoic 'reserve' means a
serious mien and attitude in speech
and conduct, and the avoidance of
deceit and insincerity in speech
which follows. The warning does
not commend brutal frankness, or

discourtesy and uncouthness in
conversation.

'Mystery' (9) suggests simplicity
and sincerity of belief. 'Mystery' was
a familiar word in the vocabulary of
ancient religion. It suggested those
deeper truths revealed or apparent
only to those accepted by the cult. In
the Christian contexts of its use
(Matt. 13: 11; Eph. 1: 9; Rom. 16:
25; 1 Cor. 13: 2), the word conveys
the idea of that knowledge of God,
his ways, and the meaning of the
Gospel, which come only after the
committal of faith has been made.
NEB renders it well: 'These must be
men who combine a clear conscience
with a firm hold on the deep truths
of our faith.' This excludes those
reservations of belief which corrupt
plain preaching. There is a test to
pass (10) and wives are involved (11,
12). To be fit for such office is
honour indeed (13). Paul ends (16)
with what may have been one of the
doctrinal antiphonal chants by
which the church, before the whole
N.T. was in its hands, propagated
and established doctrine. Pliny, the
governor of Bithynia in A.D. 110
and 111, told how his investigators
found that the Christians, at their
dawn meeting, sang alternately a
hymn to Christ as God. This may
have been part of the hymn. Its
alternation is between earthly and
heavenly, and its theme the Incarnation and its authentication. Consider John 1: 31; Colossians 1:
26; 3: 4; 2 Timothy 1: 10; Titus
1: 3; 1 Peter 1: 20; 1 John 1: 2, 3: 5,
8.

Timothy's Heavy Task
(1 Timothy 4: 1-16)

ALL the epistles speak of heretical teaching. The 'latter times' are not the end of the age. 'Later times' (ASV), 'after times' (NEB) are valid renderings. Deviant doctrine is necessarily evil (1). Deception, be it theological double-talk or plain mendacity, involves hypocrisy, and that leads to deception of self (2). Heretical forces in the early church frequently included taboos (Col. 2: 16) and fruitless legalism (3). The Lord called for self-denial (Mark 8: 34; Luke 9: 57-62). Paul gave a similar counsel (Rom. 8: 13; 1 Cor. 9: 25 ff.; Col. 3: 5). Neither suggested codified abstinence for its own sake. 1 Corinthians 8 remains a guideline, especially the last verse. 'Everything made by God has worth, and is not to be rejected if it can be received with thanksgiving' (4). Health, social impact, personal testimony, the 'weaker brother' are the guiding factors (1 Cor. 10: 31, 32).

Such is the wisdom Timothy is to teach (6). V. 7 may refer to some vocal women in Ephesus, perhaps preaching some form of ascetic 'exercise'. As for 'bodily exercise' (Greek 'gymnasia') it has its usefulness (8) but the soul, the mind, the spirit need their discipline too. Their excellence outlives the flesh. Let Timothy accept this as solid truth (9. cf. 1: 15).

Christianity is not easy (10). It demands our utmost effort (Phil. 3: 16; Heb. 12: 1). God is potentially the saviour of all (John 6: 37) but especially of those who accept and 'work out' his salvation (Phil. 2: 12).

Many texts forbid any attempt to base any form of universalism on this text. V. 11 like v. 9 calls for pause and reflection. Youth denies no man authority provided the tests of sound preaching, mature conversation, compassion, Christlike living, steadfastness in belief and clean living are passed (12). V. 13 serves the purpose of vv. 9 and 11. The laying on of hands was a symbolic transmission of authority inherited from Judaism (Deut. 34: 9; Num. 8: 10). 'Prophecy', or the divine insight of senior Christians (at Lystra? Acts 14: 23), led to the act. Again (15, 16) Paul underlines urgent solemn words.

Rules for the Church
(1 Timothy 5: 1-25)

'ELDER' (1) is here 'a senior member of the church' (JBP). Rudeness in a younger person is contemptible and will certainly be requited, for the young inevitably age. 'The grace of God is in courtesy' (H. Belloc). No blind obedience is demanded, only patient appeal. The church is a family in which elder women merit the regard of mothers, girls a chivalrous respect (2). 'Honour' is a euphemism for support. 'Look after widows who are really dependent' (Goodspeed. 3), but in other cases relatives must realise that Christian charity begins at home (4). There is pathos and pain in the widow's desolation but a spiritual contribution she can well make (5. Luke 2: 37). V. 6 probably refers to a case reported by Timothy. There is no death like failure to live (Eph. 4: 17, 18). 'Add these orders to the rest' (7. NEB); a formula of emphasis like 4: 11 and 15. A subtle and common temptation lies in the thought that the commands of duty may best be met in some place other than home (8. Mark 5: 19)' The family must not be deprived for the demands of 'Christian work', even the ministry and the mission field. Active widows, like Dorcas (? Acts 9: 36), seem to have had social obligations (9), though the verse lacks clear explanation. V. 10 supports the notion of some table of duties. The strong language of vv. 11–16 points to some major areas of trouble in the Ephesian church. It was a notable centre of immorality in which young widows must have been under strong pressures (12, 15). Paul believed in the salutary value of active occupation and had small love for the frivolous and talkative (13). A proper family life gave no occasion to the critic (14). Vv. 11, 12 are difficult in the absence of such information as Timothy had evidently supplied. Perhaps some younger women who had undertaken deaconess functions had proved restless and repudiated some vow, thus incurring adverse judgment (12)—not 'damnation' (KJV). They had made void their first pledge (12) to gain enrolment. Hold off, says Paul, and wait to see whether such younger women are serious. Vv. 17, 18 suggest a structure of paid service in the church. 'Honour' (3, 17) means 'pay' (cf. 'honorarium'). There were cases of abuse to be properly assessed (19) and publicly rebuked (20) with fairness and justice (21). But let mistakes be avoided by rushing no new convert into office (22). V. 23 touches on

Paul's anxiety for the moral health of a young man in a city which flaunted sexual vice. In more ways than one, the twentieth is more like the first than any of those that lie between. The advice to drink 'a little wine' is to be seen in context. A pure water supply was unknown in most large cities. Where it was possible, as in Rome, to drink piped water, the erosion from the lead piping was no doubt responsible for a greater or less degree of lead poisoning. In this alcohol-ridden age, with crime and death on the road lifted shockingly by social drinking, there is no mandate here for anything other than Christian abstinence. Read 1 Corinthians 8: 13. It also follows that normally Timothy did not take wine. The last two verses, abruptly closing the section, surely refer to a statement of Timothy, expressing hesitation over the moral judgments he was called upon to make in his post of responsibility at Ephesus.

Further Directions

(1 Timothy 6: 1–21)

FOR the Christian and Pauline attitude to slavery see remarks on the letter to Philemon. Paul was eager that Christian teaching 'should not be brought into disrepute' (NEB). V. 2 ends with another formula of emphasis and is followed by warning against deviant teaching (3), likely in a world apt to produce the 'pompous ignoramus' with a 'morbid appetite for discussions and arguments'. The result? 'Defamations, quarrellings, wrangling, ill-natured suspicions, recriminations, malicious innuendoes, abusive language, perpetual contention, constant friction, minds warped...' (4, 5—collected from several translations and checked against the original). Observe the metaphor of health in vv. 3 and 4—'wholesome' and 'morbidly preoccupied' ('doting' [KJV]). Paul had known the contentiousness of the rabbis and the innate disputatiousness of the Greeks. He was wearying of it. He feared the invasion of the church by the spirit of faction which had ruined Greek democracy.

In vv. 6 to 10 Paul turns suddenly to James' theme of riches and poverty. 'Contentment' is the Stoic and Epicurean 'self-sufficiency'. Christ within is the self-sufficiency of the Christian... 'religion does pay large dividends, but only to the man whose resources are within him (6)'... 'those who keep scheming to get rich, expose themselves to temptation, and lay themselves open to all manner of foolish and evil desires (9)'... 'for the love of money is a root out of which every kind of evil grows (10).' 'Man of God' is a fine O.T. vocative, a term for a prophet (11. 1 Sam. 9: 6; 1 Kings 12: 22; 13: 1). Righteousness (Prov. 15: 9; Rom. 9: 30; 2 Tim. 2: 22) is defined as justice, godliness, fidelity, love. The 'good fight' (12) is a gymnastic and athletic rather than military metaphor (1 Cor. 9: 24; Phil. 3: 12, 14; 2 Tim. 4: 7) while 'lay hold of eternal life' expands the metaphor. This is the crown (James 1: 12; Rev. 2: 10). The second coming (14) is in his own good time (16). The doxology concludes v. 16.

Three verses follow (16–19) with repeated exhortation to the rich, begging them to avoid the temptations of wealth (17. Luke 12: 16–23), and to use their wealth (18. Matt. 6: 19–24). 'Keep the faith entrusted to you, turn a deaf ear to empty and worldly chatter... (20).' The 'science' of v. 20 is probably an emerging philosophical theology.

THE SECOND EPISTLE OF PAUL TO TIMOTHY

Last Words

(2 Timothy 1: 1-18)

IT was probably about A.D. 67. Paul, arrested at Troas (4: 13), was a prisoner in Rome, no appeal case this time, but doomed by the law against the Christians which seems to have arisen after Nero's persecution of A.D. 64. Timothy was alone in Ephesus, and the recipient of some of the last words one of the greatest of all men was to write.

Paul begins a trifle formally (1) as though he had a wider audience in mind than the lonely young man in the Asian city. The church had been aware for five years or more that its written documents were beginning to form a corpus (Luke 1: 1; 2 Pet. 1: 15, 16). Paul wrote under darkening skies but in the light of the promise of dawn. It is obvious that no religion stripped of the hope of another life, can survive, or can serve in the crises of human experience.

Paul never loses the consciousness that Christianity was a definitely purposed sequel to Judaism. He himself had 'served God from his forefathers' (Acts 22: 3; 24: 14; Rom. 11: 1; 2 Cor. 11: 22; Phil. 3: 5). Timothy was an heir of two loyal generations (5). After bestowing praise and affection,

Paul now, with that same tact he showed in writing to Philippi, touches on the small anxieties he has about Timothy. He was richly endowed, honoured by an apostle's confidence. Let him therefore rise to his potential (6, 7), cast out timidity and show strength and love, practising a balanced Christian sanity. For the Greek virtue of *'sophrosunē'* see comments on Romans 12: 3. The word here is found only once in the N.T. It is *'sophronismos'*, the practice of Christian sanity as a way of living. Paul's name was not one easy to own in Ephesus. People were not all like the late Onesiphorus (16, 4: 19). There were those like two others mentioned (15), and if the Asiarchs had covered Paul's retreat (Acts 19: 31), it was no doubt for their own ends and Ephesus was closed to him (Acts 19: 40; 20: 17). Not everyone would have 'sought out' the prisoner in Rome (17) to follow up his service in Asia (18). The implication might be that friendship with Paul caused the city to sneer, a trial to a sensitive young man (8).

Vv. 9 and 10 could be another of those doctrinal hymns embedded in the text of the epistles, and designed to perpetuate and inculcate essential belief. Vv. 11 and 12 are supporting testimony, rising to splendid climax in the word 'know'. 'We have but faith, we cannot know,' wrote Tennyson, 'for knowledge is of things we see . . .', but it is true also that steadfast faith can produce through the years evidence of a guiding Mind that engenders an invincible certainty. 'That which I have committed . . .' refers to the ancient practice of depositing a valuable for safe keeping on oath to render account on a fixed date. 'That day' is the day of accounting, but it can have lesser preshadowings —my reputation against the day of vindication . . . and what one wills against what time applies (12). The metaphor runs on. Timothy had essential truth committed to him carefully expressed (13). One day he would account for that trust to God.

The Battle for Christ
(2 Timothy 2: 1-26)

CONTINUING to put steel into the young man who faced Ephesus alone, Paul stressed the sternness of the conflict. Remembering Joshua with an historic task before him (Josh. 1: 6, 7, 9), he called on Timothy to be strong (1). Like Canaan's conquest it was a daunting project. The verb is that of 1 Timothy 1: 12; Romans 4: 20; Ephesians 6: 10; Philippians 4: 13. It can be what Greek grammar calls 'middle', roughly 'strengthen yourself' or passive, 'be strengthened'. Grace and faith thus mingle —'abide in me and I will abide in you' (John 15: 4). Four generations pack v. 2, a sort of 'apostolic succession'. There was battle (3, 4) dedication (5), toil (6)

ahead. The same three word-pictures are juxtaposed in 1 Corinthians 9: 7-10, 24-27. Soldiering involves obedience, loyalty, sacrifice, wounds. KJV misses a prefix meaning 'with' in the verb 'endure hardship'. It means 'share hardship'—that is with me, with others (3, 4). In the games (5) athletes were required to state on oath that they had undergone training. The 'hard-working farmer' (6. RSV) battles with weeds and pests and sows the seed in winter mud and cold (Ps. 126: 6). Stop and think of this (7). Was not Christ the supreme pattern of one who strives, toils, battles (8)? 'Keep on remembering,' says the present imperative, 'bear continually in mind.' The term 'malefactor' was characteristic of imperial persecution (John 18: 30). Paul owed it to all to stand firm (4: 17; Phil. 1: 12, 14).

Vv. 11-13 are a fine example of Paul's rhythmic prose, probably another Christian hymn. See Romans 6: 4. 'Keep on reminding (present imperative) them of these truths (11-13) urging them with all solemnity in the sight of God to abjure wrangling about words, which helps no one, but unsettles any who hear' (14). 'Try hard to show yourself worthy of God's approval (NEB), a workman who does not need to be ashamed of his work (Knox), driving a straight furrow in the proclamation of the truth' (NEB). The metaphor is probably from the farm (15). 'Godless, idle chatter' was a problem among talkative Greeks (16). Paul makes no assault on freedom of speech. He protects freedom of hearing. Such loose talk spreads like gangrene (17), such as the heresy of two Jews who made a metaphor out of the resurrection, a party no doubt with a Sadducean (Acts 23: 8) background, or with philosophic doubts like the group in Corinth (1 Cor. 15: 12).

Paul was fond of the metaphor of the foundation (1 Tim. 3: 15; 1 Cor. 3: 10–15; Eph. 2: 19–23). Perhaps Moffatt and Knox are right in thinking that 'seal' should be rendered 'inscription'—such as the two inscriptions on Apollo's temple at Delphi: 'Know Yourself' and 'Nothing in excess'.

Vv. 20 and 21 are difficult. Perhaps Paul has in mind Matt. 13: 24–30, 36–43, 47, 48. Why must there be such a mingling in the church, folk like those of v. 17 for example? Great houses have rich silverware and common earthenware. The master alone knows the value. But unlike pots and containers we can, as free-willed beings, determine our standing with him (21). Such is the train of thought.

V. 22 was safe advice in that sex-ridden city. Carnality (22) and fruitless argument (23) must equally be avoided. Paul sought peace for the church and a gentle leader, patiently teaching (24), who remembers that the most awkward characters can be redeemed (25), is the most likely to gather and feed salvaged souls.

Last Times

(2 Timothy 3: 1–17)

THE first five verses should be read in several translations, but from KJV to the TEV the message is the same. The 'last times' are always upon us, and this list of human vices and vicious humans is as true to fact, and more true today, than it was in the first century. We live in 'difficult and dangerous times' with more voices than those of Christians warning of some day of dire reckoning (cf. Rom. 1: 29–32; 2 Pet. 3: 3; 1 John 2: 18; Jude 18).

The 'power' of the gospel (5) rests in its divine and living Christ, and v. 6 may refer to some such exponent of a diminished Christ as those of 2: 17, 18, who found acceptance among a section of Ephesian women. There were such people in the Ephesian church as Paul had warned earlier (Acts 20: 29, 30), and as John found twenty and thirty years later (7. Rev. 2: 6; 1 John 2: 18, 19; 4: 3). There were abroad specimens of the ancient charlatans of Pharaoh (8) to be resisted with confidence, for deception is shortlived, as Abraham Lincoln said in a famous dictum. The weapon against it is truth (10), which Timothy, like his father in God, must endure. He had seen Paul's own battle in his own country (11. Acts 13: 14, 45, 50; 14: 1, 2, 5, 6, 19, 22), the common fate of all good men (12. Matt. 5: 10; Acts 14: 22; 1 Thess. 3: 4). Such evil, in fact, increases (13). 'Impostors', 'pretenders', 'charlatans' swarm, but the answer is steadfastness and confidence (14) in an undamaged and authoritative Bible (15). V. 16 is rendered most in harmony with grammar, syntax and scriptural context if KJV and RSV, with most other versions, are followed: 'All Scripture is inspired by God and profitable . . .' for teaching the faith, correcting error and 'resetting the direction of a man's life' (16. JBP). It prepares a man at all points for the tasks he must undertake.

Farewell
(2 Timothy 4: 1-22)

LET the conclusion be a new translation of 3: 14—4: 5. It explains itself.

'Stand by those truths which you have learned and which you have strongly believed, knowing from whom you have learned them, knowing too that from childhood you have been familiar with the sacred Scriptures which can instruct you for salvation through the faith which rests in Christ Jesus. All Scripture is divinely inspired, and profitable for instruction, for rebuke, for straightening the character, for training in upright living, that God's man may be complete and properly equipped for every good work . . . I adjure you, before God and Christ Jesus, who will judge the living and the dead when he comes to rule, proclaim his message when you are given the opportunity and when you have to make it, break down their arguments, condemn sin, encourage with endless patience in your teaching, for the time will come when they will not tolerate healthy teaching, but will gather hordes of teachers who will tell them what they want to hear. They will turn their ears away from truth and follow fiction. But as for you, be alert in all situations; endure hardship; do the work of God's messenger, and fulfil your office' (EMB).

The metaphor of v. 6 is found at Philippians 2: 17. The drink-offering of Leviticus (23: 18) or the libation of pagan worship was in Paul's mind. 'Departure' is 'unmooring'. The word appears as a verb in Philippians 1: 23. The image of the race in v. 7 forms a third echo of the Philippian letter in two verses (Phil. 3: 13, 14).

Some fascinating biography follows. Timothy, the faithful henchman, is bidden to come to Rome, and collect a cloak and documents, before winter if possible (9, 13, 21), Demas had once run well (Philem. 24). He merits a bare mention in a letter to his hometown (Col. 4: 14). Now he is gone, and Paul uses the word for the secular world which he uses in Romans 12: 2. Was it the tug of society, the cooling of zeal, the prospect of danger, the urging of relatives? Of Crescens we know nothing. Titus was obeying orders (10). Luke, the faithful friend, was with him, and, joyously, John Mark (11. Acts 13: 1-13; 15: 36-40; Col. 4: 10). Tychicus was a trusty courier (12. Acts 20: 4; Col. 4: 7; Eph. 6: 21; Tit. 3: 12). The tense of 'I have sent' is what is called 'epistolary', the time being appropriate to the reader and recipient rather than the writer and the sender. Paul is saying: 'I am sending Tychicus (with this letter for you)'. Alexander, who 'displayed me much evil', was a renegate Christian (14). It was over a difference of doctrine (15). 'The Lord will reward him,' the words run. None had dared identification to stand by Paul (17, 18). Aquila and Priscilla, or Prisca, were now in Ephesus. Prisca was of an old Roman aristocratic family. Aquila's name looks like that of freedman (19. Acts 18: 2; Rom. 16: 3; 1 Cor. 16: 19). Onesiphorus was probably dead, perhaps in Rome (1: 16–18; 4: 19). Erastus had been city treasurer of Corinth (Acts 19: 22; Rom. 16: 23). Trophimus was a trusted Gentile (Acts 20: 4; 21:

29; 2 Cor. 8: 19–22). 'On his sickness Paley remarked: 'Forgery would not have spared a miracle.' Of Eubulus we know nothing, but Claudia was another high-born Roman. The faith was already reaching high socially. Before John died, it had touched the imperial family. Linus was probably a son of Pudens and Claudia.

And with a last word of peace a great man passes from history.

THE EPISTLE FROM PAUL
TO TITUS

Titus My Son
(Titus 1: 1–16)

THIS letter, without reasonable doubt from the hand of Paul, was probably written about the same time as the first letter to Timothy between his release from the first imprisonment, say about A.D. 62, and the outbreak of the Neronian persecution two years later. It is difficult to trace Paul's movements after 62. It appears from First Timothy 1: 3 that he had recently been at Ephesus, and had left that city for Macedonia. From Titus 1: 5 it appears that he had visited Crete, where there seem to have been Christian groups. This and the visit to the Adriatic regions (Titus 3: 12) were departures from the policy of planting churches in vital cities, which Paul had hitherto followed, though the change of strategic plan on a wider geographical pattern, does fit in with a possible visit to Spain at the same period (Rom. 15: 24, 28). Crete, Dalmatia and Spain triangulate quite strikingly the central and western Mediterranean. In Second Timothy (1: 16; 4: 13; 4: 20) place names are mentioned which suggest further journeys. In a word, scattered evidence suggests three or four years of characteristic-

ally vigorous activity in evangelism, or, more probably, in feverish organisation in face of the growing threat.

It was suggested by Eusebius that Titus was Luke's brother a theory supported by W. M. Ramsay. On this theory, Luke omitted his name from the record in family modesty. Titus accompanied Paul and Barnabas to the Jerusalem conference, and, says Paul (Gal. 2: 1, 3), was not compelled to conform to Jewish law. In all probability he was associated with some of Paul's journeys, but does not appear again until he fulfilled the office of special envoy to Corinth in a time of crisis in the church. He had served in some capacity in Corinth during the year preceding the writing of the second letter to the Corinthian church (2 Cor. 8: 16–24). The unnamed Christian who accompanied Titus on this delicate mission is thought to be Luke, and, if this is so, some weight may be added to Ramsay's theory. It would appear from the second and seventh chapter of that epistle that Paul sent a letter of some severity to the Corinthians by Titus' hand, a document which has been lost. Titus then rejoined Paul in Macedonia (2 Cor. 7: 6), bearing good news, which elicited the Second

Epistle to the Corinthians. As far as we may piece these casual and incidental references together, it would seem that Titus was an ambassador in whom both Paul and the difficult church on the isthmus had confidence, and that a most demanding task of reconciliation was managed with tact and effectiveness (12: 18).

Turning for further biographical hints to the letter addressed to him, it would appear that Titus accompanied Paul on his visit to Crete, and was left on the island to consolidate the church which was founded there (1: 5, 6). The post was not permanent, for at the close of the letter (3: 12), Paul speaks of replacing Titus by Artemas or Tychicus, and summons him to a rendezvous at Nicopolis, perhaps to conduct a mission in Dalmatia. He seems to have been in Dalmatia when Paul wrote his second letter to Timothy (4: 10). Eusebius states that he returned to Crete and served there until old age.

See 1 Timothy 3: 2–10 for the list of qualifications (6–9). It was a difficult environment with the perennial nuisance of uncultured Jewish subverters, a lower type than in the mainland cities (10, 11). Crete had a bad reputation, and Paul whimsically quotes Epimenides, the Cretan poet he had cited before the Areopagus. The line is a hexameter which can be rendered: 'Cretans are liars all, wild beasts, just indolent gluttons' (12). They required strong handling (13) especially when confronted by Jewish 'fables' (Mark 7: 7). V. 15 is often misquoted. In origin the words may have been the Lord's own. Look at Mark 7: 15–18 and Luke 11: 41. See also Romans 14: 20. The words must be set in the context of regulation-ridden Judaism, with its overwhelming list of 'unclean' things. Gnosticism, the multiform perversion of Christianity which was emerging at the moment, had this in common with Judaism, that it was beginning to list a mass of taboos, to call the body, marriage and natural practices of man 'unclean'. Paul's point is that no one can in any way define sin, unless he begins with a life committed to God. To evil men everything they touch, every human practice, joy, function, becomes evil. Horace, the Roman poet, had said a century before: 'Unless the vessel be clean, whatever you put into it turns sour.' A dirty mind soils all life. And the converse is true. If a man keeps his mind, as Isaiah put it, 'stayed on God', his conscience and judgment are steadied and purified. If the 'light that is in man, is itself darkness', as the Lord warned, no right decision in any moral question is possible.

The Minister's Task

(Titus 2: 1–15)

PAUL expected much and was not disappointed in his young men (1). He saw, too, that the character and bearing of Christians was the best commendation of the church to the watching, critical pagan world (4, 5). For the qualities he sought, a mingling of the ethical ideals of Rome, Greece and Jewry (2, 3), see comments on 1 Timothy

3: 2, 8, 11. He required as much of youth (7, 8). Dignity, wisdom, confident, sane speech (7, 8), are the mark without which age and maturity become pathetic. In youth they are a crown of magnificent achievement. On the difficult subject of Christian slaves and masters, (9, 10) see remarks on Philemon. V. 11 contains the solvent for all bonds of servitude. Slavery could not long survive the equality assumed in God's gift of grace and the salvation which both master and slave equally needed and could equally obtain. Such salvation demanded first 'a life of self-mastery, integrity and piety' (12. Moffatt) or 'lives of self-discipline, uprightness and reverence towards God.' 'Worldly lusts' (KJV) are the secular preoccupations of pagan society with which a Christian committal inevitably clashes (Rom. 12: 2; Eph. 2: 3; 1 Pet. 4: 2) The 'blessed hope' (13), a doctrine too often spoiled by clumsy hands in schemes of date-fixing and manifold folly, should not be excised from Scripture. 'Redeem' (14) is a metaphor from the O.T. (Ps. 130: 8; Mark 10: 45; 1 Tim. 2: 6). 'Peculiar' (KJV) is a dated word. It comes from Exodus 19: 5 (cf. Mal. 3: 17). It means 'a people to be his very own' (Williams), 'marked out for his own' (NEB). This, and nothing short of it is the Christian message, to be preached with authority and confidence (15).

The Commission Continued
(Titus 3: 1–15)

IF Paul visited Crete he wrote with experience of the rough islanders (1, 2). There was, as the occupying Nazis found, an intractability in the Cretan character which Paul took into account when he counselled a gentleness and submissiveness not characteristic of the independent population. V. 3 tactfully stresses that more polished communities were marked, too, by their own special faults, only to be tamed, softened and transformed by the power of God in Christ (5, 6). Man owes a debt of love and should look to his heritage (7, 8). Without a book of reference, a full N.T., the young churches must avoid profitless speculation and the controversy over trivialities which can divide and subvert (9, 10). Note the word 'heretic' (10). 'Heresy' is the Greek 'hairesis' which simply means 'a choice'. Hence its non-offensive use for 'sect' in Acts 5: 17; 15: 5; 26: 5. The Jews also called the Christians a 'hairesis' in Acts 24: 5 and 28: 22, and here the word begins to assume its pejorative colour. In 24: 14 Paul appears to object to the tone of the word, and in KJV the translation reflects his objection, though most other translations maintain consistency with the earlier verse (5), and render accordingly. Paul himself uses the word pejoratively in 1 Corinthians 11: 19 and Galatians 5: 20. So does Peter (2. 2: 1). It follows that in the present context the best translations are 'factious man' (ASV), 'sectarian' (Con.) or 'a man who causes divisions' (TCNT).

Or, better, 'a wilful dissident'. A specific case may be in mind—'recognising that such a person has a bent mind and is self-condemned in his wrongdoing'. Self-condemned, presumably by his own separation, like those castigated by John (1. 2: 19).

For the trusted courier see Colossians 4: 7; Ephesians 6: 21.

THE EPISTLE OF PAUL
TO PHILEMON

Dear Philemon
(Philemon 1–25)

PHILEMON's letter must have travelled with the letter to Colossae in Tychicus' mailbag (Col. 4: 7–9). Colossae, Laodicea and Hierapolis lay on the highway up the Lycus valley, as near to each other as any three suburban churches of the same denomination in a modern county. Paul wrote from Rome during his house-detention there (Acts 28: 30). This tiny gem of Christian literature arose from a small occasion. Onesimus had robbed his master and found his way to Rome, the roaring metropolis of the Empire, which one of Rome's own writers called the common sewer of the world. What happened there is not known. Great cities are cruel places. Perhaps the simple boy from the Lycus valley was no match for the slum-dwellers by the Tiber. Robbed, perhaps, in his turn, perhaps sick in that notoriously malarial environment, beaten by the alien horde, Onesimus may have been recognised by the good Epaphras from Colossae.

Paul led Onesimus to Christ and, in his wisdom, sent him home. He sent him, nevertheless, with his human worth underlined. He was no 'speaking tool', in the ancient phrase, 'a living instrument', 'a personal chattel', but a son, a brother in Christ. The slave came back to Colossae crowned with the love of the greatest leader of the church, more, by the love of Christ. The challenge to Philemon was sharp and clear. A foul system could not stand for long thus sapped and undermined. The epistle is a prophecy, envisaging the emancipation of the bound, the social revolution which was inevitable once men had been moved to translate into life's activity the doctrine of man's equality before God, the value of the soul, and the Christian's freedom in Christ.

Note the following details. Apphia (2) was Philemon's wife and Archippus probably his son. The family was probably brought to faith by the Ephesian ministry (Acts 19: 10). The church found a meeting place in their home (2), and Archippus was a leading figure in the Christian community (Col. 4: 17). Vv. 4–6 show Paul, with his habitual tact, preparing the way for Onesimus. Christian love, and the communion of faith can hardly tolerate the bondage of man to man. Paul mentions love first, hastens on to faith, returns to love to stress the disturbing truth that it embraces 'all the saints', and finally returns to faith to hazard the pointed suggestion that it has a work to do in the personality of the one who professes it.

Vv. 7–10 are quite exquisite. 'Paul, the ambassador', (correct for v. 9) pleads for his 'son' (10). 'Brother' comes like a handclasp in v. 7, 'Onesimus' like a catch in the voice after 'son'. 'Once he was useless to you, but now useful indeed' (11). Paul puns on Onesimus' name which means 'useful'. It was a sacrifice for a man in confinement to send him home. 'I could have wished', he continues (13), 'to keep him by me ... but I decided ...' (14). Paul uses two verbs, one of which suggests purpose, the other will. Inclination is governed by decision. Observe the delicacy with which

Paul treats Onesimus' escapade. He 'was parted' from his master, but, after the manner of God's restitution, Philemon's loss was turned to gain (15, 16). Let him charge it to Paul if anything is short (17, 18), though, to be sure, Philemon owed Paul much (19). 'Yes, brother, I would have profit of you ('*onaimên*' —another pun on Onesimus) in the Lord. Set my heart at rest in him' (20). V. 21 hints at the possibility of freedom for the repentant slave.

The epistle ends (22–25) on notes of intimacy. There was something truly Greek about Paul. The great Greek orators never placed the climax of their speech in the closing words. The oration closed on a minor note designed to bring the excited audience back to normality and rest. So here.

THE EPISTLE TO THE HEBREWS

The Old and the New are One
(Hebrews 1: 1–14)

NEITHER author nor reci-
pients of this brilliant letter
are known. It is enough to
say of the writer that he was an
educated Hellenistic Jew, heir to
two cultures, at home both with
the Greek language and Greek
thought. He is a master of style,
and coins more quotable phrases
per chapter than any other N.T.
writer (1: 1, 3, 4). He is a polished
O.T. scholar, apt at using the
Jewish Scriptures in the Septuagint
version, especially the Psalms (e.g.
in ch. 1 only, Ps. 2: 2; 104: 4;
110: 1 in that order). He seems
to have had authority in a Jewish-
Christian church. He was a
Paulinist, a friend of Timothy, and
at the time of writing was in contact
with Italian Christians (10: 32–34),
possibly refugees (Acts 18: 1, 2), if
this is not to imply too early a
date.

Those who enjoy the exercise of
such argument, have made cases for
Barnabas, Aquila and Priscilla,
Apollos and Silas, but persuasive
argument halts short of any proof.
It is clear that the letter was
written to meet the difficulties and
shortcomings of a Jewish Christian
group (5: 12; 6: 9; 10: 32; 12: 4).

Jewish Christians, often torn
between their old allegiance and
the new, had immense difficulties.
It was important to make them see
that their new faith was a logical
continuation of what they had
always heard (Paul's preoccupation). The first chapter draws O.T.
and N.T. together in its first four
verses—the prophets and all the
writers of their Jewish scriptures
(1), all of whom prepared the way
for One who had been active in
creation itself (2), and gathers in,
through one elegant paragraph of
seventy Greek words, the whole
theme of John's as yet unwritten
prologue.

Hence the aim, already visible in
the use of the O.T. in chapter 1
(4–12), to link past and present,
old and new, and to demonstrate
that Moses, and all the institutions
of Judaism, looked forward to a
higher meaning and a brighter glory
glory in the Christian revelation
(14). Those to whom the letter was
written were stumbling at this very
point. They were not faced by the
heresies which plagued the
Galatian and Colossian churches,
but rather by a slackening zeal and
diminished faith (5: 12). They had
once done well (6: 9). They had
known ostracism and loss, such as
Jews knew in the Claudian expulsion

of A.D. 49 (Acts 18: 1, 2), but not such savagery as Nero initiated in A.D. 64 (10: 33, 34; 12: 4). This fact suggests a date round the time when Peter first wrote, in the early sixties. This is supported by the fact that it seems clear that the Temple still functioned (10: 1, 2). This became impossible with the outbreak of the great revolt, A.D. 66–70. They had known the world's contempt, and needed a new infusion of spirit, zeal and a willingness to commit all to Christ (12: 3, 12; 13: 13). Such backsliding, a common fault in second generation Christians can be perilous, they are warned (6: 1–4; 10: 26–39). It comes insidiously (3: 12), laying unprepared hearts open to false teaching (13: 9). Hence the emphasis on steadfastness and confidence (11: 23; 10: 35, 38).

The Pre-eminence of Christ
(Hebrews 2: 1–18)

THE theme of the first chapter continues. Christ was the agent of creation. 'Worlds' (1: 2) can be rendered 'ages', that is the 'immeasurable content of immeasurable time'. He was the image of the 'Father', the theme of John 14: 9, the imperishable Lord (1: 11, 12). That is why 'we are bound to pay all the more attention to what we have heard lest we drift away' (2: 1, 2). RV and RSV take this as a metaphor of a ship drifting from its moorings. Cf. 6: 19. The theme of backsliding under pressure or through apathy is in the writer's words (3: 6; 5: 11; 6: 11, 12). And greater privilege involved greater

responsibilities (2). The same thought of carelessly losing a great gift, drifting rather than sailing away, lies in v. 3—'neglect' not 'reject', however sombrely one leads to the other, is the word. It is the word used of those who lightly treated the royal summons of Matthew 22: 5. The Lord and his apostles had established the great proclamation (3, 4), and commanded attention at the hearers' peril.

V. 5 picks up the theme of chapter 1, the pre-eminent Christ. A doctrine of ang.. ʼmediators had been introduced by ʼ ʼ Jewish thinking into Christian belief. Paul deals with it in the letter to Colossae, where the heresy was serious. The matter is glanced at in these verses, for Christ lost some of his uniqueness if indeed he was but one mediator among many. In a typically Jewish line of argument, the writer makes the point that man was the crown of God's creation. Christ became man, and therefore humankind is set apart in a special relationship with God. Christ, the son, 'the effulgence of God's splendour and the stamp of God's very being' (1: 3 NEB) became to man a priest and brother. The priest (17) was, in Hebrew teaching, the mediator between God and man—a man himself, yet a path to God, with no one else between. Hence perfect confidence and assurance because, since he himself has passed through the test of suffering, 'he is able to help those who are meeting their test now' (18. NEB).

The Lord is called 'the pioneer of their salvation' (10. The word of

12: 2 and Acts 3: 15 and 5: 31). It means variously in Greek the founder or originator of a school or movement, the head of an organisation, one who shows the way or initiates a process—all apply to the plan of salvation. To 'make perfect' is to ensure that the process, person or plan, is so placed that he or it will fully and adequately carry out what is designed. Then, strangely, the Lord is said to have effected this 'perfection' by suffering. In suffering he was identified with needy man, (11. Ps. 22: 22; Isa. 8: 17, 18). In suffering he also made it clear that he loves man with whom he was thus identified. And so (14–18) he gave man confidence that he could understand, sympathise and save.

A fine Christological exposition argued with Greek logic within a framework of Hebrew thought.

Today

(Hebrews 3: 1–19)

IT has been demonstrated that Christ held superiority over prophets and angels. Now, a matter of last importance to the Jew, his primacy over Moses is to be proved —'Consider him', the writer begs, using a verb which means something more than merely 'look at'. They are to observe, with discernment and thought, Christ as 'apostle' and 'high priest'. An apostle is one 'sent forth' on a special mission, and the word is here used, and only here, of Christ. Call it 'ambassador', one who speaks with the full power and authority of the one who sends him

out. His message is to be accepted. Christ's message therefore superseded that of the first ambassador, Moses. Similarly, this acceptance of one who was not a member of Levi's tribe, implied the rejection of the Levitical priesthood (1) for another (5: 10).

God had appointed Moses over all the house of Israel (Num. 12: 7) on the grounds of his faithfulness. So with Christ (2). Moses was also a member of 'the house'. Christ built the house over which he was appointed head (3), an obvious deduction being that he was superior to Moses who held a lesser appointment (4). Moses was the servant (5), but the Lord was the son (6).

The train of thought which begins in v. 7 may be this—not all who followed Moses were faithful. They hung back and disobeyed. Let it not be said that those who followed the greater messenger prove faithless in the same way. The quotation is from Psalm 95: 7–11. 'Provocation' and 'temptation' (8) are, in the Hebrew text, place names (Exod. 17: 1–7; Num. 14: 1–13; 20: 1–13). Three O.T. stories of rebellion are in the writer's mind, incidents covering forty years. Upon such spirit judgment fell (10, 11). Let their spiritual posterity beware (12). Time could be short and judgment final (10: 31). Observe the conditional clause in v. 14. To begin a Christian life is good, but it is like leaving Egypt. To continue, and reach the 'rest' of Canaan, tests the reality of the beginning. Each day matters. Hence the repetition of the warning embedded in 'today' (15). Jewish

Christians, the writer implies, finding it difficult to grasp that all was done by Christ, and that a Canaan of the Spirit awaited their entry, chose to wander on in the Sinai of the Law. They chose the less, the incomplete, the toilsome, in place of the rest of Christ.

'For who were they who after hearing provoked?' Hebrews wonderfully delivered (16). 'With whom was he angry forty years?' With Hebrews who sinned (17. Num. 32: 23). 'And to whom swore he ...?' The unbelieving (18). They had begun well, but now risked losing all (19). The theme runs on, with no break, into chapter 4.

Rest of God
(Hebrews 4: 1-13)

THE writer, in this complicated passage of typically rabbinical argument from Scripture, speaks of rest in three contexts. 'Rest' is the peace of God, or God's salvation (1), for the obtaining of which a man can 'be found to have come too late'. (The word is that of Rom. 3: 23 'to fall short of ....'.) Canaan was the symbol of God's salvation, for which the disobedient generation of the wilderness 'came too late', or which it 'failed to attain'. And why? Because grace found no faith to make it effective (see comments on John 3: 1-16).

Was then the promise of rest rounded off and concluded when Joshua, that is 'Jesus' of v. 8, finally established another generation in the land? No, because centuries later David spoke of another rest (7), still attainable,

and God himself, according to the rabbis, rested eternally after creation (4). In Genesis 2: 2 no evening is mentioned, as in the case of the other six days, and the scribes derived their doctrine from this. And so, if the Canaan rest was, indeed, historic and past, the 'sabbatismos' of God was still open. The Land of Promise, the writer argues, must have a spiritual counterpart (9), and there must also be a peace of God to be won by faith—John's 'eternal life'. To win it demands action, the old historic inroad repeated in a spiritual realm (10). The old promises come round again in a widening circle, for God's word is not dead. Indeed, the writer says, coining one of his scintillating sayings, 'the Word of God is alive and strong, more cutting than a sword with double edge. It can cut clean between emotion and intellect—to the very depths of the personality. It lays bare our real thoughts, our true motives' (12). Hence a fundamental principle of scriptural exegesis. There is multiple meaning and fulfilment, and one interpretation need not preclude another.

Christ the High Priest
(Hebrews 4: 14—5: 10)

IT was suggested above that this letter to Jewish Christians was written in the early sixties. Jerusalem, tense and slipping towards rebellion, was no fit home for those who found their faith's centre in the temple and the sacrifices. In the late sixties Jerusalem perished, a traumatic event for all Jews, and a moral shock to Jewish Christians. To them it came as a challenge to face the future without the practice of their ancient faith. Till then the danger was real that Christianity would be no more than a sect of Judaism, and that Jewish Christians would be divided from their Gentile brethren in Christ. Hence the argument. The high priest was the most significant figure of the old order, but, in Christ, the new order had a high priest subject to none of the old human limitations, the brevity of life, and the imperfections of any man holding sacred office (4: 14). How superior must be the mediation of one who is himself the 'express image of God's person' (1: 3). And how potent a mediator if, in his own person, he can assure us that God feels, knows and understands (15). In him we enter without fear the holy place (16). Christ, the writer goes on to show, had all that was demanded of a high priest appointed from among men (5: 1), compassion (2) and the office of making sacrifice (3), save that he needed to make no atonement for himself (3). God alone makes such appointment (4). So God, at an historic moment, appointed Christ (6), but not after Aaron's order. His was the more ancient order, long preceding the Law and the Levitical priesthood—to wit, a priest after Melchisedek's fashion. Thus appointed, he functioned as a high priest should, sympathetic, involved with man, enduring temptation—but victorious. V. 8 does not imply that the Lord learned obedience by the pains of disobedience. It was in his human person that he faced all the drive and

power of temptation not to fulfil God's perfect will—and submitted to that will in spite of all the shrinking of the flesh (Matt. 26: 42). It may, in conclusion, be noted that learning by suffering was a Greek concept, profoundly expressed by the great tragedian Aeschylus. The writer of Hebrews knew the great classics.

The Peril of Relapse
(Hebrews 5: 11—6: 20)

THE writer shrinks before the task of making those drilled and formed in the schools of Judaism understand the difficult truth he struggles to put into words (5: 11). The Christian faith demands the exercise of God's gift of intelligence. (Without that conviction Paul would never have written his letter to the Roman Christians.) The writer wants the Jewish Christians to digest solid food, but like babes they cling to milk (1 Pet. 2: 2; 1 Cor. 2: 6; 3: 2; 14: 20; Eph. 4: 13–15). It was time for them to be teachers, but they were still in school refusing to grow up (12–14). Abandon the alphabet of faith and push on to maturity, he begs them, build on the foundation of repentance (6: 1). All the basic doctrines of Christianity, along with the practices of its early rituals, were such that any Jew could accept (2). It was easy, if no more than this was required, to slip back, and, little changed, resume the ways and manners of the older covenant.

The Jews addressed were in peril of such relapse. When it became clear that to follow Christ meant a break with Judaism, they hesitated and sought such compromise as that which haunted the Jerusalem church, and against which Paul battled for the Galatian Christians. For such people their inadequate response and feeble committal became a barrier to all further argument, appeal and enlightenment (4, 5). In the writer's experience it was quite impossible again to bring those so conditioned to the place of salutary repentance and full surrender. Something had died in them. They are like sterile ground, burned over, in which it is impossible to grow a good crop. The stern warning is chilling, but the psychology of such backsliding is true. Those who seek to bring men to repentance and acceptance of Christ, should distrust the emotional response. Such shallow acceptance is prone to fade and to bring such defectors to saving faith may prove the impossible process which v. 6 describes in sombre terms.

After such warning the writer turns to encouragement. The Jewish Christians had shown some fruits of faith. Let them not now grow slack (9–12). Their father Abraham had shown the way. He had set out in bold faith, stumbled, and in the end saw faith win its reward. 'Thus it was that Abraham, after patient waiting, obtained the promise', which stood on the pledged word of God (13–18. Gen. 17: 5, 6; 18: 18; 22: 16–18). So their hope, like an anchor, stood firm, anchored in another world. And, mixing potently his metaphors, the writer pictures Christ,

breaking down old partitions between man and God, and fixing the outflung anchor at the very feet of the Almighty.

Melchisdek
(Hebrews 7: 1–28)

THIS chapter, placed significantly in the centre of the epistle, is a typical sample of rabbinical exegesis. The story of the gracious king of Jerusalem, who was also a priest of El Elyon—the Most High God (a title used sixteen times in the O.T.)—is of deep historical significance. To the Western and the modern mind it shows that, while the Bible follows one line of revelation, the development of God's historic plan through Abraham of Ur, there were, in the old lands of the Bible, those who also held the ancient traditions of truth and godliness. Abraham, returning from his reprisal raid on the retreating chieftains of the north, meets a man whom he recognises as his spiritual superior—a point of which the writer of this chapter makes much (Gen. 14: 18–20). Were there others? There are fragments of archaeological evidence to indicate that there may have been, but that is not important in the exegesis of this passage.

To the rabbinical scholar the historic truth was taken for granted, and of no great importance. The theological significance was his main preoccupation, equally with the mystical meaning. The last-named, as exposition in the Dead Sea Scrolls demonstrates, was sometimes fanciful in the last degree. Not so with this writer. To a Jewish student the chain of reasoning would be overwhelmingly binding. He passes from the Genesis story to Psalm 110: 4, where a Davidic king (6: 20) is named a priest of the order of Melchisedek. Jerusalem, the Salem of the story, is significant on two levels. It means 'peace', and it was David's city by right of conquest. Therefore the office of the priest-king of Jerusalem became the prerogative of David's house, by right confirmed by oath (Ps. 110: 4). The priesthood of Melchisedek was older than the priesthood of Aaron by many centuries. It was also of the tribe of Judah, the tribe of David and Christ (13, 14).

This was of immense comfort to the Jew, soon to be deprived of the old priesthood, or already deprived of it (according to the dating favoured for the epistle). They had a high priest immeasurably superior to the priest of Levi's tribe, an immortal priest (15–19), guaranteeing in his person the approach to God for which the Jew yearned, a priest who contained within his person the meaning of all the transient sacrifices, final and adequate (11, 27).

The Christian, as distinct from the Jewish mind, can lay hold of one point in the matter of Melchisedek with some interest. He is curiously described as being without father or mother or genealogy (3). This, of course, means that nothing is known of his ancestry, his people or his tribe. He breaks mysteriously into history, and as mysteriously retreats from the record, his gracious work accom-

plished. So Christ, breaking uniquely into history, and as wondrously leaving it. The angle of the Jewish writer is, of course, slightly different. The Levite could serve as a priest only on proof of his ancestry. Ezra 2: 62, 63 and Nehemiah 7: 63–65 speak of exclusions on no other grounds than lack of such proof. Of Melchisedek there is no mention of predecessor nor successor, and this to the writer suggests an eternal priesthood (16, 17). The genetic argument (3) might even, the writer suggests, imply that Levi himself and all his house paid homage to the king of Salem, in the person of their ancestor Abraham (10). A spiritual and royal priesthood was to succeed the Levitical priesthood, as a new religion of faith, based on a final sacrifice, was to supersede the whole Mosaic system (11–17). Hence a more satisfying approach to God (18, 19). Christ the new high priest was the last and complete offering— the perfect consummation (26, 27). And so 'he is able to save to the uttermost all who come to God through him—for he lives always to plead on their behalf'. John, perhaps thirty years later, was to write the words of John 14: 6, 7.

Priest Triumphant

(Hebrews 8: 1–13)

THE writer in this chapter seems to reveal his contact with a wider world than that of Jewish thought. Once or twice in the latter half of this epistle, Greek concepts seem to colour his thinking. Since Plato, a strong and haunting idea

was held by those who pondered
the deeper meaning of life. This is
an unreal world, a 'shadowland' of
C. S. Lewis' phrase. All that is here
is a reflection of reality, an approxi-
mation, partaking of final perfection
but falling short of it (5). This
notion seems to pervade the chapter. There is a truth laid up in
heaven, a perfect priesthood, a
final tabernacle (2). It was bold
thus to write to Jews of their revered
law, yet, the writer argues, inspired
minds in Israel had always seen
that the Mosaic system was not an
end in itself, but a passing phase of
history. In bondage and in exile the
Mosaic ritual was of small avail and
impossible adequately to sustain.
Paul saw that the function of the
law was to prepare for Christ, to
keep the consciousness of sin alive
in preparation for the sin-bearer.
A new covenant in fact, was promised (8, 9, 10). The covenant was
come, sealed with the blood of final
sacrifice, the heavenly perfection
of which all that went before was
the passing symbol and the foreshadowing.

The Tabernacle

(Hebrews 9: 1–28)

THE writer turns to the beautiful
symbol of the old covenant, the
tabernacle (1–10). Chapter after
chapter in Exodus (25–31, 35–40)
details the construction of this
beautiful (1–4) tent of worship. Its
message was this—God dwelt
among his people, not as a graven
image (Exod. 32: 4), but as an unseen presence, symbolised by the
empty throne above the mercy seat

(5). His tent was buffeted by the
desert winds which strained at the
goatskin covers of the multitude.
The same sun beat down on it.
John says exquisitely that Christ, in
the flesh, 'tabernacled among us',
and thus opens a world of thought.
In a kind of spiritual poem the
tabernacle pictured the Presence,
which was to be, and was.

The tent was beautiful to signify
a perfect beauty laid up in the
heavens. It spoke of awe, reverence
and submission before perfect holiness. It spoke of a mediator. The
ritual, too, had spiritual ends, and
was designed to reveal God as a
holy God, whose care and interest
dominates the very details of man's
living. There is something awesome
about the thoroughness with which
it takes in hand the moulding of a
nation's speech and thought.

In the whole majestic passage the
writer sees the tent in the desert as a
stage on which a mightier drama
was played out. The symbol occupied only a tiny corner of the world,
the reality filled the universe. He is
occupied again with the old Platonic
conception of a Vast Reality of
which all good things are but fragments and shadows. In the sacrifices Moses prefigured the basic
truth from which there is no refuge
in time or space—that where sin is
there follows death (7, 22). And in
the high priest, performing delicately his awesome ritual, is the
picture of Christ (23–28). But there
was a vital difference. Christ
entered, not 'a sanctuary made by
men's hands, which is only a symbol of reality, but heaven itself to
appear now before God on our
behalf' (24. NEB). It follows that

such a sacrifice is complete and final, and that it is folly, in a sort of nostalgia to cling to the partial and preparatory when the complete and the perfect has been revealed. No inadequacy, no continual need for repetition attaches to his sacrifice. The work is finished, the law superseded, atonement made for all time (28).

Once for All
(Hebrews 10: 1–39)

V.10 is the key to the understanding of this crowded passage. It is the will of God that man be 'sanctified'. Some remedy for sin was needed, which would relieve the conscience, and make man sure that he was reconciled to God. The law could not do this, for it contains but a shadow, and no true image of the good things that were to come. It provides for the same sacrifices year after year, and with these it can never bring those who worship to perfection for all time (1). The blood of sacrifice was a temporary expedient (2), a symbol only (3), because, manifestly, the blood of animals could be nothing more (4). That is why God 'prepared a body', by ancient promise, for his son (5), who thus gave himself, a final sacrifice (6), eternally complete (7–10). It is easy to see, from such a passage, how this epistle came to be attributed to Paul. This is exactly Paul's theology of the law and the atonement.

This is the new covenant, with its living intercessor (12), victorious over that which would destroy (13), his offering complete (14). There is

also one to indwell and to aid (15), in whom the law, as Ezekiel predicted (36: 26, 27), becomes a matter of the spirit (16). Hence assurance and peace. The past is forgotten (17, 18). Therefore let us assume our privileges. There are no barriers. The forgiven sinner has access to God's presence, more real than that of the high priest of old, symbolically entering the holy place (19). The veil was torn when the work was finished (20, 21. Luke 23: 45), and nothing, save our own lack of assurance, disbars us (22, 23).

The theme passes smoothly to practical advice. The ready way in which the writer turns doctrine into exhortation is a mark of this epistle. In view of God's goodness, he concludes, 'we ought to see how each of us may best arouse others to love and active goodness' (24), a duty not furthered by 'staying away from our meetings as some do' (25, NEB).

Then he turns to the matter of judgment (26–31). Jewish Christians under pressure from the Jews were repudiating their Lord. In chapter 6 the writer had stressed the psychological impossibility of renewing, in such backsliders, the true spirit of repentance. In chapter 10 he approaches the same dire situation theologically. If Christ is wilfully rejected, what remains? (26). Only judgment (27, 28), a grim prospect for one 'who has trampled under foot the son of God, profaned the blood of the covenant by which he was consecrated, and affronted God's gracious Spirit' (29, NEB). Remember, he begs 'the days gone by, when, newly enlightened, you met the challenge of great sufferings and stood firm' (32). The Jewish Christian church had begun well, and paid the price of resistance. Jewry cast it off. And then, like the Nicolaitans in another historic context, there arose those who tried to effect a compromise, mingle new and old, confine Christ to his own people and to circumscribe his gospel. It was a nationalistic heresy, and altogether destructive of Christian truth (39). The appeal (33–38) is strongly reminiscent again of Paul.

The Title Deeds

(Hebrews 11: 1–40)

FAITH, says the writer, picking up 10: 38, 'gives substance to our hopes, and makes us certain of realities we do not see' (1, NEB). 'Faith', as one translator dares to render it, quite legitimately, is 'the title deeds to things hoped for . . .' Faith goes on beyond where reason pauses. It is the leap in the dark after reason has reached its frontier. It involves both will and action. Faith is as old as the story of men and God (2). Still roving round the Platonic thought of perfection to which all phenomena, by God's grace, can move, he says: 'It is by faith that we understand that the universe was created as an expression of the Mind of God, its visible realities arising from that which is beyond the grasp of man' (3). Faith is basic. Grant this and the rest follows. Thus appeared Abel and Enoch at the dawn of time (5). They pleased God, not by what they did, but by what they believed (6).

Likewise Noah, of whose faith the ark itself was the symbol (7).

Abraham was the first missionary. Faith governed his life. All that was real to him was a world he could not see (8–19). The scene is Ur, 4000 years ago. At no point on the globe, in those centuries, was it more possible to grasp the spread of human life, to understand man. Pottery from Ur is found at Mohenjo-Daro on the Indus, for the dhows sailed east, met the junks of China, and carried back the products of the Malabar Coast. The caravans from 'the fertile crescent' brought knowledge of Damascus, the Nile, and the ships of Minos from Crete. A man living in Ur whose mind was illumined with a vast, clamouring idea—God was one, God was holy, and men had lost God in bestial misconception and degrading cults of human sacrifice, and animal worship, blasphemous obscenities and priestly tyranny. It was a turning point in history when Abraham found all his thinking channel into one clear voice to go and found a nation, remote from the city's corruption, a nation dedicated to a mighty truth.

Isaac and Jacob inherited the great man's faith, albeit weakly. One point only is picked in Jacob's life, the last illumination just before he died, a flash of fire which glowed bright again in Joseph (22). Moses, by nothing short of faith like Abraham's, left the glitter and the glory of high honour and career to follow God's will in the slave camps of Goshen (23–25). He saw God's plan in the Hebrew minority whose tattered horde he dared to pluck from tyranny and lead through the barriers of sand and sea to liberty (26–31). It was Abraham's vision victoriously re-created. Faith again showed itself as a moral choice, a desire to pursue truth and virtue. Faith can grow on no other ground. It is always the choice of the nobler alternative. It involves courage. Testing of the resolution inevitably follows. But John 7:17 always remains true.

The river runs on, through strange and faulty characters (31, 32) who, nevertheless, through some spark of faith, achieved something for God, through incidents over which the surge of the writer's lyrical enthusiasm hardly pauses (33, 34. 2 Sam. 8:15; Dan. 3:19–28; 6:18, 23; 1 Kings 19; 2 Kings 6:31; 20:1–17 etc.). He carries on through the brave days of the Maccabees to the dawn of Christian times, speaking of heroes and heroines 'too good for this world' (38).

And, let it be noted by Jews so ready to defect, these showed their faith triumphant in pre-Christian times, without the compelling manifestation of Christ.

The Race

(Hebrews 12:1–29)

'WITH these witnesses to faith around us like a cloud, we must throw off every encumbrance, every clinging sin, and run with resolution the race for which we have entered, our eyes fixed on Jesus on whom faith depends from start to finish ...' (1, 2. NEB). With another Pauline touch the

writer thinks of the stadium and the stripped and disciplined runners. The pageant of past heroes of faith becomes a crowd, all the past arrayed to watch the performance of today. Eyes fixed on the goal, the runner sees the watching crowd as a blur, a 'cloud' (Phil. 3:13). 'Christ is the goal, and Christ the prize.' He showed us how to run (2, 3), and inspires us in our running ... The N.T. contribution to the vast problem of pain, is one to which Job never came. God suffers, God suffered in Christ. V. 4 reinforces the suggestion made above that the epistle was written before Nero's persecution broke out. It certainly had not yet touched the provincial group to whom it was first addressed. Turning to another figure of speech, the writer likens the discipline of life to the salutary discipline of a good father, imposed and exercised because the father cares (5–11). The analogy falls short, as every analogy must do, and does not distinguish between what God permits and what he directs. The context is that of the ancient father, who held unquestioned power over the family and the words would provoke no questioning in a contemporary audience. Proverbs 3:11, 12 were also in the writer's mind, familiar and accepted thought. Life's trials, therefore, must be regarded as the discipline of God to be met by acceptance and obedience, not rebellion or resentment. 'Come, then,' he concludes, 'stiffen your drooping arms and quaking knees, and keep your steps from wavering ...' (12, 13). Straight paths must be cut for our marching. None should limp out of the way, for God can heal such stumbling (13). Peace and uprightness are the marks of Christians (14). 'Holiness' is the constant preparation for the presence of God, and the state of heart and mind must be the theme of constant vigilance (15), and no 'root of bitterness' (Deut. 29: 18) be allowed to sprout ('... no poisonous shoot be allowed to spring up' Knox). No defiled person reaches the holy presence, and let Esau's irreversible decision remind all that a moment's folly can ruin a life (Gen. 25: 28-34; 27: 1-39). In the writer's mind is the thought, springing from v. 16, that the moment's folly is commonly the breaking into sight in the glare of some testing, of what has all along been an unrevealed attitude of mind (16, 17).

Sin under Sinai and the old dispensation, stood between man and the awesome majesty of God (Exod. 19: 12, 13; Deut. 4: 11). A way had been made for Moses, but God 'came in terror, as the king of kings'. With Christ they came to another mount, a new Jerusalem, the city built by God (11: 10), a new mediator and all the immense privileges of a new covenant (18-22). But let not those so endowed treat their privilege lightly. We deal with a God of love, but that God was the God of Sinai's thunder. Judgment still lies on sin. In Christ we see God fully, and more prominent than the thunder-riven cloud upon the mount is the vision of God's love in the One in whom 'grace and truth' came visibly to earth (John 1: 17). It is true that small-minded men 'magnify his

strictness with a zeal he will not own', but it is equally true that others presume upon his goodness, as though, as La Fontaine once put it, it is 'his trade to forgive'. Forgiveness is sure but it was dearly bought and should be received, not casually, but 'with reverence and awe' (28). Our God is 'a devouring fire' (29) whose presence burns sin away.

In Conclusion

(Hebrews 13: 1-25)

ANTICIPATING John, at the end of the century, the writer opens the customary conclusion of precepts and greetings with a plea for brotherly love (1), and for the open hospitality so vital for Christians who moved about in a corrupt pagan world (2). A trifle whimsically, but in a manner sometimes true to life's experience, he mentions the incidents in Abraham's (Gen. 18) and Manoah's life (Judg. 13). It was perhaps some local circumstances which prompted the reference to persecution (3), and also, side by side, to ascetic notions of celibacy, and the sexual permissiveness which lies at the other extreme (4). The Christian is bidden cast out the greed which corrupts the soul and embitters society (5), to recognise God's overruling care (6), and to honour their leaders in the faith—'for you can see how it works out in their lives' (7). V. 8 is a 'saying', slipped in like a colophon or a 'selah' in the Psalms, to divide two themes.

Vv. 9-13 are obscure because

local context is lacking. It seems that the 'various and outlandish doctrines' (9) had to do with such dietary taboos as Paul twice encountered (Rom. 14: 2, 14, 21; Col. 2: 8, 16–23), 'various' because they resurrected now one, now another detail of the old economy; 'outlandish', it may be surmised, because they lay outside the frontiers of pure Christian teaching. It is by grace, not by select foods, he concludes, that the soul is fed (9). Such practices have not profited their devotees (9, end).

Sacrificial meals seem to have entered the controversy, and perhaps a guess might be hazarded that the Christian 'love feast' or what was to become the Christian eucharist, was being likened to the priests' partaking of the sacrifice in the 'Levitical ritual'. In some way this analogy was diminishing the atonement, or else introducing some element of form and practice which was inconsistent with the mere exercise of saving faith. From this 'outlandish' pre-occupation the writer can derive only one facet of truth. As on the Day of Atonement the priest carried the blood into the Holy of Holies, while the flesh was not eaten but burned without the camp, so Christ was rejected by society (10–13), and we who follow, bearing his reproach, must also go without the camp. So, with more guesswork than certainty, an obscure passage may be interpreted. It would be clear enough to those addressed.

What is lucid, and perennially applicable, is the associated exhortation. Let those to whom he writes not shrink from the challenge to abandon old ways and face the opprobrium of their old coreligionists. Such is the 'reproach' of Christ, and in bearing it they become one with him. The surrender of such privileges is no real loss, for the Jews live in a shadow world. The Christians inhabit a real world (14). Here is the old Platonic notion again. Plato's culmination of the argument in the *Republic* (592 A, B) runs, in Socrates' words: ' "You mean the city which we just now described ourselves as founding—the city planted in imagination, for I conceive it is nowhere on earth." "Well", I replied, "in heaven there is perhaps a pattern of it stored up for any man who wishes to see it and, seeing it, to become a citizen thereof. Whether it exists anywhere now or in the future, matters nothing; for in that city alone will he live, and not another." '

And 'outside the camp' can be offered the 'sacrifice of praise', that is 'the tribute of lips which acknowledge his name' (15. NEB)—and, 'do not neglect to do good and to share what you have ...' (16. RSV).

Whatever date in the sixties of the century is favoured, history indicates that Jewry was in a state of unrest. Jewish turbulence and revolt was not confined to Palestine, and any Roman or Greek city which had a large Jewish quarter was always aware of the problem which that restless, proud and nationalistic minority created. The writer bids Christian Jews dissociate themselves from such misconduct (17). Like the administrators of Ephesus, as the town clerk pointed out (Acts 19:

40), the city authorities had a vested interest in the maintenance of order.

Prayers were commonly requested in the epistles (18. 1 Thess. 5: 25; 2 Thess. 3: 1; Rom. 15: 30; Eph. 6: 18; Col. 4: 3). It is implied in the same context (19), that the writer belonged to or ministered to the group to which he wrote. The benediction follows (20, 21), and a request (22) which seems to indicate an irritable state of mind, either over international politics or theological division. V. 23, as has already been remarked, could imply equally that the writer was in Italy and spoke of Italian Christians around him, or was absent from Italy, but with a group of Italian Christians known to the recipients—wherever they were.

THE EPISTLE OF JAMES

Practical Christianity
(James 1: 1–27)

JAMES the Righteous, brother of the Lord, was the recognised apostolic head of the Jerusalem church from A.D. 48 to 62 (Acts 12: 17; 15: 4–29; 21: 18; 1 Cor. 15: 7; Gal. 1: 18, 19; 2: 9). Most of the recorded information about him comes directly or indirectly from Paul (1). Paul was markedly deferential towards him, even obeying the unwise command of Acts 21: 18. James, as Acts 15 shows, accepted the Gentile church, and his martyrdom in A.D. 62, reported by Josephus, suggests that Ananus the high priest saw no ally in him. He may, however, overanxious about unity, have been uneasy about Paul, especially if faced by growing Judaism in the Jersualem church. The writer of this letter knew Paul. The next verses (2–4) are almost a rephrasing of Romans 5: 1–5, written in A.D. 58, Did Paul, meticulously correct, file copies of his letters with James? Did he also know Peter's almost contemporary letter (1 Pet. 1: 7)? V. 5 is not an abrupt change. There is a verbal link apparent in the Greek. If one is to see stern satisfaction in trial (2) because it is fruitful, one needs the wisdom of God (Prov. 8), the all-discerning intelligence visible in creation, a wis-

dom available if a man is anchored in God, not tossed like a wave (Eph. 4: 14), divided in loyalties and interests (6–8), uncertain decision (Matt. 6: 22–24). The thought of testing and its steeling of the soul leads to the thought of prosperity and adversity (9), twin and common causes of tension in the Jerusalem church, and that leads nimbly to the transience of life and the imagery of the O.T. (Ps. 37: 2; 90: 5, 6; 102: 4, 11; 103: 15; Isa. 40: 7—and 1 Pet. 1: 24). James remembers that he has already alluded to a Beatitude (2. Matt. 5: 11, 12) and with v. 12 comes back to the Sermon which he remembered vividly. The crown was a common image in that athletic world (1 Cor. 9: 25; 2 Tim. 2: 5; 4: 8; 1 Pet. 5: 4). In his downright fashion he states that it is trials that are permitted of God (Matt. 6: 13; 26: 41), temptations come from within. Remembering Romans 7: 7, 8, 19–23, he quotes Peter's fishing term 'enticed as by a bait' (2 Pet. 2: 14, 18). Vv. 14 and 15 follow a Pauline sequence to 'death' as Paul conceived it (Rom. 5: 21; 6: 21). God gives no bad thing, only good, as a popular quotation has it. The opening seven words of v. 17 are a Greek hexameter. We, the privileged recipients are a special people, quick to listen, slow to speak in a perilous world, purged of violent reactions (18–20). We 'put off' the old life like a soiled garment (Eph. 4: 24, Col. 3: 8; 1 Pet. 2: 1—and Rom. 13: 14), taking the seed like the good ground (Matt. 13: 3 3–9, 18–23: Rom. 6: 5). We are free, but freedom is not negative and passive but positive and active. It invades doing and speaking, prompting, restraining (22, 26, 27). Some situation clearly demanded less talk but more social involvement by Christians. It fits the early sixties.

Faith and Works
(James 2: 1–26)

CLASS distinction (1) was forbidden by law (Deut. 1: 17). The word used here is a Hebraic formation literally meaning 're-ceiving the face of someone'. It is exclusively N.T. (Rom. 2:11; Eph.6 : 9; Col. 3: 25; 1 Pet. 1: 17). It contains the thought of ungodly pre-occupation with the outward appearance (1 Sam. 16: 7; 2 Cor. 10: 7) and disregard for inner reality (Heb. 4: 12). The Greek 'prosôpon', used to render the Hebrew for 'face' can also mean an actor's mask, and so the Greek imports a new element into the work. God is not deceived by the shell and surface of things (Acts 10: 34). Much less must the followers of 'the glorious Lord' (John 1: 14) be led by base motives to honour the well-dressed above the shabby (2, 3). Seats were provided for the elders and to notables (Matt. 23: 6; Mark 12: 38, 39). The word 'synagogue' is used for 'assembly' (2, KJV) indicative of the Jewish stance of the writer.

Such distinction is double-minded (1: 7, 8). 'Have you not made distinctions among yourselves?' (4). They become judges with evil thoughts' (RSV correctly). The word is used in Luke 5: 22, 23 for the Pharisees' reasonings. Further, reverting to the Sermon, have not the 'poor in the estimation of the world', a notable destiny? (5. Matt. 5: 3). Observe the rhetoric. James, even while he writes, is in the pulpit. What social conditions led to the outburst of v. 6 cannot be said. Persecution came from the rich and powerful (Acts 4: 1–3; 13: 50; 16: 19) but also, as at Ephesus, from the tradesmen (Acts 19: 25), unless this example also points to the rich misleading the poor. The 'royal law' would have it otherwise (Lev. 19: 18; Matt. 21: 42; Rom. 13: 10), and no man can pick and choose when confronted with the law (10–13. 1 John 3: 4). James echoes Jesus again (Matt. 5: 7; 7: 1). James, who must have been a formidable preacher, proceeds in best oratorical style to castigate sham. He does not contradict Paul, who was insistent enough about the demonstration of action (1 Cor. 3: 13; 2 Cor. 5: 10). Paul, as Peter says, was sometimes misrepresented (2 Pet. 3: 15, 16). As head of the Jewish Christians, James may have been alert to make sure that Jews should not go from the extreme of 'works' to the absurdities of a faith which did nothing. 'Can that faith save him?' (14, RV). Such 'faith' is open to obvious challenge (18). Abraham justified his faith when, thirty years after Genesis 15: 5, 6, he offered Issac. So conspicuously, did Rahab. James no more rebuffs

Paul than he does Christ in vv. 15–18 (Matt. 6: 25–34). Faith which cannot communicate, act or show movement, is like any corpse (17)—dead and doomed to corruption. James is seen again as a Jewish Christian, thoroughly Christian, but concerned to do his best, without loss of truth, to mitigate the agonising reappraisal of those who passed from law to grace.

The Tongue and the Wise Man
(James 3: 1–18)

JAMES' drastic chapter on the evils of the tongue has some contemporary explanation. Perhaps there were those who, for their own ends, thrust themselves into the teacher's rôle (in v. 1 read 'teachers', as all modern versions of standing, for 'masters') and who were doing damage by irresponsible speech. In A.D. 64 the fire of Rome was falsely fastened on the Christians, and the slander could have been made plausible by exaggeration of apocalyptic preaching (2 Pet. 3: 12). James may have also in view such fierce disputation as is found in Acts, and may have found his efforts to draw those with a Jewish and those with a Gentile background together, hampered by uninhibited controversial language. In all we know of James, moderation, a penchant for compromise, and reluctance to take extreme positions, is evident. The strong language of this chapter is mitigated by the note of intimate appeal (1, 10). Words are 'works', and the tongue can ruin integrity and testimony (2. Matt. 12: 36, 37). Let

would-be teachers, therefore, beware (Matt. 23: 8). There was a ready audience (Acts 17: 21; 2 Tim. 4: 3), and a wide sphere of damage open (Acts 15: 24; 1 Tim. 1: 6, 7). An undisciplined tongue can swerve and destroy the whole personality, like the unbridled horse, and the rudderless ship (3, 4). This is because words have a deep spring of origin (11, 12). Man speaks out of that which is accumulated in the personality (Matt. 12: 34, 35; Luke 6: 45). Trees bear after their kind (Matt. 3: 10; 7: 16, 17). Wisdom mellows speech (Prov. 8: 6, 7). Wisdom, the distillation of knowledge, issues in a worthy life (Peter's word of 1 Pet. 2: 12), and in the gentleness of Christ (Matt. 5: 5; 11: 29). The wise man is emancipated from envy and jealousy, both the bitter fruit of pride and falsehood (14). Faction and selfish ambition disqualify the one who would teach, for James still has v. 1 in mind. Self-exaltation ('glory not') can only belie truth. Truth becomes falsehood if its exponent is manifestly without its fruits. To teach God's truth demands more than the sophist's tricks, dialectics, and the subtleties of debate which professional oratory had to show (Acts 24: 2–8). Such teachers are founts of corruption (15, 16). God's wise man is a man of peace and purity, gentle, easy to approach, tolerant and outgoing, without prejudices, favouritism, posing (17). Perhaps 'James the Righteous' was precisely such a man (Matt. 5: 3–11). 'The harvest which righteousness produces grows from the seed of peace which men of peace sow' (18. Ps. 85: 10; Isa. 32:

17). The three chapters have the flavour and style of Amos and Isaiah. Chapter 4 reads like Jeremiah.

The World Invades

(James 4: 1–17)

THE early church is too commonly idealised. Were it not for the Corinthian letters, it might be difficult to believe that a Christian leader could speak to church communities as James does here. The reproaches are an argument for an early date, before persecution purged the church of corrupt adherents. It is also to be remembered that converts were snatched from the pagan society visible in Pompeii, and set forth in such writers as Juvenal and Petronius (Rom. 1: 18–32). The N.T. and its corpus of ethical teaching, was also in its first beginnings. Vv. 1–10 form a self-contained whole merging into a call to repent. Factions and quarrels marred the church (1), the manifestation of unsurrendered lives (Tit. 3: 3). 'Lusts' war against the soul, says Peter, in a similar context (1. 2: 11). It was difficult for dwellers in such great cities as Corinth and Ephesus to escape an all-pervading sensuality. The 'affluent society' slides fast towards such pleasure-ridden life. 'Killing' may not be literal murder. Death and the dealing of death has other weapons than steel (2), while adultery is a familiar image for unfaithfulness to God ('unfaithful creatures' [4], says RSV). Hence prayer which was mere words, and no answer to an 'adulterous generation' (Matt. 12: 39). Divided loyalty destroys (Matt. 6: 24). V. 5 reflects Galatians 5: 17. The verse is difficult. RV is probably correct: 'That Spirit which he made to dwell in us, yearneth for us even unto jealous envy.' So let them come to one who hates arrogance and blesses humility (6), in surrender to God and resistance to evil (7), in questing sincerity (8), in the grief of conviction of sin (9), and saving questing sincerity (8), in the grief of conviction of sin (9), and saving humility (10). So shall perish the spite and malice which enfeeble and divide (Matt. 5: 20–24; 7: 1, 2). God will undoubtedly judge (11, 12. Rom. 14: 10). The rapid fire of precept, command and exhortation ceases. A sermon from James must have been a devastating experience, no word lost, no moment of escape from the volley of truth, no hiding-place for sham, unreality, insincerity. Vv. 13–17 give a vivid picture of the Jewish business man of the great ghettos. Some of these expatriates were rich. Hence the social rifts of 2: 1–4. There is a glimpse of the typically successful business executive, cosmopolitan, hurrying abroad (Acts 16: 14), buying, selling, confident and ordering the future. Such planned living, says James (14, 15) could breed arrogance and damaging self-assurance. Let them rather hold lightly the things of a transient world and avoid what John calls 'the pride of life' (1. 2: 16).

Concluding Words
(James 5: 1–20)

THE thought of prosperous business men, and there were some in the church (1: 2–5), leads James to some indignant words about the wealthy of this world. Oppression angered him, and the poor, especially in James' own land, were pitiably deprived. It was part of the O.T. passion for justice that the wage-earner was protected (Lev. 19: 13; Deut. 24: 14, 15; Jer. 22: 13; Mal. 3: 5; Luke 10: 7; 1 Tim. 5: 18). Riches are for unselfish use. They rot and rust and ruin corrupt the stored tokens of wealth (Matt. 6: 19, 20). Used for self they rot and ruin the character (5), words which, in an age of affluence, apply to a far wider range of society than they did in James' day. The 'consumer society' of the planners' pre-occupation, can be a waster of the world's irreplacable resources. In the context of the first century he could only bid the oppressed await the coming of the king. V. 6 holds a deep pathos. James himself was so soon to die at the hands of the rich arbiters of society. Ananus took advantage of a brief hiatus in Roman procuratorial rule.

Like Paul, James uses the last paragraph of his letter to touch briefly on a variety of topics (12–20). He deals with extravagances of speech and the interspersing of what should be said in simple sincerity with protestations of truth. He also has in mind the rich hypocrisy of swearing on oath (12. Matt. 23: 16–22). He passes to prayer, that basic need for all spiritual progress (14, 15). In illness prayer was, and is, the deepest resource, and a ministry of the church had grown round it, more meaningful and both psychologically and spiritually therapeutic in that medically deprived day. Nor is it without modern validity. The anointing with oil was a Jewish practice (Isa. 1: 6; Mark 6: 13; Luke 10: 34). Here, perhaps, is another indication of the Jewish context of James' thinking. The confession of sin has been corrupted, like the ministry of healing, by human emotion and folly (16). James has no mutual wallowing in self-depreciation in view, but the proper admission of wrong done to another, a true means of restoring fellowship. And, as touching prayer, he remarks, let them remember Elijah, so human, so prone to discouragement, and yet so potent in supplication (17, 18). Finally let us care for the drifter and the weakling, bringing him back to Christ and covering his sin (19, 20). Or is it the sin of the rescuer, not the rescued? The Jews thought much of balancing sin committed by good done, and, without establishing a doctrine, James may have lifted a familiar quotation (cf. 1 Pet. 4: 8).

THE FIRST EPISTLE OF PETER

A Letter for Asia
(1 Peter 1: 1–25)

IT need not be doubted that the Galilean fisherman, Peter, who became a leader of the church and a world figure, dictated this letter to Silvanus (5: 12), for distribution to a circle of churches in the blunt peninsula called today Asia Minor. He wrote from Rome (5: 13), possibly in A.D. 63 or early 64. The savage attack on the church in the summer of 64 had not, it seems begun, for obedience to the emperor is still enjoined, (2: 17), and ordered living set forth as a means of disarming a hostile society (2: 11, 12). Persecution fed on the animosity of the crowd, as the N.T. story shows from Jerusalem to Ephesus. The frightened tyrant Nero used it, as Tacitus, the historian tells us (*Ann.* 15: 44) in the summer of A.D. 64. Hence a pointer to the date. A crisis was taking shape for Rome, and for the church. Both came in that decade. Rome, whose vast imperial system had shaped the evangelistic patterns of Paul, was now the new Babylon (5: 13), 'the Beast' of which John wrote (Rev. 13 and 17: 5).

The map shows the route taken by the bearer from Sinope to Nicomedia (1)—territory of whose evangelisation no record survives. Paul was unable to reach the area (Acts 16: 7). Pliny, the governor of Bithynia, found his province full of Christians in A.D. 111, and wrote of his dismay to Trajan (*Letters* 10. 96, 97). These unknown Christians had no N.T. Hence the theologically-loaded language of the greeting (2–4). They were a new 'chosen people' (Deut. 4: 37; Isa. 43: 21; Rom. 11: 28), strangers in an alien world (Gen. 23: 4; Heb. 11: 10, 11). The Trinity and the atonement, the resurrection, the 'new birth' (a doctrine not to appear in writing for another thirty years)— all are in vv. 2 to 4. The writer, remember, had 'seen the linen clothes lying'. (John 20: 7). He had picked up imagery and language from his colleague Paul (Rom. 1: 23; 1 Cor. 9: 25; 15: 22; 1 Tim. 1: 17; Rom. 4: 13, 14; 8: 17, 18; 1 Cor. 6: 9, 10; 15: 20; Gal. 5: 21; Eph. 5: 5). He proceeds to eschatology and the Christian hope which his readers were soon desperately to need (5–7). His words again echo Paul (Rom. 1: 16; 5: 3, 4) and a well-remembered word from the Tabgka hillside (Matt. 5: 11, 12). In vv. 8, 9 we have a lyric passage. Such language, some have said, would be beyond an 'unlettered'

(Acts 4: 13) fisherman. They forget Josef Konrad Korzeniowski, the Polish seaman, who became the figure of English literature, Joseph Conrad. Peter had seen Christ, seen the wonder of him grow, seen him defeat death.

Some of Peter's readers had the O.T., and catching up two sayings of Christ (Matt. 13: 17; Luke 10: 24—and add Luke 24: 27), he turns to others who 'had not seen', but knew him (10–12). Hence, with an incident on Galilee in mind (John 21: 7), Peter bids Christians 'gird up' their determination, be 'self-controlled' and hopeful (13), obedient, changed men, godly (14–16). In v. 14 is the first of many echoes of Romans 12: 1, 2, a passage which had deeply influenced Peter. 'Stop trying to make yourselves like the society you live in,' said Paul. Peter uses the same verb. And to be godly means awe before the price of our salvation (17, 18), and trust in a living Christ (20, 21). Observe 'call him Father'. The Lord's Prayer was clearly known.

Anticipating the theme of John's first letter, and in a church which already had members from all ranks of that stratified society, Peter stresses the levelling, binding cement of love, in the name of the eternal Word of God, the one lasting foundation then as now (22–25).

The Christian in a Pagan Environment

(1 Peter 2: 1–25)

ALL tolerated 'malice, deceit, insincerity, jealousies and recriminations of every kind', must be rooted from the recesses of the mind if the reader of the Word is to be fed by it (1–3). Peter speaks of the O.T., for the Septuagint was known in these Greek-speaking communities. Observe the common element in these corroding vices which he would see leached from his new society. They all contain the exaltation of self, the thrusting of another down that self may stand spuriously higher. Such pagan vices must be 'put off' (1) like dirty rags. Did Peter, writing from Rome, have a word from the Romans' own letter in mind about 'putting on' the Lord Jesus like a new garment (Rom. 13: 14)?

There is Jewish thinking in vv. 4–10, woven with the words and imagery of the O.T., a little alien to Gentiles, but to Jews deeply meaningful. Paul used the same metaphor of a building held together by the divine cornerstone. (See Exod. 17: 6; Psa. 118: 22; Isa. 8: 14, 15; 28: 16; Matt. 21: 42; Rom. 9: 33; Eph. 2: 19, 20.) Stones are of little use save they be bound together into an edifice, a temple, which suggests a royal priesthood (5, 9). Indeed, stones can clog the path, unorganised, uncemented (8), even the Chief Stone, if it is set aside and rejected. (Vv. 7 and 8 conflate Ps. 118: 22 and Isa. 8: 14.) See also (1 Cor. 1: 23). 'Yes, they stumble at the word of God, for in their hearts they are unwilling to obey it—which makes their stumbling a foregone conclusion' (8, JBP). A further cluster of images from the O.T. conflates Isaiah 43: 20, 21; Exodus 19: 5, 6; Psalm 107: 14. It is clear that the minds of the writer and his attentive readers, were soaked in O.T. thought. He was speaking in language they could understand. V. 11 again echoes Romans 12: 1. The words 'I beseech' are Mod. Greek for 'Please', and the word fits both contexts. They must live like resident aliens (12), under scrutiny, like all aliens, with character and conduct their front, commendation and appeal. Slander, as both Tacitus and Pliny prove, was the Christians' first testing (11, 12). Therefore let them be good citizens (13-16). This was also Paul's preoccupation (Rom 13: 1-7; Phil. 1: 27). Luke was eager to show that the new faith was no subversive doctrine. It is a sub-theme in Acts.

Even in the hideous context of slavery (18), a horror the faith was to erode and destroy, Christ's humility could be shown. In whatever state a Christian finds himself, he has Christ for his 'copy-book heading' (21). Peter rounds off the passage by slipping into the language of Isaiah 53 (22-25), perhaps a passage known by heart in the form in which Peter casts it—a catechistic piece, perhaps, from the 'oral tradition'.

The Christian in the Home
(1 Peter 3: 1-22)

THE continuing theme is the Christian in the household. The thought in Peter's mind was the problem of a wife who became a Christian while her husband was unconvinced (1, 2). The contrary problem did not arise in a context of male authority. An unconverted wife accompanied her husband to his place of worship. Peter again insists that the first appeal is Christlike conduct. Compare Paul's advice (Eph. 5: 21-24; Col. 3: 18; Tit. 2: 4). Talk, Peter saw, was of small value. A transformed character was compelling (4, 5. Rom. 7: 22). Women, in the Greek world, were not expected to be talkative (1 Cor. 14: 34). 'Silence', says Ajax in Sophocles' sombre play, 'is woman's proper adornment.' Divorce, too, was easy, and loaded against wives. Rules were formulated among Christians, and Paul and Peter agree (1 Cor. 7: 13-16). The principles still apply. Those touching adornment are still relevant, both for men and women. Gaudiness, extravagance, anything which attracts attention for absurdity, expense or ostentation, does not commend Christ. Be like Sarah (6), says Peter, with Isaiah 51: 2 in mind.

Prayer is hindered by domestic strife (7). The secret of partnership is love, sympathy, generosity, courtesy (8), never capping malice with malice, or rendering spite for spite (9). Paul is echoed again (Rom. 12: 15). Vv. 10 to 12 are probably a hymn of the church, sweet in its gentleness, Hebrew in its balanced thought, sad in its historical contrast, for these are those who, said Tacitus, echoing Rome's slander, were 'hated for their crimes'.

To men's viciousness, persecution and hatred, there was only the answer of Christ. The hostility of evil to the good is inevitable. It occurs in Christ's first recorded words (Matt. 5: 10-12). Read Bunyan's description of the jury in Vanity Fair. Such evangelism is hard, but it remains true that 'we are the sinner's gospel, we are the scoffer's creed'. 'Men trust rather their eyes than their ears', Nero's one-time tutor, the doomed Seneca, was saying at this very time. 'Make the Lord God a living presence deep within you, and always be ready, with reverence and gentleness, to answer any who ask you about the hope you hold' (15).

A messianic title used by Peter in Acts 3: 14 recurs (18). Puzzling verses follow of which no satisfactory explanation can be given. Such an admission is sometimes honest and necessary. A case might be made for an emendation of Rendel Harris and reading: 'It was in the Spirit that Enoch also went and preached to imprisoned spirits . . .' Difficulties would still, however, remain. Who were these 'spirits'? Noah's generation? The fallen angels of Genesis 6: 1-7? There is no explanation which does not leave basic difficulties or create more. Some key is lost. One point again emerges. Christ's senior disciple knew that Christ had risen. This letter is a document of the resurrection.

Peter has enough to say elsewhere to prove that, along with Paul, he preached no doctrine of 'baptismal regeneration'. Baptism meant more than the rabbis' washing (Eph. 5: 26; Heb. 10: 22). It meant, for all who had passed through it, a new life as that which awaited the survivors of the flood. Note a phrase of Peter's (Acts 2: 32-35), and his echoes of Paul (1 Cor. 15: 24-28; Eph. 1: 20).

The Coming Trial
(1 Peter 4: 1-19)

PETER'S thoughts on baptism were deeply penetrated by Paul's teaching of mystical death with Christ and a virtual resurrection (Rom. 6: 1-14). Here is the answer to the thrust and siege of sin, not only an emptying out of evil (Matt. 12: 44), but a filling and garrisoning of new life (1, 2). The picture of pagan living (3, 4), may be illustrated from Roman writers, and the walls of Pompeii. Nor is it unfamiliar. The hostile reaction of society to Christian abstention (4) is as familiar. The word clumsily rendered 'riot' in KJV (better 'dissipation') is cognate with that used of the conduct of the Prodigal (Luke 15: 13. See also Eph. 5: 18, Tit. 1: 16).

Defamation of God's children can be blasphemy against God (4). The word is used in Romans 3: 8 and Titus 3: 2, and the associated noun at Mark 7: 22 and Ephesians 4: 31. The mystery of the pre-resurrection ministry of Christ recurs (6), not, as Barclay suggests, 'a breath-taking glimpse of . . . a gospel of a second chance'. Too much Scripture precludes that explanation. Peter's readers knew what he meant. It must be admitted that we, for want of some vital information, do not. The opening words of v. 7 were sadly true. Any keen observer knew that soon, the world, as they had known it, would change. Persecution was coming, and so was the beginning of the breakdown of the Empire. The 'year of the four emperors', A.D. 69, was portent indeed. The

Christian must always live in expectation, in the light of eternity and in the consciousness of the fragility of the body, of society and the world. It is always 'the last hour' (1 John 2: 18). And what are twenty centuries beside the life of the galaxy?

Let the Christian live with alertness born of expectation, with self control which promotes prayer ('Steady then, keep cool and pray' —7, Moff.), inspires love, sweetens hospitality (8, 9. Acts 10: 6; 21: 6; Rom. 12: 13; 16: 5; 1 Cor. 16: 19; 1 Tim. 3: 2; 5: 10; Tit. 1: 8; Heb. 13: 2), prompts appropriate service (10, 11. Rom. 12: 3–8; 1 Cor. 12), disciplines preaching and commends Christ.

Peter now assumes the rôle of prophet (12). Clouds gathered. The storm soon came. Remembering many words of Christ, Peter preached hope (13. Matt. 5: 10–12; 10: 24, 25; Mark 10: 38, 39). V. 14 actually uses the signature word of the Beatitudes ('happy').

Out of 105 verses in this letter sixty refer to doctrine and sixty-five to correct conduct. Remembering how, after the Beatitudes, the Lord had passed to the corrupted salt, Peter bade his flock to continue exemplary citizenship even in a corrupt, cruel and hostile society (15). The word lamentably rendered 'busybody' in KJV, means one who meddles where he should not. Peter is deprecating Christian involvement in subversive action. Major plots were forming in Rome and there were Christian aristocrats likely to be involved. Let them stand clear and look upon suffering as purification (19).

In Conclusion ...
(1 Peter 5: 1–14)

THE first letter of Paul to Timothy and the letter to Titus were taking shape or had just been written. The leaders of the church, aware of darkening skies, were organising for survival. The eldership principle (1) went back thirteen centuries (Num. 11: 16–30). It had been known in royal days (1 Kings 20: 8; 21: 11). It was known in Judaism (Matt. 16: 21). It was early adapted by the young church (Acts 11: 30; 14: 23; 15: 2; 16: 4; 20: 17). Seniority was a norm, but there could be exceptions (1 Tim. 4: 12). Sterling character was a necessity (2–4). The passage is full of echoes and authenticity. Compare v. 1 with Mark 9: 2; v. 2 with John 21: 17; v. 3 with Mark 10: 42; v. 4 with John 10: 11.

Becoming relationships between youth and age are stressed (5). Such fellowship requires a discipline of mind. The word used for 'gird yourself' is full of meaning. Peter uses a verb related to the noun 'engkombôma'—'the apron' he had seen his Master gird about himself when he washed his disciples' feet (John 13: 4–8). It is a touching recollection. Therefore, Peter concludes, remembering the menacing tomorrow which has haunted the letter, let them cast themselves on God (6). He quotes Psalm 55: 22 and remembers Matthew 6: 25–31 (7) and Matthew 24: 42 (8). Calmness and awareness can arm the mind against such a foe (9). We all 'pay the same tax of suffering' (v. 9 can bear this rendering). Over all stands an invincible God (10). The word rendered 'perfect' (10) is the word used of James and John 'mending' their nets when the call came to Peter to fish for men, (Matt. 4: 21). Our own torn nets can find skilful mending. The benediction follows (11).

Hundreds of papyrus letters end with similar greetings (12–15). Peter took pen and added his word to what Silvanus had taken down (see Gal. 6: 11–18). Babylon (13) was Rome (Rev. 14: 8; 16: 19; 18: 5). Mark was faithfully with Peter, as he was to be with Paul (2 Tim. 4: 11). The 'holy kiss' is not imposed on less demonstrative cultures. See JBP. Even in ancient times it became embarrassing, as Clement wrote over a century later. With heads bowed we receive the apostolic benediction.

THE SECOND EPISTLE OF PETER

Peter's Witness to the Church
(2 Peter 1: 1-21)

THE first verse claims that Peter wrote this letter, and there is no final reason for rejecting the claim. For the double name, an early trait, see Matthew 16: 16; Luke 5: 8; John 21: 15-17. The recipients, according to the same verse (1), were probably Gentile Christians. The use of 'righteousness' with ethical connotations, links this letter with the first (1 Pet. 2: 24; 3: 12, 14, 18; 4: 18). The word Saviour, as applied to Christ, became more common as the first century moved on. It was a title arrogantly claimed by the deified emperors, and it appears that Christians deliberately took it for their Lord. The first letter was addressed primarily to Christians under the threat of persecution. The second, like the letter of Jude, is addressed to Christians menaced by corrupt doctrine. Consequently, if hope is the keynote of the first letter, knowledge (2) is that of the second. It is by a clear knowledge of the truth that the appeal of falsehood is countered. Knowledge of the Lord does not narrow but expands life (3). Life in Christ is not a small preserve of emotion or communion, divorced from daily living. His living presence pervades all experience. The 'knowledge of Christ' (1: 3, 8; 2: 20) with which this momentous verse concludes is, a final answer to a barren intellectualism which was invading the church. The one who wrote this epistle had 'beheld his glory'—the mark, surely, of the traditional authorship (Luke 5: 4, 8; John 1: 42-51). Such is the Being with whom the believer is 'made one' (4). Let the believer, then, promote the blessed experience of identification (5) in all the basic virtues (6)—self-control, endurance, devotion, love. All these basic virtues had small place among the sectaries who were rending the church (2: 10-16; 3: 3).

The qualities listed in vv. 6 and 7 are the marks of Christlikeness, and the believer becomes like his Master by their acceptance and exercise. Thus, indeed, he grows in the knowledge of Christ (8). It is blindness (John 9: 39-41) or short-sightedness not to see this truth (9). There seems to be a line of popular poetry, retaining its metre, in the verse. He 'squints'.

From such a plan of living flows assurance and confidence of one's salvation (10). In effect, using a metaphor from business, the verse says: 'Do your best to lay hold of the guarantee of your calling and election.' And this is done by the cultivation of the Christian graces. V. 11 proceeds to the image of a triumphal procession entering the celestial city: 'Thus you will be given a triumphant entrance into the eternal realm...' (11). No duty lies more heavily upon the writer than that of exhortation to godly living (12). Christianity faced a vicious age with standards of purity, uprightness, and uncompromising virtue, and every error contained some diminution of such demands. A 'new morality' is prompt to follow a 'new theology'. The writer has not long to live (13). The time to 'fold up his tent' was at hand. That assurance he had from Christ (14), covert reference, perhaps, to a conversation on the beach recorded in John's last chapter. V. 15 refers to the task of Mark who, said Papias (A.D. 60–130), produced the first synoptic gospel at Peter's request. Irenaeus, born about the time Papias died, speaking of Mark's writing, uses the word 'exodos' for death, a rare word used here by Peter. It seems clear that Irenaeus knew this passage. The faith, he insists, is grounded in history, factually founded, and not to be explained away or reduced to mystic experience through well-spun tales (16). A thrust is here which refers to other sophistries than those of the first century. Peter illustrates by the account of the transfiguration (18, 19) authenticated by the differences from the synoptic account. A forger with the gospels before him would have mentioned Elijah and Moses, and certainly would have included:

'Hear him' (Mark 9: 7). Thus 'we have the prophetic word made more sure' (19, RSV) by the anticipation of final glory on the mount. The phrase 'made more sure' is a legal term (2 Cor. 1: 21; Phil. 1: 7). '... to which please, take heed.' 'You will do well if ...' is a common phrase in the papyri for 'please'. In the O.T. is the word of God. Those who wrote (21) were 'driven along' (the same word is used for the Alexandrian grain ship in Acts 27: 15, 17) by the Spirit. It was clear and not a framework for exotic doctrine (20).

The Coming of False Teaching
(2 Peter 2: 1–22)

IT is sad to find the emergence of error by the middle sixties, on the very eve of the death of the last witnesses (1). John was to survive for another generation, but the coming of the Neronian persecution, as Peter foresaw, was the end of an era (1 Pet. 4: 7). There were impostors, professing to speak for God (1, 2), not an unknown or unforeseen situation (Deut. 13: 1–6; Matt. 24: 24). They 'insert' ('introduce alongside the true') false doctrines. 'Cunningly', 'secretly', 'stealthily' are various attempts to render the Greek prefix in the verb. 'The people' are the new Israel. It is a favourite idea of Peter, notable in his sermons in Acts and in the first letter, that Christians are incorporated in the new Israel of God. 'Heresies of destruction' is a Hebraism for 'destructive heresies'. For the verb 'bought' cf. 1 Corinthians 6: 20. Discredit on the faith by unworthy living is a preoccupation of the first letter (2: 11, 12, 15; 3: 15, 16; 4: 4, 14, 15). It is an old theme (2. Gen. 13: 7; Isa. 52: 5—Rom. 2: 24; Tit. 2: 5; Jas. 2: 7). The way of truth (John 14: 6) implies both a pattern of belief and a code of conduct. In Christ they cannot be dissociated.

Religion has always offered a field for gain to the unscrupulous. The clever Balaam, a man who could have known a nobler life, is the first notable example, the Sadducees with their market in the temple court, Simon (Acts 8: 9–25) who gave a name to 'simony', are of the number (15, 16). The strong language is shocking only to those who have grown tolerant of that which diminishes Christ, lowers the stern standards of God, and devalues an uncorrupted faith. Three O.T. examples follow, chosen in the style of Peter's O.T. illustrations in the first letter (ch. 2). Pride and rebellion (4), apathy before judgment on evil (5), and vice (6) were marks of the false teachers. In v. 5, 'the eighth person' means 'with seven others' (i.e. his wife, three sons and their wives). Note again an echo (1 Pet. 3: 20). 'Turning into ashes' is the word (6) used by Dio Cassius in describing the fate of Pompeii in A.D. 79.

It is a little surprising to find Lot receiving some commendation (7–9). In Genesis he has a sombre record, a self-seeker, backslidden, weak, reluctant, depraved (Gen. 13: 10–14; 19: 1–35). 'Just', he may have been on a comparison with the vileness he chose to live with—a lesson, as E. M. B. Green remarks, for television addicts. Noah and Lot, it may be granted, stood alone amid evil, but they are an illustration of the mercy of God rather than of personal worth. And Lot saved nothing save his now useless person.

'Despising government' (others variously 'scorning control', 'spurning authority') means 'undisciplined'—a mark of all social and spiritual decay. The false teachers, in Peter's view, touch the depths, presumptuous, arrogant, irreverent (11), bestial, and to be treated as such, ignorant in their blasphemy (12), dissipated and hideous table companions (12. 1 Pet. 1: 19; Eph. 5: 27) at the common meal of the church (13). They 'have eyes for nothing but women, eyes never at rest from sin. They lure the unstable to their ruin, past masters in mercenary greed. God's curse is on them' (14. NEB). Little comment is needed, only the attention of a sect-ridden church and a sex-ridden age. The word for 'luring', 'beguiling', is a fishing term. It means to catch with bait—perhaps a recollection of Galilee, as the whole verse rings of the Sermon on the Mount (Matt. 5: 20–30; 7: 15–20). The word used for 'unstable' people, echoes the Lord's word to Peter: 'When you yourself are restored, strengthen your brothers.' The word for 'unstable' is *asteriktoi*'. 'Strengthen' is *sterixon*'.

The 'Balaamites' were the Nicolaitans (Rev. 2: 6, 15). They were strong in Thyatira (Rev. 2: 20). In Numbers (22–24), Balaam is shown as the victim of avarice, but in the same book (31: 16) it is made clear that Balaam's scheme was immoral compromise to break the pure standards of the Israelite host (15, 16). A dumb beast could see through such subterfuge. Strong metaphors follow. 'Wells without water' could be disaster in a thirsty land, a deception full of death (Prov. 10: 11; 13: 14; 14: 27; Jer. 2: 13). They were mists before a driving gale (the word of Mark 4: 37 and Luke 8: 23), insubstantial, without substance like the clouds of Aristophanes' play of that name—which, oddly enough, satirises false teachers. Perhaps it was a popular metaphor. The verse, unusually, contains several words more characteristic of classical and literary Greek than of the Common Dialect. Perhaps the amanuensis was a person of culture. It seems clear that the final form of the language was left sometimes to the man who took the letter—a likely hypothesis which makes linguistic analysis a chancy ground as a test of authorship.

The lure of the sectaries (18), says Peter, using again the fishing term of v. 14, is pompous language which covers immorality with specious terms, deadly bait for those 'who have barely begun to escape from their heathen environment' (NEB). There is a stinging relevance for today. They confuse bondage with liberty (John 8: 34; Rom. 6: 6; 8: 21; Gal. 5: 13) and thus to be drawn back makes it difficult to renew them to repentance (20, 21). There is burnt-over ground in such corrupted lives, in which no good seed can root. Peter again remembers Christ (Matt. 12: 45; Luke 11: 26. And see Heb. 10: 26). Slightly rearrange the

final words of v. 22 and they fall into two metrical lines—the proverb Peter appears to quote.

The Day of the Lord
(2 Peter 3: 1–18)

PETER turns from the sustained attack on the saboteurs of the church to the tender encouragement of his own faithful people (1, 14, 17). He calls them back to Scripture and tradition (2) for comments on the deepening apostasy of the day (3). The reaction of men was foretold (Matt. 24: 3–5, 11, 23–26; 2 Tim. 3: 1–9; Jas. 5: 3). Their scorn expressed itself in a pattern of life (Isa. 28: 14–22). It was clearly a disappointment to early Christians that a generation was passing in death—and yet the Lord tarried (4). Both Peter (1. 4: 7) and John, a generation later (1. 2: 19), could speak of their time as the last hour or the end of the world. Nothing, in fact, was left in the grand plan of God for fulfilment but the final revelation of Christ. The task for Christians, as Paul told the Thessalonians, similarly bewildered a decade earlier (2 Thess. 2: 1–12), is to carry on a normal life. God is not bound by the clocks and calendars of men (5–8). 'Thousand' is not to be taken literally (8). God moves in a different pattern of time (Ps. 90: 4). Sin will not be tolerated for ever. That fact is sure (5, 6. Matt 24: 37–39). A fiery end to any final world order is a tenet of science. Nothing is immortal (7).

Furthermore, if God delays, it is to lengthen the opportunity of

grace (9). He has no pleasure in
death (1 Tim. 2: 4; Rom. 11: 32;
Ezek. 18: 23). He has warned
enough that judgment comes un-
heralded (Matt. 24: 43, 44; 25:
1–30; Luke 12: 39, 40; 1 Thess. 5:
2). Slipping into poetic, apocalyptic
language, he repeats the old warning of the prophets (Isa. 13: 10–13;
24: 19, 20; 34: 4). How else could
language express the inexpressible?
(11–13). The practical implication
is that which the Lord had himself
taught. Men with such expectation
live in the light of it (14).

Meanwhile, concludes Peter (15,
16), 'consider that God's patience is
meant to be man's salvation, as our
dear brother Paul pointed out to
you in his letter to you written out
of the wisdom God gave him.
There are, of course, some things
in his letters which are difficult to
understand, and which, unhappily,
ill-informed and unbalanced people
distort (as they do the other
Scriptures), and bring disaster on
their heads' (JBP). The reference
need not be to any specific passage
(e.g. Rom. 2: 4—and perhaps 3:
25; 9: 22; 11: 22), but to the
general tenor of Paul's teaching.
To base an argument on this passage against the Petrine authorship
of the letter is perverse and obtuse
in the extreme. The old theory of a
rift between the apostles which
came from Tübingen in the last
century is truly discredited. What
sort of Christians do some imagine
Paul and Peter to have been? The
word for 'wrested' means to 'tighten
with a windlass'. Is Peter on Galilee
again? (Rom. 3: 5–8; 6: 1; 8: 1, 2;
Gal. 3: 10).

Vv. 17 and 18 are for us.

THE FIRST EPISTLE OF JOHN

God is Light
(1 John 1: 1-10)

IT can hardly be disputed, on linguistic grounds, that this epistle was written by the author of the fourth gospel, and at about the same time. It was, perhaps a covering letter for the major work, and dealt more specifically with the deviations in doctrine which caused the last survivor of the apostles' band, in extreme old age, to write to the church.

John is earnest to make his point clear. It was the Son of God, divine, unique, with whom they had walked in those three years (1, 2). The gospel was no new mystery cult but a faith clear-cut in doctrine and built on a living Lord (3). Their eyes had looked on him (1), and he uses the verb of John 1: 14. They had touched him, he adds, remembering a moving scene (John 20: 26-29). He thus wrote that all might share the joy (3, 4). The word rendered 'fellowship' in KJV means partnership, an intimacy of vine and branches, of body and members (John 17: 3, 6, 21-23). Evil scatters. Fellowship unites in joy (4). 'Our' is the better reading in v. 4. Light (5) is a satisfying image. Light penetrates all space, infinite in extent, revealing all time. Without light

there is no vision, no confident journeying, no growth, no life. Set the image in a world which had hardly begun to conquer darkness. John is insistent on the imagery of light and darkness, because the dissident teachers, whose heresy he challenged, had much to say of 'the enlightened', a self-appointed élite, like the objects of Jude's and Peter's anger, who deviated in their pernicious practices from Christ on norms and standards.

'If we say . . .' (6, 8, 9) comes like a triple hammer blow, and points John's hatred of false profession. He held in memory John 8: 12. He had known Jewish pretensions (Matt. 23; Rom. 2: 12). To 'walk' meant habitually to live (Isa. 9: 2). But evil seeks the darkness (6, 7. John 3: 19; Rom. 13: 12). Let there be no deception. There are absolutes, principles beyond denial, moralities beyond debate (8).

John has two groups of deviants in mind. Those who denied depravity (8), the second, had made a theology of the indiscipline and hypocrisy of the first group (6). John meets the contention of those who denied the existence of sin in the 'enlightened' by a plain statement that 'the truth is not in' those who so delude themselves. By 'the truth' John always means the revelation of the true God. We sin, and it is salvation to recognise the fact. God is faithful and keeps his covenant (Heb. 10: 23). He is true to his word (Jer. 31: 34). The second adjective 'just' is the more remarkable. Not 'merciful', 'loving', or aught else. By Christ's atonement God can forgive, not by overlooking, nor by indulgence, nor by anything less than justice (9). We have all sinned (1 Kings 8: 46; Ps. 14: 2, 3; Isa. 53: 6; 64: 6; Rom. 3: 23) but God has contrived, with no diminution of his nature, to redeem.

The Undiminished Christ

(1 John 2: 1-28)

IN the first eleven verses John turns on 'the knowing ones', the Gnostics as they were later called, the pseudo-philosophers of the sort Paul had met (1 Cor. 1: 22; Col. 2: 8), who were hiding God in words and concealing truth by speculation. They were claiming an understanding of God not granted to unenlightened men. John insists that the obedient only can know God. If a man renounce sin (1) and seek in Christ to follow Christ's behests, that man may know the Lord (3, 5), and none other (4. John 15: 15-24). Doctrine is tested by what doctrine does. Unless faith involves a re-orientation of the will, and a setting of the aspirations in the direction of Christlikeness, the alleged experience is a sham, a futile stirring of emotion, unreal and transitory (6).

There is a commandment old and new, (Deut. 6: 5; John 14: 23), one perhaps that John himself, once called 'the son of thunder' (Mark 3: 17), may have taken long to learn. Enlightenment is shown by its translation into life (7-10). Profession and conduct cannot be torn apart. Nor can truth and falsehood (1: 6, 8), light and darkness (8, 9), love and hate (11) ever be commingled. If a man accepts the principle of love there is nothing in him likely to make him stumble (John 11: 9, 10). V. 10 could mean 'there is nothing in him to cause others to stumble'—no 'skandalon' or 'stumbling-block' (Matt. 13: 41; 18: 7; Rom. 14: 13). '*Skandalon*' seems to be a late form of '*skandalethron*', the trip-stick which allows a trap to spring. Perhaps John had Judges 2: 3 and 8: 27 in mind. The man who cherishes hate has chosen darkness which penetrates his whole being. He loses the faculty of sight.

A section of the letter begins with v. 12 and three verses of preparatory refrain, divided, like Hebrew poetry, into echoing parts, prepare the way for v. 15. The 'little children' of v. 12 and the 'children' of v. 13 are the 'fathers' and 'young men' of vv. 13 and 14. The change of tense ('write', 'have written') probably links the letter to the gospel, written just before. The world (15) is Satan's realm (John 12: 31; 14: 30; 16: 11). Along with its prince the world is doomed (John 12: 31 and 16: 11). V. 16 defines the world in detail. First comes the desire for carnal indulgence and its public flaunting, which has begun again, as in John's day, to penetrate all life. Next is the 'proud glory of life', the glamour which braggarts seek, self-assertion. The corresponding personal noun is found at Romans 1: 30 and 2 Timothy 3: 2. This is the world that is doomed with its open flaunting of evil. 'But the man who is following God's will is part of the permanent and can never die' (17. JBP).

This age, too, has seen its 'Antichrists', those grim parodies of Christ, whose final single incarnation is foreshadowed (Matt. 24: 5, 24; Mark 13: 22, 23; Acts 20: 29, 30; 2 Thess. 2: 3; 2 Pet. 2: 1). The actual word occurs only in John's epistles (2: 18, 22; 4: 3; 2 John 7). Some who contradicted Christ had been in the church and had left it, because they were never truly a part of it (19). But those left behind, in the light of God's Spirit, could see the truth (20) and its distinction from falsehood (21, 22). V. 20 should be rendered: 'You all know the truth'. A source of true straight thinking lay in the Presence admitted to their lives. No perversion of Christ's reality could deceive them. Lies are of Satan, the first liar. And it was a vicious lie to distinguish, as the contemporary heretic Cerinthus did, Jesus and Christ—the former the son of Joseph and Mary, the latter the Being who entered him at the baptism and abandoned him at the moment of desolation on the cross. There is little basic difference between this ancient heresy and the modern one which would separate 'the Jesus of history' from 'the Christ of faith' (22, 23).

For 'abiding' (24) see comments on John 15: 4. But they needed reminding more than teaching, for discernment was God-given (John 7: 17; 15: 26; 16: 13). V. 28 is a conclusion. Let them live consciously in him, so that, if he were suddenly to reveal himself, we should still know exactly where we stand, and should not have to shrink away from his presence' (JBP. Heb. 10: 19).

The World's Hate
(1 John 2: 29—3: 24)

THE antitheses which lace John's theme continue. Light and darkness pass into love and hate. God and the world become God's people and the same hostile system. 'Walking in the light' becomes 'practising righteousness'. The last verse of chapter 2 stresses that practical righteousness is the fruit and sign of a proper relationship to God. John takes the unity of the trinity for granted. In the final pronoun, 'him', God and the Son are not distinguished.

'What manner of love?' 'What unearthly love?' is this John asks (3: 1), using the interrogative of Matthew 8: 27 and 2 Peter 3: 11. Up to 5: 12, 'love' occurs sixteen times as a noun and twenty-six times as a verb and five times as a verbal noun. A well-supported reading inserts a parenthesis: '... that we should be called (as indeed we are) the sons of God ...' Justin, writing in A.D. 165, quotes the verse with the parenthesis in place. Can those so privileged escape the fate of their Master (1)? John wrote with Nero's sadism and Domitian's persecutions behind him. But with such glory before (2), can any man hesitate to live in the light of it (3)?

KJV obscures the antithesis

between vv. 4 and 5: 'Everyone who practises sin practises also lawlessness ... and you know that he came to take away our sin, and sin does not exist in him. Everyone who continues in sin has not seen him or come to know him' (4, 5). Observe the continuous tenses. It is habitual sin, continued and sustained rebellion, not the confessed and forgiven fault (2: 1) that John has in mind. V. 6 does not contradict 1: 8 to 2: 2. 'To the extent that he abides in him a person does not sin'. Montgomery renders: 'Whoever continually abides in him does not habitually sin'. It is most important to treat the Greek present tense carefully. The Christian may sin but rises again (Mic. 7: 8; Rom. 7: 14-25).

Vv. 7-12 contain, to be sure, repetition. Every good teacher uses such emphasis. Persistence in sin (9) and hatred (10) mark the children of the devil. 'From the beginning' (8) takes the battle back to Eden. One born again knows what Christ did (8). He 'pulls apart' (the word of Matt. 5: 19 and John 5: 18 —'break' and 'broken') the work of the devil. The indwelling Christ (9) curbs the old sinful living (Ezek. 36: 25-29). Cain was the first identifiable citizen of the devil's world, and Abel the first to suffer for obeying God (11, 12). 'And the strife goes on for ever, 'twixt that darkness and that light', as J. R. Lowell's verse puts it (13). The Lord gave warning—John 15: 18-25; 16: 1-3; 17: 14. There are two races among men. We know what we are by the side we take (14, 15. John 8: 37-47).

The rest of the chapter (18-24) is a cluster of references to the fourth gospel. V. 19 touches a natural anxiety. 'Do I love as I should love?' 'I love my brethren', (14) comes the answer. And if conscience so acquit, God, far greater than the conscience, will also acquit, comfort and confirm (20, 21). We have 'confidence towards God', says v. 21 (2: 28). The word ('parrhesia') originally meant 'freedom of speech' and then all freedom—the poise, calm, fearlessness towards all that the world can do which follows, if a man, forgiven and fortified, can so approach his god.

God is Love
(1 John 4: 1-21)

THE theme of the preceding chapter carries on to v. 6. 'Prophets', the inspired teachers of the church, functioned while the N.T. was forming and circulating. The prophet won consent by his obvious authority and insight into the truth contained in the oral tradition. Such discernment called for intelligent appraisement (1). One test all who spoke (and speak) for God must pass—the exaltation of Jesus Christ as Saviour and Lord (2-6). Heresy was abroad, and the church, about to enter a stressful century, needed this authoritative reaffirmation. There can be a misguided tolerance of error. John calls for love in every chapter, but implied no sentimental indulgence towards false teaching, which tore out the very foundations on which love stood. Christ was what he claimed to be or nothing. In the Latin Vulgate an interesting variant of v. 3 is found: 'Every spirit which divides Jesus, is not of God.' Cerinthus' heretical division of Jesus and the Christ is in view.

John has already defined God as 'spirit' (John 4: 24), as 'light' (1: 5) —and now says 'God is love' (8). In one word the manifold distortions of paganism are dismissed and God's perfect justice given the face of Jesus Christ (1: 9). Greek thinkers had grasped the thought of divine love. No one guessed at a God who could stoop and sacrifice to save.

The theme of 3: 24 resumes at v. 13. The idea of 'abiding' has haunted John's life. He turns to it again. It is the inner witness of the Holy Spirit which gives assurance, and awareness of God's presence, a deepening conviction of sustaining hands. With Christ's acceptance such moulding begins (14–16). V. 14 and John 4: 42 are the only contexts where John uses the word 'Saviour' and in both cases the phrase 'of the world' follows. He is again underlining the fact that the gift is not limited and exclusive but universal.

Absence of fear is love's measure (17, 18). If faith once grasp the fact that Christ died to save, fear of such a Lord is quenched in the conviction, for fear goes with punishment and with no punishment in store, fear dies (18. Rom. 8: 1).

Faith is the Victory
(John 5: 1–21)

THE division between chapters 4 and 5 is not a natural one. In fact 4: 19 to 5: 5 forms a self-contained section of the argument. On a superficial reading the theme might seem repetitive, but closer attention will reveal John's purpose in this re-emphasis. He feels constrained to meet the diffidence of the Christian who pauses after reading 4: 18 to ask: 'Do I, who so often feel the grip of fear, love God as I should?'

In his practical manner, John shows that love for fellow Christians is the clearest demonstration that we love God, and that obedience to God's commands reinforces it. Love for God is the inner principle, love for the brethren is its outward manifestation, and love that does not include the desire to please and to obey is not worthy of its high name. V. 2 literally runs: 'By this we know that we love the children of God, whenever we love God and keep his commandments.' This is the only place in the letter where the word 'whenever' occurs. The appeal is to experience. 'Whenever' we love and obey we deepen faith and assurance. The opening words of the verse are a converse of 4: 20 and 21, and are intended to suggest once more that love is not a mere matter of emotion. Just as love for God is demonstrated by obedience to God's command, so is love for God's people. If it merits its name, such love demonstrates itself in active benevolence.

V. 4 says 'whatever is born of God'. The neuter is used to stress that it is not the man but what has taken place in a man which wins the victory. The word 'pistis', the commonest word for 'faith' in Greek, occurs nowhere else in

John's epistles, and the classical Greek word for 'victory' occurs only here in the N.T. It is faith, not anything else, which can claim to be invincible. This, in a world where Rome was supreme from the Forth to the Euphrates... but history was to prove the claim was true.

V. 7 is found in no manuscript earlier than the fourteenth century. It is first quoted as part of John's text by Priscillian, the Spanish heretic who died in 385 A.D. and it gradually worked its way into the Latin Vulgate. Erasmus omitted the passage from the first printed Greek Testament of 1516, but undertook to introduce the words if a Greek manuscript containing them could be produced. He was faced with a late manuscript which did, in fact, contain the passage, and against his judgment kept his promise. So, by way of Erasmus' 1522 edition, the interpolation invaded the text of the Greek Testament. The action of the RV in cutting out the spurious words was tardy justice. We should treasure every word of the inspired record, but we want no invasion of that record by the additions of men, however sound the theology expressed.

The reference of v. 6 is to John 1: 32–34. 'Not by water only' was Christ authenticated, but by his death. Cerinthus' heresy of a Christ who entered a merely human Jesus is in John's mind. The water, the symbol of the Lord's consecration to his ministry, and the blood, the symbol of his atoning death, interpreted by the Spirit's testimony, contain the full significance of the gospel

In vv. 8, 9 and 10 John, old and eager to reassure those who were to outlive him, with quiet urgency points out that there is a witness greater than the last apostle. One who 'keeps on believing' (10) need not fear. He reinforces this last assurance with clear references to the gospel he had just written (11–15. John 3: 36; 6: 47, 48; 17: 2, 3). For the 'sin unto death' see comments on Matthew 12: 24–29; Mark 3: 22–29.

Three assertions sum up the letter's theme (18–20). They all three begin with a ringing 'we know'. The first combines what was said in 3: 9 and 2: 3; the second contains the essence of 1: 6, 2: 18 and 15, 3: 10, and 13; the third summarises 4: 9–11 and 5: 1–12. Together they sum up the central message of the letter, that through the coming of God's Son we have fellowship with God, and that in that fellowship we have salvation from sin and are set in complete and total opposition to the world.

Therefore, let there be no compromise with anything that symbolised that world (21). John feared the human weakness of those to whom he wrote. It was not that he expected them to take part in idolatrous rites, though, in fact, such an attitude meant abstention from every social and civic function; what he more greatly feared was lest the sheer pressure of the enveloping pagan society should encourage ways of accommodation, and ultimately damaging compromise—the old vice of 'the Nicolaitans'.

THE SECOND EPISTLE OF JOHN

Dear Lady
(2 John)

THIS small letter, probably on one square of papyrus, is like many thousands which survive from the Egyptian papyri. Some have thought the 'elect' lady (1) to be a church, but John is not writing in the style of Revelation. '*Kuria*' was common (and modern) Greek for 'lady', and the address is simply formal for: 'Dear Christian Lady'. Another slightly fanciful suggestion is that Kuria is a proper name, rendering Hebrew Martha, and that the Bethany family, along with Mary, had accompanied John to Ephesus. Some of the lady's children had visited Ephesus and their cousins (13), and John had found them fine young Christians (4).

The lady's home was a Christian centre (10) like Nympha's and Philemon's at Colossae (Col. 4: 15; Philem. 2), and John suggests discretion in whom she hospitably receives (10). Expecting that the letter would be read to the whole local congregation, John reiterates his basic message (5, 6). Purveyors of false doctrine were abroad in Asia (7), of whom all should beware (8). The only test of a Christian is, he insists, an abiding loyalty to 'the teaching of Christ' (9). Those who diminished Christ, denied an incarnation (7), or debased his saviourhood, should not be aided on their way (11). More detailed warning he deferred to his next pastoral call, generally a wise proceeding.

The letter is a vivid and moving insight into John's episcopal care, an illustration of love in action. God is revealed in the simplicities of life as well as in the major tasks of a Christian calling—in a letter from Ephesus as well as in an address to the Areopagus.

THE THIRD EPISTLE OF JOHN

My Very Dear Gaius
(3 John)

THIS letter, like its predecessor a simple personal communication, introduces a faithful Asian Christian. The name was not uncommon (Acts 19:29; 20:4; Rom. 16:23; 1 Cor. 1:14). The Gaius of the last two texts was a prominent Corinthian Christian. There was much coming and going in the Asian church (3) and the epistle suggests a tightly-knit organisation with John in constant communication (cf. Rev. 2, 3). Hospitality, in that pagan world, was a prime duty (5), and a manifestation of grace (6, 7). In such activity all participated in the preaching of the word (8).

There was trouble in an Asian church. Diotrephes, probably a rich layman, a domineering and opinionated man (9), had forbidden hospitality to a party authenticated by John (10), slandered John and sought, in other congregations than his own, to deny good men Christian hospitality. Demetrius, apparently unknown to Gaius, seems to have been the bearer of this letter of warning. He is formally commended in v. 12. The people who knew him, 'the truth' itself, John and his diocese, testified to his character—a testimonial indeed. The close of the letter, with reference to an approaching pastoral tour, suggests that the two small letters, 2 and 3 John, were written about the same time, but when they were written cannot be guessed.

THE EPISTLE OF JUDE

In Defence of Sound Teaching
(Jude 1–25)

JUDE, brother of James was also a brother of the Lord—and yet his slave (1). So three others had introduced themselves (Rom. 1: 1; Phil. 1: 1; 2 Pet. 1: 1; James 1: 1). Herein is a significant testimony to the resurrection (cf. Mark 3: 21, 31; John 7: 5). Mercy stands foremost in his prayer. ''Tis mercy all...' We need continuous remembrance (2). Jude had intended to write a pastoral letter, but had been stirred by a sudden crisis to write his brief circular (3). Perhaps Peter's second letter alerted him to an invasion. Some relation exists between Jude's and Peter's letters, as a quick collation will show. Conjecture about priority is irrelevant.

Some sinister invaders had 'slipped secretly in' (4). 'Creep, intrude and climb into the fold...' said Milton, already quoted, who knew his Greek. These people, 'self-willed rebels like Korah (11), rainless clouds, fruitless trees, noisy surf, wandering stars, a menace to the fellowship of the Lord's table' (12), had 'taken the road of Cain, and perpetrated the old error of Balaam' (11). This battery of metaphor suggests profession without reality, preaching without profit, pride and self-assertion ...

Cain (11) was the symbol of carnality in worship. His graceful altar, flower-decked, was the emblem of the easy path, of religion stripped of sternness and austerity. Balaam, in the imagery of the passage, stands for the breakdown of separation, the effacement of those differences which set apart the people of God, and the mingling of sacred and profane (11). Balaam, moreover, erred through covetousness. These seducers of weak Christians are unwilling to incur the loss which follows social ostracism and the unpopularity which is courted by the loyal and rigid Christian. Balaam strayed because he hankered for lucre and lost his fellowship with God. Abusing his influence and ability, he seduced Israel from the pure worship of Jehovah. And the weapon in his hand was the temptation to loose morality through the Moabite women, whose presence broke down the standards of God's people.

Jude's vigorous denunciation of the libertines runs on to v. 19. Vv. 20 to 23 exhort the steadfast to prayer (20), a firm, expectant guard (21) and mercy (22). 'Making a difference', the last phrase of v. 22 is a plea for discernment. Some can be won back with gentleness. Some need a stronger and more passionately urgent approach. V.

23 pictures a rescue from a fire, the rescuer shrinking from the foul clothes the victim wears. Perhaps Jude pictures the rescue of the bedraggled Lot (7. Gen. 19: 16–22).

Vv. 24 and 25 conclude with a magnificent benediction. 'Stumbling' not 'falling' should be read. God saves to the uttermost those who lay hold of his complete salvation. Vicious men may speak 'great swelling words' (16) but ages before their glib tongues seduced, and long after they have ceased to wag, 'the only wise God our Saviour' has reigned and will reign—for ever'.

THE REVELATION OF JOHN

Vision on Patmos
(Revelation 1: 1–20)

THIS book is a 'revelation', an 'apocalypse' (1), and both words mean an 'unveiling', a strange term for the most difficult book in the New Testament, but the unveiling must be understood in something like the sense in which Paul used the word 'mystery', truth hidden from those without the enlightenment of faith, but plain to those acquainted with the poetic or spiritual symbolism. To read Revelation through without attempt at analysis is to feel across the centuries the power of the early church, to catch the triumph of its faith when persecution, fierce and cruel, shadowed it, and when all its hope was in a risen and conquering Saviour. The study of the book must then be undertaken with a clear acceptance of the fact that the key to some of the imagery and symbolism has been lost. The full meaning is often elusive. There is more than one 'school' of interpretation, and all of them contain elements and facets of truth. Inspired truth is many-sided, and prophecy is fulfilled in widening circles. The arrogance of man, the endurance of the faithful, the mark of the Beast, the power of God, are still realities. The future still lies in the hands of Christ. That is why the reader is 'blessed' (3), his understanding and awareness of history deepened. Tradition, likelihood, the obvious prestige of the writer, point to the apostle John (4). The linguistic objections to such authorship can be accounted for by the conditions of exile, translation from Aramaic, a second author writing from notes.

Most of the figurative language which follows would be luminous to those steeped in the language of the O.T. In vv. 4 and 5, where the Trinity is in view, the Holy Spirit is represented as 'the seven spirits which are before his throne'. An ancient interpretation of Isaiah 11: 2 found God's Spirit there in sevenfold manifestation. In v. 6 is an echo of Exodus 19: 6, with the suggestion that a new Israel had appeared. Daniel 7: 9–13 provides background for v. 7 and 14. The cloud of Sinai (Exod. 19: 16), and of the transfiguration (Mark 9: 7) also haunt the picture. Much apocalyptic literature is lost. Though not biblical, it provided a store of symbols. For example, the rabbis seem to have used aleph and tau, the A and Z of the Hebrew alphabet, just as the first and last letters of the Greek alphabet are here used (8), to express comprehensiveness, and all-embracing communication. God has said all he has to say in Christ (5).

John probably wrote during Domitian's persecution, after A.D. 81, when the seven-branched candlestick had already lain with the Jewish loot in Rome's Temple of Peace for over a decade. But in Zechariah's day, six centuries before, the lovely article was already a symbol. The seven churches uphold the light of God's presence, but are inseparable from a central Christ (13). We know of churches at Troas, Hierapolis and Colossae, all in Asia, so why John chose the particular seven of his diocese is not clear, save that the sacred number was a symbol for perfection. Psalm 29: 3, and the noisy Aegean round Patmos may have inspired the closing image of v. 15, Paul's experience (Acts 26: 13) and Hebrews 4: 12 and Psalm 149: 6 the image of v. 16. Patmos was not so much a prison as a place of exile, even protective custody. There were elements in Ephesus favourable to Christianity in Paul's day (Acts 19: 31). This could still have been the case and Domitian was in no great favour with senatorial officials.

Four Letters

(Revelation 2: 1–29)

THE letters of these two chapters are real letters, written in apocalyptic language because times were dangerous, and a man in exile had to use his privilege of communication circumspectly. The seven churches were typical of various communities. Laodicea is chosen for a special reason.

Colossae and Hierapolis, close neighbours, are passed by. Attempts have been made to prove that the seven churches represent seven periods of history, but the project demands large distortions and adaptations of fact. All seven have been in evidence at all times, and if ages of difficulty and darkness have thrown one type into higher prominence, that is a feature of all the centuries.

It was at the beginning of the century that William Mitchell Ramsay, classicist and archaeologist, showed that an understanding of the history, geography and social climate of all seven towns, revealed that the local church, for good or ill, showed the faults and excellencies of the community in which it functioned—a truth demonstrable in any modern situation. The result was a glow of light on the meaning of the letters. If any part of Revelation reveals the efficacy of an historical approach, it is these two chapters.

At the seaward end of the Cayster valley Ephesus commanded the terminus of a great trade route. It was an ancient Greek colony, a magnificently appointed city whose greatness was past. The harbour was silting like that of the rival city Miletus at the end of the neighbouring Maeander valley, and when the church was founded there (see comments on Acts 18 and 19) the place was thriving on a tourist and pilgrim trade, and the fact that it was the proconsular seat of Asia. Right up to Domitian, in John's own day, successive rulers had adorned and repaired the old city of Artemis. It had held a great church, well-informed and devoted (2, 3), but growing weary along with the city in which it had ministered. It was free from the corruption and understood the menace of the Nicolaitan sect. The Nicolaitans of the letters to Ephesus and Pergamum are those 'followers of Balaam' who earned the contempt of Jude. And, significantly enough, in the same connection, the old sins and problems of Corinth, 'fornication and idol meat', reappear. It seems that the Nicolaitans were libertines who counselled less rigid practices, a less uncompromising stand, a wider measure of participation in the pagan life of the Greek and Roman world, a religion less austere, less unsociable. It is clear that those who claimed a spurious liberty in Corinth, and covered loose living with the name of Paul, if not of Christ, still lived (1 Cor. 3: 4). Moreover, they had formed a party, vocal, arrogant, and dangerous. Obviously they taught that the banquets of the world of guilds and paganism were no stumbling-block. Membership of one's appropriate organisation, together with the functions entailed, need not be forgone. No abstention on occasions of pagan festival was necessary. Let the Christian play his social part, and, like Naaman on his master's escort in the temple of Rimmon, let him think of Christ when the pagan smoke curls upward (2 Kings 5: 18). Thus, no doubt, their argument.

In the apocalyptic pattern of the letters each church is addressed with a phrase from the opening vision. Here 1: 13, 16. The Ephesian church was the mother church of Asia. It needed a firm grasp and a watchful presence. Hence v. 1. And each letter ends with a formula addressed to the attentive (7). Coins of Ephesus sometimes show a date-palm, sacred to Artemis and symbol of the goddess' beneficent activity. Hence the choice of a word.

Youthful Smyrna was Ephesus' rival, and to Smyrna's enduring church was promised a 'crown of life'. The Christian would fasten on the words with satisfaction, for it was the sort of poet's tag on which cities preen themselves. Athens, in Pindar's phrase was 'violet-crowned'. Of Auckland, New Zealand, where these words are written, to its citizens' delight Kipling wrote, 'last, loneliest, loveliest, exquisite, apart'. In such fashion the simile of a crown dominates all praise of Smyrna. The city was called 'the crown of Ionia'. More significantly Aristides calls the 'Golden Street', which ringed Mount Pagus with lovely buildings, 'the crown of Ariadne in the heavenly constellation'. Apollonius of Tyana, amid rich praise for Smyrna, says rhetorically that it is greater charm 'to wear a crown of men than a crown of porticoes'.

Smyrna was to suffer more bitterly than the other churches in the persecution of the day because in a great part the Christians were involved in business, well known, and unable, as in the case of the country towns, to pass unregarded (8–11).

Pergamum was a capital city in pre-Roman days, and when the last of her kings bequeathed his kingdom to the Romans in 133 B.C. it became the chief town of the new province of Asia. It was natural then that the first temple of the imperial cult should be located here. A temple to Rome and Augustus was erected in Pergamum in 29 B.C. So 'the worship of the Beast', came to Asia. But other cults beside that of Rome were endemic at Pergamum. There was the worship of Asklepios, the god of healing, whose symbol was a serpent. A coin of Pergamum shows the Emperor Caracalla standing spear in hand before a great serpent coiled around a bending sapling.

The letter is addressed to 'those who dwell where Satan's seat is', and Christians must have found something peculiarly satanic in the town's preoccupation with the serpent image. Pausanias the Greek traveller, who wrote many descriptions of ancient cities, spoke of Asklepios as 'sitting on a throne with a staff in his hand, and his other hand upon the head of a serpent'. The church in Pergamum must have found the surrounding symbolism of paganism quite diabolical.

Pausanias also mentions the magnificent throne-like altar to Zeus, which stood on the crag dominating the city, and which is now in East Berlin. The altar commemorated the defeat of a Gallic invasion of Asia. Its base was more than forty yards long and nearly forty wide; it rises to a height of perhaps fifty feet. In form it might be the entrance to some gigantic temple. Above three sides of the base a graceful colonnade runs, set with dozens of slender pillars. A flight of twenty-six wide marble steps rises up to its centre, which contains a small sanctuary. Immediately below the colonnade are set friezes which tell the story of the legendary struggle between the gods and goddesses of Olympus and the giants. The giants, in accordance with Pergamum's prevailing obsession, are represented as a brood of Titans, with snake-like tails.

Zeus, to whom the throne-like altar was dedicated, was called Zeus the Saviour, and the title would impress Christian minds as peculiarly blasphemous. They must have called the altar 'Satan's seat', and so put the phrase in the Apocalypse.

The temptation to compromise was great. Hence the warrior Christ (12) and the elusive reference to the white, pure stone of a secret covenant (17).

In the letter to Thyatira, under the figure of Balaam (2 Pet. 2: 15, Jude 11—where see comments) the Nicolaitans appear again. It is significant that Thyatira was a centre of trade and commerce. More trade guilds appear in the records than in those of any other Asian city. Inscriptions mention wool-workers, linen-workers, dyers, leather-workers, tanners, potters, bakers, slave-dealers, and bronze-smiths.

The dyers brewed a red dye, probably the modern Turkey red, from the madder root, which grows abundantly in the district. The ancient purple was a colour nearer scarlet than blue, and it was this dye, that a business-woman was selling 500 miles away in

Philippi in A.D. 52 (Acts 16: 14). It is odd that two women of Thyatira should appear in the N.T. should appear in the N.T., one the gracious hostess of Paul of Tarsus, the other the target of another apostle's scorn (20–22). Jezebel was the seal of a trade alliance with Tyre, most profitable to Israel (1 Kings 16: 28–34; Ezek. 27). The Phoenician wealth which built Ahab's palace (1 Kings 22: 39) was the return for Israel's oil, wheat and timber. The choice on Carmel may indeed have ruined a profitable commerce when its sequence brought Jezebel's death. Perhaps the dangerous woman of Thyatira was clever and endowed with persuasion. Perhaps she claimed prophetic gifts and preached compromise on Nicolaitan principles. It must have been uncommonly difficult to live apart in the small country town. Anxious men must have cried aloud for some formula of conduct by which they could maintain both their livelihood, so dependent upon their membership of the guild, and their allegiance to Christ. Was the hard choice Christ or poverty? 'No,' said Jezebel. 'Keep your heart intact. Learn the deep things of religion, and you will see that even behind pagan worship lives an acknowledgment of the Most High God. Go to the sacrifice, but think there of Christ. Attend the feasts, but set an example of purity and moderation.' 'Look' answers John, 'I set her on a dining couch, and her associates with her, and they shall have opportunity to enjoy—great tribulation, unless *they* repent, for she has shown that *she* cannot repent.'

In addressing the faithful, Christ becomes the Christ who scorned the Pharisees (Matt. 23), flashing with indignation (18), and in like character he ends (27).

Three Letters

(Revelation 3: 1–22)

SARDIS was gathered round the great fortress on a spur of the Tmolus ridge in the Hermus valley. It was the chief city of Croesus, a legend for the wealth derived from the alluvial gold of the Pactolus. It was the first centre ever to mint gold and silver coinage. It had been a great power, and the leader of the Ionian Greeks in their revolt against Persia in 499 B.C. It was once a city arrogant and conscious of its strength, but a city which had twice been easily captured by guile, surprise and stealth (3). So, too, its church had fallen short of expectations. Continue thus, says the one with 'the seven stars', and suddenly, as with Cyrus (in 549 B.C.) and Antiochus (in 214 B.C.), you will find the history of your city will be followed by the fate of the church. It will be 'blotted out'—as indeed Sardis was, and is (5). White was the colour of Roman triumph. The remnants of Christian worship are visible today in an inscription. Artemas, a physician, who may indeed have known John, 'is living' (4), and the Artemis temple seems to show signs of Christian occupation in a cross cut into the stone and a brick chapel. It is a sad ruin today, 'its lamp extinguished'.

Philadelphia, in an earthquake-ridden area of Asia Minor, was an outpost of Hellenism (8), its small and faithful church persecuted by a hostile synagogue (9), arrogant, and claiming an authority it did not hold (7. Isa. 22: 15–22). Let them hold fast (10, 11). Persecution will pass like the sufferings of the city (12). Its continuous seismic trials had made the little town unsafe to live in. People lived outside, and few pillars stood (12). The whole story of Philadelphia is in the imagery—even the city's twice repeated attempt to change its name —first in honour of Tiberius, who had been lavish in earthquake relief, and then in honour of Vespasian (12).

Laodicea, deriving immense prosperity from its position on the Lycus valley trade route, was a rich banking and commercial centre. It refused the senate's proffered earthquake relief after the great Asian seismic disaster of A.D. 60. It 'had need of nothing' (17). It was famous for its black woollen cloaks and carpets, for its medical school and its eye-salve, collyrium. The scornful imagery of the letter is based on these activities. Vv. 15 and 16 refer to the emetic qualities of the warm soda-laden water from the hot springs of the neighbouring spa of Hierapolis. Ramsay suggests that the city, vulnerable from its exposed water-supply, and noted for its wealth and easy life, had developed a sririt of compromise and worldly-mindedness, which its bishop found ruinously infiltrating the church.

The Lord comes as a friend (19). Who wills may open (20. John 10: 3, 16; 14: 23; 18: 37). To 'sup' implies the end of the day. John's vocabulary is still evident in v. 21 (John 16: 33; 1 John 5: 4).

The Other Realm
(Revelation 4: 1–11)

THE theme has moved through the valley towns of Asia, as John's mind followed his cryptic letters to the little congregations. He was helpless, bound to Patmos. But now he sees another realm than Caesar's. The imagery is built on familiar sights. As the afternoon sun slopes, a watcher on the peak of the island sees the western Aegean turn to burning gold (6) and at times a mighty pile of nimbus, intershot with lightnings and with wavering colours of pink and green around its edges caught from the westering sun, can rise high in the south and east (3). John, with the Hebrew's reluctance to describe God, seeks images of glory from nature, and the polished beauty of precious stones (3) to describe One hidden by excess of coloured light. Isaiah (6: 2–4) and Ezekiel (1: 1–28) wrestled with the same problem of language—a real one to a mind inexorably opposed to idolatry and to conceiving God in terms of art (Acts 17: 29). The worshippers (4), similarly symbolic, represented the godly of all time (12 patriarchs stood for the O.T., 12 apostles for the N.T., totalling 24). They were utterly surrendered (10) along with the representatives of all nature (7, 8). The never-ending praise was an effort to express an ordered creation eternally conscious of God's love and care (8, 11). The voices from the throne (5) represented the power of God over a world in which an embattled church might imagine Caesar supreme, the trumpet and the tramp of the legions the voice of strength and authority. The chapter is a piece of poetry in which language assumes a mystic meaning as it grapples with thought too transcendent for speech.

The Lamb That Was Slain
(Revelation 5: 1–14)

THERE was a scroll, sealed like a Roman will, on (not 'in') the hand of the Presence on the throne, a scroll which none could unroll for it contained the future which is beyond the reach of every man. It was a full scroll for, as was sometimes done, the writing was on the back as well as on the front of the papyrus (1–4. Ezek. 2: 9, 10). Only Christ was able to break the wax; '. . . the future all unknown, Jesus we know, and he is on the throne.' He is in the vision, somehow involved and fused with the whole scene, Christ in all his aspects. He is the Lamb of sacrifice, but also the Lion of Judah and the royal Lord. Lewis had this thought in mind when in his Narnia books he made Christ Aslan who 'was not a tame lion' (Gen. 49: 9; Ezek. 19: 2, 3, 5, 6). The Lamb has horns and the horn, linguistically and symbolically in Hebrew signifies power (Deut. 33: 17). Nothing is beyond the Lamb's perfect strength. (Seven is the perfect number.) Seven eyes signify his all-seeing awareness (6, 7. Zech. 4: 10). He took the book (8. John 1: 1; 17: 14). God now

works through Christ (Acts 17: 31; Phil. 2: 5–11) in whom prayer avails (8). A new cause for praise and confidence thus enters life (9. Ps. 33: 3; 40: 3; 96: 1; 144: 9; 149: 1). It requires an effort of the mind to remember that John writes of one whom he had known as a man in Galilee and Judaea. Such was the conviction the resurrection brought. The chapter ends in a union of praise. They 'make one music as before, but vaster . . .' (11–14). It is a strange pageant to be apprehended as a poetic whole.

The Four Horsemen
(Revelation 6: 1–17)

THE Apocalypse is a preview of Rome's future by one who knew that moral issues determine history, that the precarious frontiers could hold only while worthy hands held them, hands strong because evil was not finally triumphant in the minds that guided and the hearts that planned, and because in a sense they still fulfilled a plan of Providence.

The declaration of war on the church was a turning-point. In that act Rome followed the Jews, and rejected the offered faith. At that moment, John knew, judgment became inevitable, and how could judgment come, save down the old invasion routes, from the outer reservoir of barbarism, in the long grim sequence of interwoven tribulations to which the precarious civilisation of man, laboriously held and toilfully defended, has ever been exposed?

Hence the sombre poem of this

lurid chapter. First rides a bowman on a white horse 'conquering, and to conquer' (2). The figure is strangely like a Parthian, old terror of the Middle East, whose arrows had proved the answer to the Roman legion in 53 B.C. on the plains of Carrhae. The disaster to Crassus' legions had been a fearful lesson, and it was Rome's good fortune that political obtuseness and internal tension in the Parthian realm prevented the triumphant raiders from following up their victory, and overrunning the Middle East and Asia. A bowman on a horse was a symbol of invasion, and terribly was the oracle fulfilled.

The second rider followed on a red horse (4). In the writer's memory Rome had known the horror of civil strife, and this was the symbol's meaning. The world had watched in fascinated fear as the legions clashed in northern Italy in A.D. 69, and had wondered at the vitality of a power which could rise from such carnage and internecine strife (13: 3).

A black horseman follows close behind (5). He makes a grim proclamation. The horseman is famine, and his horse is black like the casual corpses emaciated by the drought-stricken roadway. Famine follows war and civil strife. A denarius a quart was twelve times the usual market price for the vital commodity of life. In the midst of such starvation oil and wine remain mockingly unharmed. They are not dependent on a yearly sowing neglected in times of trouble. The vines and olive trees are not so easily trampled by the passing hosts.

Last in the vision comes a livid horseman (8), the colour of a corpse long dead. The picture is strife among hungry multitudes, disease stalking abroad, the very beasts slinking into abandoned and undefended villages to rend the weak and the dying. The dreadful vignette of the rider on the livid horse is an inclusive vision. All the ills of his predecessors, after war's cumulative fashion, are summed up in him. He is general chaos . . .

Now follows the cry of those who, not meriting such sufferings have nevertheless been involved in them (9, 10. Ps. 79: 5–10). Let those who have never suffered from the sadism and vileness of the persecutor sit in comfort and condemn the call for retribution (10). Historically it always seems to come, slow though the mills grind (11).

The apocalyptic imagery which follow is from the stock of imagery which this type of literature affects. The Hebrew apocalyptic moved within an accepted range of imagery and symbol, and communicated clearly with those familiar with that field of thought. Part of our difficulty in the interpretation of the Apocalypse is that some of the sources of its imagery are no longer accessible, and the keys to the symbolism consequently lost. Some of the imagery of vv. 12–14 can be actually traced in the O.T. (e.g. Amos 8: 8; Ezek. 38: 19; Joel 2: 10; Hagg. 2: 6; Isa. 13: 13; 50: 3; Joel 2: 31—in order of sequence). Other details can be recovered from extant apocalypses. It is sufficient to see breakdown, disruption of established order, chaos . . . 'and whoso hears aright, can only hear the plunging of the nations in the night.'

The Redeemed
(Revelation 7: 1–17)

THE symbolism is clear. We still speak of the earth as a square with 'four corners', and having 'ends'. So did the prophets (Isa. 11: 12; Ezek. 7: 2). The winds often symbolise the unseen power of God—a device aided by the fact that the same word, in both Hebrew and Greek, signified wind and spirit (Ps. 18: 15; 83: 15; Isa. 66: 15; Jer. 4: 13; 23: 19; 30: 23; 49: 36; Ezek. 37: 9; Nah. 1: 3; Zech. 6: 1–5; 9:14; John 3: 8). The tornadoes of disaster were to be held in check until God's own were sealed. The metaphor of sealing will be discussed on chapter 13 but the key to the image, apart from some surviving non-canonical apocalyptic literature, is found in Ezekiel 9: 1–7. They were 'sealed' as God's property (and see Gen. 41: 42 and Esther 3: 10; 8: 2). So then catastrophe is held (1–3) and the sealing proceeds. The number signifies completeness $(12 \times 12) \times (10 \times 10 \times 10)$, i.e. the square of 12, basis of the duodecimal system (which was Babylonian: cf. English 'dozen') and the cube of 10, basis of the decimal system. All tribes are represented. They are, of course, the new Israel (Rom. 2: 28, 29; Gal. 3: 29; 6: 16; Jas. 1: 1; 1 Pet. 2: 9, 10). The spiritual Israel (4–8) is 'the great multitude' of v. 9 and the rest of the chapter. 'Thousand', of course, also meant 'clan' or family group (Mic. 5: 2—and cf. 'hun-

dreds' in old English administration). They were upright and confident (9) in worship (John 12: 13), of all languages, such as John must have seen in Ephesus and Smyrna, they were washed (Ps. 51: 1–7; Isa. 1: 18; 64: 6; Rom. 3: 25; 5: 9; Col. 1: 20; Heb. 9: 14). They had come out of great distress (14) and at all times some of the church so lives. With the knitting of mankind into unity it becomes increasingly possible for some malign power (2 Thess. 2: 8) to render global what has always been known regionally. The close of the chapter (15–17) contains some of the tenderest verses in the whole book.

'Mills of God'
(Revelation 8: 1–13)

THIS chapter, surely, cannot be interpreted, as much in the book can, on historic or futuristic principles. Two verses only might tempt such explanation—v. 8 could be imagery based upon the eruption of Vesuvius, on August 24, A.D. 79, which overwhelmed Herculaneum and Pompeii. One Jew or Christian in the latter city, whose evil is glaringly obvious in its surviving remnants, certainly saw God's judgment in the catastrophe. Why else would he write SODOMA GOMORA on a wall? Vv. 10 and 11 might prompt a reader from the age of nuclear peril to see reality in the blazing thing which fell to pollute the tormented seas. Wormwood is the Artemisia, named after Artemis ('Diana of the Ephesians', Acts 19: 24–37) the bitter juice of which was proverbial (Deut. 29:

18; Prov. 5:4). Red seas after volcanic activity were known in the Aegean, for example after eruptions of the notorious Santorini. Red rain, the sand of the Sahara, borne on the devastating, searing sirocco, was well known. Melbourne experiences a similar phenomenon from Australia's 'Red Centre', when a period of northerly wind and intense heat gives way to a cold front from the south, and the dust, which can darken the skies, falls in crimson stains. Like the plagues of Egypt, which are in the writer's mind, the disasters of this chapter are visitations not unknown in the Mediterranean world, but given meaning and a theological context by those who saw in them a judgment of God (7-12). V. 2 would make a better sequence if placed after v. 6. It is not impossible that the present order results from the early misplacement of a verse.

Certain truths emerge from the turmoil of symbolic catastrophe. There is a listening God (1). Amid all the heavenly pageantry described, God must not be thought remote and uncaring while the embattled and lonely Christian strives with the world's authority, seemingly supreme in unjudged evil. The prayers of the saints do prevail (3-6) and 'though with patience stands he waiting, with exactness grinds he all'. Taken as a whole, and poetically interpreted, the significance is real. It is like the message of Jeremiah's first visions. God is not asleep.

The Mills Grind On
(Revelation 9: 1-21)

THE phantasmagoria of vivid and violent imagery continues, even more difficult to interpret in this chapter than the last. A locust plague was, until modern methods of control mitigated the periodic catastrophe, one of the most destructive evils which could fall on mankind (Joel 1 and 2). But the locust horde (3-6) seems to merge into the horror of a Parthian invasion (7-11), numberless mounted bowmen, trained to fire even in retreat (19). The Romans never solved the problem of the Euphrates frontier (14) and invasion from that open door, where pressure from the nomad tribes of the Gobi, set moving by periods of drought and dessication, was never solved. Nero had mounted a campaign of conquest (A.D. 58-62). Trajan was to launch another, but Rome could never hold fast a frontier on the Persian Gulf. The Parthians continued to plague the eastern provinces. Through the Euphrates door came Huns, Mongols and the Turks who finally destroyed the Eastern Empire. That door is not yet shut, and the poetry of this timeless vision could yet find imagery turn to fact again. But conjecture must in such contexts, never be confused with truth. Was the star which 'had fallen' (1) the gospel which, rejected, leaves man to reveal the abysmal depths of his evil (2)? Or was it Nero, fallen in A.D. 68 to leave the world a prey to the horrors of quadrilateral civil war in A.D. 69, when the legions learned in Tacitus' phrase 'what authority had kept hidden—that an emperor could be set up elsewhere than in Rome'? Vespasian, marching from the East, and denuding the Euphrates frontier to further his ambitions, finally brought healing to a bitterly wounded Rome (14, 15). It is idle to seek literal meaning in v. 15 but the length of time of Rome's mortal agony was a little over a year. The Empire's travail in no way softened the leaders of Rome or the proletarian hordes towards the Christians (21). That much can be seen in a morning's walk round Pompeii.

The Little Book
(Revelation 10: 1–11)

CHAPTER 10 and the first 14 verses of chapter 11 form an interlude between two trumpets of doom. Chapter 10 is none the less a unit. The messenger (Ps. 104: 3) appears, trailing some of heaven's glory (Ezek. 1: 28). The seven thunders may reflect seven 'voices of God' from Psalm 29. Other Scriptures tangle with the language (Joel 3: 16; Hos. 11: 10; Amos 3: 8). So much for the mighty messenger (1–3). The last conflict is about to begin (3–7) and the final message is to be eaten in the form of a small book (8–10. Ezek. 3: 1–3). The prophet makes the divine oracle his own (10. Jer. 15: 16). The last hour is about to strike, and since the messenger, like a colossus, bestrides earth and sea, the message is to be for all (11), and the small book must be the ultimate roll of judgment about to fall upon the earth. The first touch of that knowledge would be sweet. The sufferers under man's tyranny were to see their tormentors felled, but in such cataclysm is no final joy (9, 10). To delight in the death of anyone is not godlike. The call comes again. It is not only on the world of Nero and Domitian that catastrophe falls, but on all rebel men of whom, in all times, those tyrants were but the types and forerunners (11).

The Two Witnesses
(Revelation 11: 1–9)

TO understand this chapter, perhaps the most difficult in the book, it is important to hazard a guess as to how the seer's mind was working. In imagination he stood where once he stood and heard the words of the Lord's apocalypse, Matthew 24. He was on the Mount of Olives, the place where not long afterwards they received the great commission, and whence the Lord ascended. It was calcined ruin when he wrote, but in imagination he heard old words again. Begin, he said looking at the hostile city, the cruel citadel of their foes, 'at Jerusalem'. To the right of them, olive-green and uncluttered with the rival buildings which crowd that sacred spot today, they could see Gethsemane where they slept through his hour of agony. They could see the steps he climbed, amid a flare of torches. Out to the right of the gleaming beauty of the temple, which he had cleared of evil, they could see Tower of Antonia, where he stood on the flagstones still to be seen, scored with the marks of the brutal soldiers' games.

They looked at Jerusalem, where they were told to begin, the city where they had seen the dream of a kingdom die, a kingdom for which they saw no substitute, where they had trembled before one of the most terrible spectacles evil has to show, a mob howling for blood, and a people calling for a man of violence. 'Not this man, but Barabbas.'

It had not dawned on them that the dream was still to come true but as always with the affairs of God, in a manner infinitely more wonderful than they had ever imagined it. But it was a daunting sight, a sombre command. To be sent back into the dreaded place of sin, to wait there indeed until he spoke again, was hardly what they hoped. And beyond lay Samaria, where barriers of their own hatred and prejudice had to be surmounted, further still Galilee, where it all began, the Lake, Capernaum, Nazareth ... Their eyes could imagine no more distant scene, but beyond lay the world John was to know, and beyond that the world we know.

Perhaps that is how he came to see Jerusalem as the world. It can hardly be literally Jerusalem, because he immediately calls it Sodom and Egypt (8). It is organised mankind, coherent, ungodly, hostile (9), foe of the witnessing church, and maker of martyrs (9). The church in the midst is represented by the temple (1 Cor. 3: 16; 1 Pet. 2: 5), part of which the world's feet may trample but the centre of which is safe and unpolluted (2). But the witness of the church is represented by two active figures (3), two, on the principle of Deut. 17: 6, and prob-

ably seen as Moses and Elijah (3-6. 1 Kings 17: 1; Luke 4: 25; Jas. 6: 17; Exod. 7: 14-20).

In John's imaginary time chart of the world to be, the witnesses testify until their message is finally rejected, and the Antichrist destroys them in a final spurious victory. Until then they are as indestructible as the olive tree (3. Zech. 4: 3) whose roots survive all burning. There seems a link between the forty-two months of v. 2 and the three and a half days of v. 11, and the period of time is symbolic. Antiochus Epiphanes 'trampled' and profaned Jerusalem with massacre and blasphemy from June 168 B.C. to December 165 B.C.—a time of horror which left a mark on every Jewish mind. As Antiochus seemed triumphant, so will seem the Beast. The church will seem dead, its body cast out in the streets of the godless world. Then, like its Lord, it shall rise (11) and like its Lord be taken to its reward (12. Acts 1: 9). At the trumpet blast of retribution (13) the nations rage (18. Ps. 2: 1). Thus the chapter seems a preview of the rest of the book, the church's tribulation, the Beast's ephemeral triumph, God aroused to intervene, and the new Jerusalem in the last verse.

The Ancient Conflict
(Revelation 12: 1-17)

TWO truths emerge from the tumult of imagery. First there is ancient strife beyond human imagining between God and that which challenges his rule. Secondly, in the story of man, a facet of the ancient conflict is revealed in which man is involved. The woman, royally apparelled, is the 'church' of the O.T., the real Israel of the twelve tribes (1), whose destiny was to bring forth Christ (2). Stephen sought to explain to the Sanhedrin (Acts 7) that only thus did Israel's history make sense (Gal. 3: 24). God's intrusion into man's history was viewed as a vital front of conflict by a Being of Terror—Satan (3, 4). Pause to realise that the reality of Satan is demanded if the N.T. is granted authority. It postulates a personal being who opposes, accuses, tempts, seduces, corrupts and deceives (Matt. 4: 1-11; 6: 13; 13: 39; Luke 4: 2-13; 8: 12; 13: 16; 22: 3, 31; John 12: 31; 13: 2, 27; 14: 30; 16: 11; Acts 5: 3; 2 Cor. 12: 7; Eph. 6: 11 and elsewhere). This 'malevolent critic of creation', libels the good, and plays cosmically the despicable part of the 'delator', that scandal of first century imperial law, the common informer. Satan is a being eternally vigilant against the good (3). The Child, the destined ruler (Ps. 2: 9), is protected (Matt. 2: 13) and given refuge in the old place of security (1 Kings 17: 1-7; 19: 1-8). The wilderness was deep in Hebrew consciousness (Heb. 11: 8), annually celebrated by the Feast of Tents, and illustrated by the desert communities—the Essenes and Qumran (5, 6). The child was 'caught up' (5. Acts 1: 9), but Satan, defeated cosmically, (7-12. John 12: 31), fights a rearguard action against the woman, who is now the church of the N.T., the continuation of the true Israel (13). Obeying Mark 13: 14, the church

fled to Pella in the Decapolis when the Romans closed on Jerusalem for the usual limited time of tribulation (14). Such phenomena as that of v. 15 had taken place in the Lycus valley near Colossae.

The Beast

(Revelation 13: 1-18)

THE seaways to Rome lay westward from Patmos, and Patmos was a landfall for galleys on their way to Asia. Perhaps John built his apocalyptic imagery on a scene from the island's coast as courier ships swept east. The Beast, like the ship's hull rose out of the sea, a thing with the speed and ferocity of the leopard, the crushing power of the bear, and the terror of the lion —an agent of Satan. Seven heads were seven emperors under whom Caesar-worship had become established (Tiberius, Caligula, Claudius, Nero, Vespasian, Titus, Domitian). Augustus had played the cult lightly, and perhaps John regarded him, as he sought to be regarded, as merely the last of the republican magistrates. Add three for the ten horns—Galba, Otho, and Vitellius, the three short-lived contestants of the ghastly year A.D. 69 (1, 2). That was the year of the deadly wound (3). Rome was a thing of blasphemy because of Caesar-worship (4-6). Under Nero, and after the Great Fire of A.D. 64, Rome had declared war on the church.

The period of Paul's hope—that the empire could be won for Christ was gone. The Roman authority, up to Nero, had accepted and indeed favoured the church—in

Philippi (Acts 16), Corinth (Acts 18), Ephesus (Acts 19), and Jerusalem (Acts 21, 22). Paul had commanded obedience (Rom. 13: 1-6; Phil. 1: 27; 1 Tim. 2: 2). He saw Rome as a restraining force (2 Thess. 2: 6, 7). Peter was as clear (1 Pet. 2: 13-17). All now was changed, by Rome's own folly. Yet, let no one form an armed resistance movement (9, 10), as Jews were doing all over the world. It would be futile, since it is a notable fact that the proletariat at large favoured the power which had brought them peace. The second beast (11) is either the governor of Asia or the imperial priesthood. 'Magic' and trickery associated with this cult can be documented (12-15).

To 'receive a mark' (16) or be sealed meant to become the property of the imperial power. This appears to be the use of the verb which Paul had in mind in Romans 15: 28, a verse which has produced an astonishing variety of renderings. Paul seems to mean: 'When I have secured this fruit for them to hold and to retain.' Seals were set on sacks of grain to guarantee the correct weight or measure of the contents. There was also a red stamp, which was required for all documents of exchange. It showed the emperor's name and the year of his reign, and was technically known as 'the seal'.

If, therefore, the basic interpretation of the Beast is Caesar himself, John's picture of the seal stamping hand and brow of the duped multitude becomes shockingly true to life. They are sealed with the sign of the false god of Rome, upon the hand which creates, and before the brain which plans. And without the stamp, which stands symbolically for conformity, and tacit acceptance of the worship and divinity of the Emperor, a man could 'neither buy nor sell'. The trade-guilds with their stranglehold upon a man's livelihood are in view. This sombre century, in which the battle for liberty has been fought over again in three continents, and still continues to be fought in large tracts of the globe, has produced many illustrations of the tyranny over hand and head, and the despot's threat to livelihood and thought, which John thus symbolized.

And what of v. 18? Note first that a far from negligible manuscript tradition gives 616, not 666. In both Greek and Latin the letters of the alphabet had numerical value, and the fact was very commonly used to build puzzles. Among the wall scratchings from Pompeii is an election notice in which the vowels are cryptically exchanged for numbers, and another inscription speaks of a girl called Harmonia. 'The number of her name', it says, 'is 45.' The key to the puzzle seems to be that Harmonia suggests the nine Muses, and 45 is the sum of all the digits from 1 to 9.

The churches of Asia probably knew the key to 666 or 616, but it was early forgotten. In Greek 616 adds up to 'Caesar God', but 666 is not so simple, and much ingenuity and juggling with spelling has been employed to fit the number to 'Nero Caesar', or 'Caius Caesar'. It is also plausibly suggested that 666 falls short of the perfect trinity 777 in all counts, and thus presents a grisly picture of the power and baseness of Antichrist. Perhaps some papyrus scrap, still undiscovered or undeciphered, some inscription under a Turkish doorstep or embedded in a wall, contains an answer to John's cryptogram.

Obviously, the historical interpretation in no way precludes a futuristic one. The N.T. seems to indicate a final mobilisation of evil before the consummation of the age and the coming of Christ. And today needs to look no further than a computerised and docile proletariat under totalitarian rule, the church itself rent between conformists and the brave, to see peculiarly diabolical reality in vv. 16, 17.

The Choice

(Revelation 14: 1–20)

AFTER the vision of evil come the pageant of good and the scene of judgment. John is on the familiar vantage point of Jerusalem, Mount Zion this time, not Olivet. The 144,000 are the rounded number of the saved. The sound of the surrounding sea is a background to Patmos, and like the sea was the sky-filling voice, rising to the roll of the Aegean thunder, which the Seer heard (2). Theirs was a new song, because only they can sing who have known and felt the theme of their singing (3). They were the steadfast and uncompromising. Spiritual unchastity, of course, must be the meaning of v. 4 (Exod. 34: 15; Deut. 31: 16; Judg. 2: 17;

8: 27, 33; Hos. 9: 1). They are true and unblemished (5). Sincerity is a prized mark (Ps. 32: 2; Isa. 53: 9; Zeph. 3: 13; 1 Pet. 2: 22). 'Unblemished' was a word of sacrifice (Eph. 1: 4; 5: 27; Col. 1: 22; 1 Pet. 1: 19).

A triple vision of angels follows, telescoping the age of the gospel (7), the fall of Rome (8), and judgment on the deluded horde which has conformed to the Beast. Rome did fall, and that catastrophe was the great traumatic event of European history. And there is no doubt that, had Rome at the great turning-point in the sixties accepted the gospel and banished the Caesar-cult, the Empire could have survived. The death of slavery, an outward envangelical contact with the barbarians of the hinterland, the taming of the destructive power of the army—all this would have restored Rome, provided an êthos, and obviated the Middle Ages and the catastrophe of continental disintegration. Instead Rome poisoned the world (8). Caesar-worship was the cause of the clash with the church, and the cult was accepted with enthusiasm by its debilitated victims (13: 4).

The last half of the chapter sweeps into a cataract of imagery which cannot be related to events and must be symbolic of final disintegration. Our own age cannot brush aside a vision of unimaginable mortality (20) covering a land the length of biblical Palestine with death. It cannot dismiss the bitter harvest of an earth sown thick with the weeds of hate, rebellion and godlessness (14, 15). Julia Ward Howe, viewing a Washington camp

during the first of modern, techno-
logical wars, over a century ago,
wrote of God 'trampling out the
winepress where the grapes of wrath
are stored' ... We too have seen
'the lightning of his terrible, swift
sword'. Who can see hope for man
save in Christ? He, or 'Armageddon', is the still open choice (7).

Interlude
(Revelation 15: 1-8)

WHEN the sun drops into the sea
west of Patmos the view can
be precisely that of v. 2, a blazing
golden floor on which the swell
seems to sway flames of submarine
fire. Such, thought the Seer, was the
sea of pain through which those
who had died for Christ had passed.
On the shore they sing like those
sang who passed through another
sea to a Promised Land—the song
of Moses (Exod. 15: 1). The 'new
song' is composed largely of fragments of the Psalms (in sequence:
145: 17; 86: 9; 99: 3; 111: 9; 86:
9; 98: 2). Then the heavens open to
reveal the beautiful tent built with
such expenditure of art and devotion in the wilderness. Its specifications and construction had followed
significantly the sin of idolatry
under Sinai (Exod. 32). Its message
to a depraved people brainwashed
by servitude in idolatrous Egypt,
was that God did dwell among his
people, not visibly but wreathed in
beauty, not as an image, but symbolised by the empty throne above
the blood-sprinkled mercy seat and
the stern tablets of the moral law.
God's tent was buffeted by the
desert winds which strained at the

goatskin covers of the nomad
horde. The same sun beat on it. In a
kind of spiritual poem. the Tabernacle pictured the Presence just as
Christ did 'who tabernacled among
us' (John 1: 14). So here the
tabernacle fulfils its role as the
symbol of the unseen God among
men. And from that presence come
the avenging angels.

Vials of Wrath
(Revelation 16: 1-21)

THE plagues which fall upon the
earth are reminiscent of the
plagues of Egypt and the dire visitations of chapters 8 to 11. There is no
sequence and they were all phenomena of evil known in the centuries
of the Empire and in the first century in which John wrote. Bubonic
plague came out of the east periodically (2). As early as 430 B.C. a
most grievous epidemic, difficult to
diagnose, fell upon Athens. The
legions who came back in A.D. 166
from yet another attempt to solve
the Parthian problem, brought
home a plague which devastated
Italy and killed half the population
of the Empire. It recurred six years
later. In the mid-third century
whole areas of the Empire were
depopulated. Polluted rivers and
streams (4), drought from the
burning Sahara winds, and perennial frontier problems (12), were
known in the world of John as they
are known today. If men 'break the
everlasting covenent' (Isa. 24), as
they break it still, the result is inevitable—nature retaliates. The
Mediterranean world was exhausted, its topsoil gone. Roman

depredation of North Africa had given whole provinces to the Sahara. Fertile Asia Minor and Greece, along with Italy itself, were becoming eroded wastes. What is new in the list of plagues is what the world is facing today—a sound of finality. Man still had time to repent but blasphemed. He still has time to repent, now that Revelation 15 assumes global warning. God was 'sifting out—*is* sifting out—the souls of men before his judgment seat'. The sin of man in John's vision proves mortal. Sin has a sequence. First stands fleshy sin, so obvious, so disreputable and withal, at times, so pitiable. In the second place comes spiritual sin, pride, vanity, lust for power and the legion of their like, respectable, yet treacherous, too often well-concealed, and altogether damnable. Thirdly, follows diabolical sin in which evil becomes an object of love for its own sake, sin's judgment on itself, the final fruit of unrepentant wickedness. Finally comes blasphemy, that conscious and determined hostility to God in person, which the Bible defines in its final consummation as the 'sin unto death', and which finds no repentance because it is never committed until all desire or opportunity for repentance has been consciously and wilfully rejected (9, 11, 21).

Global war (19–21) seems to close the chapter, vaster, deadlier than any Parthian inroad (12). Misled (13, 14), deceived, polluted, the Empire was ripe for destruction. It stood for a whole world.

Babylon the Great
(Revelation 17: 1—18: 8)

BABYLON, enemy and persecutor of the Jews, was the evil power of the O.T. She is reproduced in Rome, enemy and persecutor of the Christians. Babylon sat astride the Euphrates (Jer. 51: 13) and in the midst of a mighty system of irrigation canals. Rome sits on the Tiber but on the waters, too, of all the inland seas, whereon all the peoples of the Empire also dwell (15). Babylon poisoned the world (Jer. 51: 7). So did Rome (5). The woman is identified with the Beast (3. 13: 1). The horns were the seven hills (9). Then, by a swift change of imagery, they become seven emperors (Augustus, Tiberius, Caligula, Claudius, Nero —the five who have fallen— Vespasian who was emperor from 69–79—Titus, who lived only two years as emperor). He who was to be (10, 11) must be Domitian. This solves one difficulty to raise another. John was writing, most probably, under Domitian, who, on the testimony both of Pliny and Suetonius, was the vilest and bloodiest of men, but he can hardly be called Antichrist unless it is as the representative, through all time, of evil in the supreme place. The ten kings of v. 12 cannot be identified in any framework of historical interpretation, but it has been more than once observed that the historical approach does not preclude, and indeed can fuse with a futuristic interpretation. In such case the chapter opens up. The tyrant Domitian is simply a type, a forerunner of Antichrist. The scarlet woman stands for those who, through all time have assumed autocratic power, drunk the blood of the persecuted, and blasphemed God. The ten kings express in a round number all that foul successor host of persecuting dynasts. And the fall of the tyrant power is typical of all who before her (Isa. 13, 14, 21; Ezek. 26–28; Jer. 50, 51) have held nations in sanguinary servitude and have corrupted satellite peoples to their final destruction. And the fall of the persecutor foreshadows the fall of every state or institution which, drunk with power, defies God and looses death upon the world. With the leader go the led (18: 1–3). Thus in very deed went Rome. Our own age has seen the fall of other tyrannies. And the end is not yet. Haunting the whole apocalyptic poem is the ultimate Antichrist.

Taunt Song

(Revelation 18: 9–24)

As Nahum's book was a taunt song over the old oppressor Nineveh, so this chapter is a taunt song over Rome. The Empire, its stability recovered (13: 3), stood high when John wrote. The world accepted her Peace (3), puppet rulers and governments like the Herods of Judaea and the authorities of Ephesus, found comfort in Rome's authority (9). Only the embattled church, despised and rejected by society, found itself outcast (4). And it was all to pass away. Chapters 17 and 18 envisage the consummation without restraint. The former oracle, passion-

ate in its imagery, as we saw, shows Rome like a woman of sin, infecting the world with the pollution of her vice, arrogantly astride the nations, flattered, foully worshipped, but doomed for her hatred of 'the Lamb'. Under different imagery the same evil despotism haunted Chapter 13, demanding loyalty beyond question and protest, marking hand and mind with a seal of blasphemy, denying callously a common livelihood to those who dared to stand on conscience, and fettering the souls of men. In Chapter 18 the tone is less apocalyptic, and takes on the strain of an Old Testament taunt-song. The deluded world laments its overturned idol (9). The merchants bewail its passing (15, 16). In some Asian port the writer had seen the galleys loading their cargoes. There was 'merchandise of gold, and silver, and precious stones, and of pearls, and fine linen, and purple, and silk, and scarlet, and ... vessels of ivory, and ... precious wood, and of brass, and iron, and marble, and cinnamon, and odours, and ointments, and frankincense, and wine, and oil, and fine flour, and wheat, and beasts, and sheep, and horses, and chariots, and slaves, *and souls of men*' (12, 13). The climax is bitter, and it was for the last-named cargo that the Seer knew there was a price to pay in blood and ruin. He seemed to picture Ostia, the Tiber post, in the stark ruin in which it stands today, Rome under the smoke of her burning, and the voice of the harpers stilled (22). So Nineveh had lain of old under Nahum's taunts, Babylon under Isaiah's contempt,

and Tyre under Ezekiel's bitter
scorn. But here was an audacity
equal to them all. The Seer saw a
world Empire doomed for persecution's sake, consigned to nether
Hell because she warred against the
weak and gentle, and those who
wished her well (20–24).

Consummation

(Revelation 19: 1–21)

THE doom-song is followed by
the paean of triumph. 'Halle-
lujah' opens thirteen of the psalms
of the last book of the psalter, the
theme of which is dominated by
the fall of Babylon and the return
of the oppressed. And now another
Babylon is down, her smoke lingering like an evil memory (1–3.
Isa. 34: 9, 10). The elders, represent-
ing the true remnant of all the ages,
and the living creatures standing for
tormented nature (4. Rom. 8: 22),
join in jubilation (1, 2). It is the
marriage feast, the last consummation. The symbol of the Messiah's
banquet (Matt. 8: 11; 26: 29)
merges with the concept of the
final union of redeemer and redeemed which carries on from O.T.
to N.T. (7–10. Isa. 54:5; Jer. 3: 14;
Hos. 2: 19, 20; Matt. 22: 2, 10, 11;
25: 1; Mark 2: 19; John 3: 29;
Eph. 5: 21–33).

Conscious that he has said much
of angels, and aware that Colossae,
in his own Asian diocese, had been
badly afflicted by a heresy tied to
the worship of heavenly inter-
mediaries, John stresses that such
messengers are also servants. Testimony centres on Christ, he concludes (10). There is no other theme
for those who speak the mind of
God ('prophets').

A symbolic picture of victory
follows (11–21). There are echoes
of John's first description of the
glorified Christ and of his doctrine
of the Word which was made flesh,
God's last message to the world
(John 1: 1). The poetic interpretation now takes over. Armageddon
is connected with that meeting
place of history and crossroads of
marching armies, the Esdraelon
plain, north over the low pass of
Megiddo. But this final battle is
wherever man's perennial strife
finds final confrontation with the
good, and this almost static picture
of the Rider's triumph must be read
in the framework of its imagery. It is
rewarding to read the whole book as
a poem, and to seek to apprehend
its main movements without detailed exposition, to experience in
short its powerful impact on the
mind without yielding to the
Western obsession with logic, and
its passion for analysis. Poetry
demands a certain surrender on the
reader's part, and anyone who will
read the Apocalypse through with
sympathy as a poem, will gain a
vivid impression of the daring faith
of early Christians, utterly convinced that their unequal battle
could only end in victory, of their
scorn for the Empire which had
turned foully to persecution, and
of their complete certainty that
judgment, fierce and fast, would
fall.

The Great White Throne

(Revelation 20: 1-15)

THE millennium, the 1000 years of peace, after which the bound prince of evil is allowed abroad again to do his deadly work is a concept beyond explanation (1-3). The doctrine has divided churches on trivialities of interpretation, and no interpretation so far published can claim to be adequate. The approach here adopted to Revelation, as to the rest of the N.T., is that it is authoritative, that the text bears divine sanction beyond that accorded any human document. Without this presupposition the line taken by liberal scholars would be relevant. The idea of a millennium of peace, often with the earthly pleasures of a Moslem paradise, was, they say correctly, not unknown in non-canonical apocalyptic literature, and John simply adopts and adapts. This exegesis is not available here. Shall it rather be said that the key to John's meaning is lost? There is some symbolism which eludes. And does it in any way diminish the worth of a commentary if it expresses inability to elucidate all contexts? Let the millennium and the two resurrections therefore be set aside as mysteries, the 'second death' (6, 14) left as an elusive phrase to ponder on, and the attention directed to the fact of final judgment (11). The justice of God demands an ultimate accounting, and the majesty of the great white throne adequately ennobles the idea. In the mind of God all events, all deeds, all words are stored, and if he is perfect justice, all will be judged aright and with perfection assessed. There is a day appointed (Acts 17: 31; 2 Tim. 4: 1). The judge stands central (11). All else vanishes. It is at last the moment of truth.

The New Creation

(Revelation 21: 1-21)

THE theme merges into pure poetry. John struggles with a new dimension. Lewis invented Narnia, adopting at random the name of an ancient Italian city to form his 'other world'. And then mystically he seems to discover a Narnia within Narnia, even an England within England. There are thoughts too insubstantial to confine in words, eluding even imagery, which can only find a clothing of symbol and metaphor. From this wealth of mysticism we can pluck some precious coin. The notion of a new Jerusalem which was yet clothed like a bride (2) and yet a glittering mass of stylised ramparts, gates, jewels (10-21) outstrips any attempt to visualise. It simply means that the life of the redeemed shall be replete with inconceivable beauty, and true wealth beyond imagining, with a Presence that envelops, and satisfaction only there attained (6). To find meaning in the distribution of the gates is rather an homiletical exercise than a scheme of exegesis. Let us simply hold the thought that those things which mar this life, tears, death, pain (4) shall disappear in God's new world. Evil is purged, consumed, banished (8). It is Isaiah's mystic dream at last come true

(54: 12; 60: 11–22). The very dimensions of this imperfect world are gone. The eye could not compass the size of the New Jerusalem (16), even if the mind could encompass its beauty. This is not our world, nor can we understand another (1 Cor. 2: 9).

Paradise

(Revelation 22: 1–21)

THE poetry comes a little closer to earth with the final imagery. The river of life (Ps. 46: 4; Ezek. 47: 1–7; Joel 3: 18; Zech. 14: 8) and the tree of life (Gen. 3: 6), are familiar. Read both in the contest of a region where living, running water, and fruitful trees stood in stronger contrast to the scorched earth than they do in many other lands. But the poetry intentionally transcends all experience. The Seer is caught up into his vision and melts into it. There is little order now. It is as though the writer emerges into quiet after the tumult of his experience. Let every man choose the life which he wills

to project, with his immortality, into another dimension, but John has shown what can be (11). No one is compelled, but blessedness is open for the choosing and the right choice is urged by the most winsome invitation (17). In v. 18 John asseverates his authority—like Paul in Gal. 1: 8, 9. The truth is not to be tampered with in any way (Deut. 4: 2; Prov. 30: 5, 6). In the days of the manuscript it was the strongest temptation of a copyist to alter, subtract, comment, and comments ('glosses') could intrude into the text. The warning deprecates distortion. It does not suggest that a Christian can forfeit salvation by misinterpreting the Apocalypse. It does imply that only those out of tune with the gospel, and in rebellion against God will treat its message disdainfully. The book offends only those who are repelled by the gospel and its Christ. John has nothing to say to them but this word of warning.

And so we close the Book and the Testament. The grace of our Lord Jesus Christ be with you all— Amen.